The Royal Norfolk Regimental Museum

Sponsored by

FRANCIS HORNOR
BROWN & CO

Estate Management
Farm Consultancy
Residential sales and Letting
Renovations and Repairs

COMMERCIAL
AGRICULTURAL & RESIDENTIAL
PROPERTY CONSULTANTS

Professional Strength in the City and Country

Old Bank of England Court,
Queen Street,
Norwich NR2 4TA

Telephone: (01603) 629871
Fax: (01603) 760765

Surveyors to the
Royal Norfolk War Memorial Cottages

Offices throughout the region

The
Royal Norfolk Regimental
Museum

A Soldier's Life in the County Regiment in peace and war.

Follow the men and their families around the world since 1685.

NORFOLK MUSEUMS SERVICE

Shirehall
Market Avenue
Norwich NR1 3JQ

Raising the 9th of Foot

The 9th Regiment of Foot was raised for the Catholic King James II in 1685 to quell a rebellion. Over the next three centuries the Regiment's name was changed from time to time until it became The Royal Norfolk Regiment in 1935. As the name suggests the soldiers travelled and fought on foot. In 1688 the Protestant William of Orange was invited, from what is today the Netherlands, to seize the throne of England. The Regiment fought its first battle against James - the Battle of the Boyne in Ireland in 1689.

The Colours

Like all regiments the 9th of Foot carried flags called colours. Colonel Henry Cornwall who formed the Regiment had one and so did his senior officers. They were used as rallying points and to show the regiment's position to the generals directing the battle. They came to symbolise the regiment itself and they were fiercely defended. Later the number was reduced to just two; one representing the Sovereign, the King's or Queen's Colour and the other representing the Regiment. For a particularly brave or sustained action a regiment may be given an Honour which can be recorded on the Colours. On The Royal Norfolk Regiment's Colours the following Honours appear :-

A junior officer holding the Regimental Colours escorted by a Colour Sergeant whose role it was to protect them. From a print in the National Army Museum dated 1813.

Seven Years War (1756-1763)
Belleisle, Havannah

French Revolutionary War (1793-1805)
Martinique 1794

Peninsular War (1808-1814)
Rolica, Vimiera, Corunna, Busaco, Salamanca, Vittoria, St. Sebastian, Nive, Peninsula

First Afghan War (1838-1842)
Cabool 1842

First Sikh War (1845-1846)
Moodkee, Ferozeshah, Sobraon

Crimean War (1854-1856)
Sevastopol

Second Afghan War (1878-1880)
Kabul 1879, Afghanistan 1879-80

Boer War (1899-1902)
Paardeberg, South Africa 1900-02

First World War (1914-1918)
Mons, Le Cateau, Marne 1914, Ypres 1914, Somme 1916 & 1918, Hindenberg Line, Landing at Suvla, Gaza, Shaiba, Kut al Amara 1915 & 1917

Second World War (1939-1945)
St. Omer La Bassee, Normandy Landing, Brieux Bridgehead, Venraij, Rhineland, North West Europe 1940 & 1945, Singapore Island, Kohima, Aradura, Burma 1944-45

Korean War (1950-1953)
Korea 1951-52.

There are many others too numerous to fit on the colours. Regiments still have colours today but they are no longer carried into battle.

Victoria Crosses

Six members of the Regiment have been awarded the Victoria Cross for exceptional valour; they are as follows :-

During the First World War

Lieutenant Colonel John Sherwood-Kelly V.C., C.M.G., D.S.O., 20th November 1917 at Marcoing, Canal du Nord in France.

During the Second World War

Colour Sergeant Major George Gristock V.C., 21st May 1940 on the River Escaut in France.
Captain John Neil Randle V.C., 4th May 1944 at Kohima in Assam.
Corporal Sidney Bates V.C., 6th August 1944 at Sourdeval in France.
Captain David Jamieson V.C., 7th August 1944 at Grimbosq, River Orne in France.
Lieutenant George Arthur Knowland V.C., 31st January 1945 at Kangaw in Burma.

Officers

Whilst the rank and file of the Army was recruited from a reluctant population there was considerable competition and expense in becoming an officer. This was particularly true of older and more fashionable regiments. Being the ninth regiment of foot The Norfolk Regiment, as it later became, was a desirable regiment to be in. Officers were given their authority called a commission by the Crown or a Lord Lieutenant. Commissions could then be bought and sold, to obtain a higher rank. Rising in rank was not a question of ability but of wealth. In the 1700s in a regiment like the 9th of Foot the lowest rank cost about £450 rising to £4,500 to become the commanding officer, a lieutenant colonel. At the time these were vast sums of money and even these were often exceeded. The system of buying and selling commissions was eventually abolished in 1871.

Recruitment

Recruiting sufficient numbers of soldiers was always a problem. From each regiment an officer, a recruiting sergeant, a drummer and a small number of private soldiers would travel the country trying to find men to join. In a large town several regiments might be attempting to recruit at the same time. Until well into the 1800s the Army was looked upon with distaste by ordinary people and it would bring shame on the family for a son to join up. The unemployed and prisoners could be forced to join and debtors could be released from their debts if they signed up. The Army would even take convicted criminals who would otherwise be hanged.

Soldiers of the 9th of Foot in 1751. From left to right, a private soldier, grenadier and an officer. From a 20th century water colour by R. Simkin.

DISEASE

During the 1700s the 9th of Foot fought a number of campaigns in the West Indies. The prospect of being sent there terrified soldiers. When troopships left Europe sometimes the soldiers would not be told they were bound for the West Indies until they were at sea to prevent them deserting. They might be killed in action but even more certainly by disease. The heat, humidity, bad food, dirty water and poor hygiene could destroy an Army. Even when stationed in the British Isles the death rate amongst soldiers was greater than that of the civilian population. It was not until the 20th century that the numbers killed in action exceeded those who died of disease.

THE SQUARE AND SKIRMISHING

The traditional square formed as an exercise in India in the late 1800s.

During the first 200 years of the Regiment's existence battles were fought with very set manoeuvres. Troops were drilled to make strict formations one of which was the square. This was a defensive measure meant to withstand the onslaught of cavalry. Soldiers formed a square which might be several ranks deep. Whilst one rank was firing the others could load. By this means a constant barrage of fire was maintained. Formal methods were still employed in the late 1700s but were of little use, for example in the woods of North America and especially against men who used the stealth and skills of hunters. These experiences and the development of the more accurate rifle led to a less formal method called skirmishing.

THE WAR OF AMERICAN INDEPENDENCE (1775-1782)

The French were the common enemy of both the British and their American Colonies. In the Seven Years War which ended in 1763 the British had defeated the French. Now they no longer needed protection from the French, the American Colonists began to resent British taxes, the presence of British troops and rule from London. The discontent led to war in 1775 and the Americans declared independence from Britain in 1776.

Lieutenant General E. Ligonier, First Earl Ligonier K.B. Colonel of the Regiment at the time the 9th of Foot was involved in the War of American Independence.

4

The 9th of Foot took part in the conflict but had to surrender as part of General John Burgoyne's Army. Lieutenant Colonel Hill hid the Colours in his personal baggage to prevent them being seized and they were presented to King George III by Hill when he returned to England.

FEEDING AN ARMY

Armies at this time carried practically no food with them but took it from the people in the country they passed through. For this reason warfare was to a large extent seasonal. Battles took place in the summer months because in the winter there was little food to be had and in addition the roads became impassable. There was a continual battle within a battle where the local people tried to hide their stores of food from the soldiers.

Men of the 9th of Foot burying the body of Sir John Moore, Commander-in-Chief of the British Army in Portugal. He was killed at Corunna on 16th January 1809.

Some of the Regiment's cooks on a journey from Dagshai to Lahore in 1893. By this time the provision of food was much better organised.

THE RETREAT AT CORUNNA

In the winter of 1808-9, during the Peninsular War, Napoleon's armies in Spain had defeated the Spanish leaving the British and their allies outnumbered. Retreat was the wisest course although the reasoning was not conveyed to the troops and many resented not being allowed to attack the enemy. The journey was made in appalling conditions and many died on the way including women and children who froze to death on abandoned baggage wagons. Ships intended to pick up the soldiers at Corunna were delayed and Sir John Moore who commanded the British was killed before embarkation was complete. Soldiers of the Norfolk Regiment buried the General's body in January 1809 and were the last to leave. Only 60 of them remained to sail away. From then on drummers in The Norfolk Regiment wore black braids to commemorate the Regiment's part in the tragedy. Later the Regiment returned to Spain and took part in Napoleon's defeat.

THE "HOLY BOYS"

The Regiment's badge is the figure of Britannia. During the Peninsular War the Spanish mistook the image for that of the Virgin Mary. Other British regiments on hearing about this began calling the Norfolk Regiment the "Holy Boys" and the nickname has stuck ever since.

DISCIPLINE

Discipline in the Army was harsh. Very few men enlisted in the Army as a career and recruits were found amongst criminals and the poorest men for whom enlistment was an act of desperation. Such men were forged into coherent fighting units with brutal punishment for any misconduct. Men were lashed in front of the whole regiment with a cat of nine tails wielded by the regiment's drummers. Sentences of up to 1000 lashes were meted out. Up until 1817 the cat was also used on women who were attached to the regiment. Persistent offenders could be branded on the hand, arm, or chest ; "BC" for Bad Character and "D" for Deserter.

In 1846 a Society for the Abolition of Flogging in the Army and Navy was founded. Through the 1800s sentences were gradually reduced. The maximum number of lashes was brought down to 50 in 1846 and abolished altogether in 1881.

The port of Balaclava in 1855. It was the main supply base for the British Army during the Crimean War.

THE CRIMEA (1854-1856)

Russia was threatening to invade the Turkish Ottoman Empire. British soldiers joined with allies to fight the Russians in the Crimea on the north coast of the Black Sea. Among the allies were the French and it was difficult for the British to get used to the idea of fighting on the same side as their traditional enemy. The organisation and supply behind the war was chaotic and soldiers fought in freezing cold with no warm clothing or bedding. Medical aid for the injured was minimal. Newspapers at home printed more accurate reports of the war more quickly than had been possible before and the news shocked the public. Steps were then taken to improve the soldiers' conditions.

It has been said of warfare that it consists of days and months of waiting and boredom punctuated with periods of intense action. This was certainly true for The Norfolk Regiment in the months they spent in the Crimea. In appalling conditions they went just once into battle during the siege of Sevastopol.

It was in the Crimea that Florence Nightingale set up her hospital at Scutari.

Uniforms of officers and men of the 9th Regiment of Foot in about 1854.

Alexis Soyer a famous French chef at the Reform Club in London developed a field kitchen to improve the preparation of meals on the battlefield.

INDIA AND MARRIAGE

Regimental wedding photograph taken in India in about 1903.

The Norfolk Regiment first set foot in India in September 1835 and continued to serve there from time to time until India's Independence in 1947. Although the campaigns were fought in India, Afghanistan and Tibet against local rulers, the ultimate threat was thought to come from Russia. In the wars to conquer and keep India, strangely enough, some of Britain's fiercest enemies like the Gurkhas and Sikhs later became its most steadfast allies.

During the 1700s Europeans in India described themselves as Indians, just as those who settled in America called themselves Americans. They often wore Indian clothes and some married Indian women. In time the notion of being Indian disappeared particularly following the Mutiny in 1857 and the opening of the Suez Canal in 1869. Today the Mutiny is seen by many Indians as their First War of Independence.

The Suez Canal made a shorter route for the "Fishing Fleet". This was the unflattering name given to the women who sailed to India to find husbands amongst the officers in the Army and the Indian Civil Service. In fact marriage in the Army was discouraged and only a limited number of men in each regiment were allowed to marry. The wives were then deemed to be "on the strength" of the regiment. If a soldier married without permission he was treated as if his wife and children did not exist and he received no extra pay to keep them.

Private soldiers' wives undertook work for the regiment like washing and cooking. The sergeants' wives did washing for the officers. They and their children lived with the soldiers in the barrack rooms; the only privacy was a screen of blankets. When a regiment went abroad not all the wives were allowed to go. Others often followed as best they could, even those whose existence was unacknowledged.

Lieutenant Hadow on the 1903-4 British Expedition to Lhasa in Tibet. He led the Machine Gun Section of the 1st Battalion of the Norfolk Regiment.

Boer War (1899-1902)

In the late 1800s most African countries were colonies of European countries or were ruled directly by people of European descent. Conflict flared up in the southern states of Africa between the Boers, of Dutch descent, and the British. Among the prizes fought over were the rich gold fields.

At the outset of the Boer War the British Army still wore red tunics but they were soon abandoned in favour of the hard-to-see khaki which had been worn in India since the 1840s. The Boers did not fight set battles but were skilled marksmen who used horses to move quickly and knowledge of the country to hide and spring surprises. Against such an enemy it was a hard struggle but the British eventually succeeded.

Since 1859 the Regular Army had been enthusiastically supported by Volunteer soldiers, sometimes mockingly called "Saturday Night Soldiers". They were the predecessors of today's Territorial Army. Volunteers fought abroad for the first time alongside the Regulars in The Norfolk Regiment during the Boer War. At this time Volunteers in Yeomanry Regiments, who were mounted soldiers, were not allowed to serve abroad but many of The Norfolk Yeomanry joined The Imperial Yeomanry which was raised to do so. The assassination of the Austrian Archduke Franz Ferdinand in Sarajevo sparked off a series of events which led to Germany attacking Belgium as the first step in invading France. The war spread and drew in men and women of many nationalities and races from all over the world.

A group of Boers.

First World War (1914-1918)

Soldiers leaving Thorpe Station, Norwich during the First World War.

"Old Contemptibles" and the "New Army"

The 1st Battalion of The Norfolk Regiment was part of the British Expeditionary Force sent in 1914 to drive the Germans out of Belgium and France. Germany's Kaiser Wilhelm II called it "a contemptibly little army". Later these men were to call themselves proudly "The Old Contemptibles". There were insufficient numbers of these Regular Army soldiers for the ensuing war and Lord Kitchener called for volunteers to form a "New Army". The Norfolk Regiment expanded from 2 battalions to 14. Men were encouraged to join up together from clubs, factories and football teams and were promised they would stay together throughout the war. Colmans, the mustard manufacturers of Norwich, promised to pay their recruits wives 5/-

(25p) per week whilst they were away. The practice of recruiting and keeping men together was later abandoned. By 1916 too few men were coming forward as volunteers and conscription came into force.

The Battle of the Somme

At first it was a war of rapid movement over a broad area but soon it slowed to one of mass destruction fought from an amazingly intricate network of trenches and tunnels beneath them. The Norfolk's 7th, 8th, and 9th Battalions were there on the first dreadful day of the Battle of the Somme, 1st July 1916. Between them they lost 1042 men. The 8th lost a further 662 in the next week.

Gallipoli

The 1\4th and 1\5th Battalions fought in a disastrous campaign in Gallipoli in Turkey. The 5th Battalion was recruited in the northern part of Norfolk including one Company of men from the Royal Estate at Sandringham. On the 12th August 1915 the Battalion attacked Turkish positions. They received conflicting orders and advanced beyond the point where they could be supported by other troops. In consequence they were surrounded and slaughtered. Their unmarked graves were discovered in 1919. Despite the facts being published immediately after the war, the fate of the 5th Battalion has given rise to all kinds of wild speculation and mystical explanation up to the present day. The remaining Norfolks in Turkey were brought up to strength and went on to fight in Gaza. In 1916 the Second Battalion of the Norfolk Regiment was part of an army which was so reduced in numbers and starved that it had to surrender at Kut in Mesopotamia (Iraq).

The Norfolk Yeomanry

At the beginning of the war the Norfolk Yeomanry was still organised as cavalry but fought as an infantry battalion of about 500 men in the Gallipoli campaign. They became true infantry as the 12th (Yeomanry) Battalion of the Norfolk Regiment whilst serving in Egypt in 1917. Later they fought at Gaza and advanced northwards to be at the relief of Jerusalem.

Women of the 3rd Norfolk Regiment, Queen Mary's Auxiliary Army Corps in about 1918.

The Armistice

In March 1918 when Germany was thought to be a spent force it summoned a great counter offensive which almost resulted in defeat for the Allies. The 1st, 7th, and 9th Battalions of the Norfolk Regiment were still in the trenches. They were joined by the 12th (Yeomanry) Battalion and took part in the fierce battles to push the Germans back. At last on 11th November 1918 the war came to an end.

In August 1914 the 1st Battalion had sailed from Belfast for France; from those men only a Captain and 50 men were still serving at the end. Few towns or villages are without a memorial to the those who died. The long lists and the repeated family names point to the terrible effect this war had on a county like Norfolk.

The Second World War (1939-1945)

Marquees forming extra wards at the Norfolk War Hospital. This was the name given to St. Andrew's Hospital at Thorpe during the First World War.

The consequences of the First World War and a world wide depression caused Germany to fall into severe economic decline. Adolf Hitler, leader of the NAZI party, came to power as Chancellor in 1938. He promised a better future with economic growth and renewed national pride. Hitler's troops marched into demilitarised zones and into Austria and Czechoslovakia. In 1939 Hitler invaded Poland, an ally of Britain, which caused Britain to declare war on Germany.

In the Far East Japan too had been expanding its empire by invasion. On 7th September 1941 the Japanese launched a surprise attack on the American Fleet in Pearl Harbour in the Pacific Ocean. This action brought the United States of America into the war.

The Western Front

Dunkirk

The 2nd Battalion of the Royal Norfolk Regiment arrived in France in September 1939 to be followed by the 7th Battalion in January 1940. Resistance to the German invasion soon collapsed in Holland, Belgium and Western France. By May 1940 the Allies had retreated to the Channel coast at Dunkirk. Any vessel capable of making a Channel crossing was pressed into use and more than 338,000 British, Belgian and French troops were carried back to England. A few of the 2nd Battalion escaped but others were captured, some of whom were massacred at Le Paradis whilst they were in captivity. The 7th Battalion which had been raised only six months previously were to be evacuated from the coast between Le Havre and Dieppe. The 51st Highland Division, of which they were part, had no food or ammunition remaining and the boats never arrived. The General commanding the Division had no alternative but to surrender.

"D" Day

The 1st Battalion were in India at the outbreak of war. They were brought back to Britain where they were part of the force kept at home for the defence of the United Kingdom. Whilst carrying out this duty they trained for assault landings using beaches and cliffs in the North of England and Scotland. This training was in preparation for "D Day" where thousands of Allied troops were carried across the Channel for the invasion which was eventually to lead to the defeat and occupation of Germany. They landed on what was named Sword Beach in the third wave of troops on "D Day" the 6th June 1944. The 7th Battalion landed on "D Day" plus 22, that is 28th June. This

Soldiers of "D" Company, 1st Battalion, Royal Norfolk Regiment dashing across a street in Kervenheim, Germany in 1945.

was an entirely new battalion since the previous 7th had been captured in 1940.

The battle strategy was to push south and west to divide the German Army in two. One of the first objectives was the capture of the city of Caen. The fighting was harsh and little of the city remained standing after the battle. Following these first days the 1st Battalion fought through France, Belgium and Holland sometimes meeting little resistance but at other times having to fight from street to street. On 25th February 1945 the 1st Battalion crossed into Germany itself and the cease-fire came on 5th May. But in South East Asia and the Far East the war still continued.

THE WAR IN THE EAST

India & Burma

Following the defeat in France in 1940 the 2nd Battalion was reformed and sent to India in 1942 to be trained in jungle warfare. In 1944 the Japanese launched an attack in Burma, intending eventually to conquer India. The Battalion was flown to Assam in north eastern India and then travelled on to defend Kohima. For the Japanese the capture of Kohima was a necessary step to conquering India. Here the Battalion won a Battle Honour and the Allies' victory proved to be a turning point in the war. Before final victory over the Japanese the 2nd Battalion was called back to India where its long experience in that country was used in trying to contain the violence which marked the country's Independence. Finally in 1948 the Battalion was disbanded.

THE FAR EAST

The 4th, 5th, and 6th Battalions of the Royal Norfolk Regiment were not full time Regular Army soldiers but Territorials who trained as soldiers as well as doing their normal day to day jobs. At the outbreak of war they too became full time soldiers. These battalions were trained for desert warfare. At some point in their sea voyage to what was probably the Middle East plans were changed and they were sent to Singapore Island at the tip of the Malayan Peninsula. What training in jungle warfare there could be took place on board ship. The three Battalions fought at first on the Malayan mainland but soon withdrew with the British Army to Singapore Island which was to be the last stand against the Japanese. They were constantly shelled and bombed and vastly outnumbered. The British surrendered including the 4th, 5th and 6th Battalions. After 17 days fierce fighting they were to endure three and a half years captivity. Many died through the brutal treatment, others of tropical diseases and still more in building the notorious "Railway of Death" through Thailand.

The Norfolk Yeomanry in the Second World War

The Norfolk Yeomanry had been disbanded after the First World War but were raised once more in 1923. At the outbreak of the Second World War they were part of the Royal Artillery. They landed in France in 1940 but were evacuated from Dunkirk having to leave much of their equipment behind them.

After a period of training in the United Kingdom they sailed to the Middle East. The Italian Army had been defeated and the Allies were moving westwards through the desert. Progress was halted and reversed following the arrival of the Afrika Corps under the command of the German General Rommel. The Allies were pushed back to the border between Libya and Egypt. A turning point came with the Allies' victory at El Alamein. From there a push westwards brought final victory in Tunisia. After fighting briefly in Italy the Yeomanry were shipped back home to prepare for "D Day". They landed in France beginning on "D Day" plus 3. They took part in the fierce fighting to secure Caen and then fought eastwards. Every river crossing presented a well defended obstacle but at last the Seine was reached in August 1944. Eventually they crossed the Rhine and received news of the cease-fire outside Hamburg. The Norfolk Yeomanry then stayed in Germany for a period after the cease fire but was disbanded in February 1946.

NATIONAL SERVICEMEN JOIN THE "REGULARS" IN KOREA, CYPRUS & ADEN

After the Second World War men continued to be called into the Army to do up to two years National Service. Men from all backgrounds were mixed in together and many resented their studies or careers being interrupted. Despite this men often say they would never have joined voluntarily but in fact it did them a great deal of good.

Tactical Headquarters in Pegasus village in Aden in about 1965.

In 1951 the Royal Norfolk Regiment joined a United Nations force which was employed to prevent the Communist North Koreans invading the southern part of the country. In fact most of the men in the Regiment at this time were National Servicemen.

The island of Cyprus in 1955 was a British colony where EOKA, a Greek Cypriot organisation wished to force out the British and bring about unity with Greece. The Regiment spent a year there in operations against small gangs who were using guerrilla tactics to achieve their aims. Self government for the island was granted in 1959.

AMALGAMATION

In 1959 the Royal Norfolk Regiment was amalgamated with another regiment with a long history, the Suffolk Regiment (12th Foot), originally raised in the same year, 1685. Together they formed the 1st East Anglian Regiment. It was this successor regiment which for just over a year fought Arab terrorists in what was then the British Protectorate of Aden.

The 2nd Battalion, Norfolk Regiment at Fermoy in Ireland in 1898.

IRELAND

Ireland was the scene of the 9th Foot's first battle for the Protestant King William III against the deposed Catholic King James II. This was the Battle of the Boyne won by William in 1689 and still commemorated by the Protestants of Northern Ireland today. Until 1922 all of Ireland was ruled by the British and the Regiment served there frequently from 1689 onwards. Regiments were moved about all over the British Isles, particularly before the building of permanent barracks in the late 1700s. Ireland was a convenient place to keep troops. They were less obvious to the majority of the population of Britain and possible foes in Europe. They were also paid less when stationed there.

During the 1920s the Norfolk Regiment was in Ireland and in September 1920 an attempt was made to assassinate the Colonel of the Regiment, Major-General Sir E. Peter Strickland who was commanding the troops in Southern Ireland.

Irish Independence was finally granted in 1922 except for Ulster, six counties in the north, which remained part of the United Kingdom. The population of these six counties was mainly Protestant. Some Catholics living in Ulster wished it to be part of the Republic of Ireland as well. Open conflict on this issue broke out once more in 1968. In 1969 British troops were called in to maintain order. From 1970 the 1st Battalion The Royal Anglian Regiment, successor to The Royal Norfolk Regiment, has had periods of duty in Northern Ireland of up to two years.

Men of the Royal Anglian Regiment regrouping after a charge during a disturbance in Londonderry in Northern Ireland in August 1971.

Text: D Jones
Design: J Maxwell
With additional material by R Bird

Printed by Balding + Mansell, Norwich

Supported by the
Royal Norfolk Regimental Museum Trustees

and

FRANCIS HORNOR BROWN & CO

Norfolk Museums Service

THE HISTORY OF
THE NORFOLK REGIMENT

THE HISTORY OF THE NORFOLK REGIMENT
1685————————————1918

BY
F. LORAINE PETRE, O.B.E.
AUTHOR OF "NAPOLEON'S CAMPAIGN IN POLAND," "NAPOLEON AT BAY"
ETC., ETC.

VOL. II

4th August, 1914, to 31st December, 1918

ERRATA OR CORRIGENDA TO VOL. I.

Col. Shepherd, C. H. *not* C. R.   P. 397.

Col. Phillips, L. H. *not* L. W.   P. 401.

Turnell, *not* Tunnell.   P. 427.

P. 431. Read after third paragraph :
From Bloemfontein the 2nd Battalion moved to Pietermaritzburg in March, 1907, and from Pietermaritzburg to Gibraltar in September, 1908.

Plate facing p. 288—date 1845 *should read* 1846.

P. 334, line 11—for 1885 *read* 1855.

P. 156, line 13—for July 29, 1808, *insert* June 29, 1808.

P. 334.   Becher, C.B.E.

P. 335.   Hamilton, C.B., D.S.O., C.S.I.

,,   Massy, C.M.G.

,,   Ballard, C.B., C.M.G.

,,   Shepherd, D.S.O.

P. 336.   Peebles, C.B., C.M.G., D.S.O.

P. 339.   Buxton, V.D.

Brigadier-General Longe died in 1916.

For Sprixworth *read* Spixworth.

MAPS (FULL PAGE)

	FACING PAGE
PART OF THE WESTERN FRONT IN FRANCE AND BELGIUM	1
MESOPOTAMIA	61

SKETCHES IN TEXT

	PAGE
BATTLE OF MONS (ELOUGES), AUGUST 24, 1914	3
BATTLE OF LE CÂTEAU, AUGUST 26, 1914	6
BATTLE OF THE AISNE	9
FESTUBERT FRONT	11
NEIGHBOURHOOD OF YPRES	14
THE ALBERT FRONT	17
LONGUEVAL AND DELVILLE WOOD	25
FULFEMONT FARM AND MORVAL	30
LA COULOTTE	37
THE BATTLE OF SHAIBA	68
THE TIGRIS ABOVE AND BELOW KUT	72
THE BATTLE OF CTESIPHON	81
SUVLA BAY AND ANZAC	123
THE GAZA FRONT	141
PLOEGSTEERT—ST. ELOI FRONT	172
THE ARRAS FRONT	185
BATTLE OF ARRAS (FEUCHY CHAPEL)	187
THE BATTLEFIELD OF CAMBRAI	195

	PAGE
MONTAUBAN	216
THIÉPVAL	222
SCHWABEN REDOUBT	224
BOOM RAVINE	229
IRLES	232
GLENCORSE WOOD	240
POELCAPPELLE	244
THE QUADRILATERAL	255
FIRST BATTLE OF CAMBRAI—ATTACK OF 9TH BATTALION	273
QUÉANT—PRONVILLE	281
BEERSHEBA AND SHERIA	310
ADVANCE OF THE 74TH DIVISION NORTH OF JERUSALEM	315
NIEPPE FOREST AND VIEUX BERQUIN	323

LIST OF ILLUSTRATIONS
VOL. II

1. His Majesty King George V
2. Mons
   Stanley Barwell
3. Field-Marshal Sir William Gomm, G.C.B.
4. Uniforms, 1698 and 1745
5. Uniforms, 1790
6. Shaiba
   Stanley Barwell
7. Regimental Sergeant-Major Robert Semmence
8. Colours, 1685
9. Colours, 1759 and 1767
10. Gaza
    Stanley Barwell
11. The Sandringham Colours
12. Types of Uniforms
13. Types of Uniforms
14. Peninsula Colours
15. (i) Uniform, 1830 ; (ii) Lace Point
16. The War Memorial of the Norfolk Regiment
17. Colonel John Patteson's Colours
18. Arms of the XVIIth and XVIIIth Centuries
19. Colours, 1827–1848, 1859–1896
20. Silver. 1st Battalion
21. The South African Cup

FIELD-MARSHAL SIR WILLIAM MAYNARD GOMM, G.C.B.
(This portrait came too late to be included in *Vol. I*).

MONS, August 24, 1914.
Looking north from a point 1,000 yards south-west of Elouges village, shortly before the attack. From a sketch by an officer of the 1st Battalion.

GRENADIERS. OFFICER AND PRIVATE, 1790, *circa*.
From a painting by Captain H. A. Armitage, Adjutant, 1st Battalion, 1879.

GRENADIER, 1745.

From the original by Morier at Windsor Castle, painted for the Duke of Cumberland. By permission of His Majesty the King, Colonel in Chief.

MUSQUETEER, 1698.

From Colonel Walton's History. By permission of Mrs. Winterne.

ROBERT SEMMENCE.
Regimental Sergeant-Major, 2nd Battalion.   Killed at Shaiba.

SHAIBA, April 14, 1915.

SARATOGA COLOURS, 1767 AND PORTIONS OF A COLOUR OF 1759.
(No. 2, Schedule, *Appendix IV.*)
Supposed to be the oldest known Regimental Colours in the British Army.

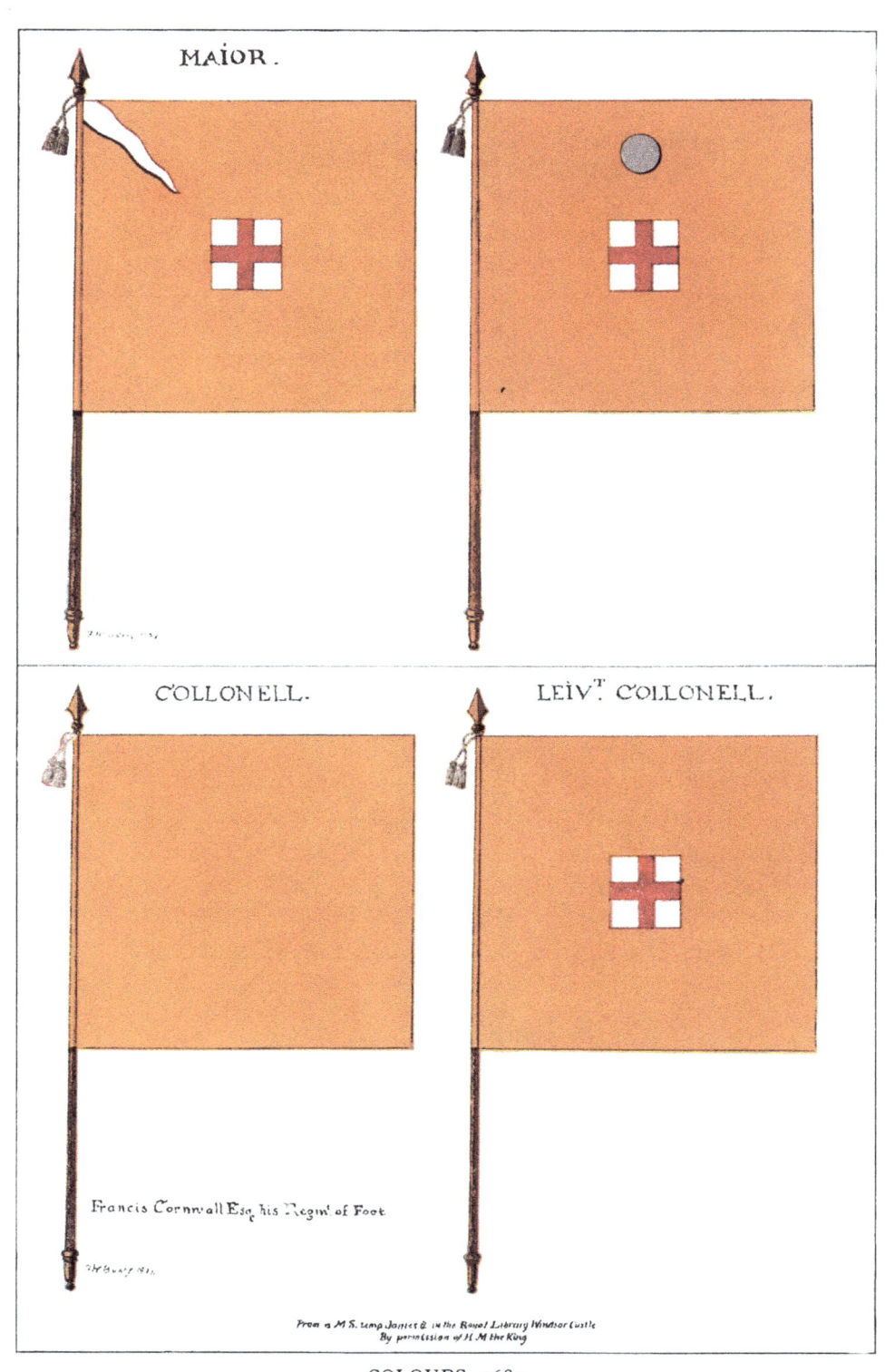

COLOURS, 1685.
From a MS. Temp. James II in the Royal Library, Windsor Castle.
By permission of His Majesty the King, Colonel in Chief.
(No. 1, Schedule, *Appendix IV*.)

THE SANDRINGHAM COLOURS.
Crimea, 1848–1887.
No. 8.
(Schedule, *Appendix IV.*)
By permission of His Majesty the King, Colonel in Chief.

1st Battalion, 1887–1909.
No. 9.

2nd Battalion, 1892–1919.
No. 12.

GAZA, 1917.
From details given by an officer of the 5th Battalion.

9th East Norfolk Regiment, 1798.
Private and Officer.

1812.
Grenadier.

1812.
Drummer and Drum-Major.

1832.
Officer, Grenadier Company.

1807.
Sergeant and Officer.

1832.
Corporal, Light Company.

1864.
Bandsman and Officer.

1864.
Officer, Undress.

The Norfolk Regiment, 1887.
Sergeant-Major and Adjutant.

TYPES OF UNIFORMS.
From a picture given by Lieutenants C. H. Renwick and H. G. Levinge, 1887.

TYPES OF UNIFORMS.

From a picture given to the 1st Battalion by Captains B. de M. Leathes and S. D. Shortt, 1887.

9th Foot

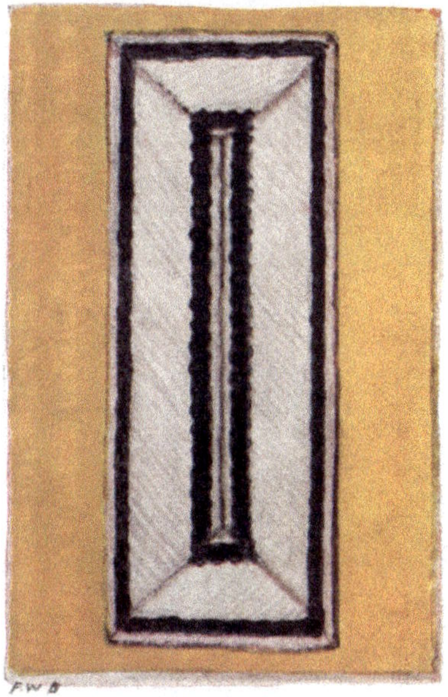

From the original pattern, 1768 at Windsor Castle

LACE POINT. See Plate 5.

OFFICER OF THE LIGHT COMPANY, 1830.

From a sketch by a French officer. In 1830 the lace was changed from silver to gold.

PENINSULAR COLOURS.
1st Battalion and portions of the Colours of 1798. (Nos. 4 and 5, Schedule, *Appendix IV.*)

COLOUR OF COLONEL JOHN PATTESON BATTALION OF VOLUNTEER INFANTRY,

enrolled as Local Militia, 1808, and drafted into the East Norfolk Militia. By permission of Colonel Sir Charles Harvey, Bart. (No. 17, Schedule, *Appendix IV.*)

THE WAR MEMORIAL OF THE NORFOLK REGIMENT

(2) 2ND BATTALION COLOURS, 1859–1896.
(No. 11, Schedule, *Appendix IV*.)

(1) KABUL-SUTLEJ COLOURS, 1827–1848.
(No. 7, Schedule, *Appendix IV*.)

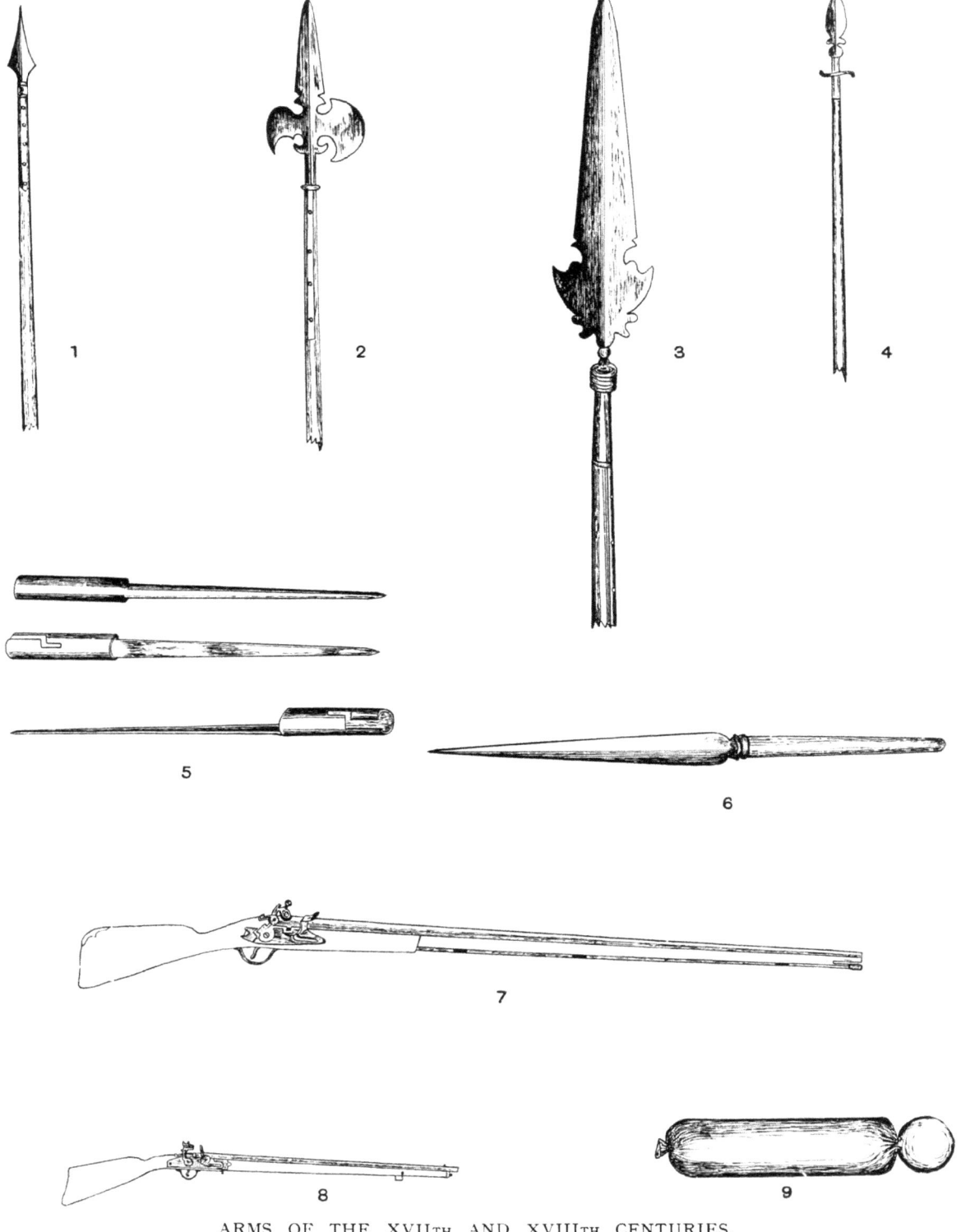

ARMS OF THE XVIIth AND XVIIIth CENTURIES.

1. Pike, XVIIth Century. Carried by sergeants of Battalion companies after 1792 till 1830.
2. Halbert, XVIIth Century. Carried by sergeants of Battalion companies till 1792.
3. Partisan, XVIIth Century.
4. Espontoon, 1786. Carried by officers of Battalion companies till 1786.
5. The first socket bayonet, 1690.
6. The plus bayonet, 1678–1684. This took the place of the pike for the rank and file, 1696.
7. The flint lock musket, XVIIth Century.
8. The fusil, 1790. Carried by officers and sergeants of Grenadiers till 1792 and retained by sergeants of Light Companies.
9. The ball cartridge, 1680.

Presented by the Citizens of Norwich and Residents of Norfolk to the 2nd Battalion the Norfolk Regiment on its return from the South African campaign, and on the occasion of its first visit to the City of Norwich since 1804. February 14, 1903.

TO THE 1st BATTALION

From the 1st Dorset Regiment, Belfast, 1914; The 57th Regiment, Limerick, 1881;
The 1st Battalion, 7th Royal Fusiliers, Dublin, 1876.

CONTENTS

VOL. II

CHAPTER		PAGE
	INTRODUCTORY REMARKS	xiii
I.	THE 1ST BATTALION IN BELGIUM AND FRANCE	
	(a) 1914: MONS (ELOUGES)—LE CÂTEAU—THE MARNE—THE AISNE—LA BASSÉE—YPRES	1
	(b) 1915: YPRES—THE SOMME FRONT	14
	(c) 1916: LONGUEVAL—FALFEMONT FARM—MORVAL—GIVENCHY	19
	(d) 1917: VIMY—OPPY WOOD—YPRES—ITALY	36
	(e) 1918: ITALY—NIEPPE FOREST—THE FINAL BATTLES	44
II.	THE 2ND BATTALION IN MESOPOTAMIA	
	(a) 1914: SAHIL—BASRA—KURNA	61
	(b) 1915: KURNA—SHAIBA—THE ADVANCE TO AND BATTLE OF CTESIPHON—SIEGE OF KUT	66
	(c) THE COMPOSITE BATTALION—FEBRUARY–JULY, 1916	98
	(d) THE PROVISIONAL BATTALION, OR RECONSTITUTED 2ND BATTALION	103
	(e) 1917: PASSAGE OF THE TIGRIS—BAGHDAD AND BEYOND	105
	(f) 1918	111
III.	THE 3RD (SPECIAL RESERVE) BATTALION	114
IV.	THE 4TH AND 5TH (TERRITORIAL) BATTALIONS	
	(a) 1915: GALLIPOLI AND EGYPT	120
	(b) 1916: EGYPT	138
	(c) 1917: PALESTINE	139
	(d) 1918: PALESTINE	156
	THE 2/4TH, 2/5TH, 3/5TH, AND 4/5TH BATTALIONS	160

CHAPTER		PAGE
V.	THE 1/6TH, 2/6TH, AND 3/6TH BATTALIONS	169
VI.	THE 7TH (SERVICE) BATTALION IN FRANCE	
	(a) 1914–1915: ORGANIZATION—ST. ELOI—GIVENCHY	170
	(b) 1916: HOHENZOLLERN REDOUBT—THE SOMME—OVILLERS—RIDGE TRENCH—BAYONET TRENCH	175
	(c) 1917: ARRAS—CAMBRAI	184
	(d) 1918: ON THE LYS—THE ANCRE—THE FINAL ADVANCE	197
VII.	THE 8TH (SERVICE) BATTALION IN FRANCE AND BELGIUM	
	(a) 1914–1915: ORGANIZATION—THE ANCRE	208
	(b) 1916: THE SOMME FRONT—MONTAUBAN—DELVILLE WOOD—THIÉPVAL—SCHWABEN REDOUBT	214
	(c) 1917–1918: THE ANCRE—IRLES—YPRES—POELCAPPELLE—DISBANDMENT	228
VIII.	THE 9TH (SERVICE) BATTALION IN FRANCE	
	(a) 1914–1915: RAISING—THE QUARRIES NEAR HULLUCH	249
	(b) 1916: THE SOMME FRONT—THE QUADRILATERAL—MILD TRENCH	252
	(c) 1917: TRENCH RAIDS—SUBURBS OF LENS—HILL 70—BATTLES OF CAMBRAI	262
	(d) 1918: THE GERMAN OFFENSIVE OF MARCH AND APRIL—THE FINAL BRITISH ADVANCE BY LE CÂTEAU—THE MARCH TO THE RHINE	279
	(e) THE 10TH (SERVICE) AND 11TH (TERRITORIAL) BATTALIONS	299
IX.	THE 12TH (YEOMANRY) BATTALION IN GALLIPOLI, EGYPT, PALESTINE, AND FRANCE	
	(a) 1915–1916: GALLIPOLI—EGYPT—SOLLUM	301
	(b) 1917: PALESTINE—GAZA—BEERSHEBA—SHERIA—JERUSALEM	307
	(c) 1918: NORTH OF JERUSALEM—FRANCE—NIEPPE FOREST—VIEUX BERQUIN—THE LAST ADVANCE	318

APPENDICES

		PAGE
I.	THE SUCCESSION OF COLONELS AND LIEUTENANT-COLONELS. BIOGRAPHICAL NOTES	333
II.	ESTABLISHMENT OF THE REGIMENT AT VARIOUS DATES	352
III.	UNIFORM, ARMS, AND BADGES	359
IV.	COLOURS AND BATTLE HONOURS	376
V.	REGIMENTAL BANDS AND MUSIC	396
VI.	OFFICERS KILLED OR DIED IN THE WAR, 1914–1918	400
VII.	EXTRACTS FROM MESS-BOOK AND COURT MARTIAL SENTENCES	422
VIII.	WRECK OF THE "ARIADNE," 1805	427
IX.	FRIENDSHIP BETWEEN THE NORFOLK REGIMENT AND THE WORCESTERSHIRE, ROYAL FUSILIERS, MIDDLESEX, AND DORSETSHIRE REGIMENTS	429
X.	THE NICKNAME "HOLY BOYS"	433
XI.	THE NORFOLK REGIMENT WAR MEMORIAL	434
XII.	THE NORFOLK REGIMENT PRISONERS OF WAR HELP ORGANIZATION	436
XIII.	NORFOLK NATIONAL RESERVE	438
XIV.	MISCELLANEA	439

INTRODUCTORY REMARKS

THE GREAT WAR, 1914–1918

WHEN, in August, 1914, the greatest of all wars that the world has so far seen broke out, few probably foresaw a fraction of the developments which were to make of it a world war, or of the character which it was to assume. The majority, including of course the Germans themselves, believed it would be of short duration, and financial opinion generally held that, on grounds of expenditure alone, it could not last long. All these anticipations were falsified at a comparatively early date, and the world settled down to a belief in the prophecy, attributed to Lord Kitchener, that it would be an affair of at least three years.

Amongst other developments was the creation in the British Empire of armies of a strength of which the wildest dreamers before it probably never thought. Regiments which had never before consisted of more than four regular battalions at the most, found themselves with territorial and "service" battalions which, in some cases, raised their strength to that of a whole division, or even a corps, according to the old conceptions.

The Norfolk Regiment was not one of those which reached the largest dimensions; still it had in the end twelve battalions,[1] (not counting the so-called 13th Battalion, which was only a provisional organization created later for purposes of record of graves and collection of the scattered dead), of which no less than eight actually served abroad.

---

[1] Besides reserve and garrison battalions.

At first the old 1st and 2nd Battalions alone went abroad, and it was not till the latter part of 1915 that the 4th and 5th Territorial, and what was afterwards the 12th (Yeomanry) Battalion went to Gallipoli, and later to Egypt and Palestine. The "service" battalions (7th, 8th, and 9th) began to go abroad for active service in the second half of 1915. The services of the 1st (excepting a short period in Italy in 1917–18), 7th, 8th, and 9th were entirely on the Franco-Belgian front; the 2nd Battalion fought in Mesopotamia only; the 4th and 5th in Gallipoli, Egypt, and Palestine; and the 12th served on these fronts and in France and Belgium.

As a rule there was little change of each battalion from one brigade or division to another; but corps and armies were different, and the battalions found themselves frequently changed, with their brigade or division, from one corps to another, and the corps from one army to another. There were more changes of brigades and divisions on the Eastern fronts (2nd, 4th, 5th, and 12th Battalions).

The only satisfactory way to treat the various battalions is to give the history of each separately, seeing that, on the Western front, no two battalions of the Norfolk Regiment were ever in the same brigade or division. At the same time it seems desirable to show generally the distribution of the regiment on the Western front. On the Eastern fronts the 2nd Battalion was alone in Mesopotamia, whilst of the 4th, 5th, and 12th Battalions the two first were so much together that it is convenient to treat them in one section. The 12th, except in Gallipoli, was generally separated from them and ended its service on the Western front.

The following table will serve to show, for the Western front, where the various battalions were at the principal epochs after the first year of war. It strikes us that the separation of the battalions of a single regiment between different brigades and divisions, especially when so many of these battalions were new creations for this war only, might have tended to make esprit de corps base itself on the exploits of the brigade or the division, rather than on those of the regiment. But in the war diaries of the other battalions of the Norfolk Regiment, and in other documents, we find frequent references to the regular battalions, and hopes expressed that the new battalion is rendering itself a credit to the regular battalions and the regiment as a whole. This is all the more remarkable in that the "service" battalions often contained many officers and men from other counties and other regiments, and that at times some of them were commanded by officers from other units, whose employment in that capacity for a time was rendered necessary by the losses of senior officers in the battalion.

STATEMENT SHOWING THE LOCATION SYNCHRONICALLY OF THE BATTALIONS ON THE WESTERN FRONT FROM JULY, 1915

(The positions are only indicated very generally.)

Date.	1st Battalion.	7th Battalion.	8th Battalion.	9th Battalion.
1915 July	Verbranden, Molen	Ploegsteert	North of Amiens	—
Aug.	Albert and Fricourt	Do.	West of Albert	—
Sept.	Maricourt and Morlancourt	Do., and St. Elie and Vermelles	Do.	Montcavrel
Oct. Nov. Dec.	Trenches about Carnoy and Mametz	Trenches, Vermelles, Festubert	Albert Area On the Ancre Do.	Loos. Ypres Area. Do., St. Jean
1916 Jan.	Do.	Festubert	Near Albert	St. Jean (Ypres)
Feb.	Trenches west of Arras	Festubert and Hohenzollern Redoubt	Do.	Do.
March	Trenches N.E. of Arras	Hohenzollern Redoubt	Albert, Maricourt, and Bray-sur-Somme	South Side Ypres Salient
April	Do.	Do., and Lillers and Canchy	Maricourt, Somme Front	Calais, Wormhoudt

Date.	1st Battalion.	7th Battalion.	8th Battalion.	9th Battalion.
May	Trenches N.E. of Arras	Béthune Area	Vaux en Amienois, Somme Front	La Bassée Canal
June	Do.	Start for Somme at Vignecourt	Do., and to Carnoy	Do.
July	To Somme Front, Longueval, Delville Wood	Ovillers, Beaumont Hamel, etc.	Somme Battle, Montauban, Delville Wood back to Godewaerswalde	Do.
Aug.	Abbeville, and back at end to Somme Front	Ovillers, etc., Arras	Training south of Bailleul, etc.	Somme Front, Mailly-Maillot
Sept.	Falfemont Farm Morval	Arras Front	Thiepval, Schwaben Redoubt	Quadrilateral Ville-sur-Ancre, etc.
Oct.	Béthune Front Trenches	Somme Front, S.W. of Longueval, Arras	Schwaben Redoubt, Miraumont	Geudecourt, Mild Trench, etc.
Nov.	Do.	Arras Front	Warloy and Ovillers, Abbeville	Béthune Area
Dec.	Do.	Do.	Near Abbeville	Do.
1917. Jan.	Trenches, La Bassée Canal	Arras Area	Do.	Vermelles
Feb.	Do.	Do.	On the Ancre about Miraumont	Mazingarbe and Béthune
Mar.	Do.	Do.	Irles	Béthune Area
April	Vimy	Do.	Near Béthune	Do., and Hill 70
May	Fresnoy	Do.	Arras Front	Vermelles, Hulluch
June	Fresnoy and Oppy	Do.	Do.	Lens

Date.	1st Battalion.	7th Battalion.	8th Battalion.	9th Battalion.
July	Fresnoy and Oppy	Arras Area	Ypres Front ..	Lens and Armentières
Aug.	Do.	Do.	Do.	Armentières and Hill 70
Sept.	Beaumont, and back to Ypres Area	Do.	Rubrouck Training Area	Do.
Oct.	Polderhoek ..	Do.	West Bank Yser Canal, Poelcappelle	Do.
Nov.	Do., and Boulogne	To Peronne neighbourhood; battles of Cambrai	Poelcappelle ..	Ribécourt-Cambrai Battle
Dec.	Italy	Resting; eventually Merville, near Hazebrouck	Do.	2nd Cambrai Battle, Bailleuval
1918 Jan.	Do.	On the Lys about Sailly	Elverdinghe	Frémicourt, Bapaume-Cambrai, Railway
Feb.	Do.	Do.	Battalion disbanded	Quéant-Pronville Sector
March	Do.	Do.; on 24th to Albert neighbourhood; German Offensive	——	Do.; German Offensive
April	Forest of Nieppe	On the Ancre near Albert	——	Ypres Salient
May	Do.	Do.	12th (Yeomanry) Battalion	Do.
June	Do.	Do.	Nieppe Forest area	Do.
July	Do.	Do. ..	Do.	Do.
Aug.	Doullens and forward ..	Do., and forward by Falfemont	——	Do.

Date.	1st Battalion.	7th Battalion.	12th Battalion.	9th Battalion.
Sept.	Beugny	Forward by the Somme	⎫	Corbie (East of Amiens)
Oct.	Le Câteau	North of the Scarpe	⎬ Forward in final advance	Forward in final advance to Cologne
Nov.	Forest of Mormal and forward	Landas	⎪	
Dec.	Forward to Grand Lees	——	——	——

The sacrifices of the Norfolk Regiment in the Great War were perhaps not greater than those of many another regiment, but how heavy they were is shown by the return of those who lost their lives—a return which takes no account of the many thousands of wounds, of which many resulted in permanent, total, or partial disablement. Of these it is not possible for us to give a statement.

The losses in dead alone of the eight battalions which served abroad were:

```
1st    Battalion  -  -  -  -  -  -  -  1,201
2nd    do.        -  -  -  -  -  -  -    557
1/4th  do.        -  -  -  -  -  -  -    359
1/5th  do.        -  -  -  -  -  -  -    519
7th    do.        -  -  -  -  -  -  -  1,114
8th    do.        -  -  -  -  -  -  -    673
9th    do.        -  -  -  -  -  -  -  1,019
12th   do.        -  -  -  -  -  -  -    134
                                        -----
                                        5,576
```

The total number of men raised during the war was 32,375.

The accounts of the doings of the several battalions are based mainly on the War Diaries of each, and of the brigade and division to which it belonged. All these vary in fullness. Where the battalion War Diary is brief and incomplete, which it must be said is not usual, fuller accounts of actions have been got from War Diaries of the brigade or the division. To supplement these the writer has in some cases had the great advantage of personal narratives by officers engaged, though it is to be regretted that these are not more numerous.

Other officers have given useful help by correcting errors and furnishing supplementary information for the drafts of the history of their battalions.

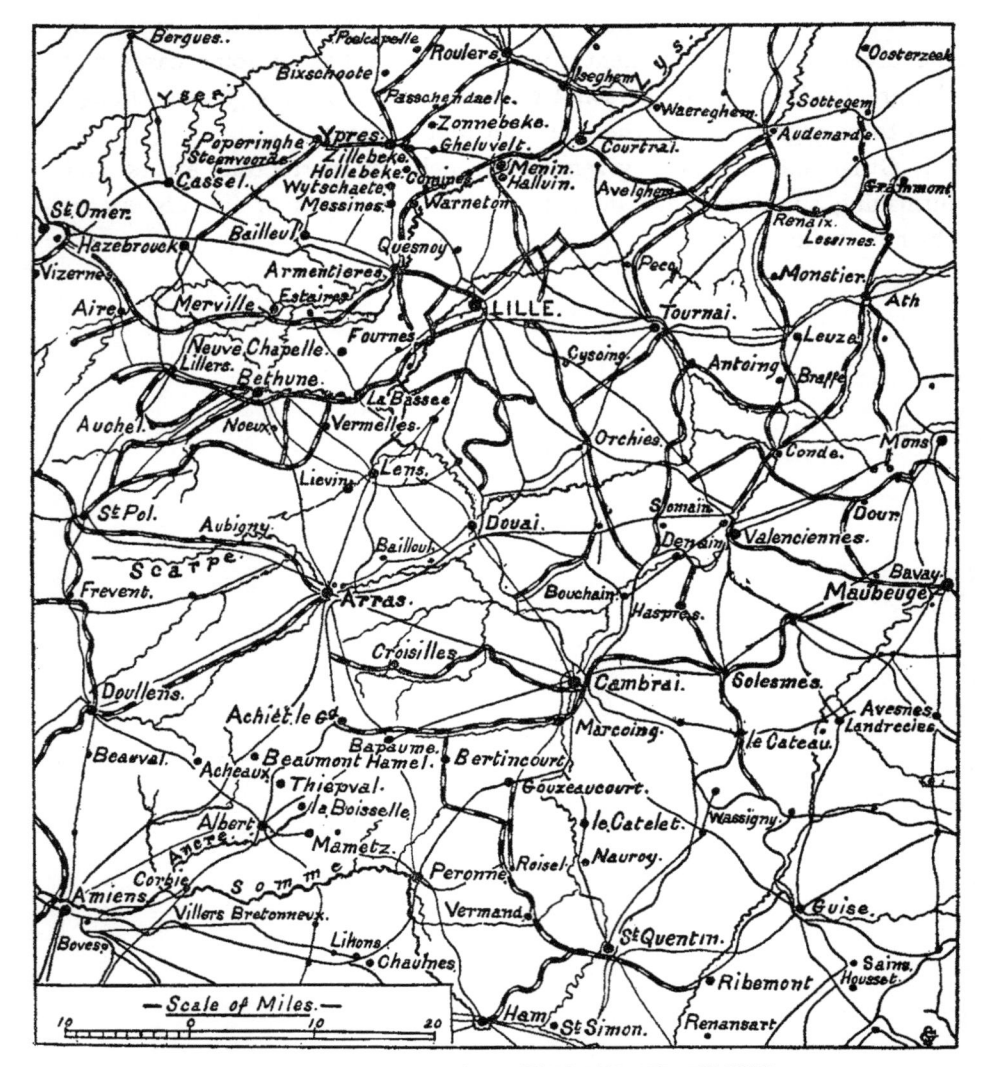

PART OF THE WESTERN FRONT IN FRANCE AND BELGIUM

HISTORY OF THE NORFOLK REGIMENT

CHAPTER I

THE FIRST BATTALION IN BELGIUM AND FRANCE

(a) 1914: MONS, (ELOUGES)—LE CÂTEAU—THE MARNE—THE AISNE—LA BASSÉE—YPRES

THE 1st Battalion was quartered at Belfast when, in the evening of the 4th August, 1914, it received the order to mobilize for the Great War which was now inevitable. Mobilization was complete by the 10th, and on the 14th the battalion embarked on two transports. It formed a unit of the 15th infantry brigade, the commander of which was Brigadier-General Count Gleichen. The other regiments of the brigade were the 1st Battalions of the Cheshire, Bedford, and Dorset Regiments. The Bedford and Cheshire battalions continued with the 1st Norfolk in the brigade till the end of 1918. The 1st Dorset left it after 1915, in which year the 6th Cheshire and 6th Liverpool were temporarily attached to it. In 1916 the 16th Royal Warwickshire Regiment took the place of the 1st Dorset, and the two battalions added in 1915 gave place to a 15th Brigade Machine Gun Company and a Trench Mortar Battalion. There was no further change in the composition of the brigade till 1918, when the Machine Gun Company ceased to belong to it, and became part of the 5th Battalion Machine Gun Corps.[1]

The brigade, with those numbered 13 and 14, constituted the infantry of the 5th division under the command of Major-General Sir

[1] "The 5th Division in the Great War," Appendix I.

Charles Fergusson. The 13th and 14th brigades sailed from Dublin. The 5th and 3rd divisions constituted the 2nd corps commanded by Lieutenant-General Sir Horace Smith-Dorrien, in succession to General Grierson, whose sudden death had deprived the British Army of one of its most valued chiefs.

Havre was reached without mishap, and the Norfolk battalion marched, with the rest of the brigade, to Rest Camp No. 8, on the hill six miles off. There was some difficulty in finding the way in the dark, especially as a motor lorry had broken down on the road.

The Officers originally with the battalion were:

Head Quarters.
Lieutenant-Colonel C. R. Ballard,
Major J. B. Orr, D.S.O.,
Captain and Adjutant F. J. Cresswell,
Lieutenant and Quartermaster E. Smith.

"A" Company.
Major H. R. Done,
Lieutenant R. C. Nixon,
Lieutenant M. D. Jephson,
2nd Lieutenant G. N. Paget,
2nd Lieutenant A. E. Reeve.

"B" Company.
Captain R. H. Brudenell Bruce,
Captain W. C. K. Megaw,
Lieutenant M. F. R. Lightfoot,
Lieutenant J. R. Holland.
Lieutenant H. M. Openshaw.
2nd Lieutenant O. S. D. Wills
2nd Lieutenant F. C. Boosey.

"C" Company.
Captain C. E. Luard, D.S.O.,
Captain T. R. Bowlby,
Lieutenant G. C. Lyle,
Lieutenant T. A. F. Foley,
2nd Lieutenant R. W. Patteson.

"D" Company.
Captain E. N. Snepp.
Captain R. C. Clark,
Lieutenant E. V. F. Briard.
Lieutenant E. H. T. B. Broadwood,
2nd Lieutenant J. B. Oakes.

In the night of August 17th, the brigade entrained for the front, and arrived at Le Câteau next day. On the 20th the battalions were paraded and addressed by the G. O. C. 5th division. On the 21st and 22nd they marched to Dour and Bois de Bossu, where the brigade was in support of the 13th and 14th brigades spread out along the Mons-Condé Canal, the 5th division being on the extreme left of the British Army, with the 3rd division on its right. On the 23rd, whilst engaged in digging trenches, the battalion received its first German shells, but had no casualties.

With this exception the 1st Norfolk battalion was not engaged actively on the first day of the battle of Mons. Their turn was to come next day under circumstances now to be related.

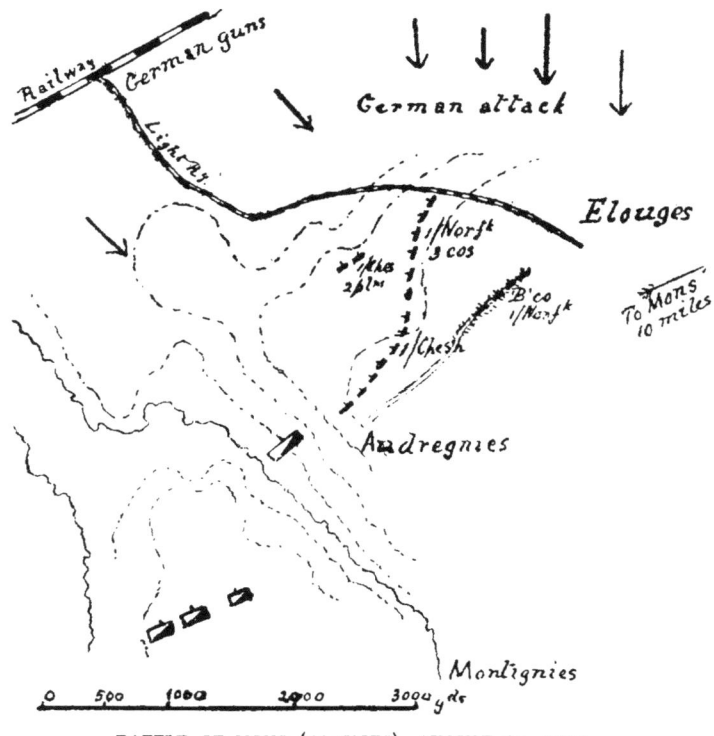

BATTLE OF MONS (ELOUGES), AUGUST 24, 1914

At 4.30 a.m. on August 24th the battalion was relieved by the 1st Suffolk in the trenches on the railway running south of, and parallel to, the Mons-Condé Canal. Then it marched southwards to Dour in divisional reserve. About 11 a.m. the 13th and 14th brigades of the 5th division had begun their retreat. The 15th brigade was on the left of these, and about 11.45 it became clear to the commander of the 5th division that his retreat was threatened by large German forces advancing from the north beyond his left, which was now uncovered by the retirement of the 19th infantry brigade and the cavalry division on that side. He at once called on the cavalry to return, and created a left flank guard for his division by placing the 1st Norfolk and 1st Cheshire battalions, a squadron of the 19th Hussars, and the 119th battery under the command of Colonel Ballard. At first this force advanced northwards to counter-attack, but was very soon diverted to a position facing west, about 1,000 yards west of Elouges. Here the 1st Norfolk battalion was posted with its right resting on the railway running from Elouges to Quièvrain. On the left of the 1st Norfolk battalion the line was continued southwards by the 1st Cheshire as far as the outskirts of Audregnies. The position was a good one, with a glacis slope falling from it to the west.

About 12.30 p.m. the 9th Lancers and part of the 4th Dragoon Guards charged northwards from Audregnies along the Condé road but were stopped and forced to retire by heavy German artillery fire. These squadrons rallied and reformed in the sunken road in which was the reserve Norfolk company. This delayed the German attack, which was covered by the fire of at least seven batteries. The 119th British battery came into action about 200 yards behind the reserve company of the Norfolk Regiment, and engaged the German batteries. The British gunners under the storm of fire were as cool as if it had been a field day. Some of the German shells meant for them were short and fell amongst the Norfolk reserve company. The attacking force was the whole of the German 4th Corps. Still the infantry of Colonel Ballard's force seemed safe against a frontal attack, and it was not till about 2.30 p.m. that he found it necessary, owing to threats to his right flank from the north, and to his left by an extension of the German envelopment, to order his troops to follow the retreat of those on his right rear.

The Norfolk battalion had already suffered heavy losses, among them those of Captain and Adjutant F. J. Cresswell, killed whilst carrying a message, and of Major J. B. Orr, second in command. Owing to these two deaths, one platoon in an advanced position did not receive the orders to retire, and remained with the Cheshire Regiment, whose orders likewise failed to reach them, though Colonel Ballard had sent three messages. The consequence was that this battalion and the Norfolk platoon were cut off, and, after fighting till their ammunition was exhausted, and they were completely surrounded, they were compelled to surrender. The Cheshire battalion only mustered two officers and about 200 men on the following morning. The 1st Norfolk too had suffered heavily. Four officers (Major Orr, Captain Cresswell, Lieutenant Openshaw, and Lieutenant Briard) were killed or mortally wounded; four more (Lieutenant M. D. Jephson, and 2nd Lieutenants A. E. Reeve, J. B. Oakes and G. N. Paget) were wounded, and about 250 other ranks killed, wounded, or missing. The battalion and the 1st Cheshire had made a most gallant stand against enormously superior forces, and had effectually covered the retreat of the brigade. About a hundred of the wounded had to be left in Elouges.

That night they bivouacked at Bavai, and on the following morning continued the retreat, in sweltering heat, along the western edge of the Mormal Forest to Troisvilles, three miles west of Le Câteau. It had been intended to continue the retreat on the 26th, but the commander of the 2nd corps found himself compelled to make a stand before doing so.

The position assigned to the 1st Norfolk Regiment on the morning of August 26th was in second line along the sunken road running east from the southern part of Troisvilles to Le Câteau. Their position was marked by a large solitary tree about 1,200 yards east of Troisvilles.

The 1st Bedford Regiment was in first line 1,000 yards north and the 1st Dorset was in front of Troisvilles on the left of the 1st Bedford, on the right of which the 2nd King's Own Scottish Borderers continued the line. During the earlier part of the battle even the front line in this part was not seriously attacked, and the Norfolk battalion, dug in on the sunken road, was not disturbed at all. The 2nd corps was threatened and attacked on both flanks, and about 1.15 p.m. the 1st Norfolk was sent back to Reumont, about 2,000 yards south of the tree near the sunken road.

It was about 3.30 p.m. when General Smith-Dorrien decided to break off the action and continue the retreat.

The spur running south-eastwards from Reumont was held by a party of the infantry and a battery. Behind them were the 2nd Royal Welsh Fusiliers, 1st Scottish Rifles, and 1st Norfolk Regiment, except one and a half companies of the latter sheltered in a quarry south-west

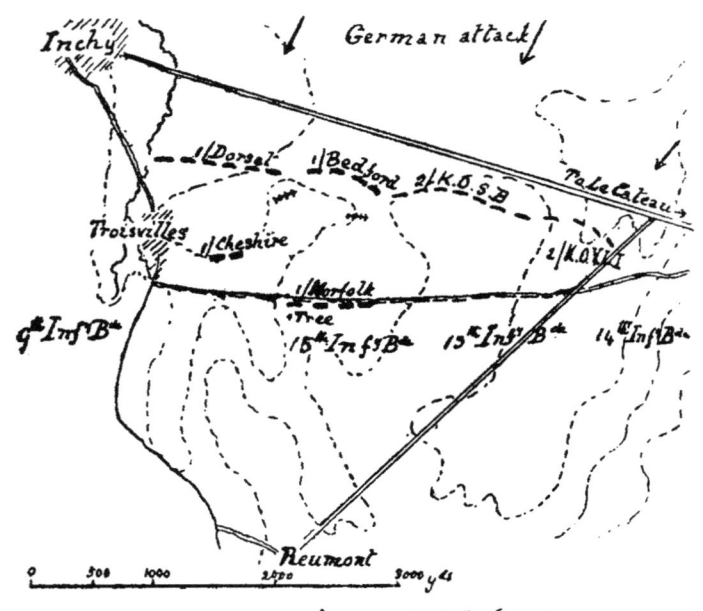

BATTLE OF LE CÂTEAU, AUGUST 26, 1914

of Reumont, which were at this time the troops nearest the enemy. This detachment fired on the advancing Germans north-east of it, and presently retired through a company of Royal Welsh Fusiliers, which took over the rear-guard from them.

The battalion now passed farther to the right to the edge of Honnechy, where they found a better field of fire against the Germans advancing up the valley of the Selle from Le Câteau. On these they opened an effective rifle fire. The Germans advancing by the road in the valley came to a standstill some 1,500 yards before they reached the Norfolk position. Falling back by successive companies, their fire kept back advancing parties of Germans. The main road to St. Quentin was reached at Busigny, the Norfolk Regiment still acting as rear-guard in this direction.

All that night the retreat went on. The diary of the 15th brigade, after describing the terrible congestion on the road, where infantry, guns, and motor transport were almost inextricably mixed up, adds significantly : " It looked like the break up of an army." It is hardly surprising that the Germans thought that French's " contemptibles " were destroyed. Yet, by the time it reached St. Quentin in the morning of August 27th, the 15th brigade was more or less together, and by noon the various units had got fairly sorted out into their separate rest camps.

During the 28th, at one of the numerous halts, Sir John French, when he met the brigade head-quarters, assured them that their action at Le Câteau had " resulted in saving the left flank of the French Army." His words of praise addressed to the units raised the spirits of all. During the first twenty-four hours after Le Câteau the 5th division marched about thirty miles. The Norfolk battalion, doing rear-guard to the division, was holding the line of the Somme Canal on the morning of the 28th, when a breakdown on the road checked the retreat for an hour. Fortunately, the Germans did not appear, and the march continued through Noyon to Pontoise, and on the 29th to Carlepont. Passing by the eastern edge of the Forest of Compiègne, the brigade retreated, with the rest of the army, through Crépy-en-Valois on the 31st, Ormoy Villers on the 1st September, and Montgé on the 2nd. The 1st Norfolk had now been relieved of their rear-guard duty and returned to the 15th brigade. They were almost in sight of Paris, but still the retreat continued, with various alarms but no serious fighting, till Tournans,[1] less than twenty miles south-east of Paris, was passed on September 5th. Then came the unexpected and joyful news that the retreat had ended, and was to be converted next day into an advance. The effect on the spirits of all was marvellous. The reasons for the sudden change were not known, but men at once began to march, no longer desponding,

[1] 1st reinforcement under 2nd Lieutenant A. C. O'Connor joined the battalion here.

but cheerily singing and whistling as they returned through Tournans and through the Forest of Crécy to La Celle. Thence, on the 7th, the march continued to the Petit Morin. On the 9th the Marne was crossed. Beyond this river the first serious resistance of the Germans since the advance commenced was encountered by the 15th brigade at Hill 189, south-east of Montreuil aux Lions, from which a battery opened on the 1st Norfolk, killing one man and wounding thirteen. They were then sent forward to attack the hill in front with the 1st Dorset, whilst the 1st Bedford moved round it to the right, the 14th brigade being on the left. The Norfolk and Dorset battalions crawled forward under a rather heavy fire from some distant unseen heavy guns, but could not get beyond a low ridge, whence they could fire effectively on the enemy infantry entrenched within 120 yards from them, and where eventually they dug themselves in for the night. By next morning the German rear-guard had disappeared, leaving behind them their field battery on Hill 189, surrounded by its dead. The cavalry were now in front rounding up convoys, and leaving the traces of their action in the shape of broken-down German motors and dead men.

On September 12th the 1st Norfolk and 1st Dorset battalions were at Nampteuil; on the 13th the brigade was approaching the Aisne, with orders to cross by rafts in the ensuing night. The crossing, near Bucy-le-long, above Soissons, was made without fighting, though with considerable difficulty; but, as they marched into Ste Marguerite, on the 14th, the troops came under heavy fire of all sorts. They were moving eastwards to Missy, a village lying near the foot of the heights on the top of which runs the famous Chemin des Dames. From Missy the brigade had orders to clear the spur leading down from the north and having on it the Condé fort. After 4.30 p.m. a somewhat mixed force, consisting of twelve companies[1] of battalions belonging to the 13th, 14th, and 15th brigades, had been collected in Missy and was sent forward northwards to the attack of the spur. There were too many men for the passage of a space enclosed on either side by a six foot wire

[1] Three on the right from the 1st Norfolk, four in the centre from the 1st Bedford, three on the left from the East Surrey, with two from the Cheshire and Duke of Cornwall's Light Infantry in support.

netting in the wood above. Some of them did get through into the wood, where some Germans were killed. Farther on in the wood there was a horseshoe shaped road where the men lost direction, and the right closed in on the centre, with the result that there was a good deal of confusion and some firing on friends, who were mistaken for Germans. There was also a belief among the men that their own artillery were

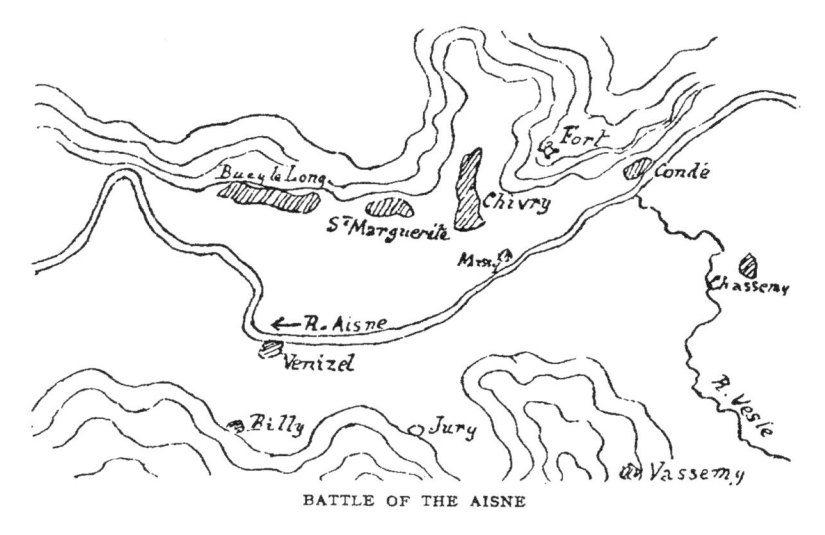

BATTLE OF THE AISNE

firing on them, and they began to fall back in considerable confusion on Missy, where they were heavily shelled by the Germans.

Of the 1st Norfolk, twenty-five men, with Captains C. E. Luard and T. R. Bowlby, appear to have got far forward in the wood, where both these officers were killed, and the rest either taken or killed. These were of C. company. A and D companies got back in good order to Missy. In addition to the officers above named, Lieutenant J. R. Holland and 2nd Lieutenant O'Connor were wounded, and about one hundred other ranks killed, wounded, or missing. The attack had failed.

On the 15th a renewal of the attack was ordered, the 1st Norfolk leading about 8 a.m., with the 1st Bedford in support, and the 1st Cheshire in reserve. The Norfolk men again got into the wood, but were unable to make much progress, and eventually, after a second attempt to advance, which was stopped at a wire net six feet high, withdrew to the line Missy–Ste Marguerite. That night the brigade was relieved and sent back to Jury in a valley of the southern border of the Aisne valley. Thence the 1st Norfolk were moved to Chassemy to reinforce the 3rd division. On the 27th they went into billets farther back at Vasseny, and on October 2nd they were back with the 15th brigade at Droizy. They had been shelled more than once at Chassemy, but had suffered few casualties. 2nd Lieutenant Teeling was killed by a shell on the 24th.

They were now to be moved farther north, and on the morning of the 7th they entrained with the rest of the brigade from stations near Compiègne, passing by Creil, to Abbeville; whence, partly by march, and partly by motor buses, they reached Béthune on the 11th. They now moved forward to the La Bassée front, a perfectly flat country, very different from the hills near the Aisne. It has been described as resembling the Black Country of the English Midlands, with fen lands interspersed among the coal mines and factories. At first the 1st Norfolk was kept in divisional reserve till October 19th, when they were in front between Festubert and Givenchy, where, on the 20th, a heavy shelling wounded Captain E. N. Snepp, Lieutenant E. H. T. Broadwood, and about twenty men. By the 21st the 1st Norfolk was about half way between Canteleux and Violaines, which latter place the 1st Cheshire had reached. The 22nd was a day of battle. At 6 a.m. the 1st Cheshire, on the left, were driven back from Violaines with heavy loss. All that day the Germans made frequent attacks, but never made much progress in that way, though they did a good deal of work in pushing forward their trenches. Lieutenant Budgen (wounded) was apparently the only officer casualty on that day. That night the whole brigade fell back to a line just east of Festubert and Givenchy, where they dug themselves in.

On the 25th a heavy bombardment was followed by a more determined German attack, which was beaten off with the loss of Lieutenant T. A. F. Foley and twenty men killed and thirty wounded. The Indian (Lahore) division now reinforced the exhausted 15th brigade and shared the trenches with them. The Indian infantry in the Norfolk trenches had a strength of four men to each man of the 1st Norfolk. French troops were also fighting with the 15th brigade.

On the 29th, during a heavy attack on the Devonshire Regiment, one company of the 1st Norfolk was sent to help the latter regiment, and presently a French battalion sent two companies as reserve to the other three companies of the 1st Norfolk. The fighting was over for the

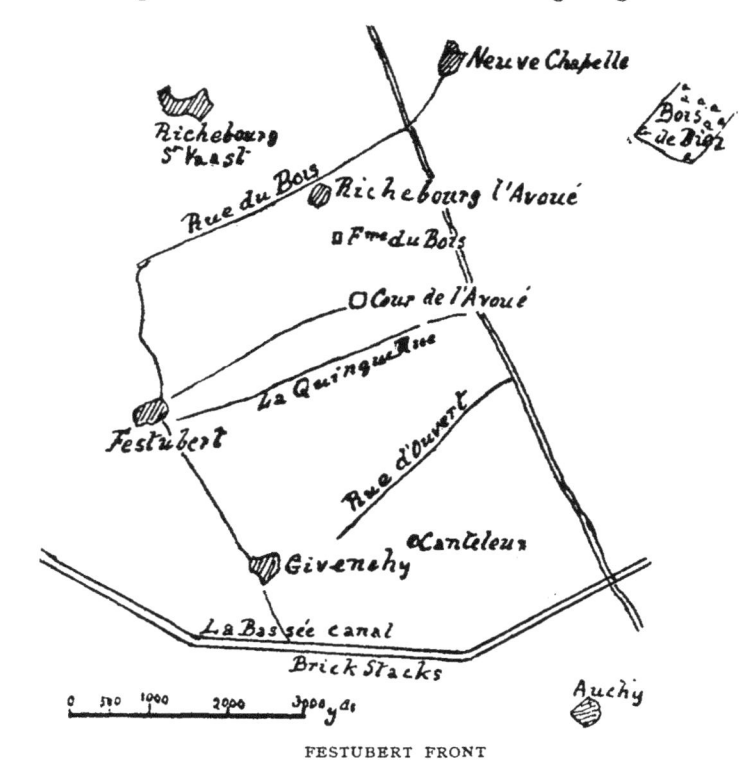

FESTUBERT FRONT

day by between 9 and 10 a.m. During this day Colonel Strickland, the present colonel of the Norfolk Regiment, was engaged with the 2nd Manchester Regiment, which he then commanded, in support of the Devons.[1]

On October 30th the 15th brigade was relieved by the Lahore

[1] He was an officer of the Norfolk Regiment, and had been with them at Belfast before the war. On appointment to command the Manchester battalion he joined it in Egypt on its way home.

division and sent north. But the whole of the Norfolk, and half the Bedford battalion, were left behind to initiate the new-comers into what, to them, was a novel form of fighting.

It was not till November 13th that the 1st Norfolk marched off northwards to the Ypres front, where the first battle of that name was in progress, and where they were temporarily attached to the 14th brigade. At this time there were a great many changes of organization on the British front, battalions being constantly shifted about from one brigade or division to another. On the 18th the 1st Norfolk, in very cold weather, took over the French trenches at Kemmel, just east of the commanding hill of the same name. Ten days later they returned to billets at Dranoutre, and on the 29th once more joined the 15th brigade.

They were now settling down for the winter trench warfare, and we must pass very briefly over the next few months of monotony. The trench warfare of the Western front has been described as consisting of long periods of intense boredom, punctuated with moments of intense excitement. The trenches of the front about Messines and Ploegsteert were unutterably miserable in the winter of 1914–15. The weather was vile, constant rain alternating with frost and snow. In a low-lying, swampy country there was a superfluity of Napoleon's fifth element of the campaign of 1806–7—mud. Men in the trenches were constantly in varying depths of water or mud; "trench-feet" became the fashionable complaint, and, work as they might, the men were never able to improve the trenches up to anything like the standard which was attained in later years. The history of the 5th division describes the work as "a very labour of Sisyphus; no sooner had one part been built up, than, weakened by rain, another portion slid down into the water at the bottom of the trench." It was only by the spring of 1915 that conditions in the front and support trenches became even tolerable. In brigade reserve positions conditions were less bad, and the 15th brigade was lucky in having as a reserve position the village of Dranoutre, which hardly ever received the attentions of the German artillery. The paradise of the troops on this front was the divisional reserve at Bailleul.

All through this period, from November, 1914, to March, 1915, the routine for all battalions was the same : so many days in the supreme misery of the front trenches, as many more in the almost equal discomfort of support trenches, then a turn of the comparative comfort of brigade reserve, and a short enjoyment of divisional reserve. Whereever they were, the men were working hard. If they had not to supply working parties for the improvement of trenches, they were busy at training, either general or in special subjects, attacks, machine gun or Lewis gun instruction, or one of the innumerable special branches which characterize warfare in the twentieth century. In the front and support trenches it was always the same—utter discomfort, constant shelling by the German artillery in varying quantities, and with varying results in the shape of casualties. One day there would be no casualties, the next perhaps fourteen or fifteen, the next two or three.

On Christmas Day occurred the famous meeting with the Germans in " No Man's Land " which drew down the wrath of G.H.Q. and a demand for the names of officers, who, it was held, should have prevented it. The matter was eventually dropped, and no harm was, as a matter of fact, done, seeing that our men managed to have a good look at the German defences, and took good care that the fraternization did not spread over to their own trenches. Visits of the King, the Prince of Wales, and the King of the Belgians made some break in the monotonous existence of those troops who were not at the time in the forward lines.

At the end of February, 1915, the 15th brigade was moved from the neighbourhood of Messines to the southern face of the Ypres salient, in relief of the 84th brigade of the 28th division, about St. Eloi, where the trenches were, if possible, worse than those they had left.

By this time, of the officers who had left Belfast in August, 1914 there remained in the 1st Norfolk only five.[1]

During the period from the middle of November to the end of February, the casualties from enemy action, bombardment, snipers,

---

[1] " The Doings of the Fifteenth Infantry Brigade," p. 282. The author, Brigadier-General Count Gleichen, was at this time promoted Major-General and handed over command of the brigade to Brigadier-General Northey.

etc., had been four officers killed and four wounded; of other ranks nineteen killed and forty-seven wounded.

(b) 1915: YPRES—THE SOMME FRONT

From March 3, 1915, when the 1st Norfolk first occupied the St. Eloi trenches, till the 14th matters were quiet. On the latter date the enemy commenced bombarding the front between the canal on the British left and St. Eloi on the right. A mine was at the same time exploded under the " Mound " and a heavy infantry attack followed.

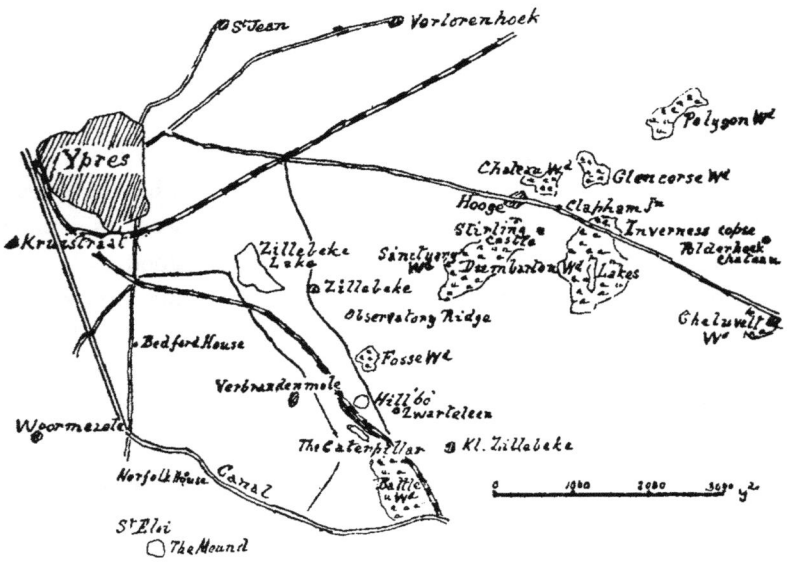

NEIGHBOURHOOD OF YPRES

St. Eloi fell into the enemy's hands, thus exposing the right flank of the 15th brigade. The 13th brigade, from reserve, was sent up, and during the night the 27th division recaptured all the ground they had lost, except the " Mound." During this day, the 1st Norfolk, on their way to the front from Kruistraat, had just left that place when the German bombardment began on it. Luckily for them, they were not caught formed in it; but, as it was, they lost Lieutenant McCurdy and six men killed, and nineteen wounded. No further attempt on St. Eloi was made after its recapture by the British.

In the beginning of April the 5th division held a line from the "Mound" at St. Eloi, running north-eastwards on the west side of Hill 60, with the 15th brigade still in the right sector south-west of Hill 60, on which an attack was being prepared. The 1st Norfolk had lost, on March 31st, Captain and Adjutant Megaw killed, and were in reserve from the 7th to the 9th at Zevecoton. On the 10th three companies relieved the King's Own Scottish Borderers in the trenches at Verbranden Molen, the fourth remaining in reserve at Ypres, and moving up on the 11th. In those trenches they remained till the 17th, on which date, at 7 p.m., three British mines were exploded under Hill 60, about 150 yards to the left of their position. Immediately afterwards a heavy bombardment and rifle fire was opened by the British artillery and the infantry in the trenches. The German artillery replied at once, their shells falling all around the 1st Norfolk men, who, however, encountered little rifle fire.

What is known as "Hill 60" was only in reality a large mound, formed of earth excavated from a cutting on the Ypres-Comines Railway. On the opposite side of the cutting, south of Hill 60, was a similar mound called the "Caterpillar," from its shape. On the same side of the cutting as the Caterpillar, about 300 yards to the northwest, was another smaller mound known as the "Dump." The trenches of Verbranden Molen were south-east of the "Dump." The cutting itself was through the highest part of the ridge south-east of Ypres. At the time of the attack the 15th brigade had been moved to the left sector facing Hill 60, with the 14th brigade on its right, and the 13th in reserve at Ouderdom. The 1st Norfolk was on the west of the cutting, the 1st Dorset on the east of it, the Bedford and Cheshire battalions on the left of the Dorset. The night before the attack the 13th brigade took over the front trenches from the 15th with the King's Own Scottish Borderers and West Kent battalions. These two battalions, covered by the fire of the 15th brigade and numerous machine guns on their left, rushed Hill 60 with small loss and got some distance beyond the crest into the German position.

On this occasion the German artillery for the first time used gas and lachrymatory shells, which, in the absence of masks, caused many casualties. The German shelling went on till after midnight, the 1st Norfolk still remaining in their trenches. At 3 a.m. on the 18th they were firing vigorously on a German counter-attack, and assisting thereby in its repulse by the troops on Hill 60. At 6 p.m. they again assisted with their fire in an attack by the British to improve their position on the hill. In these two days the casualties of the 1st Norfolk were Lieutenant Todd, died of wounds, and Lieutenant Bryans wounded; of other ranks eleven killed, forty-six wounded. On the 20th the 1st Norfolk again assisted with their fire against a counter-attack which forced the holders of Hill 60 back to the line originally taken on the 17th. Casualties: Captain P. V. P. Stone and Lieutenant Withington wounded; seven other ranks killed, and thirty-one wounded. They were heavily shelled during the 21st and 22nd till, on the latter date, the centre of interest in front of Ypres moved farther north, to the great gas attack by which the Germans hoped to force their way to the Channel.

During the early part of May the 1st Norfolk remained in the same trenches till, after suffering seventy-five casualties from gas on the 5th, they were relieved on the 6th. They retired to the camp at Ouderdom, after being for twenty-six days continuously in the trenches. In this period they lost ten killed and fifty wounded. All June was spent in and out of the trenches at Verbranden Molen, with a loss in the month of twenty-two killed and 123 wounded. They were still there for the first thirteen days of July, during which Lieutenant L. C. Wilson died of wounds; seven other ranks were killed, and thirty-nine wounded.

After that followed a period of training and recuperation up till the 29th. On the 23rd the battalion was inspected by the army commander, General Plumer.

The 15th brigade had again lost its commander owing to General Northey being wounded. He was succeeded by Brigadier-General M. N. Turner. The division was commanded by Major-General C. T. Kavanagh, after the promotion of General Morland to the 10th corps command. The 5th division was now destined to the Somme front.

On the night of July 29th–30th the 1st Norfolk entrained at Godewaersvelde and, after travelling all night, reached Corbie, just east of Amiens, at 6.30 a.m. and marched thence to La Houssoye. On August 2nd they

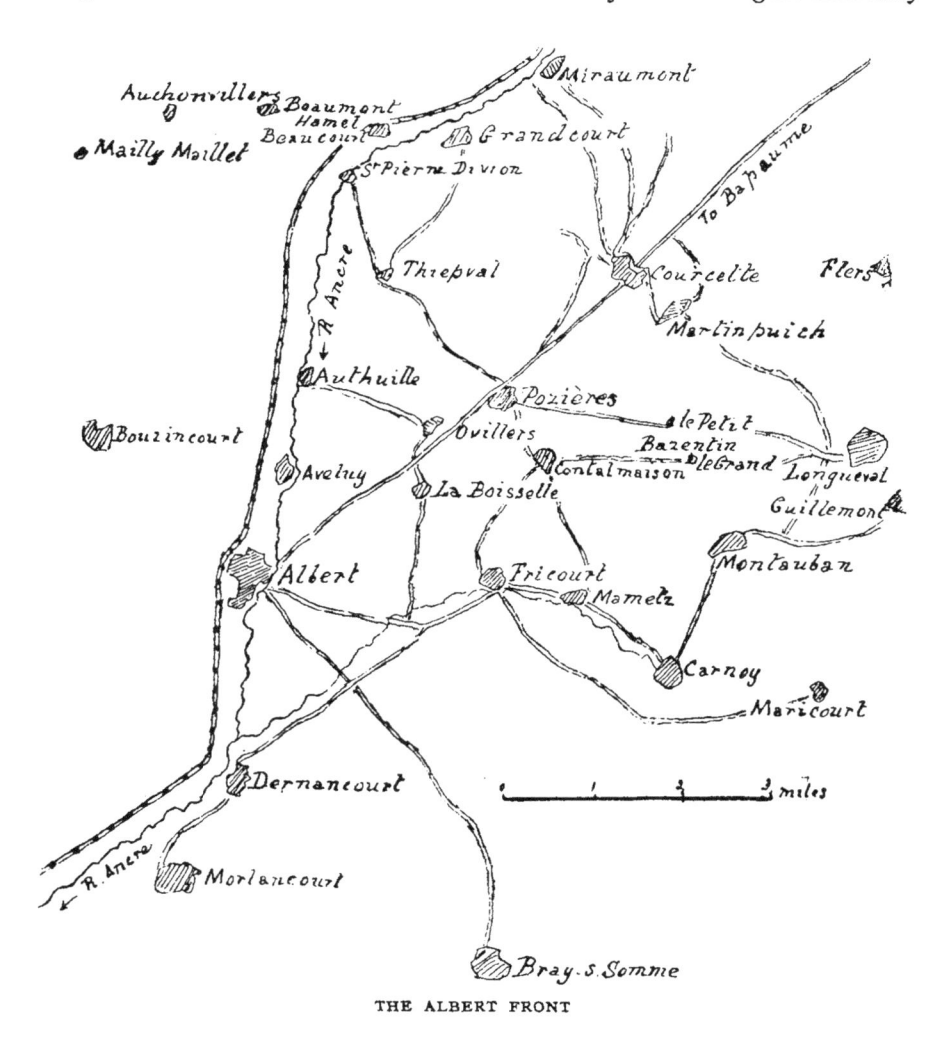

THE ALBERT FRONT

relieved the French 119th in trenches at Fricourt, east of Albert. From the 2nd to the 22nd was a quiet time, the total casualties being six killed and eleven wounded. During the remainder of August the

1st Norfolk was in billets at Morlancourt and other places, supplying daily parties to work in the neighbouring support trenches.

On September 1st they began a series of alternate reliefs with the East Surrey Regiment at Maricourt, returning to Morlancourt during the days they were not holding the trenches, and supplying working parties. From the 16th they held the trenches at Carnoy, which they took over from the 10th Essex. On the last day of September a heavy bombardment resulted in the death of Captain J. P. Longfield, and the wounding of Lieutenant Klein and another officer. Of other ranks four were killed and eight wounded.

On the whole, the trenches were a great improvement on anything the 5th division had held before. The centre of the divisional front at Carnoy faced due north, whilst the right flank bent back from Maricourt to the Somme, beyond which were the French; the left flank, about Fricourt, bent forwards to face east.

From September till the close of 1915 was generally a very quiet time as regards fighting, though, of course, there were the usual bombardments of varying intensity. The 1st Norfolk were, during their periods of front trench service, in the trenches between Carnoy and Mametz. When out of them, they were kept constantly employed in supplying working parties, or in training of various kinds, including the training of the whole battalion as grenadiers. In those days the trench artillery (Stokes mortars were not yet to the fore), consisted of weird weapons, including adaptations of the ancient Roman catapult and similar weapons, the use of which had to be learnt.

On October 25th the battalion was one of the two representing the 10th Corps at the King's inspection at Ribécourt. On December 1st, just as the battalion got into the trenches, the Germans exploded a mine in the sector, causing several casualties among the mining and tunnelling fatigues. In rescuing buried men gallant service was done by Lieutenant Burlton, Sergeant Dunbabbin and Private Doughty. For this the officer received the M.C. and the others the D.C.M.

On December 15th Lieutenant-Colonel H. R. Done, who had commanded the battalion since November, 1914, was translated to the command of the 145th brigade, and was succeeded by Captain T. F. Wall, who presently made over to Major P. V. P. Stone.

On December 29th the battalion began occupying trenches rather more to the left which were found to be an improvement.

(c) 1916: LONGUEVAL—FALFEMONT FARM—MORVAL—GIVENCHY

January, 1916, passed in the usual routine up to the 29th, when one platoon of " C " company under Lieutenant Borton was sent from Bray to Cappy, and two more (Lieutenants Montgomerie and Martin) to Froissy, the whole under Captain O'Connor. Their object was to keep in touch with the French on the left bank of the Somme who had been driven from Frise on the day before, and were now counter-attacking. Both Cappy and Froissy were heavily shelled all day, and at 9 p.m. " A " company was placed under the orders of the 90th brigade at Suzanne, for the same purpose of keeping touch with the French. " A " Company returned to Bray on the 30th. The 5th division had at this time been replaced by the 30th, but the 15th brigade was left behind for the moment. The other two brigades of the 5th division (the 13th and 95th)[1] had gone to Corbie, where they were rejoined by the 15th brigade on February 2nd.

On February 6th the 5th division moved to the area just north of Amiens, and on to the Cavillon area, where they hoped to have a rest— a hope which was soon disappointed. The great German attack on Verdun had begun on February 21st, and the 5th division was required to set free French troops holding the front about Arras. The weather was terrible; heavy snow and frost rendered the roads almost impassable. On one occasion the infantry had to drag the transport up a hill on which the horses were unable to keep their feet; moreover, the roads were much blocked by French troops on their way to Verdun. Passing

[1] This brigade, commanded by Brigadier-General Ballard of the 1st Norfolk, consisted of three battalions of the 14th Brigade, with four battalions of the new (Kitchener's) army. It had replaced the 14th Brigade in the reorganization necessitated by the appearance on the front of the new army.

from the Vidame area by Belloy sur Somme, Candas, and Doullens, the 1st Norfolk first occupied the French second line trenches west of Arras, and then, on March 9th, relieved the 15th Royal Warwickshire Regiment in the front line trenches north-east of Arras, across the road to Bailleul. The 1st Bedford were on their right, the 95th brigade on their left as far as Roclincourt. The weather continued horrible till March 12th, when it cleared up. The remainder of March was spent in the usual trench routine, Arras being the reserve position. On March 29th Captain H. S. Cameron was wounded in the trenches, and Lieutenant A. W. Bates died of wounds. On the previous day Major Stone had again been wounded. Thanks to the severe training they had undergone, the men were at this time in the height of condition.

The early days of April were on the whole quiet, though a few casualties were caused on two occasions by the explosion of German mines. The monotony of the time was relieved by an inspection by the G.O.C. 5th Division, and by inter-regimental football matches between battalions in the back areas. Otherwise things went on as usual into May, with occasional severe outbursts of German shelling. On the 7th May the wire on the front of the 1st Norfolk was extensively cut by "Minenwerfer," in consequence of which a regular system of wiring and patrolling on alternate nights was started, each company sending out ten men on the patrol nights. Another plan which was adopted at this time was the "obstacle trench" system, consisting in evacuating the original fire trench and filling it up with wire. The line actually held was some distance in rear of this, beyond the area of German mines; the line so held being connected with the "obstacle trench" by small posts. On May 19th the Germans fired a mine on the left of the 1st Norfolk, to which they replied by blowing a "camouflet" in another place.

On the 20th there was fighting about the crater of the German mine, and Lieutenant Hoare and the Norfolk stretcher-bearers succeeded in digging out an officer and a non-commisioned officer of the 15th Warwickshire who had been buried. On the night of the 21st Lieutenants Hoare and Hall, with a party, covered the right of a trench raid by the 15th Warwickshire, when a German bombing party was encountered, but no casualties occurred on our side.

A German bombardment on June 1st wrecked the left trench on the Norfolk front. On the 2nd and 3rd the storm fell on the trenches on the right, killing four and wounding eight men. On the 4th, the two trenches on the left of this right-hand group being no longer tenable, the men in them had to move to their left. At 9.17 p.m., after three hours of bombardment, the enemy exploded three large mines, of which two were on the Norfolk front and the third just to the left of it. The explosion was immediately followed by an infantry attack along the Bailleul-Arras road. The 1st Norfolk opened fire, supported by artillery fire directed on the newly formed craters. Only a few of the enemy reached the obstacle trench; some of them began bombing a disused trench between the obstacle and the front line trench, but none of them reached the Norfolk firing line. The reception they met with was so hot that they fled, leaving behind a quantity of bombs and other material. This evening's work cost the 1st Norfolk twenty-one killed, twenty-five wounded, and nineteen missing. Among the latter were Lieutenants G. P. Burlton, L. Edwards, and L. J. Row (afterwards ascertained to have been killed). The battalion was relieved the same night and retired to billets at Agnes-lez-Duisans.

The following is the gist of the report on this affair as described in the 15th brigade War Diary :—

After firing their mines the Germans at once launched their attack. In the attack on the right company (" C "), the enemy at once seized their lip of the crater and sent forward twenty or thirty men, who were stopped. Another small party, following the Chantecler-Arras road, got into the obstacle trench and solemnly bombed it. Our troops then established themselves on the near lip of the crater. At 9.32 two red lamps were shown by the Germans on their parapet. This was interpreted by Lieutenant Hoare, commanding the right platoon, as meaning " Home," so he at once concentrated his fire on the space between the lamps, about 200 yards. This platoon did excellent work, and Captain A. C. O'Connor, commanding " C " company, is specially mentioned. Though partially buried by an explosion in July Avenue, he returned to company head-quarters and conducted working parties for digging out buried men till 8 a.m.

In the centre, when the mines exploded, Lieutenants Burlton and Edwards went out to the sap-head. Since then Burlton had not been seen, and was believed either to have been killed or captured by the bombers of the obstacle trench. Lieutenant Row was undoubtedly blown up, and the command of the company devolved on Lieutenant Hall, who held the rear lip of the crater in front of the centre, ready to bomb the enemy if he attempted to get a footing.

On the left, Lieutenant Francis, realizing the difficulty of maintaining communication with the Warwickshire Regiment on his left, secured his front and " stopped " the trench on his flank. He also brought up a Lewis gun to sweep the ground in front of the " Gridiron," 200 yards north of the Bailleul road, and awaited the attack, which never got beyond our wire.

The following extract from divisional orders shows how the action of the battalion was appreciated :—

" The Divisional Commander congratulates the 13th and 15th brigades and the divisional artillery on their work on the night of the 4th June, especially the 15th Warwickshire Regiment and the 1st battalion Norfolk Regiment, who, in spite of an extremely heavy and prolonged bombardment, prevented the enemy from gaining any permanent advantage from the attack. Information from prisoners shows that 500 or 600 of the enemy were employed in the attack, which can therefore be looked upon as something greater than a trench raid. In spite of the mines and bombardment, the enemy was repulsed by our first line on far the greater portion of the front attacked. Had not the first line been held with the greatest resolution, it is probable we should have lost the high ground in K.1 sub-sector. The casualties were heavy, but would have been much heavier if we had been forced to retake this ground by counter-attack.

" (Signed) R. B. STEPHENS, Major-General
" Commanding 5th Division."

The rest of June passed on the whole quietly. On the 12th General Stephens, commanding the 5th division, presented the Distinguished Conduct Medals gained by Sergeant Battey and Lance-Corporal Moore, and Military Medals to Lance-Corporal Collins and Sergeant Tidd. On the 25th there was another presentation by the 6th corps[1] commander, General Keir, when Sergeants Cross and Smith and Privates Green and Clarke received the Military Medal and the battalion was congratulated by the general on its exemplary conduct on the 4th.

From the 16th to the 18th German "camouflets" were blown against the work done by the New Zealand tunnellers, who were assisted in their labours by working parties of the Norfolk. A great deal was done by the battalion in improving the trenches and artillery positions.

The 5th division was now about to take part in the great offensive on the Somme, which began on July 1, 1916. By the 16th July the Norfolk battalion, after several hard marches in great heat and dust, were back at their old position on the Somme. On the 19th the division was ordered to reinforce the 7th, then holding the line between Longueval, nearly east of Mametz on the right, and High Wood to the north-west of Longueval. For possession of Longueval a furious battle was raging. On the right of the 15th corps, through the centre of Longueval, the line was continued eastwards by the 13th corps through the southern portion of Delville Wood, and thence due south to the west side of Guillemont.

Up to the 21st the 1st Norfolk were in reserve about Montauban. That night they were ordered to reinforce the 13th brigade in its attack on the south-east of High Wood.

At 6 a.m. on the 23rd "D" company advanced in four waves on a frontage of one platoon, with intervals of six yards between each man, and occupied the front line from the south-west corner of High Wood. In this advance Lieutenant Hall was wounded; one man was killed, and fourteen were wounded. "C" company occupied a trench north of Bazentin le Grand, whilst "A" and "B" remained in the old German front trench, to which "D" was presently withdrawn.

At 8.45 the battalion relieved the 1st West Kents in the firing line,

[1] The 5th division had been transferred from the 10th to the 6th Corps early in March.

from the south-west corner of High Wood along a line running towards Longueval. The relief had to be carried out by dribbling up men singly under heavy fire. "A" and "B" companies were in first line. On the right were the 1st Bedford, on the left the 4th Seaforth Highlanders. "C" company remained in its old position north of Bazentin, with "D" on its right. All night of the 23rd–24th work went on in constructing a new trench a short distance forward of the present front line.

The battalion was to have been relieved on the 24th, but so intense was the German bombardment that the operation had to be postponed till the early hours of the 25th. When that time arrived there was still pouring upon the position a constant rain of the heaviest projectiles mixed with gas shells.

They were at Pommiers redoubt till 10.45 p.m. on the 26th, when they moved forward to assembly posts for the attack of the following morning. Again they were in the midst of the same terrible shelling, enfilading and almost taking them in rear. Gas still compelled the wearing of masks, and for five weary hours this nerve-shattering ordeal continued. The strain on the mental and physical powers of the whole battalion under such trying circumstances can be imagined, and it is wonderful that officers and men should have been able to achieve the success they did a few hours later when called on to storm Longueval.

Longueval village was situated immediately west of Delville Wood, the main portion being opposite the south-west corner of the wood. The main street of the village, running north and south, was known to our people as "North Street." The wood had been passed completely through by the British on July 15th and part of the German defences of Longueval had been occupied. On the 18th, however, a counter-attack by the enemy had enabled them, on the 19th to regain their hold on the northern part both of the wood and the village. For a week there had been furious fighting in both, but the British still held the southern portions of Longueval and Delville Wood. The objective of the attack on July 26th was the complete capture of both, and it fell to the lot of the Norfolk Regiment chiefly to carry out the operation in the village, with the support of the 1st Bedford and 16th Royal Warwickshire Regiments.

The following account of the fighting on the 26th and 27th is based on Colonel Stone's report to brigade head-quarters. Colonel Stone adds special acknowledgment of the gallant and capable services on this day by the Brigade Major, Major W. T. Brooks of the Duke of Cornwall's

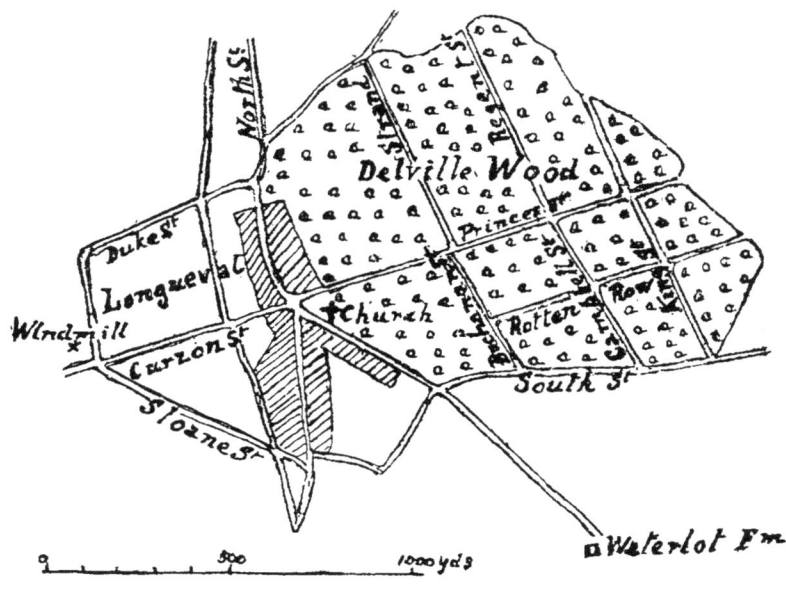

LONGUEVAL AND DELVILLE WOOD

Light Infantry. When everything was at its very worst, when the shelling was so intense that no messages could be got through, he came several times to Longueval, arriving perfectly cool and cheerful, and able to explain what was happening elsewhere and to give invaluable advice, as well as to take back full information as to the position of affairs at Longueval. It must be remembered that though Longueval could in ordinary circumstances be clearly seen from brigade headquarters, it disappeared on this day in the dense cloud of smoke, dust, and flying debris from the uninterrupted bursting of German shells. Colonel Stone is anxious to acknowledge fully the invaluable assistance the battalion received from Major Brooks during the whole Somme battle. Colonel Stone was in command of the whole force at Longueval, consisting of his own battalion, the 1st Bedford, and 16th Warwickshire Regiments, with trench mortars and one company Argyle and Sutherland Highlanders.

The battalion reached Longueval at 2.30 a.m. on the 27th; "A" and "B" companies relieved the 12th Gloucestershire in front line, whilst "C" occupied a trench in the western part of the village, with "D" on its right. "A" and "B" were supported by "C" and "D". The enemy bombarded heavily all the 26th and 27th, and Longueval, as a salient, was open to bombardment by enemy artillery from every direction except southwest. At 5.10 a.m. on the 27th the British artillery opened fire, and the German reply was so violent that, by 6.50 a.m., "A" company could hardly muster one platoon, most of the rest having been buried by the shelling, including Captain Francis and Lieutenant Hunn. "B" also reported their position untenable. "C" and "D" were therefore ordered, from support, to attack simultaneously with "A" and "B," and the 1st Bedford battalion were asked to reinforce "A" and "B."

At 7.20 our barrage lifted, and at 7.30 two companies of the Bedford battalion closed up to our original first line.

From this point the action of the companies is described separately.

The German barrage had fallen specially heavily on the two left platoons of "A," which were practically completely buried and unable to advance. What remained of the other two went forward with the barrage.

"C" also had to move to its right, being unable to attack over the left area, where the German barrage was still furious. The German trench running westwards was carried and its occupants killed.

Owing to the impossibility of advancing in that direction, a German strong point remained in action on the left rear of the actual advance. This necessitated blocking the captured trench on the left, which operation, and the clearing by bombers of the houses on the left of North Street, occupied some time. About fifty prisoners were taken in the houses where 2nd Lieutenant Howlett was last seen alive leading the bombers.

At 8 a.m. a second shallow trench was captured by a forward movement and consolidated. Part of " C " company, under Lieutenants Martin and Windham, went still farther, but was obliged to return, as it ran into our own barrage. The next obstacle was a sunken road where " A " and " C " were held up by machine guns and snipers.

It has been mentioned that a German strong point had been left behind. Against this Captain A. C. O'Connor led a force. Both he and 2nd Lieutenant E. W. Martin were killed in the attack, and 2nd Lieutenant Steer was wounded.

At this time German reinforcements were approaching from the ridge in front, but they were so cut up by the fire of British and their own artillery that they had to go back. For some time " A " company had not a single officer in action, and " C " had only 2nd Lieutenant Windham, who thus found himself in command of all the battalion to the west of North Street.

Meanwhile " B " company, having formed on the road leading south-east from the centre of Longueval, assaulted at 7.20 a.m. They met with no opposition until they advanced about seventy-five yards beyond the Church. Here they found a very strong redoubt on their right, with a house and cellar in it. The centre of the company had got a little beyond this redoubt. The line had to be stopped whilst the redoubt was attacked in front and rear by bombing parties of " B " and " D " companies, who took it with about a hundred Germans in it.

The Norfolk men then dug in, and the Bedford battalion (some of whom had moved to the east side of North Street) passed through. A small temporary advance was made on the left of " B " company, where a few more of the enemy were killed and captured, and touch gained with "A" Company on North Street. "D" Company had advanced in support of " B." No. 13 platoon took part in the original assault, and later joined the Bedford men in their advance. Part of No. 14 platoon assisted " B " in the capture of the redoubt, whilst the rest went forward to just north of the church, where Lieutenant Clode, at their head, was wounded.

On the right of " D " the Royal Berkshire were busy constructing a strong point in Delville Wood.

The original idea had been for "A" and "B" companies to advance to the first objective, indicated by a line on the map just beyond Longueval. "C" and "D" would then pass through to capture the second objective, a line passing through Delville Wood some distance beyond Longueval; but the orders came too late to be given out to their subordinates by company commanders, and, in the end, the whole battalion had to go straight through. The final objective was 300 yards north of Longueval, but the line actually attained was the northern edge of the village. Further progress was impossible, as, when the attack was held up whilst the houses and cellars of the village were being cleared, the barrage had passed on and the infantry were left without its protection.

Colonel Stone says that the capture of the north-west end of Delville Wood was far the most difficult operation prescribed, since it was commanded by machine guns in High Wood, Switch Trench, and many strong points in the open just outside it, the operations in this sector being in full view of them. Save for the losses by shelling before the attack the battalion's chief casualties were in Delville Wood.

The casualties in this very heavy day of fighting were serious. Of officers, Captain A. C. O'Connor and 2nd Lieutenant E. W. Martin were killed, and the wounded and gassed were Lieutenant Brown, 2nd Lieutenants Clode, Windham, Howlett, Steer, Hunn, Jackman, Beale, and Captain Scott (R.A.M.C.). Of other ranks there were killed fifty; wounded, gassed, etc., 157; missing, believed killed, fifty.

The total casualties of the battalion in this one week of fighting at High Wood, Longueval, and Delville Wood amounted to seventeen officers and 412 other ranks. Total 429.

During the 28th the new positions were held and consolidated, and on the 29th the battalion was relieved and sent back to Pommiers Redoubt.

A brigade order of the 28th says: "The Brigadier-General commanding wishes to express to all ranks of the brigade his great admiration at the magnificent way in which they captured the village of Longueval yesterday. To the 1st Norfolk Regiment, and the 1st Dorsetshire Regiment, and some of the 16th Royal Warwickshire Regiment who were able to get into the enemy with the bayonet, he offers his heartiest congratulations. He knows it was what they have been waiting and wishing for for many months. . . . The way in which the troops behaved under the subsequent heavy bombardment was worthy of the best traditions of the British Army."

On July 31st and August 1st the 1st Norfolk were again in Longueval, which was still suffering one of the heaviest bombardments in the war, and was on fire, with explosions frequently occurring; 2nd Lieutenant Hoare was wounded. 2nd Lieutenant West was killed on July 31st in Delville Wood.

On August 2nd and 3rd the battalion, with the rest of the 5th division, moved back by train to the south-east of Abbeville for a period of rest from fighting, but of vigorous training. Here, when quartered at Le Quesnoy, they received strong drafts from the 2/6th battalion, ninety per cent of whom, having not yet served in the field, required training in the conditions prevailing on the front.

On August 24th the division returned to the Somme front and the battalion bivouacked near Bronfay Farm, south-west of Maricourt, on the 26th, where they were employed digging for the 13th brigade. The division was now attached to Lord Cavan's 14th corps.

The front line had, in the interval since August 2nd, moved well forward, and was now on the eastern slope of the Maltz Horn ridge, with the French operating against Combles on the right of the 14th corps. The 15th brigade was on the right of the 5th division, touching the French left and facing the end of the spur on which stood the Leuze and Bouleaux woods running in a long strip from south-west to north-east. At the south-west end of this ridge was Falfemont Farm, a locality glorious in the annals of the Norfolk Regiment.

The capture of this farm was a necessary preliminary to the French advance by the valley on its right leading to Combles. The attack on the farm was begun by the 13th brigade on September 3rd. On that evening the 1st Norfolk were acting as reserve to the 95th brigade on the left of the line attacking Guillemont, but had no fighting. On the 4th they were returned to the 15th brigade and sent to the right opposite Falfemont, in relief of the 1st Cheshire. "B" company was on the right next to the French, "A" on the left, "C" and "D" behind "A" and "B" respectively.

At 8 a.m. on the 4th orders were received for the attack on Falfemont, against which the 13th brigade, though suffering heavily and reinforced from the divisional reserve, had not succeeded.

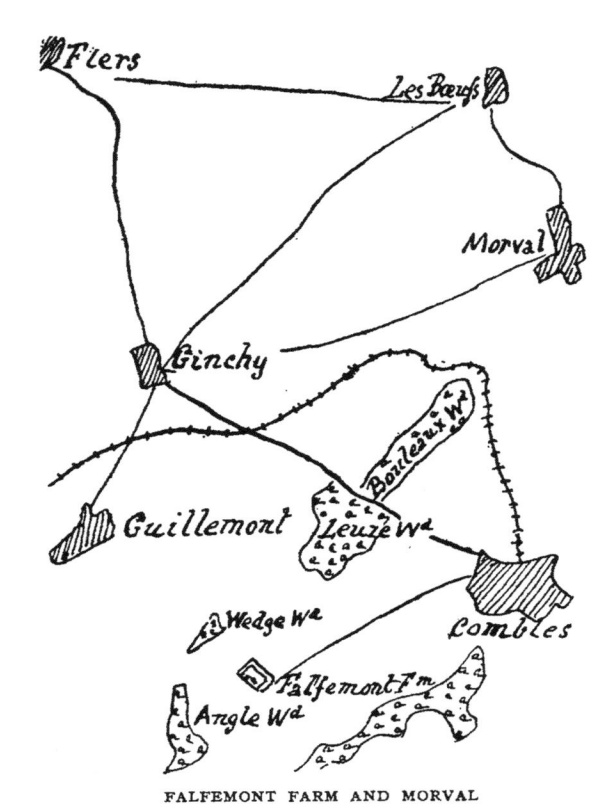

FALFEMONT FARM AND MORVAL

At 3.10 p.m. the assault was commenced by "A" and "B" companies on a front of 500 yards, over a space of 350. Captain Francis, who had been slightly wounded at 6 a.m., got with a few men of "A" company to the south-west corner of the farm, but was bombed out of it. The rest of the attack was held up by a cross fire of machine guns. All but two officers on this front were killed or wounded, and progress was only possible by crawling from one shell hole to another. Whilst the enemy's attention was directed to the front, the Bedford and Cheshire battalions, on the left, were able to get into the trench line north of the farm. As "A" and "B" went forward, "C" and "D" occupied their trenches, and at 3.20 started to assault the south-east face of the farm. They too were held up. Lieutenant T. Brown, with the reserve bombers and two Lewis guns, was sent to work round west of the farm and capture the quarry.

At 4 p.m. the left of the Norfolk battalion was within fifty yards of the farm, but the right was still held up by a terrible machine gun fire.

At 6.40 p.m. orders were issued for an attack on the farm with the co-operation of the 95th brigade, reinforced by two companies of the 16th Warwickshire and the 1st Bedford (both of the 15th brigade) on the left. At 6.45 all companies advanced on the objective, with the two companies of the 16th Warwickshire reinforcing them. Failing to take the farm then, the Norfolk men dug themselves in and waited for dusk. The ground in front was a network of shell holes which heavy rain had made still more difficult to pass.

At 8.30 p.m. part of "A" company on the left again rushed the south-west edge of the farm, whilst the Warwick battalion behind them were busy digging communication trenches up to it. By 3 a.m. on the 5th "A" and "C" companies had captured and held the whole of the farm. Beyond the south corner of the farm the position was less certain, and the Norfolk battalion began working down the German trenches and sending out patrols to link up with the French on the right. Machine guns in that direction were still causing heavy casualties. By 7.30 a.m. the whole of the objective was taken and the French were up on the right. Unfortunately, the 1st Norfolk, as well as the French, were under fire from our own 18-pounders, which could not be stopped till 10.30 owing to the difficulty of cut telephone communications. Consolidation, till then, was difficult and dangerous in the newly acquired line. Lieutenant T. Brown and his two Lewis guns, sent as above mentioned against the quarry in the afternoon of the 4th, were held up by machine guns, and Brown himself was killed. When the companies were reorganized at 11.30 a.m. on the 5th "A" held Falfemont Farm, "B" the German trenches on the right down to the French left, " C " and " D " were in the original British firing line.

At 3.15 p.m. on the 5th the Norfolk men were relieved, with the exception of two officers and one hundred men left in the German trenches south-east of the farm. After resting in the trenches north of Hardecourt till 8.30 p.m. the whole battalion, including the detachment temporarily left behind, bivouacked at 1 a.m. on the 6th at Billon Farm.

Such a feat as the capture of Falfemont necessarily involved serious casualties. Of officers six were killed—Captain W. J. H. Brown; Lieutenants H. S. Cameron and E. P. W. Brown; 2nd Lieutenants L. C. Coath, T. Brown, and W. F. Bice. Wounded, seven—Captains Sibree, Francis, Youell, Grover; Lieutenant Swift; 2nd Lieutenants Cullington and Watson. Of other ranks there were killed fifty; wounded 212; missing, believed killed, ninety-four. Total 369, including officers.

The battalion now went for a short rest to the Morlancourt area, whence it supplied working parties to the trenches. On the 16th and 17th it again went forward to Waterlot Farm, a little south-east of Longueval, and on the 18th the 5th division was sent towards Morval to relieve the 6th. Here the battalion found itself with the 1st Bedford on its right and the Coldstream Guards on the left. On the night of September 24th it again went into the firing line preparatory to attacking the German trenches on the west of Morval, a village 2,000 yards north-east of Combles. At 12.35 p.m. on the 25th the 15th brigade who were formed on a one battalion front, with the Norfolk battalion leading, started the assault on Morval. In view of the great importance of the capture of the first objective, and also looking to the recent heavy losses of the veterans of the battalion, Colonel Stone decided to lead it in person to the assault. He went over the top at the head of the centre, and each company and platoon was also headed by its own commander. On the previous day a special battalion order had recited the victories and sufferings of the battalion, and urged the men to rival those exploits in carrying out an operation of which the importance was explained.

On the right, in front, was " D " company, with " C " on the left; " B " and " A " respectively were on the right and left of the support line. The first objective—the German trench—was taken the moment the barrage lifted from it. The Germans had mostly got out of it into shell holes behind. A few were killed in the trench, most of them behind it, and about 150 surrendered. Bombing patrols pushed on along the communication trenches till they had to stop on catching up the British barrage. Three machine guns and a bomb-thrower were captured under a violent machine gun fire from every direction except the rear.

The battalion now dug in and joined up with the Devons of the 95th brigade on the right. Here the advance was stopped by order whilst other units pressed on beyond Morval.

Next day the 1st Norfolk went back to the rear. The casualties on the 25th were:

Officers wounded, six—Lieutenants Woodthorpe, Rose, Read, Soddy, Clarke and Spencer.

Other ranks—seven killed and seventy wounded.

On October 1, 1916, before the battalion left the Somme area, the following special battalion order was issued by Colonel Stone:—

" Before leaving the Somme and all it will mean to us and to the history of the Regiment, I wish to convey my most sincere thanks to all ranks for what they have done. We were no new regiment, fresh and keen from home, who had rested in billets well at the back for months, but an old regiment who had been continuously engaged since the start of the war with practically no rest at all—trench worn and suffering from overwork and over-exposure. You had everything against you, but you have been through the heaviest fighting of the war and come out of it with a name that will live for ever.

" At Longueval, your first battle, you were given your first and severest test, and no praise of mine can be too high for the extreme gallantry and endurance shown on that occasion. The severest test of discipline is for men to stand intense shell fire and to hold on to the ground they have won under it—and this you did. At Falfemont Farm you again had a difficult task and a severe fight, but you stuck to it and eventually captured it—a position whose importance cannot be over-estimated. Then, during the most trying weather conditions, you were in the open making trenches, and at one time the limit of complete exhaustion had almost been reached, but when one final effort was asked of you at Morval, you carried out a brilliant assault. These things could have only been done by the finest troops in the world.

"I cannot sufficiently express my admiration of your gallantry and splendid conduct throughout. You came to the Somme battle-field with a very high reputation, which you had rightly earned during twenty-three months of strenuous warfare—you leave the Somme with the highest reputation in the British Army.

"(Signed) P. V. P. STONE, Lieut.-Colonel
"Commanding 1st Battalion The Norfolk Regiment."
"1.10.16."

The capture of Morval elicited from Sir H. Rawlinson congratulations to the 5th division, and an expression of his regret at its approaching transfer from the 4th army under his command.

On September 29th the 1st Norfolk entrained at Dernancourt for Longpré, where, on the 30th, General Morland, commanding the 10th Corps, presented the following ribbons for services at Falfemont and Morval:—

Military Cross - - - -	C.S.M. Pryer.
Distinguished Conduct Medal	C.S.M. (now Lieutenant) Ambrose and Corporal Cook.
Military Medal - - -	Privates Leggatt and Lark.

On October 1st the battalion entrained at Longpré with the 5th division on its way to join the 1st Army on the Béthune front, where it had been in October, 1914.[1] The country had not changed much in appearance, and there were still the same breastworks in a tract where a high water level forbade the sinking of trenches. Such trenches as there were, were still waterlogged and deep in mud when the weather

[1] See Map, p. 11.

was wet. On October 4th the battalion was in the front line near Quinque Rue, overlooked on the left by the Bois du Biez, on the right by the Givenchy ridge. There was much work at this time in making strong points, the system in vogue then being to hold the firing line with such posts. In the intervals behind were machine guns and Stokes mortars. Behind this advanced line was a very strong support line.

On October 14th a very successful raid was carried out by the 1st Norfolk against the farm of Cour d'Avoué. At 6 p.m. 2nd Lieutenant C. F. Harrison went out with an assaulting party of twenty men, supported by two Lewis gun detachments. Crawling for 150 yards, he turned to the left to the moat of the farm. He left three men on either side and the rest to complete the wire cutting, which had been begun in the previous night. Then, with only three men, he rushed the German post with the bayonet, capturing its two occupants, men of the 6th Bavarian Regiment. The party was fired at on its way back, but had no casualties. During the rest of October, and all November, nothing happened to break the usual course of trench warfare with its alternation of service in the front trenches, in support, or in reserve.

In the night of December 1st–2nd an elaborate raid by "C" company was attempted. At 1.15 a.m. the raiders had crawled to their assembly position. So far all was well, but as they advanced they came on some very thick wire, which, being out of sight in a depression, had escaped cutting by trench mortar fire. There was no getting through this, and the raid had to be called off. Though the men had had a hot meal before starting, the cold was so intense that many were half frozen before they got home again.

A period of training at Essars followed, from the 3rd to the 20th December. On the 17th the army commander presented the Military Cross to Captain R. G. Davies and the Military Medal to Private J. Riches. On the 20th, after a heavy snowfall on the previous day, the battalion moved to Beuvry, and on the 22nd, in heavy rain, to Le Quesnoy. On the 24th it was back in the trenches, this time on the left of the brigade, which had moved to its right astride of the La Bassée Canal, two platoons only of "A" company being south of the canal as far as Cuinchy. The front trenches were very bad, with an average of one foot of water in them. In this neighbourhood nothing noticeable happened during the rest of December, 1916 to January, 1917, or up to the night of February 26th–27th. The work in the trenches was very strenuous, with constant fatigues night and day, and a number of casualties from trench mortar fire. The battalion had nine days' rest at Beuvry from January 22nd, and then returned to the trenches about Richebourg l'Avoué, where they had been in November. On the 12th Lieutenant-Colonel Stone was promoted to the command of the 17th brigade, and was succeeded in command of the battalion by Major R. W. Patteson.

(d) 1917: VIMY—OPPY WOOD—YPRES—ITALY

On the night of February 26th–27th three raiding parties, under Captain Kelly, assembled at 11 p.m. in "No Man's Land." They were lying down, but were discovered by German Vérey lights. Captain Kelly, thinking there was still time to do something, dashed forward covered by a barrage. The Germans, however, were prepared and the raiders had to withdraw from the enemy's parapet, where they left two dead.

On March 5th the 1st Norfolk again moved to the south of the canal, in support at Cambrin. On the 10th a German raid was beaten off with a loss of one killed and one wounded of the Norfolk battalion. On the 17th the battalion went back to Béthune, and on the 25th to Le Pugnoy, where they were training till April 7th, when they began to move towards the famous Vimy ridge, which runs south-east from the Souchez River near Givenchy en Gohelle and sinks down into the plain west of Bailleul. On April 9th the ridge was taken by the Canadians. In this great achievement the 15th brigade had no share, but on the 13th the 5th division relieved the Canadians, and next day moved over the Vimy ridge, with the 95th brigade on the left of the 15th, the left support battalion of which was the 1st Norfolk, in trenches just east of Givenchy. On the right of the 15th brigade was the 12th

Canadian brigade. Fifteen hundred yards ahead of the 1st Norfolk the 1st Cheshire and 16th Warwickshire came to a standstill in extended order in front of strong uncut wire.

Up till the 23rd nothing special happened. The 1st Norfolk were in the front line on that day, under the command of Lieutenant-Colonel Carroll, when at dawn they started their advance against the German first line in front of La Coulotte. The German wire had been reported the previous evening to be damaged, but not completely cut.

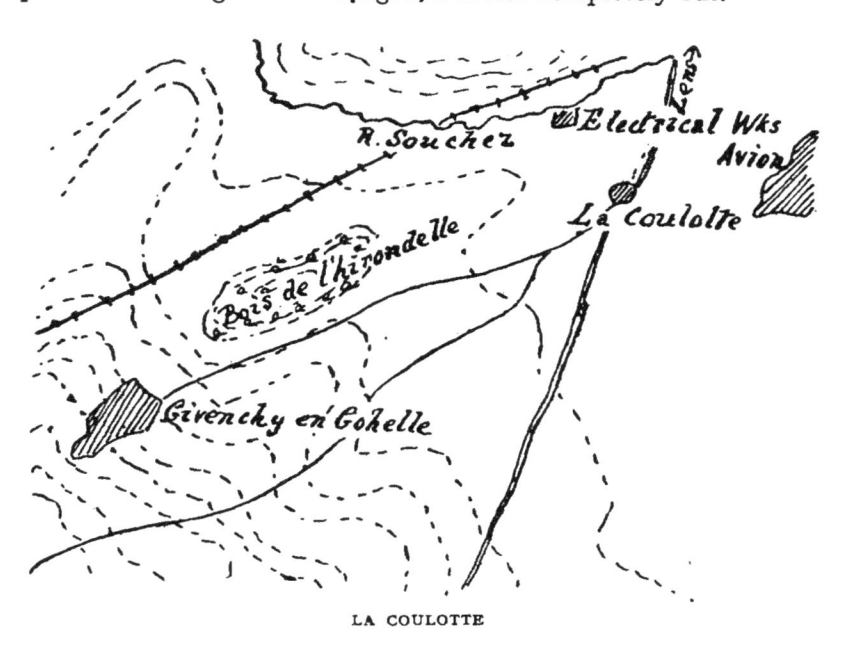

LA COULOTTE

At 4.45 a.m. the British barrage opened, closely followed up by the infantry attack. In the front line of the 15th brigade was the 1st Norfolk with a strength of twenty-four officers and 745 men, on the right of the brigade, with the 52nd Canadians on their right, and the 1st Bedford on their left. "A" and "C" companies were in first line, "B" and "D" in support. Very soon, as the leading platoons arrived at the German wire and saw the enemy already showing signs of surrender, they came under a heavy machine gun fire from the railway and its cutting, and found themselves held up by uncut wire. "B" and "D" also were held up in the same way, but the left platoons, with the right platoons of the 1st Bedford, found a way through a zigzag opening, left by the Germans for their own use, and proceeded to bomb outwards along the trench. A party of "A" and "D", bombing along the German trench, took four machine guns, which they destroyed, as they were unable to remove them when they found themselves stopped by a German strong point. Other parties, which got forward as far as the enemy's support trench, found little opposition on the way, but were then stopped by an enfilading fire of machine guns from the railway and the neighbouring houses.

From 10 a.m. to 7 p.m. the battalion was under a very heavy German barrage. The remains of "B" and "D" companies were withdrawn at dark to the original outpost line. The failure of the attack was almost entirely due to the uncut wire.

The casualties were heavy: Officers killed, seven—Captain J. C. F. Magnay; 2nd Lieutenants L. S. Ling, F. C. Coleman, J. Soddy, H. N. Fox, A. C. Cockrill, and F. W. Hoare. Officers wounded, eight—Captain Clode; 2nd Lieutenants Davies, M.C., Ingle, Tower, Kirby, Stuart, Harrison, and Evans. Other ranks: Killed, thirty, wounded 124, missing twenty-four. Total casualties: fifteen officers and 178 other ranks.

On the 24th the battalion was withdrawn to corps reserve, where, from then till the 7th May, they were busy clearing up and reorganizing. The 5th division was now attached to the 13th corps commanded by Lieutenant-General Sir R. Congreve, V.C. On May 8th the 1st Norfolk moved from Roclincourt into support of the 95th brigade near Fresnoy, which had just been lost. A counter-attack ordered for 7 p.m. the same day was postponed till the early hours of the 9th, when, at 1.45 a.m., the battalion was in assembly positions, with "C" and "D" companies in front, and "A" and "B" in support. At 2 a.m. the barrage opened and was replied to by a German barrage directed largely on the back areas. As the infantry advanced the waves were broken up by intense machine gun fire, and eventually, though small bodies penetrated into the woods around Fresnoy, it was found impossible to retake the village and the battalion fell back to Farbus Wood beyond Arleux, where only thirty-six men and five Lewis guns remained. The casualties on this day were:

Officers wounded, six—Lieutenants Needham, Tuck, and Finch 2nd Lieutenants Crosse, Case, and Scott.

Other ranks—Killed six, wounded 103, missing eleven.

On the night of May 24th the battalion, in the front trenches at Willerval, was being relieved by the Highland Light Infantry. At 11 p.m. a German barrage was directed on and behind the left of the firing line; five minutes later an officer and eighty-four men of the 13th Bavarian Regiment gained a footing in the trench in front of Arleux, which was held by three officers and fifty men of " B " company. Captain Kelly at once reorganized his men fifty yards behind the captured trench and counter-attacked with bombs and the bayonet. A hand-to-hand fight ensued in which the Bavarians were driven out and back to their own trenches, leaving eight dead and three wounded in our trench, twelve more a little beyond it, and others near their own. Captain Kelly and Lieutenant Chapman held the left of the trench, flanking the German right with their fire, in which they received assistance from the Bedford Lewis guns, breaking up the German flanking party. The 1st Norfolk lost twenty other ranks wounded, two men prisoners, and about twenty more dead in or in front of the recaptured trench.

Nearly all June was on the whole quiet, though the Germans did a great deal of shelling of the back areas, as well as of the trenches and batteries, the latter suffering very severely.

On June 28th occurred the attack on Oppy Wood, in conjunction with the attack of the 31st division on the trenches south of it. The attack of the 15th brigade was led by the 1st Norfolk in the centre, 1st Cheshire on the right, and 1st Bedford on the left. At 7.10 p.m. they broke out from the " Marquis " trench in two waves, the first of which, being within twenty-five or thirty yards of the barrage, suffered some casualties from " shorts." The German first trench was taken against some opposition, chiefly from thirty men in a concrete machine gun emplacement. From this the garrison was driven with bombs and Mills' grenades. The German barrage had been late in beginning, and the trench was already taken when it did so. Oppy Wood was entered with little opposition, and a line was established eighty yards into it, with posts fifty to seventy-five yards farther on. By 9 p.m. the Norfolk and the other battalions were busy consolidating. The Norfolk battalion's share of the captures was one officer and seventy other ranks, one light and one heavy machine gun. Their losses were comparatively light: Lieutenant Chapman was seriously and Lieutenant Scott slightly wounded; other ranks, fifteen killed and forty-six wounded.

A fighting patrol going forward next day towards Oppy village had to retire on finding it strongly held by the enemy.

It was at this time that the use of burning oil was successfully used as a reply to the German "flammenwerfer," and a liberal dosing of Fresnoy with oil is believed to have drawn the enemy's attention to an expected attack there and to have facilitated the surprise at Oppy Wood.

July was a very quiet month for the battalion, which was mostly in reserve and had not a single casualty.

The only notable events in August were an attempt on one of "A" company's posts, on the 7th, which was driven off, and another similar attack on the 8th, in which only one particularly fine specimen of the German warrant officer got into the trench, where he was shot. A curious incident occurred on the 29th, when a German, who had either lost his way or gone mad, wandered over towards the Norfolk trenches near Oppy. Being invited to come into them, he shook his head and turned back, but was shot before he could get home.

During the greater part of September the battalion was in the back area about Beaumont.

On September 25th it returned to the Ypres area for the third battle of that name, which had already been in progress since July 31st with the gain of much ground by the British 2nd and 5th armies. On the 29th the 5th division, less the 13th brigade detached as reserve to the 5th corps, marched to the area east of Hazebrouck; next day the whole division was about Meteren and Berthen, and on October 1st moved up, partly by bus, to the front line, where it relieved the 23rd division that night. It was now part of the 10th corps. The 1st

Norfolk remained with the 15th brigade in divisional reserve just east of Dickebusch Lake. The weather was again wet, which rendered this low country most obnoxious. Movements had to be made largely by " duck-boards," and shell holes and craters were often the watery graves of men who fell into their depths.

The front of the 5th division had its right about 1,000 yards short of Gheluvelt on the Menin road, its left at Polygon Wood. On October 5th, when the 15th brigade moved into front line, the Norfolk battalion found themselves facing the Polderhoek Château, with the 1st Cheshire on their left and the 16th Warwickshire on their right.

During the next two days they had several casualties from shell fire, and on the night of the 7th moved into support trenches in front of Inverness Copse. The German position at Polderhoek Château had been made into one of great strength, with numerous machine guns and " pill-boxes." It had been attacked on October 4th by the other two brigades of the 5th division with partial success, but the final objective had not been reached, and some of the ground gained had subsequently been lost in the great counter-attacks launched by the enemy. The 13th brigade, which the 15th now relieved, had suffered heavily in the fighting, and both sides were recovering their breath after the struggle. The Diary of the 1st Norfolk about this time contains a good many complaints of the miserable weather, and the hard labour imposed on the men by constant fatigues for improving defences, making huts in the back areas, and bringing up supplies of all sorts. On the evening of the 8th orders were received for a renewal of the attack on the Polderhoek position in the morning of the 9th.

By 4 a.m. the battalion had moved from the support trenches to the point of assembly, under the command of Major Lambton, who reports on the action. " C " company on the right and " A " on the left were to lead the advance, with " B " in close support, and " D " in reserve ready to make counter-attacks. The early morning was very dark, with heavy rain, and there had been great difficulty in finding the way to the assembly point.

As the barrage lifted at 5.20 a.m., the 1st Norfolk and the 16th Warwickshire, leading the advance of the 15th brigade, went forward, the latter on the right. In the darkness and rain "A" and "C" companies of the Norfolk battalion inclined too much to the right and found themselves right in front of the Château, instead of to the left of it. They were falling back when the officer commanding threw in "B" to reinforce them. By this time the enemy had opened a terrific cross fire of machine guns on them and the British barrage had passed forwards, leaving them unprotected. The losses under these circumstances were very heavy, and no farther progress could be made all day. Farther to the left, two platoons had also lost direction and gone leftwards, which brought one of them, after an advance of about 400 yards, in front of the right of the 1st Cheshire on their left, where they held on all day, isolated and out of touch with the rest on their right. To add to their difficulties, the men had no hot food after they started for the assembly point in the very early morning.

At 9 p.m. the battalion was back reorganizing in its original firing line, where they were relieved between 10 and 11 p.m. The casualties during this unfortunate day were:

Officers killed—Captain L. W. Clements; 2nd Lieutenants W. D. C. Sharp, F. Entwistle, and Coxens.

Officers wounded—Captain Dickinson; 2nd Lieutenants C. B. Smith, R. P. Scott, and Livingston.

Other ranks—Killed thirty-eight, wounded 144, missing 112.

The failure of the attack is attributed, in Major Lambton's report, to the exhausted condition of the men and the terrible weather. Next day, when they were back in their old position, only one officer was left to reorganize the remains of the three leading companies. Many wounded had been lying out for a long time, and stragglers continued to come in in a ghastly condition during the 10th and 11th, on which latter date the battalion was back at Berthen reorganizing and training in very bad billets. On the 17th a draft arrived with 148 men—a smart, well trained lot, but mostly men from the north-east counties, and few of them Norfolk men. Another fair draft of 144 arrived next day.

Training continued at Berthen till the 23rd, when the battalion moved to Ridge Wood. On the 25th it was in divisional reserve at

Bedford House, and on the 26th it was again at Stirling Castle, where the line was nothing but a network of shell holes. The rest of the month was spent in improving these defences, and on November 1st the battalion again went up to the firing line opposite Polderhoek Château, an operation in which it had about twenty casualties, due to the unsheltered nature of the approaches from the rear. The trenches were very muddy and wet. In the operation which resulted in the temporary capture of Polderhoek on the 26th October the battalion took no part. During November, when the battalion was on the usual routine of in and out of trenches, training, digging, and being shelled, nothing worthy of note happened. The casualties for November amounted to six other ranks killed, forty-one wounded, and two missing. The 5th division had been relieved in front of Polderhoek, sent back to the Westoutre area, and then had gone by rail to the area between Lumbres and Boulogne, where there was a period of rest, refitting, and training from the 11th to the 26th November, when the division began concentrating for transfer to the Italian front.

The month of November, 1917, had seen the great Austro-German offensive on the Italian front, when the Italian army, demoralized by German propaganda, had given way and could not be stopped till it was behind the Piave, where its tenure was still far from secure. To reinforce it there were sent seven French and five British divisions, amongst the latter being the 5th. From December 1st to 6th half the 1st Norfolk were in the train, passing by Versailles, Lyon, Avignon, Marseilles, Nice, Savona, and Mantua to Montagnana, near Padua, where they were billeted in the church. The other half battalion only entrained on December 10th and joined their comrades on the 16th at Marsango. Here the rest of the month was spent in training, inspections, musketry, football, etc., which continued till January 23rd, when the battalion began its march to the front, reaching St. Andrea on January 25th and remaining there till February 2nd, with nothing more exciting than an occasional bomb from the enemy's aeroplanes, which were very active. The men, who had had a decidedly good time since arrival in Italy, thoroughly appreciated it after all the mud and other miseries of the Belgian front.

(c) 1918: ITALY—NIEPPE FOREST—THE FINAL BATTLES

The 5th division had been originally intended for the northern front in Italy, and much reconnaissance of the mountains had been done. Eventually, however, its destination was changed to the plains of the Piave. That river flows, like other North Italian rivers, in several channels, generally fordable, and extending to a total breadth of from 400 yards to a mile and a quarter. In floods the islands between the channels are apt to change their positions, and consequently maps are not for long reliable.

The position of the 5th division was in the plain on the right bank of the Piave, after it has passed round the long Montello hill and finally left the mountains. The firing line occupied by the 1st Norfolk, on relieving the 2nd King's Own Scottish Borderers on February 2nd, was about 800 yards long, with the railway and road bridges of Ponte Priula in its centre. Both bridges had been destroyed for 110 yards on the Austrian side of the river. The 16th Warwickshire were on their left, the 12th Gloucester (95th brigade) on the right, the 1st Bedford in support. The deepest and swiftest channel of the Piave was on the Austrian side.

During the whole of February the enemy was quiet, and the battalion went through the usual routine of firing line, support trenches, and reserve, the latter periods being enlivened by plenty of football. The weather was, on the whole, beautiful, with only occasional rain.

Nothing particular happened in the first half of March. Various attacks and raids were projected, but cancelled. On the 17th, after the heaviest shelling experienced on this front, the Norfolk battalion was relieved by an Italian regiment and went back to Visnadello. Thence a return was made to the Padua neighbourhood, and the uneventful share of the battalion in the Italian campaign had ended. If it had not added to its laurels, the battalion had gained much in the refreshment and rest which it had enjoyed, in generally beautiful weather and easy times, after the many trials it had undergone in three years of warfare under the most trying conditions on the Western front. It was now thoroughly recuperated, and ready again to play its part in the defence against the great German offensive of March, 1918, and later.

The first train carrying the Norfolk battalion to France left Vicenza at 2.30 a.m. on April 5th. This time the route was by Milan, Turin, and the Mt. Cenis tunnel. On the 8th, at 3 p.m., Amiens had to be avoided, as the German attack had brought the enemy within ten miles of that place, and, even on the diversion to the west, a train carrying another regiment of the 5th division was very nearly hit by a shell.

The 1st Norfolk detrained at Doullens on April 8th, and marched to billets at Neuvillette, under orders to relieve the 2nd Canadian division south of Arras. They started to do so on the 10th, but, just as they were reaching their destination, fresh orders arrived sending them back to billets, ready to proceed the same evening northwards by train. The German offensive against the 5th Army about Amiens had come to a standstill ere this, and now news had been received of their fresh attempt to break through towards the forest of Nieppe and Hazebrouck. Armentières had been taken and, it was reported, Messines also. The Portuguese had been attacked and driven in towards Neuve Chapelle, and it was in this neighbourhood that the 5th division was required to stem the tide.

The 1st Norfolk arrived on the night of the 11th, very uncertain as to where the enemy was. At one p.m. on the 12th they moved as advance guard of the brigade to St. Venant, south of the Nieppe Forest, occupying it just in time to prevent the Germans doing so from Merville, where they had wasted time in ransacking the cellars after its capture.

The first orders required the 5th division to retake Merville, which lies opposite the south-eastern projection of the irregularly shaped forest.

The divisional artillery not being up, the attack on Merville did not materialize, and the 5th division, now part of the 11th corps, took up a position with its front just outside the eastern edge of the forest. As the Norfolk battalion came up, the enemy was making an attack on the 95th brigade, to which the battalion was temporarily attached as reserve, but was not engaged in the action which ended, on the 15th, with the failure of the German attack and the stoppage of their advance on Hazebrouck.

For the rest of April, and on till early in August, the front on the east of the forest of Nieppe remained stationary, and the routine was similar to that in other cases of entrenched fronts. There was a great deal of hard work in creating and improving the new front, and work inside the forest was peculiarly hard and dangerous; for the German plan was to drench the forest with mustard and other gas, which hung for long periods in the undergrowth. Being devoid of odour, and not giving immediate signs of its presence by its effects, mustard gas was very difficult to detect, until the unfortunate man who had inhaled or come in contact with it began to suffer tortures. The 1st Norfolk were, at this time, commanded by Lieutenant-Colonel E. W. Montgomerie, the 15th brigade by Brigadier-General Oldman.[1] Of most of this period there is little to be said; but the following incidents which occurred during the battalion's periods of service in the front trenches must be recorded:

On the 11th May, at 2 a.m., No. 6 platoon ("B" company), under Captain Taylor and 2nd Lieutenants West and Howe, dashed out under cover of a barrage for a raid on two houses in which the enemy were believed to have machine guns. The houses were on the north side of the canal. 2nd Lieutenant West, with a Lewis gun, was on the left, 2nd Lieutenant Howe on the right. The former took up a very advanced position to protect 2nd Lieutenant Howe's left. Howe, pushing along the canal bank eastwards towards Merville, bombed some Germans behind a hedge projecting northwards from the canal. Then he sent Corporal Burton, with a machine gun, round the German right behind the hedge to enfilade a deep trench there. Still advancing, he reached his objective three minutes before scheduled time, and proceeded, though he had only three men with him, to search the two houses, in which he was joined by Corporal Burton and one other man. The houses were found not to be prepared for defence and had been evacuated. After the search, Howe collected his men and returned unharmed to the trenches. In the German trench behind the hedge about six of the enemy

[1] Of the Norfolk Regiment.

had been killed; six prisoners were taken and a machine gun. This very successful little raid was approved in congratulatory telegrams from the commanders of the brigade, the division, and the corps. General Oldman's telegram highly commended the three officers concerned and the dash of the platoon.

At the end of May a direct hit on battalion head-quarters seriously wounded Captain Musters, the adjutant, and Captain Mann, second in command.

In the middle of June the enemy appeared to be negligent by day, and our patrols could move about easily in front of the British lines. On the 16th a daylight patrol, consisting of 2nd Lieutenant Bowstead, D.C.M., M.M., Corporal Mallett, and Private Collins, all of "D" company, crawled forward through the crops and German wire to an enemy post in a shell hole. Finding it empty, they crossed a muddy stream fifteen yards wide, five feet deep, and smelling strongly of phosgene and proceeded fifty yards to another unoccupied German post. Turning back towards their own lines, they came on another trench, about four yards long, in which lay four rifles, the German owners of which were resting in a shelter. With a shout of "Hands up!" the patrol fired three shots, one of which wounded a German lieutenant in the abdomen. Another German, who seized a bomb, was wounded by two shots from Bowstead's revolver, but managed to throw his bomb. By this time fire had been opened from the enemy's main trench, and the patrol was forced to retire without gaining information, beyond the fact that the trenches here were held by Prussians. For this affair 2nd Lieutenant Bowstead received the Military Cross.

The next day, at 7 a.m., Lieutenant Cubitt, M.C., of "A" company, with Colour-Sergeant Shawe, crawled through the crops and the enemy's wire to what was believed to be his main trench. It was empty where they struck it, so they went about 120 yards along it till they heard a sentry cough. There they saw two blankets covering shelters under the parapet. From under each blanket protruded two pairs of German boots, the wearers of which appeared to be sleeping in the shelters. It was not possible, under the circumstances, to take away prisoners, so the two Englishmen crept quietly to within three yards of the shelters, threw Mills' grenades under the blankets, and made off by the road they had come. Jumping out of the German trench where they had entered it, they got back unharmed to their own trenches.

On the 27th June, at midnight, Captain Wood and 2nd Lieutenant Shaul, with twelve other ranks, sallied forth against a house occupied by enemy bombers. After bombing and destroying this nest, and bombing some other posts, they returned at 1.20 a.m. without loss. The same officers successfully carried out a raid on the 28th. On the 29th there were more raids, one of which was driven back by machine-gun fire in the bright moonlight.

June 28th saw an advance by the 5th division to a position well east of that which they had hitherto held, with the forest close behind it. In this the 15th brigade took no part. During July evidence was found during raids of the demoralization which was already setting in amongst the enemy. The forest was terribly stuffy, full of mosquitoes in some places, and German gas in others, which was very trying in the prevailing hot weather.

On August 7th the 5th division, being relieved by the 61st, retired to rest about Aire, where they were visited by H.M. the King, to whom the commanding officers were presented.

All during this trying period the tedium had been relieved for the men, as far as possible, by sports, boxing, and other amusements.

In July the curtain had risen for the last act of the great drama, and the first scenes had been played when, on August 18th, the 5th division moved once more southwards to the area east of Doullens and north-east of Amiens. The division was now attached to the 4th corps, of which the other divisions were the 37th, 63rd, and New Zealand, under Lieutenant-General Sir G. Harper.

The advance on this front was fixed for August 21st, the 5th division to follow the right brigade of the 37th division and to pass through it when it had carried the first objective, the heights east of Beugny, and continue the advance. The 95th brigade was to lead on the right and the 15th on the left of the 5th division, with the 63rd division beyond, on the left, passing through the left brigade of the 37th division.

At zero hour (4.55 a.m.) on the 21st there was a dense mist. Ninety minutes later the 5th division passed through the 37th to carry the attack through, with the New Zealand division on the right of the 95th brigade. Seventy-two minutes later the second objective was carried. During this advance the 1st Norfolk were in rear of the leading battalions (1st Cheshire and 16th Warwickshire), and when the 1st Cheshire were nearly cut off, owing to the 63rd brigade on their left being held up, the 1st Norfolk were sent to reinforce them and fill the gap between them and the 63rd brigade. The fog was still thick, and apparently owing to it the Norfolk battalion failed to reach the Cheshire. That night they were in position near Achiet le Petit. The casualties were Captains Taylor and Wood, 2nd Lieutenants Hammond and Rivett wounded, and a few casualties only among other ranks.

The night of the 21st and the 22nd were spent in consolidating the new position, and on the latter day the battalion suffered badly from the tremendous German shell fire. Lieutenant-Colonel Humphries, now commanding the battalion, and Captain G. C. Tyler, his adjutant, were both wounded and died soon after. Captain T. A. K. Cubitt was killed and Lieutenant Shaul seriously wounded. There were heavy casualties among other ranks. Major G. de Grey, D.S.O. assumed command of the battalion.

On August 23rd the general advance continued against the Arras-Albert Railway up a glacis-like slope. In the valley on the right were many machine guns, which caused serious losses to the Bedford battalion, who were leading the brigade. Before the railway was reached three lines of wire had to be passed, and the left was held up until tanks broke through the wire and put out of action many of the troublesome machine-guns. The advance of the 37th division on the left enabled the 1st Bedford to reach their objective, where their depleted line was thickened by two companies of the 1st Norfolk. The battalion in this advance had only a few casualties amongst the men, and 2nd Lieutenant Cosham wounded. Its position for the night was eighty yards in front of the objective line. Next morning it was withdrawn to the trenches east of Achiet le Petit.

On August 25th the 1st Norfolk moved forward across the railway to the trenches near Achiet le Grand. In the shelling of this day Major de Grey was wounded, two other ranks were killed, and fifteen wounded. Major de Grey was temporarily succeeded in the command by Major H. S. Walker of the 1st Cheshire. That night the 15th brigade took over the line on the left of the 5th division, the battalion in front being the 1st Cheshire with one company of the Norfolk. On the 28th the brigade, by a side slip, took over the front occupied by the 13th brigade.

At 4.45 a.m. on the 30th the 15th brigade moved forward towards the Sapignies-Bapaume road, in support of the attack of the 95th brigade north of Bapaume. By 2.30 p.m. the 95th brigade was firmly established in the " Old Army Line " west of Beugny, and the 15th brigade passed through it to trenches facing that village, whence they were withdrawn next day under heavy gas and high explosive shelling which gassed Lieutenant and Adjutant Field, killed one man, and wounded eighteen. Earlier in the day, 2nd Lieutenants Jordan and Fretwell had also been wounded. In the night of September 1st–2nd the 1st Norfolk were again moved up for an attack on the 2nd, with the Norfolk battalion leading on the right and the Cheshire on the left, against Beugny and the ground to the south of it. The assault started at 5.15 a.m. and the Norfolk men reached their objective with few casualties, capturing 250 prisoners. The Cheshire battalion at the same time established themselves in Beugny, as far as a sunken road in the middle of it. An enemy counter-attack on the right was repulsed. Lieutenant Burry was wounded, and the casualties in other ranks on the 2nd September were twenty-one killed and eighty-five wounded.

By one p.m. the enemy had dribbled back and penetrated the line between the right of the Norfolk battalion and the left of the New Zealanders. This compelled the advanced companies of the 1st Norfolk to withdraw slightly; but they held on firmly to their general position south of Beugny. By 4 p.m. the new line had been formed, with the assistance of two companies of the 1st Bedford, and was held all night.

The following extract from battalion orders testifies to the conduct of the Norfolk men on this day:

" The divisional commander has asked the commanding officer to inform all ranks of the 1st battalion the Norfolk Regiment how much he appreciated the extraordinary good work carried out by the battalion during the operations from August 21st to September 2nd. During this time the division has recaptured a depth of over fifteen miles of enemy territory, which is more than any other division in the whole army has been able to accomplish in the same time, and has captured an enormous amount of booty and prisoners.

"During the operations near Beugny village on September 2nd the 1st battalion the Norfolk Regiment was the only battalion, out of three divisions, that reached the final objective in its entirety, and it was only due to the fact that the battalion held on throughout the night to the high ground south of the village that the village became untenable to the enemy, and he was forced to retire. . . . The fruits of the victory were made clear to all ranks by the advance that was made, almost without opposition, on the following morning."

On the morning of September 3rd the brigade again attacked, two companies of the Norfolk battalion following 500 yards behind the front line to assist in consolidation of a line at Delsaox Farm, south of Beugny. Little resistance was encountered, as most of the enemy had retreated in the night. At one p.m. the battalion passed forward again as far as the western edge of Le Brucquière village, where Major de Grey rejoined it in billets. By this evening the 5th division, as the result of almost continuous fighting since August 21st, had driven the German line back some fourteen miles, though not without a loss of about 4,300 in casualties. It was relieved by the 37th division. From the 4th the 1st Norfolk were resting or training in the back areas till the 20th, when they relieved the 13th brigade in the support area about Neuville, moving forward again on the 25th to Metz en Coûture, where "A" company was in the front line, attached to the 1st Cheshire, the other three companies remaining east of Metz. "C" company had ten casualties from a heavy bombardment.

On the 26th the whole battalion was in assembly positions for an advance on the 28th, which began at 10 a.m. and was again carried forward at 5 p.m. as far as the railway from Gouzeaucourt to Cambrai, on which "C" and "D" consolidated, with "A" and "B" in support and reserve. On this day Lieutenant Rickwood was wounded, and fourteen other ranks. This day was signalized by the capture of "African" trench, north-west of Gouzeaucourt, which had been the scene of a fresh stand by the enemy. In the actual capture of this trench the 1st Norfolk do not appear to have participated. The early hours of the 29th saw the battalion advancing on "Fusilier" ridge, which was reached but had to be evacuated, as the right flank was in the air. A position was consolidated, with two supporting companies in a sunken road behind. There was much gas and high explosive shelling, and the battalion's casualties on this day rose to nine killed of other ranks and forty wounded.

On the 30th the 1st Cheshire led the advance to the first objective ("Barrack" trench), where the Norfolk battalion passed through to attack the second. As they moved on Banteux they saw the enemy evacuating it, and the casualties were slight—2nd Lieutenant T. Boast killed and five other ranks wounded. On the 29th and 30th, 200 prisoners were taken by the battalion.

On October 1st the 37th division again took over from the 5th, and a period of rest and training followed for the Norfolk battalion about Metz, La Vacquerie, Ligny, etc., where the 5th division was in corps reserve till the 9th. On the 13th it took up the line on the Selle, the stream which passes by Le Câteau of glorious memory, nearly northwards to Denain, with the 13th brigade in front line from Neuvilly on the left bank to Briastre farther north on the same side of the river.

On the 22nd the 1st Norfolk went up into the support line. Here the Rev. R. W. Dugdale, M.C., C.F., was killed, and on the 23rd the Norfolk battalion took over the front line at Beaurain from the Bedford and Cheshire battalions, withdrawn to rest after suffering heavy casualties in the fighting of the previous days, in which the 1st Norfolk had not taken part. They were relieved the same evening and went back to Caudry for reorganization and training. Their total losses in October had only been two killed and three wounded.

On November 3rd they once more moved forward by Beaurain to positions for the attack on the forest of Mormal from Neuville. The German defence had for some time been gradually weakening, and the end was approaching.

At 5.30 a.m. on November 5th the Norfolk battalion led the attack, with the 1st Bedford at Jolimetz in immediate support. The weather, which had been splendid, had now broken and the advance was made in a downpour. At first no opposition was met with, and by 7.30 a.m., when the first objective had been gained well within the forest, the Bedford battalion passed through to continue the attack. The 1st Norfolk reformed at the cross-roads at Le Godelot, ready to give assistance, which, however, was not required.

On the 6th the battalion went on to La Haute Rue, near the eastern edge of the forest, for a further attack. At 5.30 p.m. it was ready for an attack across the Sambre, which flows north-eastwards along the eastern edge of the forest. A bridge in front had been reported safe, but by 7.30 p.m. it was found to have been blown up by the retreating enemy, as well as a foot bridge.

Late that night a working party was detached to help in the reconstruction of the bridge at the lock. By 6 a.m. on the 7th work had to be abandoned owing to the hostile machine-gun fire. At 7.30 the attack was launched across the river, with the railway running north to Maubeuge as objective. The passage was made by a pontoon bridge constructed during the night by the Royal Engineers. The railway was reached and made good by the Cheshire battalion and a platoon of " B " company of the Norfolk battalion.

About 4.30 p.m. the Devonshire battalion of the 95th brigade passed through the Norfolk and Cheshire battalions to continue the attack. Fontaine, on the right, was taken, but the Devonshire men were held up at St. Remi-Mal-bâti on the left. At 5.30 a.m. on the 8th the Devonshire battalion were attacking the Avesnes-Maubeuge road, and at 9.30 the 1st Norfolk were withdrawn to the railway, whence, on the 9th and 10th, they went back to rest and reorganize at Jolimetz on the west of the Mormal Forest. Here, on the ever-memorable November 11, 1918 they learnt that hostilities were to cease at 11 a.m. From the history of the 5th division it appears that the news of the Armistice was received with none of the wild rejoicings and enthusiasm which characterized the day in London. The troops had been for four years and a quarter constantly engaged in the most desperate struggles with a powerful and obstinate enemy, and it is easy to imagine that they could hardly believe that all the misery and dangers they had endured were at an end. To quote the words of the history: " The lifting of the ever-present cloud of death, which had been before them for four and a half years, was not at first apparent to the muddy, rain-soaked, and exhausted troops, and, though the dramatic events of the past few days had prepared us for it, it took some time before its tremendous import could be realized."

The subsequent movements of the 1st Norfolk up to the end of 1918, when this history ceases, require but few words.

The rest of November, and the first thirteen days of December, were passed at Le Quesnoy, whence the battalion moved gradually forward into Belgium, through Nivelles and Sombreffe—names famous in the Waterloo campaign—to Grand Leez, where they arrived on December 23rd and remained till the 31st.

At the Armistice there remained of the full complement of officers and men who had sailed from Belfast in August, 1914, but one officer (Captain and Quartermaster E. Smith, M.C.) and fifty other ranks. A few of the officers had been transferred or promoted to higher ranks, but the vast majority of both officers and men had laid down their lives for their country, or been incapacitated by wounds or disease incurred in its service.

The following extracts from the diary kept in Germany by 6324 Private R. Sheldrake of the 1st battalion are of interest on the subject of the German treatment of prisoners of war.

Private Sheldrake was badly wounded in the left arm (nerve severed) and back, apparently in Captain Luard's fight above Missy on the Aisne on September 14, 1914. He was taken prisoner by the Germans, and, after being kept in hospitals in France for some time, was sent back to Germany in the second week in November. He writes regarding the diary :

" This diary was wrote by me in the Prisoners of War Camp, Zwickau, Saxony, Germany, with the exception of the part wrote in Millbank Hospital, 14.12.18. This book, and two smaller ones, and a few more papers, I smuggled home by making a secret case (a false bottom) in a cardboard box about a foot square, then filled it up with printed books and curios, etc., for them to examine."

The "printed papers" were the polyglot "Illustrated War Courier," "War Chronicle," etc., prepared and circulated among prisoners of war for propaganda purposes. Of these there are many copies in England.

The extracts hereafter quoted are copied exactly, save correction of a few slips in spelling and punctuation, from the diary.

"We entered Germany about 6 p.m. that night. A German lady came and laid two cigars on each of our tables that night, but I think she was mistaking us for German wounded, as there were several carriages full of them on our train. I don't think civilization has got so far as Germans giving cigars to their prisoners, not even if they are wounded. . . .

"We had arrived at our destination, which turned out to be Zwickau in Saxony. We had a drink of coffee given us here; the Germans received coffee and rolls of white bread at several stations coming along, but not the prisoners. . . . When we arrived into some wooden huts that held about thirty men each (built since the war begun) we were stripped and put into nice, clean hospital clothes and spring beds. Our clothes were taken away, labelled in bundles with our names on, but afterwards they appeared to have been fumigated and all mixed together, so when we left the hospital we had any old thing that came first given us. . . ."

After describing how, as they moved quarters, the German onlookers sneered at the "Engländer," the diary goes on:

"The next to share the German 'honours' were a few Arabs of the French army; there was about a dozen of them. The Germans, looking on them as comrades, giving them milk two or three times a day, and placed them in a room together and preached the Holy War to them. They were ignorant enough to think they would get them to fight against their benefactors the French, these being loyal soldiers who wore the Morocco medal. The last three of them were moved to a camp near Berlin (Wiensdorf), leaving here the 12th July (1915). I heard there was an interpreter there preaching the Holy War to them, and if they would go to Turkey and fight against the French, English, and Russians, for the Sultan of Turkey, they would send them there."

Of his ill-treatment by the Germans the diarist gives the following instances:

"One we nicknamed 'Big Head' . . . One very cold night he came and pulled a second blanket off my bed (one I had taken lying on a spare bed) saying 'We give Englishmen nothing.' When he used to bring round the small ration of meat at dinner-time he used to always fish me up a bone, or a piece of fat, and to sneer out that detestable sounding word 'Englander.'"

The following gives credit to a German doctor who took the place of one who had treated the prisoners brutally. The new man "was very kind to us all":

"We were very sorry to hear later on that an old civilian Frenchman (who had had his leg taken off in his ward, and received the best of treatment from this most experienced doctor and his colleagues) went home to France and reported in the press that he had been treated badly by the German doctors. I think I am speaking the minds of all our French soldier comrades here by saying it was a wicked lie. It greatly annoyed this officer, as he showed us the report and asked us if it was true, and if we had any complaint to make to him he would be pleased to hear it, and he would do anything in his power to rectify it. Some of the Frenchmen wrote a letter to the editor denying the false accusation, but it was not forwarded. . . . This officer and his colleague, a private soldier (but a doctor and a gentleman), used to dress my wounds with all the kindness and gentleness any person could desire."

The following passages paint another picture :—

"Two parties of convalescents were sent on the 2nd and 24th December from Zwickau to another camp, probably Chemnitz. Our comrade Griffiths, the Welshman, left with the second party; they looked a helpless lot marching over the snow with the scant clothes they had given them. Griffiths had an old pair of trousers large enough for three like him to get into, a half shirt, a leg of stocking for a sock, etc.; some men with trousers legs that had been cut off the wounded."

"When we arrived in the large prisoner camp, on the 8th May, we found they were not receiving more than half a pound a man. They gave a half loaf to last five days. Some young men, still growing and hungry, used to eat it the first day, then would be very hungry till bread day arrived again. The bread will just give an ordinary appetite satisfaction for breakfast; then at dinner time and supper we receive about a pint of what is called soup. Up till Christmas we hospital patients used to receive a small piece of meat each dinner-time; then after that time we used to receive a small piece of meat, sausage, or fish every alternate day. When we arrived in the large camp, all we got was sometimes a mouthful, mostly on Sundays, in our soup. Well, now for trying to describe the different kinds of soup. First of all for its bad taste was what I call 'Black Soup'; looks like rye meal boiled in some water with a little salt and pepper to flavour it, sometimes a bone, but we never (*sic*) feel sick from the grease. Then we had a lot of 'white water soup', made from a handful or two of white flour mixed in water, but if you used it to paste paper on a wall it would be too thin for that purpose, though we had to make a meal from it. . . . The Russians and the French, who cannot receive any food in parcels, are half starved, look like skeletons. . . . In June we had some mangolds. To see them all rotten in a heap, some persons would hesitate in giving them to a pig, but they were mixed up in some more vegetables and went down with them. The end of August a lot (French and Russians) refused to go down the mines, as it was not their profession. A lot of men who had never wielded anything much heavier than a pen were warned to go mining. These men were put under close arrest with only a blanket to sleep on and bread and water to eat for several days; they gradually gave in, finding it useless to kick against the last backer-up of justice, for good or bad, military force."

Private Sheldrake generally gives credit to the Germans where he can. Whilst dealing with the shortage of prisoners' food he recognizes that the population also was short of food owing to the blockade.

The diary is very long and impossible to quote in full. We can only afford a limited space for quotations from it, and will conclude with the following on propaganda :—

"Another (Frenchman) had a bullet taken from his back after being wounded ten weeks. The Germans said it was an English bullet, but if it was the English had a hit early, as he told me he was wounded about 4 p.m. the 22nd of August. They said they would show us the bullet, but did not do so; they were very fond of trying to prove these little accidents against the Allies. Anything they can find to try and break up the Entente Cordiale of France and England is acceptable to the Germans' ears. They say here when this war is over the Germans will be comrades with the French, but not so with England. How pleased they are of repeating that myth that England will hold Calais after the war. I suppose the French would rather have the English hold it than the Germans. . . . We had some tracts given us telling us the German views of the causes of the war, and pointing out the barbarous acts of the Cossacks and French and the good qualities of the German soldiers."

Private Sheldrake was eventually sent home, in the end of 1915, as incapacitated for service owing to his wounds.

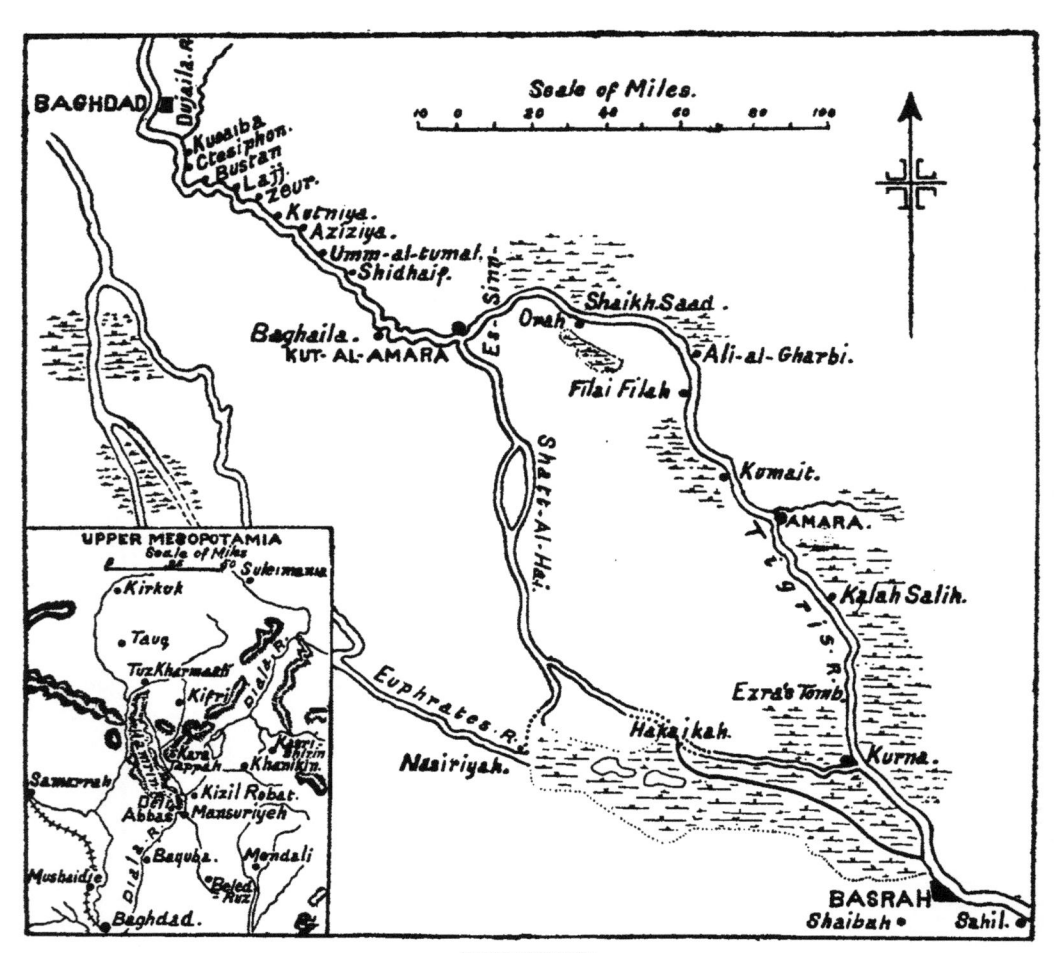

MESOPOTAMIA

CHAPTER II

THE 2ND BATTALION IN MESOPOTAMIA

(a) 1914: SAHIL—BASRA—KURNA

THE 2nd Battalion had been at Belgaum since 1911 when the Great War commenced in Europe. There they remained, no doubt wondering if and when they were going to have a hand in the great events which were in progress. The question was answered when, on November 3, 1914, they entrained for Bombay, and three days later sailed, on the transport "Elephanta," for the Persian Gulf. The officers embarking with the battalion were:

Lieut.-Col. E. C. Peebles, D.S.O.
Major F. de B. Bell
Major W. E. Cramer Roberts
Captain C. V. Lanyon
Captain H. L. Willett
Captain W. J. O'B. Daunt
Captain R. D. Marshall
Capt. and Adjt. G. de Grey
Captain G. B. Northcote
Lieut. R. A. Downs
Lieut. A. J. Shakeshaft
Lieut. A. B. Floyd
Lieut. L. W. Blakiston
Lieut. H. E. Hall
Lieut. R. T. Frere
Lieut. J. O. C. Orton
Lieut. F. W. Hudson
Lieut. H. S. Farebrother
2nd Lieut. H. L. Peacock
2nd Lieut. J. H. Brownrigg
2nd Lieut. H. J. Bullock
Lieut. and Q.M. J. T. Richardson, D.C.M.
Captain A. Hendry, R.A.M.C.

The strength at embarkation was twenty-three officers, five warrant officers, and 907 other ranks.

By November 13th the "Elephanta" was nineteen miles from Fao at the mouth of the Shatt-al-Arab, the river formed by the united streams of the Tigris and the Euphrates after their first junction at Kurna. Next day the transport steamed up the river as far as Saniyah, some thirty miles from Fao. On the 15th the battalion disembarked, the small enemy forces in the neighbourhood having been driven off from their camp four miles away on the same day by the troops already landed under General Delamain, the 16th (Indian) Brigade. The Norfolk Regiment formed part of the 18th (Indian) brigade, commanded by Major-General C. I. Fry. The other regiments in the brigade were the 7th Rajputs, 110th Mahratta Light Infantry, and 120th Rajputana Infantry.

On the morning of November 17th two brigades (16th and 18th) of the 6th (Indian) division, had landed, and the general advance began at 6 a.m. along the right bank of the Shatt-al-Arab. Along this bank was a fringe of palms, sometimes a mile in breadth, which was left 1,500 yards on the right of the Norfolk Regiment. The march was at first nearly north, parallel to the course of the river. The day was hot, after a night and early morning of bitter cold.

When the advance had progressed six miles, the cavalry reported the enemy in position near a police station and an old fort. So far the 2nd Norfolk Regiment had been with the main guard. They were now sent up on the right of the 7th Rajputs. Opposite Sabeh Nakhlat the enemy's artillery had opened fire from the old fort, but had caused no casualties.

At this juncture a heavy shower turned the desert into a quagmire, through which progress was only possible at a slow walk. The hostile artillery now began to be more effective, but was mostly directed on a mountain battery on the British right.

The Turkish position faced nearly west, with its left resting on the old fort, and its right at the village of Sahil. The whole front consisted of a long trench parallel to the fringe of date palms, extending back on its left towards the old fort at the edge of them.

At 11 a.m. a halt was called to enable the 16th brigade to come up on the right. Then the whole line advanced eastwards in the teeth of a heavy rifle fire from the Turkish trench about 1,000 yards in front. On the left were the 7th Rajputs, with the 2nd Norfolk Regiment on their right, and the 110th Mahratta Light Infantry in reserve. Against the Turkish left flank the 16th brigade advanced nearer the palms. The 2nd Dorset Regiment (16th brigade), opposite the left of the trench, suffered severely from rifle fire. Nothing, however, could stop the advance, and, though heavy casualties were incurred from rifle fire, and from a gun firing percussion shrapnel, the defenders of the trench were presently driven from it. As they left the trench, they were almost annihilated by the fire of two British batteries behind the left of the 16th brigade.

At 2 p.m. the whole line was pushing on, still annoyed by the fire of the gun above mentioned. During the whole action the troops on land were aided by the fire of H.M.S. " Odin " and " Espiègle " on the river, though it was rendered less effective than it might have been by the intervening fringe of palms.

At 4 p.m. the pursuit was stopped and the troops went into camp a mile south of the old fort. The outpost line was held by the 16th brigade and the 48th Pioneers. The Norfolk battalion's casualties on this day were seven other ranks killed and forty-eight wounded.

The night was again very cold, with a gale blowing, and the camp was sniped by Turks from the palm trees on the right. As the men had brought neither great-coats nor blankets with them, they spent a very miserable and almost sleepless night.

During the 18th a company of the Norfolk Regiment cleared the snipers out of the palms, but that did not prevent many of them returning to their job in the ensuing night. That night was rather less uncomfortable for the Norfolk men, thanks to a supply of waterproof sheets, great-coats, and blankets, found in a deserted Turkish camp by " B " company when out rounding up some Arabs.

The 19th and 20th were employed in clearing up, when fifteen dead of the Dorset battalion were found.

On the 21st the Norfolk Regiment again embarked on the S.S. " Medjidieh " for Basra. The embarkation was not an easy matter, and, as the Turks had endeavoured to obstruct the passage by sinking ships in the river, a way through had to be discovered.

Basra, where the 2nd Norfolk arrived at 10 a.m. on the 22nd, had been evacuated by the Turks and left to the tender mercies of the predatory Arabs, who were happily looting it when the British warships arrived, just in time to prevent its total destruction, and to save the European inhabitants.

The rest of November was uneventful, the battalion being chiefly employed in rounding up the neighbouring Arab villages and searching for arms. On the 26th it collected 162 rifles from a village six miles away.

The next move was made on December 3rd, when " D " company, under Captain Lanyon, Lieutenants Downs, Frere, and Bullock, with 183 other ranks, embarked for Kurna, the point of junction of the Tigris and the old branch of the Euphrates.[1] The force, under Lieutenant-Colonel Frazer, sent on this expedition consisted, besides the company above mentioned, of one section Royal Field Artillery, half a company of Sappers and miners, the 104th Rifles, and 110th Mahratta Light Infantry.

At 6.45 a.m. on the 4th the " Lawrence " and " Espiègle " were engaged with the enemy at Kurna. An hour later Colonel Frazer's force landed at Swaib Creek on the left (east) bank of the Shatt-al-Arab, which was defiladed from the enemy's fire from Kurna by the usual fringe of palms. The first mile of the advance northwards was through a reedy marsh, which fortunately, owing to recent dry weather, was passable by all arms.

At 11 a.m. the infantry were in artillery formation south-east of Kurna, facing the enemy's position, which extended north-eastwards from the junction of the Tigris and Euphrates along about a mile of palm trees, the village of Mazera, and what appeared to be mud walls. The latter eventually turned out to be reed screens in front of trenches. The

---

[1] This channel is nearly stagnant. The main channel of the Euphrates is now that which meets the Tigris at Gurmat Ali, a few miles above Basra. Kurna lies in the angle between the Tigris and the old channel of the Euphrates, on the north side of the latter. It is from Kurna that the river becomes the Shatt-al-Arab.

enemy had good cover in the palms and irrigation channels, whilst the approach to their position was over flat ground offering no shelter. One section, moving round the north of the position, was held up by rifle fire, but the rest of the infantry worked through the village and enfiladed the Arab defenders, who retired northwards. By 2.30 the village and palms had been cleared, and the force was close to the bank of the Tigris, which rose about ten feet above the ground level and gave some protection from fire from beyond the river. At 3.10 p.m. the force retired to bivouac at the landing-place, as it was not strong enough to attempt the capture of Kurna.

During the 5th nothing happened; Lieutenant Downs, who went out with a platoon, saw no signs of the enemy. Reinforcements were now sent up to enable an attack to be made on Kurna. The rest of the Norfolk battalion left Basra by steamer on the 5th, with the 7th Rajputs, half the 120th Infantry, and four guns. They were at Swaib Creek by 6 a.m. on the 6th, and two hours later the advance was resumed against Mazera, where the Turks had again occupied their former position, from which they had been driven on December 3rd. They were busy entrenching, and a reconnaissance, from a brick kiln 2,000 yards northeast of the British camp, enabled an estimate to be made of their numbers, which appeared to be about 2,000 men with four guns. The latter fired on the reconnaissance. Captain Lanyon, with half of "D" company, had been left behind to guard the camp.

At 10 a.m. the attack on Mazera was ordered, the 2nd Norfolk against the centre of the village, with the 120th Infantry on their left, whilst the 110th Mahrattas were sent to the right to turn the enemy's left flank. The 104th Rifles and 7th Rajputs followed in support of the frontal attack. It was 11 a.m. when the guns had been got through the swampy ground of the first part of the march and the infantry were able to attack. The ships also were firing from the river on the enemy's right.

At 11.35 the Turks had strongly reinforced their right, and were enfilading the British line by rifle fire from a trench between Mazera and the Shatt-al-Arab. The artillery was turned on to this, and then the 120th Infantry cleared the Turks out with the bayonet. At the same

5

time the Norfolk battalion and the 7th Rajputs cleared Mazera, also with the bayonet.

As the Turks fled from the whole of their position on the east bank, they came under the rifle fire of the 110th Mahrattas on the right, and suffered severely. In Mazera two field guns were taken.

The casualties of the Norfolk battalion were, Captain W. J. O'B. Daunt and 2nd Lieutenant H. J. Bullock wounded, two other ranks killed, and thirty-five wounded, of whom two died of wounds.

On the 8th the 104th and 110th crossed the Tigris above Kurna, under cover of the fire of the Norfolk battalion from the left bank, where they remained till next day, when they heard of the surrender of Kurna with 1,010 prisoners, two field guns, and two mountain guns.

Crossing to Kurna on the 11th, the battalion was employed for the rest of the month on the defences of their camp there. Beyond occasional shots from Arabs in the desert beyond, there is nothing to note before the close of 1914.

(b) 1915: KURNA—SHAIBA—THE ADVANCE TO AND BATTLE OF CTESIPHON—SIEGE OF KUT

During the early part of January, 1915, matters were fairly quiet. On the 6th " A " and " C " companies, with the 7th Rajputs, went by steamer up the Euphrates nearly to Cubaish, where they anchored but did not land; they returned next day to Kurna. On the night of the 6th there was a small attack by Arabs on Norfolk Hill, a small elevation on the right bank of the Tigris north of Kurna which had been fortified towards the end of December, when news came in that the Turks were collecting troops about ten miles higher up. The attack was easily stopped by " B " and " D " companies holding the position. There were no casualties on our side.

On the 19th the battalion was again at Mazera, in the south-west corner of the series of trenches and forts which had been built there. Early on the 20th the 17th brigade were engaged in a reconnaissance from the northern end of the defences of the left bank, and the Norfolk battalion acted as reserve to it. Half a dozen shells fell among them, but did no harm, and that evening they again crossed the Tigris to Kurna, where they spent the rest of the month uneventfully. The annual floods had commenced ere this, and the whole country about Kurna was practically a swamp, though on the left bank of the Tigris, north of Mazera, the ground was much drier. Kurna was altogether an unpleasant place, though in Mohammedan tradition it is the reputed site of the Garden of Eden.

On February 7th the Norfolk battalion furnished the guard of honour on the occasion of the visit of H. E. Lord Hardinge, Viceroy of India, to Kurna.

On the 17th " A " and " C " companies were sent back to Basra, where they were followed by " B " and " D " on the 21st. At first the Norfolk battalion were told off to hold the Custom House post. On the 25th they were sent to the Ashar Barracks, where they suffered some discomfort owing to the reduction of the ground by rain to a quagmire.

March was passed in Basra. The only event of note was the despatch, on the 11th, of Lieutenant Farebrother and fifty men with the expedition under Major Farmer up the Euphrates. The object was to prevent the arrival of supplies by " mahela "[1] to the Turkish camp at Nakailah. There was a good deal of bombardment by the ships, and many " mahelas " were destroyed, but the details of these operations are of no special interest to the Norfolk Regiment, who were not engaged on shore. The expedition returned to Basra on March 31st.

On the 22nd it had been decided to organize the Mesopotamian Expeditionary Force as a complete army corps, under the command of General Sir J. Nixon.

The Turks had for some time been collecting both regular troops and Arabs at the camp at Nakailah on the Euphrates, with the object of attempting a blow at Basra from the west by Shaiba. This place lies some eight miles west of Basra, and is used by the wealthier inhabitants of the latter as a summer refuge from the intense heat. It had

[1] " Mahela," a sailing barge carrying from fifteen to seventy tons on the Tigris and Euphrates—something like the Nile " dahabiyah."

been held as an outpost by the British since the capture of Basra. Nakailah lies some twenty miles to the north of Shaiba on the new channel of the Euphrates. The Turkish threat became serious by the beginning of April, 1915, and it was necessary to meet it. On April 5th the 2nd Norfolk Regiment was ordered to march to Shaiba with the rest of the 18th brigade,[1] the 16th brigade being already there with the cavalry and three batteries. Marching at 6.45 a.m. the battalion did

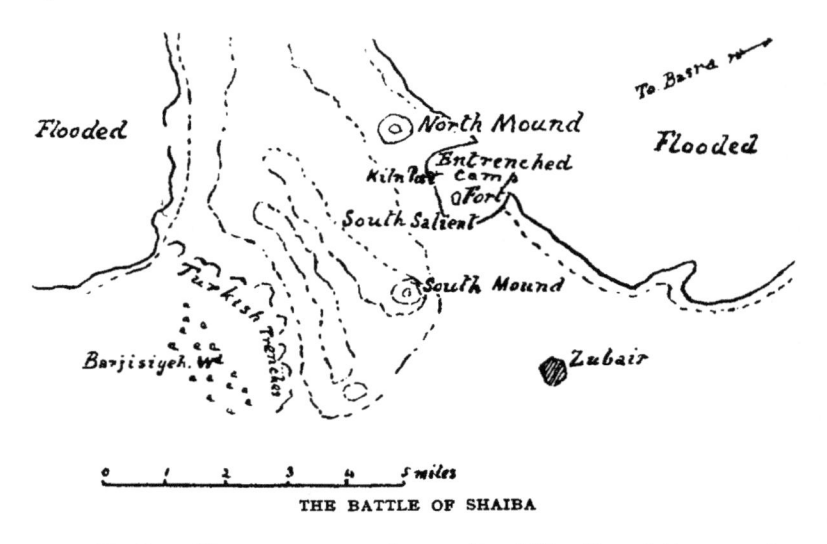

THE BATTLE OF SHAIBA

not reach Shaiba till 7.30 p.m., owing to the difficulty of the march across the intervening flooded desert, through which the men had to wade, the depth of water being from six inches to five feet in places.

The Shaiba position was on a low ridge running north and south. The main portion of it was about an old mud fort and was about a mile from north to south and half that breadth. Near the north end of the west face was a mound known as "Kiln Post," about half a mile north of the old fort. There were two advanced knolls outside the position—South Mound about two miles south and North Mound a mile away on the north front. In front of the position were other slight ridges, with Barjisiyeh Wood about six miles to the south-west in a depression.

[1] The 48th Pioneers had taken the place in the brigade of the 7th Rajputs employed at Ahwaz.

The position was strongly fortified with barbed wire, trenches, gun emplacements, and redoubts.

The Turks had collected some 10,000 or 12,000 men, whilst the British force consisted of three regiments of cavalry, eight battalions, and four batteries, including one of horse and one of mountain guns.

The Turkish force had advanced to within four miles of Shaiba, on the hither side of Barjisiyeh Wood, and were expected to attack on April 12th.

At 5.15 on the morning of April 12th heavy rifle fire was opened from the south, followed by artillery as the British piquets fell back. Of the Norfolk Regiment " C " and " D " companies were held in reserve, under the orders of the G.O.C. just east of Shaiba Fort ; " A " and " B " with the machine-gun section (less one gun lent to the 48th Pioneers)[1] were in reserve in trenches behind the south salient of the fort. Artillery fire from about ten guns continued all day. At 11 a.m. the whole battalion was ordered to cover the arrival of reinforcements (the 30th brigade) from Basra. The order was presently cancelled ; the reinforcements failed to get through, except the 24th Punjab Infantry, which came over in bellums with General Melliss in the evening. The artillery fire continued all day, and some of the enemy succeeded in digging themselves in within sixty yards of the south salient works ; but the attack was never pressed home. The Norfolk battalion's casualties on this day were Major W. E. Cramer Roberts, Lieutenant H. S. Farebrother (who received the M.C. for his conduct on this day) and thirteen other ranks wounded. Major Cramer Roberts was wounded when in a trench with Colonel Peebles and Captain de Grey.

The night of the 12th–13th was much disturbed by rifle fire and attacks by the enemy with hand grenades. The main assault was repulsed at 9 p.m. In the morning of the 13th the enemy was found to be withdrawing and the rifle fire ceased. During this day two trenches containing seven Turkish officers and 120 men, surrendered, after some resistance to the 16th brigade. Later in the day a sweeping movement was undertaken by the 16th brigade towards the village of Zobeir in the

[1] Corporal Waller received the D.C.M. for the gallant manner in which he fought this gun (of which he was in charge) after he was wounded.

south-east, pivoting on the Norfolk Regiment, who only had one man wounded. A number of Turks surrendered.

On the 14th, at 8 a.m., a similar sweeping movement, starting towards the south-west, was undertaken by both brigades, the 18th being on the left and the 2nd Norfolk Regiment being echeloned on the left rear of it. The objective was to clear all the ground between Shaiba and Zobeir.

At 10.30 a.m. the Norfolk battalion and the 120th were sent across from the left to the right of the line, and by 11 a.m. found themselves echeloned to the right rear of the 119th (16th brigade) near South Mound. The sweep was now continued towards the south-west, and as the 16th brigade moved rapidly in that direction the Norfolk Regiment was directed to prolong its line on the right. The 16th brigade had continued southwards for some time and consequently, at one time, there was a gap of nearly 2,000 yards between their right and the left of the 18th brigade. As the Norfolk Regiment advanced they encountered heavy rifle fire, and a few shells, from the right, in which direction their line was continued by the 120th, with the 110th in reserve.

The main body of the enemy had been located in well-sited trenches north of Barjisiyeh. When the Norfolk battalion had got within 350 yards of these trenches, they had suffered heavy casualties and found themselves held up by intense rifle and machine-gun fire. On reporting this to headquarters, they were ordered to hold firm where they were. The 120th had suffered still heavier losses.

At 3 p.m. orders were received that the trenches must be taken "at all costs." They were practically invisible, being concealed by thorn bushes, so much so that it was not till they were taken that the Norfolk men discovered the whereabouts of two machine guns which had caused the majority of their casualties.

Fortunately, at this time Lieutenant Gilpin, R.A., reached the battalion and concerted measures with Colonel Peebles for signalling to his battery, which very much improved the artillery support.[1] The

---

[1] As all the head-quarter signallers were either killed or wounded, Captain de Grey very gallantly took a flag and kept up communication, which it would have otherwise been impossible to keep up.

guns did great damage to the Turkish trenches. Colonel Peebles now decided that a bayonet charge was the only way of carrying out his orders. The battalion charged forward cheering, and, thanks to the improved artillery fire, was able to cover the last 200 yards with a loss of only one killed and one wounded![1]

The charge was more than the Turks could stand; they fled from their trenches before the Norfolk men could reach them. The trenches were found to be full of dead and wounded; 147 dead were counted in 200 yards of trench, and a trench farther on was even worse.

On the left the 16th brigade soon afterwards overcame the resistance in their front, and the whole Turkish force was now in rapid and disorderly retreat. The British were not in a condition to pursue. There had been seven battalions engaged on this day, the other two being left to guard the camp; their casualties had amounted to 1,100, and they owed much to the work of the artillery in stopping the Turkish reserves.

The Norfolk Regiment had very severe losses:

Officers, killed—2nd Lieutenants J. H. Brownrigg, R. A. Wynn, and Burnett (R.A.M.C.),

> *Officers wounded*—Major F. de B. Bell (died of wounds); Captains C. V. Lanyon and R. D. Marshall; Lieutenants J. O. C. Orton, R. T. Frere, and H. Richardson.

> *Other ranks*—Killed or died of wounds, twenty-nine (including Sergeant-Major Semmence and Colour-Sergeant Ewin); wounded, ninety.

The 2nd battalion was at very low strength on this day; Major de Grey thinks only about 300. Many men were sick, and a detachment under Blakiston only rejoined in the evening.

The success achieved by the resolution of the commander and the

[1] The message ordering the attack was received at 3.5 p.m., from Brigade-Major 18th brigade. It was: " Push forward at all costs. Take enemy's trench." As Colonel Peebles rose to lead the charge, he waved his sword (it was the last occasion on which officers carried swords in action), and shouted: " Come on the 9th," a call which was answered in the same words by the men. The instinctive reversion to the old number at a supreme moment when few expected to return unharmed from the desperate charge, is noticeable.

courage of the troops was as complete as it was opportune. The result of this battle gave immediate and permanent relief to a situation which, in its military and political aspects, was fraught with difficulty and even danger.

At 5 p.m. when the Turks were gone, orders issued for retirement to the Shaiba camp. The wounded were to be carried off, but, even then, it was considered unsafe to attempt the removal of the dead, who were left on the field for the night. The Norfolk battalion were back in camp at 7.30 p.m.

THE TIGRIS ABOVE AND BELOW KUT

The 15th was spent in collecting and burying the dead, and bringing in the ammunition and supplies abandoned in the enemy's camp. General Melliss congratulated the troops on a complete success. The Turkish commander, Suleiman Askeri, committed suicide after his defeat. Nothing more of note happened till the battalion again reached Basra, after a very difficult march in pouring rain through six miles of flood, mostly waist deep, on April 22nd.

On the 27th the Norfolk Regiment was again in Ashar Barracks, where they replaced the 4th Hampshire, gone to Ahwaz. Here they were inspected on May 8th by General Townshend, the new commander of the 6th division. Life at Basra up till May 28th was as tolerable as it could be with a day temperature rising to 120° or over at times.

On May 28th the battalion started again for Kurna, the beginning of the advance which was destined to end in Kut in April, 1916. Travelling by river steamer, it reached Kurna next day with the thermometer standing at 118°, but it was only on June 1st, when it was wrongly reported that Norfolk Hill was in the enemy's hands, that it landed at Bahran. May 31st had been spent on board watching, but taking no active part in, the battle of Kurna, which, by the evening of that day, had resulted in the capture by the 17th brigade of Norfolk Hill and the other small eminences which rose as islands from the surrounding floods, and the retirement of the Turks to the ridge running north from Bahran. During the night the Turks had abandoned this position, and the landing of the Norfolk Regiment on June 1st only afforded them an opportunity of stretching their legs on shore. At 5 a.m on the 2nd they again proceeded upstream by boat, with orders to push on to Ezra's Tomb; thence they were sent on, at 2.30 p.m., to Kala Salih. The steamer was held up by congestion of traffic in the narrow part of the river near Ezra's Tomb, and it was not till 11.45 a.m. on the 3rd that Kala Salih was reached, where orders were received to follow General Townshend to Amara, which he had taken with a handful of men.

The night of the 3rd–4th was spent at anchor a little below Amara, and by 6.40 a.m. on the 4th the 2nd Norfolk battalion were disembarking at that town, just in time to give support to the utterly inadequate force with which Townshend had "bluffed" the surrender on the previous day.

Arabs were looting the town, and the battalion was employed most of the day in suppressing them, which was done in the town by a company under Lieutenant Blakiston, whilst a detachment was sent over to the right bank of the Tigris till it could be relieved by the arrival of the 104th.

Amara itself is situated on the left bank of the Tigris, in the angle between it and the Jahala Canal, which leaves it on the upstream side of the town. Half the Norfolk Regiment, including the head-quarters, was quartered in Government House (renamed "Norfolk House"), close to the outflow of the canal, the other half in the Turkish barracks farther down the left bank of the Tigris.

Amara, being a definite stage in the advance up the Tigris, was organized for defence, the forces there being divided into (*a*) the striking force and (*b*) the minimum garrison. The defensive position was in the angle between the canal and the river, with bridge-heads beyond both.

All June was spent at Amara doing nothing much more than cleaning up and furnishing working parties, or escorts for Turkish and German prisoners. On the 17th eight officers joined from England, including Major F. C. Lodge, who took over the command from Colonel Peebles, who was sick. The weather was terribly hot, especially when the wind dropped, and there were many cases of heat-stroke. At the end of the month 227 men were proposed for change of climate to India, but the medical officer reduced them to 187, certifying the other forty as fit only for garrison duty. Even the 187 appear not to have gone in the end.

On July 6th the battalion paraded at 5 a.m. for service beyond the canal with the striking force. Nothing, however, happened, and there was no fighting.

On July 9th Major Rumbold (East Surrey Regiment, attached 2nd Norfolk) was sent up the river for duty at Kumait, in consequence of a report that 200 of the enemy with guns had been located at Filah-i-Filah on the 8th. With him went Lieutenant Campbell and twenty-five men of the Norfolk machine-gun section, and two machine-guns, besides a barge with a naval 4.7 inch gun. Next day Colonel Peebles, who had returned, was also sent up to reconnoitre and, if the enemy were not found in force lower down, to bombard Ali Gharbi from a range of 6,000 yards. He took with him four officers and 100 more men of the Norfolk battalion, two more 4.7 inch guns on a barge, and H.M.S. "Shaitan" as escort.

The expedition passed Kumait at noon on the 11th, and was at Ali-ash-Sharki by 7.30 p.m. At 6.15 a.m. on the 12th a Turkish steamer was sighted at Filah-i-Filah, and some Turkish cavalry on a mound. The latter were soon driven off by artillery fire, which also compelled the steamer and a motor boat to retire upstream. The fire against the mound was replied to at a range of 7,000 yards, and the enemy's guns were counted and other information gained by the "Shaitan," which pushed farther up. The reconnaissance returned to Amara at 8.30 a.m. on the 13th.

On July 6th intelligence had been received that General Gorringe's force on the Euphrates had pressed up, in the face of stubborn resistance, as far as the bifurcation of the old and new channels of the river. The 18th brigade was now sent to reinforce him in his advance against the Turks at Nasariyeh. The Norfolk battalion embarked for Kurna on July 16th, changed ships there, reached Azami camp on the left bank of the Euphrates, and disembarked at 7 p.m. on the 18th.

Beyond some desultory artillery fire nothing happened till the 23rd, when orders were issued by General Gorringe, G.O.C. 12th division, for the attack next day. The attack was to be northwards on both banks of the Euphrates, by which the Turks also were divided into two bodies. Both sides were of course connected by craft on the river.

In the fighting on the 24th the Norfolk Regiment played but a small part.

The 18th brigade formed the reserve, on the left bank, to the 12th division, the 120th Rajputana Infantry alone being sent to the right bank. As the Turks were driven upstream on both banks, the Norfolk battalion was sent over, at 2 p.m. to the right bank. At 3.30 p.m. they again embarked on the S.S. "Medjidieh," which steamed slowly up, shelling the enemy's position at the junction of the Euphrates and the Shatt-al-Hai. At 7 p.m. the battalion landed on the left bank, took fifteen or twenty prisoners and four 15-pounder guns in an abandoned Turkish position, and encamped for the night. They had only one man wounded and had only fired 1,130 rounds of rifle ammunition.

In this neighbourhood they remained till the end of the month, clearing up and reconnoitring, but not otherwise disturbed.

On August 2nd they started back via Kurna, with the rest of the brigade, to rejoin Townshend's force at Amara. Owing to delays on the river, they only reached Amara on the morning of the 7th, when Colonel Peebles took temporary command of the left bank of the Tigris, pending the arrival of the officer commanding the 18th brigade. Training, classes of instruction and route marches filled the time till August 25th, when Colonel Peebles, who was again ill, had to go to

Basra, making over the command to Major Lodge, who had been temporarily commanding the 4th Hampshire Regiment.

On the 27th the machine-gun section, which had been left at Ali-al-Gharbi, rejoined.

General Townshend, who had been to India sick, was now back with his division, ready for the advance on Kut-el-Amara. General Fry, of the 18th brigade, had commanded the 6th division during his absence. The Norfolk Regiment[1] started on September 7th and reached Ali-al-Gharbi that night, remaining there till the 13th, when they moved up by steamer to the village of Mandali, where the brigade took up a position covering the ships on the river, the 16th and 17th brigades being on the right bank. On the 14th the 18th brigade moved up by river and anchored above Shekh Saad, the 16th and 17th brigades reaching the same neighbourhood by march on the right bank.

After steaming up beyond Sannaiyat on the 15th, the battalion disembarked there, and next day "A" and "B" companies were sent across to the right bank to support the cavalry there. Nothing more of importance happened from the 17th to the 24th, when the brigadier-general explained the coming operations to the battalion commanders.

On the 26th the battalion, supplied with extra shovels and very flimsy wire cutters, was landed one and a half miles east of Nakailah on the left bank, where the men dug trenches and prepared an aerodrome.

The enemy on the left bank were entrenched on a line extending from the Tigris on their right to the Suwada marsh, and again beyond it towards the small marsh south of the great Suwaikieh swamp. On the right bank the line was extended south-eastwards along the Es Sinn ridge. Behind this was their general reserve. On the morning of September 27th the 18th brigade began its advance up the left bank, the 7th Rajputs next the river on the left, then the 120th, and the Norfolk battalion on the right, with the 110th in reserve. The advance

---

[1] Sir C. Townshend says their strength on September 22 was 660. Major de Grey says that of these at least one-third consisted of drafts received from the 5th and 6th East Surrey, 9th and 10th Middlesex, 4th and 5th Queen's, and 2/4 D.C.L.I. who joined, to the number of 350, at Basra about the end of April, 1915.

was continued to within 3,500 yards of the Turkish position, with the front line as far forward as another 1,500 yards. The enemy's position was plainly seen, with high wire in front, loopholed parapets behind, and guns in rear again. A party of the enemy opposing the Norfolk advance was easily driven into the Suwada Marsh by "C" and "D" companies. Another party was taken in hand by Sergeant Friston[1] and six snipers, to whom thirty-two Turks surrendered in the evening.

The positions reached were held all day, and strengthened during the ensuing night. There was good cover from the Turkish artillery in the irrigation channels. The firing line had eventually worked forward to within 800 yards of the enemy.

On the right bank a demonstration only had been made against the Es Sinn position by another column. During the night of the 26th–27th the principal mass of the British force had been secretly passed from the right to the left bank at Nakailah, and had started to turn the whole Turkish position by passing between the Suwada and Suwaikieh marshes and then wheeling to its left on Kut.

The function of the 18th Brigade was to simulate a decisive frontal attack along the left bank, but not to press it home till the turning movement had had its full effect.

At 6 a.m. on the 28th the advance was resumed, but the 110th took the place, on the right, of the Norfolk battalion, who remained as reserve in the trenches. Up to 8.50 the 2nd Norfolk had suffered hardly any casualties from the heavy Turkish artillery fire. Captain J. J. Lecky (Royal Fusiliers, attached 2nd Norfolk) was killed by a shell. At 9.30 came the news that Column "A"[2] had taken the enemy's position between the marshes. But the successes of this column were by no means so rapid as had been expected by General Townshend, and it eventually encountered the Turkish general reserve, which had crossed from Es Sinn by the boat bridge north of Kut.

Meanwhile the 18th brigade had been ordered to turn its holding attack into a real one. The Turks in front held firm and little progress could be made; indeed, at 4 p.m., "D" company of the Norfolk

[1] Sergeant Friston received the D.C.M. for this exploit. He was afterwards killed at Ctesiphon.
[2] The force referred to in the previous paragraph but one.

battalion had to be sent to support the 110th. Though the company was heavily shelled, it had no casualties.

That night the brigade held very much the same positions as on the previous one.

When it again advanced at 5.30 a.m. on the 29th it occupied the position which the Turks had abandoned in the night. It was found to be very elaborately fortified and wired. When the wire was cut the nippers, which had recently been served out, were found to be so bad that all were broken in cutting a twelve-foot passage through thinner wire than that used by the British.

At 10 a.m. the brigade, with the Norfolk battalion on the right, was covering the Horseshoe marsh behind the position on the west. At noon the Norfolk battalion were ordered to embark on the "Blosse Lynch" by 2 p.m., but, as a ramp had to be made, they only got on board at 5 p.m., when they went up and anchored just above the boat bridge, a little below Kut. It took the whole of the next day (30th) to get the ships past a bad bit of river to Kut itself.

The casualties of the 27th and 28th were slight—Captain Lecky and two other ranks killed; Lieutenant Cooke and three men wounded.

With the controversial question of the wisdom of the advance from Kut to Baghdad a regimental history has no concern.

On October 1st the 2nd Norfolk, on board the "Blosse Lynch," steamed up the Tigris, frequently delayed by their own or other ships sticking on banks. So bad was this that nearly every ship had some experience of it. It was sometimes even necessary to disembark the men to lighten the boat, and on the 2nd only eight miles were covered in the whole day.

On the 5th Azizieh was reached, and the battalion disembarked for several very hard days of work at unloading stores and guns, R.E. bridging, and fatigues of every kind.

The pursuit of the Turks under Nur-ed-din Pasha, defeated at Kut, was delayed by difficulties of navigation, and the whole of the British troops only reached Azizieh, about fifty miles upstream, on October 6th. Here, on the 11th, it was ascertained that Nur-ed-din had halted at Ctesiphon, after leaving a covering force of about 4,000 men at Zeur, some twelve or fourteen miles short of it. Altogether his strength in numbers was probably about equal to Townshend's. The latter commander looked upon the three British battalions (Norfolk, Dorsetshire, and Oxford and Bucks. L.I. Regiments) as the backbone of his little army.

The battalion had left Es Sinn on September 29th 611 strong, all fit. On October 8th ninety-two were reported sick, of whom seventy were held unfit to fight. About half the " fit " men ought by rights to have been in hospital. In addition, thirty-three had been admitted to hospital. As the diary plaintively says, " 103 men out of action in eight days without a shot being fired ! " The sickness was greatly increased by lack of proper food. Tons of vegetables from India and elsewhere had to be thrown into the river to get rid of the stench due to their rotting.

Work on fortifying the camp at Azizieh continued, and the rate of sickness remained high. About thirty-five cases of " beriberi " occurred. The battalion took its share of working at or garrisoning a protective post, and there was occasionally an alarm of an attack which did not materialize.

On the 15th General Fry fell ill and had to go on sick leave, being relieved in command of the 18th brigade by Brigadier-General W. G. Hamilton, who had commanded the 1st Battalion Norfolk Regiment in 1904.

On October 27th it was estimated that the enemy had a force of 1,500 camel corps, 1,000 cavalry, and four guns at El Kutuniè, which General Townshend proposed to attack next day. The whole force, except two battalions and the unfit men left to guard the camp, proceeded on this expedition.

The force marched in two parallel columns at 11.30 p.m. on the 27th. Deploying at daybreak, the enemy soon appeared to have been completely surprised. There was some firing from light camel guns, but the Norfolk battalion had no fighting, as the Turks promptly fled northwards, carrying off their guns and not pursued by the cavalry.[1]

The battalion guarded the sappers engaged in destroying an old

[1] Major de Grey states the ground was barely practicable for infantry and not at all for cavalry.

building in El Kutunie, which the Turks had fortified. They then returned with the rest of the force to Azizieh.

The battalion was still with the rest of the brigade at Azizieh on November 4th, when its winter kits were brought up from Amara, the arrival of which was very welcome, as the nights were getting very chilly, though the days were still warm.

On the 11th the 18th brigade marched from Azizieh to El Kutunie, the scene of the affair of October 28th, the Norfolk battalion acting as advance guard. The few Arabs occupying El Kutunie being quickly driven out by the cavalry, the battalion was installed in the old building near the river which had been partially destroyed on October 28th, and which was now put in a state of defence. One company was detached next morning to reconnoitre in the neighbourhood of a wood one and a half miles farther up the left bank of the Tigris. On the 13th the Norfolk battalion stood to arms during a cavalry reconnaissance, but were not called up. On the 15th the rest of the force came up, as well as Sir J. Nixon, who inspected the battalion on the 16th. The 17th brigade arrived also, completing the concentration of the 6th division.

The force which advanced on the road to Baghdad, on November 19, 1915, consisted of the 6th division, the cavalry brigade, the 30th brigade (12th division), and forty-two guns of all sorts—a total strength of under 14,000 combatants, of whom 8,500 were infantry. It was divided into four columns, all of which were to operate on the left bank, the Turks on the right bank being left out of consideration.

"A" column, under Major-General Delamain, included the 16th and half the 30th brigade, with one field battery, and half a company of sappers and miners.

"B," under Brigadier-General Hamilton of the 18th brigade, consisted of that brigade, with one battery.

"C," under Brigadier-General Hoghton, comprised his 17th brigade, with sappers and miners.

The flying column, under Major-General Sir C. Melliss, was the cavalry brigade, with the 76th Punjab Regiment from the 30th brigade.

The 18th brigade was the first to move, with the 110th as vanguard, followed by the Norfolk battalion.

When ten miles of the road had been covered, an advance guard of 1,000 enemy horse was found at Zeur and quickly put to flight by the cavalry brigade. The night was spent in the enemy's position of Zeur, which was hastily fortified.

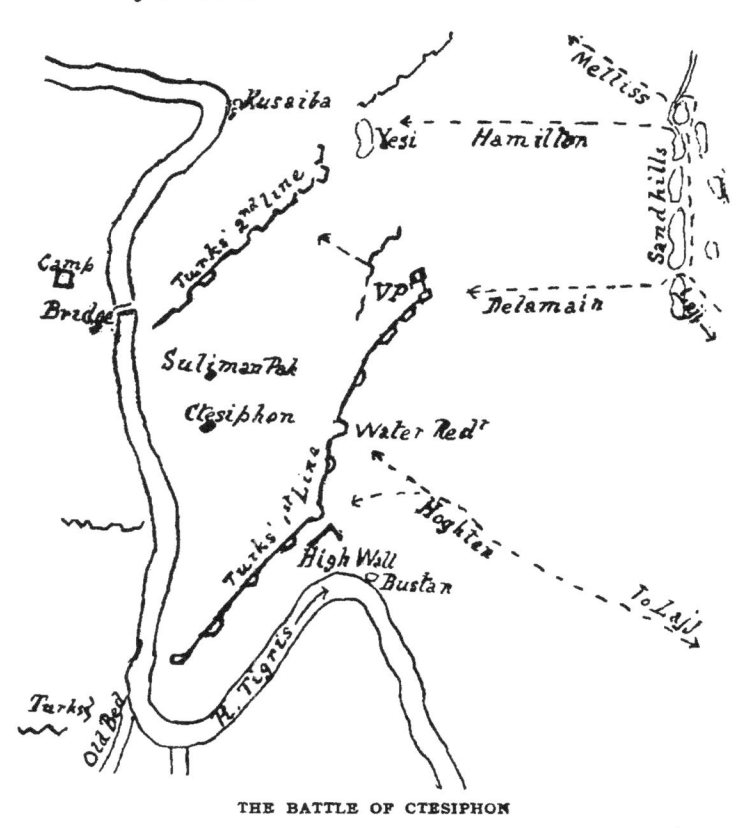

THE BATTLE OF CTESIPHON

On the 20th the 18th brigade again acted as advance guard, reaching the village of Lajj about noon, after a seven mile march on the very dusty Baghdad road. Marching through the place, the brigade took up a position protecting the rest, about a mile farther on on the bank of the Tigris. From here the famous Arch of Ctesiphon was clearly seen dwarfing the neighbouring small buildings and indicating the position of Nur-ed-din's army. The night of the 20th–21st was passed by the British force at Lajj, with the 18th brigade covering it on the Baghdad road. The Norfolk battalion was sent out on the afternoon of the 20th with the artillery staff to reconnoitre and take ranges. The enemy's position at Ctesiphon was about eight miles distant.

A few Arabs rode up and fired from the saddle in the morning of the 21st, but were quickly driven off by a few rounds of shrapnel, and the 18th brigade then retired to Lajj, on being replaced by column " C."

The Turkish position on the left bank of the Tigris about Ctesiphon had been very strongly fortified. Its right was at the apex of the southerly bend of the river, due south of the Arch of Ctesiphon, whence it extended a little east of north for nearly six miles to two fortified mounds known to the British as " Vital Point " (or shortly as " V. P. ").

In front of the first line, on the road from Lajj to Ctesiphon, was the High Wall, which consisted of hard clay banks, forty feet high in places, with very steep sides. It is supposed to be the remains of the citadel of the Roman fortified city of Ctesiphon. It formed two sides of a rectangle, the angle being open towards the British side. The north side was about 400 yards long, whilst that running south from its western end was about 600 yards.

Looked at from the British side, the whole position was perfectly flat; the only features visible were the Arch of Ctesiphon, the High Wall, the mounds of V.P., and the slight rise of ground on which was sited the Turkish second line. This second line had its right on the river, about a mile behind High Wall, and extended parallel to the first line, but considerably overlapped its left.

On the right bank of the Tigris, beyond the right of the Turkish first line on the left bank, were more Turkish troops, probably the 35th division of about 4,000 rifles;[1] and here also were their heavy guns, which played a considerable part in the battle, not only by their fire on the attack, but also by preventing the passage up the river of the British ships.

General Townshend's plan of attack disregarded the Turks on the right bank, and dealt only with the position on the left bank. The

[1] Bird: " A Chapter of Misfortunes," p. 55.

general idea was for column " C " to hold the Turkish right by a frontal attack. When its attack had developed, the next move would be a turning one round the north of V.P. against the Turkish second line. This would be carried out by " B " whilst the flying column would proceed still farther to the right, and endeavour to get behind the second line.

When this turning movement began to take effect, the main attack with column " A " would be launched against V.P.

Column " C," the object of which was to pose as the main body and attract as much as possible of the Turkish attention, started from Lajj at 2 p.m. on November 21st, and eventually halted for the night near the river, about five miles short of the Turkish front line between V.P. and High Wall.

The other three colums, whose movement it was so important to conceal, did not move till darkness had fallen, about 7.30 p.m. All talking and smoking and the use of lights of any sort were strictly forbidden, and the march over the featureless country had to be by compass bearing only. The three colums proceeded north-westwards till they reached the southern portion of some sandhills with an old canal embankment running along their western face. Here column " A " was dropped, whilst " B " and the flying column went on another one and a half or two miles through the sandhills. Here " B " halted, under shelter of the old canal, whilst the flying column went on yet another mile and a half before halting.

It was one a.m. when the Norfolk battalion, with " B ", reached and lay down to rest in their deployment position, where they were to remain in concealment till the attack of "C" on the left was in progress.

They were about three miles north-east of V.P. Fortunately, the Turkish cavalry screen, which had been in evidence on the afternoon of the 21st, had been withdrawn and the march had been unmolested.

About 8 a.m. General Hamilton sought and obtained permission from General Townshend to commence his advance, though he had not yet heard the attack of Column " C " on the left. His ultimate objective was the village of Qusabah on the Tigris behind the Turkish second line. This point, in this flat country, could not be seen. The first objective was the Turkish second line, from which the column stood about four miles to the north-east.

The 18th brigade advanced, with the 2nd Norfolk Regiment on the right and the 110th Infantry on the left in front, supported by the 7th Rajputs and the 120th.

After half an hour's advance in artillery formation they came under heavy rifle fire from rifle pits in front of the Turkish second line, which were evacuated as the advance continued.

Casualties in the Norfolk Regiment and the 110th were already beginning to be heavy; Major Lodge and Lieutenant Cooke were both wounded. By 11 a.m., the whole battalion was in the firing line, and by 11.30 had taken two advanced trenches in front of the Turkish second line. Here, however, they came under such heavy concentrated fire, and casualties were so heavy, that further progress was impossible for the 18th brigade, the right of which had been reinforced by the 76th Punjabis from the flying column.

That column had been forced back by the attack of 2,000 Turks and numerous Arabs from behind the second line.

Meanwhile V.P. had been taken by column "A," which pushed on beyond it against the second line.

At one p.m. the right of the Norfolk battalion was reinforced by a company of the 120th, and soon after this Major Cramer Roberts (now commanding, *vice* Lodge, wounded) ordered a fresh advance.

This gained another 100 or 150 yards, and brought the battalion within 1,000 yards of the Turkish second line trenches, which were so concealed as to be invisible from the ground.

The left of the Norfolk battalion was now threatened by about three Turkish battalions, which were driven off by artillery and rifle fire.

A general Turkish counter-attack appeared to be in progress. The troops on the left of the 18th brigade were compelled by the heavy counter-attack to retire a short distance. Though the situation in that quarter was shortly restored, the 18th brigade had been compelled, by the exposure of its left flank, to fall back from the ground it had gained.

Many officers and men were hit in the retirement. Captain Shakeshaft's diary specially mentions the gallantry of Corporal Edwards in going out three times to fetch in wounded men.

The casualties in the Norfolk battalion had been terrible; half the machine-gun section had been wiped out, but the rest of it were doing splendid service, for which Lieutenant Campbell afterwards received the Military Cross; all the officers of "D" company were casualties; Captain de Grey had been wounded, and all the wounded had to suffer tortures from the jolting of transport carts in the absence of proper ambulances. Some of them could not be brought off the field.

Towards evening the Turks began to develop an attack, from the direction of the Diala against the right flank of the 18th brigade and the flying column, then echeloned somewhat to the right rear of the brigade. Artillery fire from this attack was annoying, but the Turkish infantry, held back by the flying column, had not come into action by dark.

At nightfall General Townshend decided to establish his force in the captured Turkish first line trenches, and the 18th brigade was withdrawn unmolested to V.P. The wounded were removed in every sort of vehicle, including gun limbers, but, from want of conveyance, the dead could not be brought in.

The cold of the night was so great that sleep was hardly possible, and men had to get up and walk about to keep warm.

The casualties in the Norfolk battalion on this day were:

Officers killed, four—Major Rumbold, Lieutenants F. G. Boosey, R. A. Ritchie, and F. Hogben.

Officers wounded, nine—Major F. C. Lodge; Captains G. de Grey, G. B. Northcote (died of wounds), L. W. Blakiston, and F. W. Hudson; Lieutenants Shilcock (died of wounds), Chappell, and Cooke; 2nd Lieutenant Richardson.

Other ranks—Twenty-seven killed, 225 wounded, two missing.
Total casualties—267.

The total losses of the force were over 4,000; of the 18th brigade alone 1,214. Of the Norfolk battalion there remained fit for duty seven officers and about 250 men, just fifty per cent of those who went into action.

When day dawned on November 23rd the results of yesterday's battle were clearly seen on the bloodstained field, strewn everywhere with the dead of both sides; for, if the British had suffered heavily, the enemy had lost still more. He was gone for the moment no doubt, but it was known that he had been reinforced strongly, and a fresh advance was to be expected.

The ration carts arrived from Lajj and the Norfolk men had a regular meal, the first since they had left Lajj on the evening of the 21st. After breakfast the Turks began shelling Vital Point, and the Norfolk battalion had to seek cover behind a mound. At 2 p.m. the 17th brigade was left at V.P. to cover the evacuation of the wounded.

The Norfolk battalion had nearly reached High Wall about 6.30 p.m. when the enemy were seen advancing from the north-west in long lines against their old front position. Shortly afterwards the Norfolk battalion and the 120th were sent to reinforce the left of the 16th brigade.

This brigade, under General Delamain, was holding the Turkish first line trenches of November 22nd on the left of V.P., its centre being about the Water (or Delamain's) Redoubt. The 7th Gurkhas were pushed out on to "Gurkha Mound," close to Ctesiphon. Their splendid defence of this mound is beyond the scope of this history.

The Turkish attack was now falling mainly on the right (V.P.) and centre (Delamain) of the British line. There was no attack towards High Wall, where General Hamilton had the 110th and 7th, with some sappers.

The 2nd Norfolk now took over some of the trenches from the Dorset Regiment on the left of the 16th brigade. On their left, between them and High Wall, were the 120th Rajputana Infantry. They did not have to deal with heavy attacks such as those which fell upon the troops on their right, or on the Gurkhas in front, and which were repulsed with difficulty. General Townshend, who was with Delamain, says that there were at least six of these attacks on the latter's position from 9 p.m. onwards.

During the night a Turkish officer, with a party throwing bombs, approached the Norfolk position by a communication trench. These were met by a party of Dorset and Norfolk bombers, who killed them all. Earlier, before the great attacks began, Lieutenant H. E. Hall had been sent out to get into touch with the 120th. On the way he was shot through the head, probably by a Turkish sniper, and his body was found by an officer of the 120th.

The 24th was passed at High Wall, burying the dead and covering the retirement of the 17th brigade from Vital Point. On the 25th twenty-five more men were buried by a party of the Norfolk battalion at 10.30 a.m., whilst the rest were employed improving the trenches. Occasional shelling by the enemy during the day did no harm, but General Townshend had now decided to retire on Lajj to await reinforcements. At 4.30 p.m. a British aeroplane reported that about 10,000 Turks were advancing from the Diala. The retirement was ordered to commence in two hours, anything that could not be carried being burnt or buried.

The 18th brigade acted as rearguard in this retreat, the Norfolk battalion being the last of all to leave High Wall at 8.30 p.m. and reach Lajj at 2 a.m. on the 26th, after an unmolested march which was rendered very unpleasant by a heavy thunderstorm.

During the 26th, and the early part of the 27th, prospects seemed more cheery and the army began entrenching and settling itself down to wait for reinforcements. At 12.45 p.m. came news of a fresh Turkish advance, and there was nothing for it but to pack up and be off. At 2.30 retirement to Azizieh was ordered, all tents to be left standing, in order to deceive the enemy, who had already been in contact with the cavalry brigade. The rear-guard arrangements were as before, the 2nd Norfolk again having the honour of being the last in the column. It was twenty-one miles from Lajj to Azizieh, and the battalion was thoroughly weary when it reached the latter at 10 a.m. on the 28th. Here a small reinforcement arrived, in the shape of the 14th Hussars and half a battalion of the Royal West Kent Regiment.

The 29th passed quietly in improving defences and loading stores on barges.

It had been intended to continue the retreat at noon on the 30th, but the advance of the Turks caused the time to be advanced by four hours. Rear-guard was as on previous days. The march covered about ten miles to Umm-at-Tabul, where rifle and artillery fire at night showed that the Turks were on the heels of the British. Nevertheless, patrols sent out 500 yards from the front of each company early on December 1st reported "all clear."

At 6 a.m. warning was given that the G.O.C. intended to attack the pursuers, who were believed to be in the direction of and beyond a mound about 2,800 yards on the Azizieh road.

Half an hour later the Norfolk battalion deployed for attack, with the 7th Rajputs on their right, and took post in a large nullah just outside the camp. To their astonishment, as it became light, they perceived officers' tents and men's bivouacs which had sprung up in the night on the mound just mentioned. As soon as this camp was seen, the British field batteries got on to it with their guns, and in an instant all was in the wildest confusion.

Two companies of the Norfolk battalion now advanced 200 yards from the nullah, the other two remaining in it in reserve. Turkish shrapnel was soon bursting over them, and about 8.15 a.m. orders were received to retire as soon as the 16th brigade was clear of the camp.

The enemy, who were estimated at 12,000, were endeavouring to envelop the British right. The artillery was turned on to them with great effect, and the infantry of Delamain moved forward, whilst the cavalry was ordered to envelop the Turkish left. Before this counter-offensive the attack came to a standstill, and the enemy began to fall back. The attempted envelopment, in particular, was thrown into complete disorder. Townshend promptly seized the opportunity to break off the engagement and continue his retreat.

The retirement was in alternate echelons of brigades, commencing with the left (16th brigade). The 30th brigade on this day took over the rear-guard duties hitherto performed by the 18th. The losses of the day had been some 500 killed and wounded on the British side, and the ships "Comet" and "Firefly" were lost. The losses of the Norfolk battalion are not ascertainable. Captain Shakeshaft was slightly wounded. The next halt, at Shadie, was reached at 10 p.m., and after a thirty-six mile march and the battle of the morning, all were exhausted.

The march of December 2nd was unmolested, except by the usual firing by Arabs, and carried the force to Shumran, a short way above Kut, into which it marched on the morning of the 3rd. In the last thirty-three hours it had marched forty-six miles. The Norfolk battalion halted just outside the town and received orders to occupy the "Serai." They were then sent to line the river bank, as the Arabs were looting the village opposite, and the 110th and 120th were being sent across to stop it. This operation was covered by the fire of the Norfolk battalion across the river. About 10 a.m. two companies were employed for an hour restoring order among the Arabs in the town of Kut.

From this date onwards, till the surrender at the end of April, 1916, the battalion formed part of the garrison of Kut. There were many attempts to relieve them from outside which ended in failure. An account of these will be given later in connexion with the composite battalion of the Norfolk and Dorset Regiments formed in February, 1916. For the present we shall confine ourselves to the doings of the original 2nd battalion during the months of the siege. For this purpose Captain Shakeshaft's diary is of the greatest assistance; for of course all war diaries, and other documents which would have been useful or interesting to the enemy, were destroyed before the capitulation.

Kut was a collection of Arab houses on the left bank of the Tigris, with a population of about 6,000. The minaret of the mosque was visible for many miles round. The town had a river frontage of about one and a half miles at the apex of a southerly bend of the river; to this frontage ran, through the town, six or seven streets. The covered bazaar was parallel to the river front and the Tigris opposite Kut was about 600 yards broad, though it contracts to 250 lower down. From opposite Kut there runs the channel known as the Shatt-al-Hai, connecting the Tigris with the Euphrates near Nasariyeh. When the Tigris is low it is almost dry, but in the flood season there is a stream about one hundred yards wide. The defence was organized in three sectors:

Northern.—Major-General Delamain and the 16th brigade.
North-Eastern.—Brigadier-General Hoghten and the 17th brigade.
Southern.—Brigadier-General Hamilton and the 18th brigade.

The 30th brigade, under Major-General Sir C. Melliss, constituted the general reserve.

The Southern sector, with which we are mainly concerned, included the town of Kut and the garrison (at first of one and later of two battalions) of the Arab village beyond the river and the adjoining walled enclosure commonly called the liquorice factory or wool press. The "Serai," where were the Norfolk head-quarters, was in the north-west corner of the town. The fort was below Kut, on the right of the defences stretching across the neck of the peninsula. They were little more than a wire fence to keep out the Arabs, with four blockhouses at points in it.

The "Serai" Captain Shakeshaft describes as "a large building, with a number of small rooms looking on to the square; the officers were billeted in these rooms. . . . There was one big room upstairs which we appropriated as a mess-room. There were a number of small rooms downstairs in which we managed to put two of our weak companies; the remaining two had to bivouac in the square."

For the first few days the Norfolk battalion was, like the rest of the troops, very busy digging trenches, putting up cover in the "Serai," digging gun pits, and making good lateral communications between the streets leading to the river front.

Turkish shells began falling in the town on December 6th, which Captain Shakeshaft calls "the official day of commencement of the siege." The first of many shells dropped in the "Serai" on the 9th, by which date habitable dug-outs had been made there. On that day three men were wounded on fatigue on the river front, and four more next day. After this all digging work had to be done at night. On the 12th five of the Norfolk men, of whom two died, were wounded by a shell in the "Serai." On the 14th the battalion went into the second line trenches for the night, and after that were required to sleep in one or other of the trenches each night, thus affording some relief to the troops who had occupied them during the day.

The same routine prevailed for the Norfolk battalion for some days; fatigue parties, intermittent shelling, sometimes replied to by the British, and nights in the trenches. By the 22nd the river was so shallow at the south-east end of the town that the Norfolk battalion spent the night in the gardens of the neighbourhood, in case the enemy should attempt a crossing.

Christmas Eve saw the heaviest bombardment so far, a prelude to an attack on the fort, into part of which the enemy penetrated, but was again driven out at 12.45 p.m. There were evidently going to be more attacks on the fort, so the Norfolk battalion was sent in the evening into the north-eastern sector. The fort had been again attacked, and the enemy were once more in the north-eastern bastion when Major Cramer Roberts (temporarily commanding owing to Major Lodge's illness from wounds) was asked to send up two companies to reinforce it. Arriving at the position assigned to them, " B " and " D " companies found it occupied by the 48th Pioneers, and were sent to a nullah in reserve, whence they could prevent attempts of the enemy to cut off the fort by an advance up the river bank round the British right. At 2 a.m. on Christmas Day the companies were ordered into the fort and relieved the 48th Pioneers near the north-eastern bastion. By 3 a.m. the Turks had given up the attack on the barricade and abandoned the bastion, which was reoccupied later by " B " and " D " companies. The bastion was a mass of ruins, strewn in all directions with dead and fragments of bodies. The other two companies were now also in reserve in the fort, and Major Lodge had resumed command. The day was spent in clearing up the bastion and putting it in a state of defence. There was some sniping, by which two men were killed and two wounded, in the course of the day. For the ensuing night " A " and " C " companies relieved " B " and " D " in the bastion, and next day the battalion, on relief by the 76th Punjabis, returned to the " Serai " to eat their Christmas dinner a day late.

They were back at the fort again on the 28th, and on the 29th two Turkish officers, one of them a major, decidedly drunk, applied for an armistice to bury their dead, which was refused as the application did not come from the enemy's head-quarters. Whilst the white flag was flying, both sides stood up and had a look at one another. The Turkish trenches were full, says Captain Shakeshaft, of " very sturdy, thickset, bronzed-faced fellows, just ideal fighting men." They were working hard at sapping up to the fort.

For some time after this there is little to record ; one day was much the same as another, with constant Turkish sniping, bombardments, hard work for the defenders on fatigue parties, and frequent bombing at night on both sides. The guns of the relieving force were heard from Shekh Saad, and, later, news was received of General Aylmer's heavy losses and only partial successes.

Floods, about the middle of January, compelled Turks as well as the British to abandon their front trenches. On January 23rd the Turks had no posts nearer than 450 yards from the fort, and the opportunity was taken to destroy their saps and fill in part of their trenches.

The weather during the whole of January was bad, and as low a temperature as 11° of frost was registered. Nevertheless the health and even the spirits of the men remained good. Company Sergeant-Major Dermott and the battalion snipers made a good bag of Turks. It was about this time that General Townshend telegraphed to General Aylmer: " It is my handful of Norfolks, Dorsets, and Oxfords who are my sheet anchor here." On January 24th supplies had begun to run short, and rations were reduced to three-fourths of the normal. February began like January, but by the 8th brown bread containing one-third barley meal was issued instead of white. On the other hand, starlings shot in the trees, where they were plentiful at that season, made a welcome change of food.

On the 13th the 76th Punjabis relieved the Norfolk battalion in charge of the fort, and the latter returned to the " Serai," with one company billeted in the aeroplane yard. On this date, for the first time, an enemy aeroplane dropped bombs on Kut. They were some that had been lost at Azizieh. A variety in the bombardment occurred when the enemy used a gigantic and ancient Turkish mortar firing 200 lb. balls from the right bank of the Tigris. On the 18th the spirits of the garrison were damped by the announcement that General Aylmer was suspending his attempts to relieve the place till the arrival of the 13th British division from Egypt. The next day (19th) General Hamilton, commanding the 18th brigade, was wounded on his house-roof by a Turkish sniper, and command was assumed by Colonel Evans, R.E. On the 29th there was a downpour of rain.

March began with a specially heavy bombardment and bomb-dropping from three aeroplanes. On the 4th scurvy broke out among the Indian troops, mainly owing to the total want of fresh vegetables, milk, or any anti-scorbutic diet.

On March 8th and 9th the Norfolk battalion, as part of a composite brigade under Colonel Evans, assembled in the aeroplane yard, ready for a projected attack on the right bank against the Turkish position at Dujailah redoubt, which was attacked by Aylmer's relieving force. They had six casualties by bombs from an aeroplane which had seen the concentration. Aylmer's attacks on the Dujailah redoubt failed; there was no opportunity for the intervention of the Kut force, and the Norfolk battalion, except "B" company, returned to the "Serai."

The killing of horses, to provide meat and save grain, now commenced, 417 being killed on the 10th.

Two days later jam and dates gave out, and the daily ration for British troops was reduced to ten ounces of bread and one pound of horse or mule flesh. On the 18th two ounces were knocked off the bread ration, and hunger began to be felt.

During the rest of March there were several specially heavy bombardments, inducing a belief in an approaching attack which did not materialize.

In the early days of April bombardments and bomb-dropping continued. The effects of starvation were visible, for Captain Shakeshaft writes: "Men are frequently seen sitting down resting in the street Sentries have to lean against walls." On the 5th came news that Gorringe's 13th (British) division had taken the first five lines of the Turkish position at Hannah, on the left bank; the river had been rising for some time with the melting of the snows at its source. By the 10th Gorringe's advance had failed, and rations in Kut were reduced to five ounces of meal and one and three-quarter pounds of horse-meat.

For a long time meat and bread were the only food. There were no extras, no tea or sugar, fat, or vegetables. Young weeds were eaten as vegetables for a time, until, owing to some cases of poisoning ascribed thereto, this diet also ceased. All the latter part of the siege there was no fuel but crude oil. Of the sufferings of the garrison from starvation Sir C. Townshend writes: "Such was the state of weakness of the troops that men fainted on sentry duty and could not work at any fatigue. . . . The garrison was now absolutely done. Men were dying at an average rate of fifteen a day, dysentery and scurvy claiming many victims."

Of the Norfolk battalion General Hamilton, commanding the brigade in which they served, says : " In spite of all the trying conditions of the prolonged siege, the discipline, good order, and soldierly bearing of the battalion were maintained to the end. The daily guard mounting in the street at the entrance to the "Serai" was in itself a soul-stirring revelation of the unquenchable spirit of the Norfolk Regiment. Though worn to shadows of their former selves with starvation, constant duty, and frequent sickness, though their clothing was grimed and ragged, the men were still steady under arms, their drill punctiliously correct."

The " nights in bed " were few ; only about one off duty to four or five on it. Even the nights off duty were often broken by heavy fatigue work.

Hopes of relief were again raised, only to be disappointed. British aeroplanes dropped bags of food, but all they could bring went but a very short way in feeding the large garrison. The men were too weak to give any assistance to the relieving force. The last gallant attempt o the S.S. " Julna " to bring in supplies by river failed, and on the 26th General Townshend began negotiations for a capitulation. With these we need not concern ourselves, though a very full account is given in the diary of Captain Shakeshaft, whose knowledge of French caused his selection as translator of the communications passing between General Townshend and Khalil Pasha, the Turkish commander-in-chief.

On April 29, 1916, after a siege of 146 days, Kut surrendered unconditionally, and the remains of the Norfolk battalion, along with the rest of the garrison, passed into captivity.

Their casualties, excluding followers, during the siege, up to the end of March, are shown in Sir C. Townshend's book as one officer wounded ; rank and file killed or died of wounds, seventeen ; wounded, forty-six ; died of disease, nine. Their effective strength on March 15th was seven officers and 303 other ranks. No later figures are given. The Norfolk officers who became prisoners of war with the battalion were

Major F. Lodge, D.S.O.　　　Lieutenant J. F. W. Read
Major W. E. Cramer Roberts　Lieutenant H. S. Bullock
Captain A. J. Shakeshaft　　Lieutenant F. V. Portsmouth
Lieutenant H. L. Peacocke　　Lieutenant T. Campbell
　　　Lieutenant and Quarter-Master J. T. Richardson.[1]

We cannot follow them in detail in their captivity, but Captain Shakeshaft's diary conveys the impression that the officers were, on the whole, not badly treated after they got away from the neighbourhood of Kut. If they were short of shelter and food before their removal, there is some excuse for the Turk in his habitual negligence in such matters, and in his finding on his hands so large a force in addition to his own. With the other ranks, generally separated from their officers, it was very different, as is shown by the following.

EXTRACTS FROM CAPTAIN SHAKESHAFT'S DIARY

BAGHDAD, 17*th May*.—The troops soon began to arrive, a dreadful spectacle to see British troops in rags, many barefooted, starved, and sick, wending their way under brutal Arab guards through an Eastern bazaar. A few men who were too bad to walk rode on camels. Mr. Brissel, whom we frequently saw, did his best for the men; he sent them food, but the Turks did everything they could to hinder his good work. The troops were in these black tents on the hot 'maidan' (plain) without any water; a few barrels of water used to be brought up every morning, but what was that to hundreds of men? The American Consul asked that the men might be moved down into the belt of palm trees near the river. When nearly all the men had departed by train, the few remaining, nearly all convalescents, were moved down to the river bank. The men got no meat ration, except what the American Consul sent, only some bread and 'bulgour,' a sort of wheat which makes good porridge. The rations sent to our own orderlies were most excellent,

[1] This officer was seriously and permanently injured by a shell in the "*serai*" and was eventually, some time after the surrender, sent down on exchange from Baghdad.

and they had no cause for complaint. From men in hospital I heard many stories of the horrors of the march from Shamran. Several told me that Sergeant-Major Aldridge had behaved splendidly on the march. Many men had been maltreated by the Arab guards. Quarter-Master Sergeant Eastell had been knocked down and beaten by the brutes.

"10th June.—We met (at Tekrit, between Baghdad and Mosul) a number of unfortunate British and Indian soldiers who were standing at the door of a miserable yard where they were herded together; they looked ghastly; they were sick left behind by one of the columns. . . . They were in a miserable plight, many suffering from dysentery, others were fairly fit, but had no boots for marching. There were about eighty British and Indians. They received only a ration of wheat; the Arabs used to bring milk and eggs to sell and asked exorbitant prices, consequently they would soon have no money and would die of starvation and neglect. There were no guards over them, and they were completely abandoned. Sometimes, when a sick man would crawl out of the house they lived in, Arabs would throw stones and chase him back into the yard. I will spare the reader any description of the dark, filthy hovel where they slept. Some of the men told us that, a short time before, they were simply left on the river bank without any cover under the cruel sun; many of the men were without helmets, some had nothing more than a vest and a pair of shorts. I believe a Turkish officer, passing by with his regiment, had made the local commandant put them into the house, or rather hovel, where we saw them. Many had died here. Immediately a corpse was buried, the Arabs used to dig it up and take away the blanket. There was an Indian assistant surgeon to look after them, a good fellow, but what could he do? For he had no drugs.

"General Melliss sent for the commandant, an old Arab captain, but nothing could be got out of him, and a letter to Khalil Pasha was probably never sent. The general and his companions did what they could for these poor men and left them some money and clothes; but it is terrible to contemplate what their fate probably was."

A less unfavourable account of matters at Mosul is given on the

"*17th June.*—There were only a few convalescents in barracks, except British and Indian officers. The food for the men appeared good, we saw it being prepared in great cauldrons, but they did not get enough of it. Most of them looked half starved and very ill. The place was in a filthy condition, and words would fail to express the sanitary arrangements. The officers were closely packed in rooms upstairs, British on the left of the archway, Indians on the right. . . . We then went to the hospital; there were about eighty men here under Captain Spackman; all the men were very well looked after; every man had a bed and were all in clean rooms."

At Demir Kapee, on the way to Aleppo, Captain Shakeshaft writes :

"*20th June.*—A British soldier came and told us that there were about half a dozen of his comrades in a room at the post, two of whom were dangerously ill. We went in and found six British soldiers in a fearfully emaciated condition, lying in a filthy stable. Of course the Turks had done nothing for them. One of the men said: 'We are like rats in a trap, and they are just slowly killing us.' They said that the German machine-gun section had been most kind to them; the officers had given them money, and the men had given them part of their rations. . . . We saw the Turkish official in charge, a warrant officer; he was quite useless and could do nothing—the usual sort of thing, '*Ce n'est pas mon affaire.*'"

With reference to this entry it may be remarked that Captain Shakeshaft appears to have found the German in the East much more humane than his brother on the Western front. He speaks of the Germans he came across out there almost invariably favourably.

"*24th June* (crossing the mountains beyond Aleppo).—Just about at the top of the hill we came to a spring, and lying around it were three British soldiers, none of my regiment; all were horribly emaciated and in a dreadful state; they told us that they had been left behind by a column that had passed about two days ago, as they could not march. They had nothing to eat from the Turks, but the German wireless section that we had met had given them some food. We took these men on our carts to bring along with us."

A little farther on, on the same day,

" I saw a German warrant officer talking to twenty-four British soldiers. He told me that they had been left here the night before by the party going out, as they were too ill to travel. He had seen the commandant several times and begged him to put the men under shelter (they were lying by the roadside) and to give them food, but each time the commandant gave an evasive reply and nothing was done."

General Melliss eventually succeeded in getting the men sent on in carts with rations. Throughout their journey he and his party had done what was possible to help the unfortunate prisoners, but had everywhere met with indifference where there was not positive obstruction. The more important officers communicated with were full of polite promises, which it is to be feared were rarely carried out by subordinates, even if the promiser really exerted himself. As for the subordinates in immediate charge, when remonstrated with, they generally replied that, if things were wrong, " *Ce n'est pas mon affaire.*"

The above extracts are by no means all Captain Shakeshaft's accounts of the miseries of prisoners of war, at least of the lower ranks, in the hands of the Turks; but they will suffice to show generally that they were not dissimilar to those suffered at the hands of the Germans in Europe. The only thing to be said for the Turk is that less was expected of him than of a nation pretending to a high standard of European civilization, and that he was habitually equally negligent of the sufferings of his own soldiers.

(c) THE COMPOSITE BATTALION (*February-July*, 1916)

When the 2nd Norfolk and 2nd Dorset battalions had gone on the expedition which ended with Kut, and were already blockaded in that unhappy place, there were available drafts, and recovered sick or wounded of both regiments, from whom it was decided, on February 4, 1916, to constitute a composite battalion. Of this two companies were Norfolk and two Dorset men, and the whole battalion was known commonly, if not officially, as the " Norsets." It was attached to the 21st brigade of the 7th (Meerut) division. Till the 1st of March it was commanded by Major H. A. Carroll of the Royal Munster Fusiliers, and then, for the rest of its life of five months, by Major H. A. Case of the 2nd Dorset Regiment.

When first constituted, on February 4th, it mustered forty-five officers and 858 other ranks. On the 8th it was sent into the trenches facing the Turkish position of Umm-el-Hannah on the left bank of the Tigris, as part of General Aylmer's force, then endeavouring to relieve Kut by threatening the Turkish position on the left bank of the Tigris below the beleaguered town. On the 15th it was in the front trenches facing the Turkish right, with its left resting on the left bank of the Tigris. On the 22nd it moved to the northern end of the British line and faced the Turkish left. Being close to the Suwaikieh marsh, which was apt to overflow when banked up by a strong wind, the trenches here were very bad and liable to flooding.

At the beginning of March the command was taken over for a few days by Captain Lanyon of the Norfolk Regiment, *vice* Carroll, sick. Permanent command was taken by Major Case on the 7th. From the 14th the " Norsets " had a brief spell out of the trenches, to which they returned on the 21st. They were again out of them on April 2nd, and on the 5th were moved up to the trenches evacuated by the 13th division when it moved forward on that day.

On April 6th the " Norsets," with the 9th Bhopalis on their left, occupied the enemy trenches which had been captured on the previous day. At 2.15 a.m. the rest of the 7th division passed through to the attack of Sannaiyat, the 21st brigade following in reserve. At 6 a.m. the last-named brigade was moving in artillery formation. Arriving 200 yards in front of the artillery, they remained there all day, whilst the 19th and 28th brigades were held up before the Sannaiyat position. The " Norsets " dug in 1,500 yards from the enemy position.

On the 7th the 21st brigade took part, with the rest of the 7th division, in the advance on Sannaiyat. It was on the left of the 19th brigade, filling the space of 600 yards to the Tigris. The attack was led by the 6th Jats, followed by the Mahratta battalion, supported by the 9th Bhopalis, the " Norsets," and twelve machine guns. At 11 a.m. the Jats, on the left nearest the river, and the Mahrattas on their right, deployed and advanced westwards in three or four lines. The Bhopalis supported the Jats, the " Norsets " followed the Mahrattas, on whose right were the 92nd Punjabs of the 19th brigade. The 19th and 21st brigades found themselves much crowded together by the northward sweep of the river, and impeded by the swampy ground. A terrible machine-gun and rifle fire met them, and by the time they reached the irrigation channels, still 900 yards short of the enemy's position, the leading battalions had lost twenty-five per cent of their men.

At 2 p.m. the " Norsets," Bhopalis, and machine-guns dug themselves in some 1,600 yards from the enemy's trenches. At 5 p.m. the 21st brigade took over from the 19th a length of 500 yards from the river bank. At 10.30 p.m. the " Norsets " relieved the Jats and Mahrattas, and dug a new trench 150 yards farther forward, which was connected up with those in rear. During the night a breach in the river embankment, the cause of the flooding on the left of the line, was repaired.

All April 8th the 21st brigade remained where it had consolidated, till relieved by the 40th brigade (13th division), which was about to renew the attack next day. One company (" A ") of the " Norsets " remained in the front trench nearest the river; the others went with the 7th division into reserve in the position occupied on April 6th. The attack of the 13th division on the 9th failed. During this day the " Norsets " lost one officer killed and six other ranks wounded, all apparently in " A " company, which rejoined the others at nightfall.

On the 10th the 21st brigade relieved the 28th in the right sector of the trenches facing Sannaiyat, where they remained till the 22nd. The Turks were now further protected by floods, from the Tigris on one side and the Suwaikieh marsh on the other, which formed a sort of moat in front of their position.

During the night of April 21st-22nd, the 21st brigade was arranged in a series of lines on a front of about 175 yards. In the first line were the "Norsets" with their machine-guns; behind them the Bhopalis, Jats, and 1/8th Gurkhas.

At 7 a.m. on the 22nd the 7th division attacked on a front of one brigade, the 19th brigade leading. At 7.25, on a report that the 19th brigade had taken the enemy's first line, the 21st was ordered up to support it on the right. The "Norsets," leading the advance, found their front reduced by the encroachment of the marsh to one of two platoons—about 170 yards. At first the distance between platoons in depth was fifty yards, but it had presently to be doubled on account of the heavy fire and the difficulty of crossing the flooded trenches of our front line. The going was terribly heavy, and the men had to try and double through ten or twelve inches of water with mud below. The last twenty yards before they got into the enemy's front line of trenches were dry. The trenches themselves were found to be badly damaged by the British artillery fire and full of water. Many of the rifles had got jammed and useless in the advance through the mud.

At 8.8 a.m. the Bhopalis were sent up to reinforce the "Norsets," who were held up in these trenches. Meanwhile, the 19th brigade had given way before a Turkish counter-attack, and, owing to the condition of their rifles, the "Norsets" were unable to support their right flank, by fire across their front, as much as was to be desired.

By half-past eight they also were compelled to fall back with the 19th brigade, and a quarter of an hour later the Turks had regained the front line, from which they had been at first ejected, and were bombarding the British trenches. Their farther advance was stopped by the artillery.

At 11.45 a.m. the enemy put up a red crescent flag and began collecting their dead. From this hour till 2 p.m. there was an informal armistice, quite in the style of the wars of the nineteenth century. The following extract from brigade orders by Brigadier-General C. Norie is significant:

"I have been credibly informed that an enemy officer, supposed to be a German, came out of the Turkish trenches under cover of the red crescent flag, and was seen to kill four wounded Highlanders with an automatic pistol. Also that a Turkish officer apologized for this brute's conduct to one of our officers."

The conduct was quite in accordance with German practices. The apology was characteristic of the Turkish officer, who, if he was brutal in his treatment of prisoners, generally fought like a soldier and a gentleman.

The casualties of the " Norsets " on this disastrous day were thirteen officers wounded; other ranks, twenty-two killed, 146 wounded, twenty-two missing. Of the officers wounded, the following belonged to the Norfolk companies: Captain Lindsay; Lieutenants King and Cooke, 2nd Lieutenants Gillett, Peake, Little, and Stocker.

On April 24th the 21st brigade, on relief by the 28th, was sent across to the right bank of the Tigris at Abu Roman, where it remained in corps reserve for the rest of the month, suffering like the rest of the army from temperatures and a climate which made them think of the hottest and unhealthiest parts of India as a health-resort.

On April 29th Kut surrendered to the Turks, and there was no longer any reason, for the present, for continuing to hurl troops on the Turkish defences on both banks of the Tigris, which had so far defied the many desperate attempts to break through them. The season was not one for fighting, if it could be avoided, and the British force was now about to be reorganized by the great leader who, in the following cold weather, was to solve the problem of Kut and Baghdad.

On May 1st the " Norsets " were in trenches at Beit Aiessa, on the right bank, and later at Chahela. Cholera had broken out, and the temperature was too high even for the weaker spirits amongst the flies. The sandfly alone retained his full powers of annoyance.

In June, and up to July 21st, the " Norsets " remained at the front, sometimes on the right bank, sometimes on the left. On the latter date the Norfolk part of the battalion was sent down the river to join the newly formed Provisional Battalion of the Norfolk Regiment.

(d) THE PROVISIONAL BATTALION, OR RECONSTITUTED 2ND BATTALION

When Kut surrendered the remains of the 2nd Norfolk battalion who had landed in Mesopotamia in November, 1914, had gone into captivity. The two companies of recovered invalids and drafts were still with the "Norsets," and it was decided to dissolve the composite battalion from July 15th, returning its component parts of Norfolk and Dorset men to join the provisional battalions now being formed to replace the 2nd battalions of the Norfolk and Dorset regiments respectively.

The new battalion of the Norfolk Regiment, formed at Basra on July 16th, was joined on the 25th by the Norfolk part of the "Norsets," and at the end of July was organizing at Gurmat Ali, the point of junction of the new course of the Euphrates with the Shatt-al-Arab.

Of the Provisional Battalion ten per cent of the men were old soldiers of pre-war days, the remaining ninety per cent equally divided between Kitchener men and Derby recruits, the latter being very young and practically untrained. Without the training they were now to receive they would have been almost useless at the front.

The officers of the Provisional Battalion (which for convenience sake we shall speak of as the 2nd Norfolk battalion) were as follows. The battalions or regiments from which they came are stated in all cases in which they were not of the original 2nd Norfolk.

Captain F. Higson, C.O.
Captain G. de Grey, D.S.O., Adjutant.
Lieutenant F. Monaghan, Acting Quartermaster.
Captains—E. T. Horner, N. P. Shand, F. W. Hudson.
Lieutenants—G. C. Keighley (3rd Norfolk), B. H. Chappell (2/4th D.C.L.I.),
2nd Lieutenants—H. Richardson, H. T. Kenny (1st Norfolk), W. Abbott (10th Norfolk), A. E. C. Daniel (3rd Norfolk), M. J. Farquharson (3rd Norfolk), J. H. Woodger (9th Norfolk), A. O. Lyus (3rd Norfolk), C. T. Price (3rd Norfolk), R. S. Lloyd (3rd Norfolk), F. St. J. Bell (10th Norfolk), G. E. Peden (3rd Norfolk).

On August 13th command of the battalion was assumed by Major L. N. Jones Bateman, C.M.G.

There was a great deal of sickness, especially among the young officers, much diarrhœa and one case of cholera, which puzzled the doctors as the camp was irreproachably clean. On the 21st diphtheria broke out, which seems astonishing to those who know India, where it is generally supposed to be a very unusual disease. It hung about amongst the Norfolk men for many months. On August 22nd 2nd Lieutenant H. J. Farquharson died, and the effective strength of the battalion was reduced by sickness to 498.

August and the first half of September were spent in training, beginning with the most elementary courses. On September 13th the battalion proceeded up the Tigris to the rest camp at Shekh Saad, which it reached on the 18th with fifteen officers and 488 men. The accommodation in tents was insufficient. As a result, sickness did not improve, and by the 30th there had been seventy-one admissions to hospital. Nothing of note occurred till October 2nd, when the battalion took over the redoubts at the bridge-head on the left bank. As 266 men were required for this duty, it may be imagined how little rest there was in a weak battalion in a very unsatisfactory state of health.

On the 10th the 2nd Norfolk battalion moved to Blockhouses 1 to 14 at Sodom Point, and on the 12th received a draft of which the War Diary says : " There are three men who have been in France, 157 from the 3rd and 10th battalions, and thirty-five ' Bantams ' from the Suffolk Regiment. How men of such miserable physique as the latter are expected to perform the ordinary duties of a soldier in a country like this is a mystery." Thirty-seven men had been left on the way in hospital, though the climate at this season was no longer trying. It is stated elsewhere that one of the " Bantams " was so short that even the top of his helmet did not show over the parapet. A War Diary does not concern itself with such matters as patriotism ; but it is not possible for us to refrain from paying a tribute to these gallant and patriotic little men, whose high spirit led them to volunteer and press to be employed on active service, when their physical shortcomings would have justified them in the eyes of all in not doing so.

Nothing particular occurred in October, though there is a quaint complaint of the jackals firing the trip-wire rifles, and eating everything, even cartridges!

November was again a month of training which was much hampered by sickness, the daily average in hospital being about seventy, and inoculations for diphtheria taking a hundred men at a time off duty. December was the same

(e) 1917: PASSAGE OF THE TIGRIS—BAGHDAD AND BEYOND

Early in January the Norfolk battalion moved from Sodom to Twin Canals, a post which the Diary forcibly describes as "a stinking place." Nevertheless, the health of the battalion was improving; there were only sixty admissions to hospital in the month, and a daily average of five per cent off duty for minor ailments.

At the end of the month, having replaced the 4th Devonshire in the 37th brigade, the 2nd Norfolk moved to the Shatt-al-Hai, the connecting link between the Tigris at Kut and the Euphrates at Nasariyeh. There they had several days of practice at embarking and disembarking on the Shatt-al-Hai, in preparation for the passage of the Tigris, which was eventually fixed for February 23rd. At 4 p.m. on the 22nd, guided by Captain de Grey and 2nd Lieutenant Tate, I.A.R.O., the battalion started for the Tigris at a point previously reconnoitred. At the head of the column were thirteen pontoons for the crossing, and fifty rowers under Lieutenant Lloyd. Behind them followed "A," "B," "C," and "D" companies in the order given. After marching two miles they halted in sight of Kut, waiting for darkness to fall. They then marched to within a mile of the Tigris, and again halted. Presently "A" company moved through a gap in the wire to a deep nullah leading to the point of embarkation, which was at the southern extremity of the bend where, after flowing south past Shumran Fort, the Tigris turns north-east towards Dahra above Kut. There were to be three points of passage for the brigade, of which the Norfolk battalion took the left, the other two being assigned to the 2nd and 9th Gurkha Rifles. At the river end of the nullah "A" company lay down to sleep, with "B," "C," and "D" behind them. The movement had been difficult in the dark, but was successfully accomplished. The pontoons were carried in sections by their crews to the river bank, ready to be put together and launched.

At 5.15 a.m. on February 23, 1917 the pontoons were put together, after being carried over the embankment of the river, and placed on it. At 5.30 the first half of "A" company embarked in semi-darkness, which saved them from all but slight casualties. Each pontoon carried ten men and two boxes of ammunition, besides its crew of five rowers. The Tigris was 340 yards wide at the point of passage. Rowing rapidly across the river, Lieutenant Horner was the first to set foot on the left bank. Practically single-handed, he put out of action a Turkish machine-gun which was just about to fire. For this act of gallantry he was afterwards awarded the D.S.O. Sergeant Williams, who helped him with the machine-gun, and in capturing a trench and thirty-five prisoners, received the D.C.M. This trench was of great importance as commanding the head of the ferry. The pontoons had returned for the other half of "A" company and the other three companies, who gradually got over. Moving to the right, one half of "A" established a ferry-head, whilst the other half moved to the left, followed by the other companies as they arrived. The Gurkhas were crossing on the right of the Norfolk battalion, who moved leftwards till held up by a Turkish strong point, when they occupied a trench north of the river embankment and parallel to it.

When this line was firmly established, "D" company took over the guard of the ferry-head and the rest pushed forward. The Norfolk ferry alone of the three, was kept going all day; the other two broke down and were completely out of action after a few men had got across. The whole battalion was across by 8.30 a.m. C. S. M. Arthur Fisher got the M.C. for his conduct on the river bank, of which Major de Grey speaks very highly.

At 9.20 bridge construction commenced at a point some distance above the Norfolk ferry, and an hour later the Norfolk battalion was relieved by the Gurkhas, who, with their rowers, had suffered severely from the enemy's fire, now that it was light. "D" company then, after some delay, rejoined "C" on the right of the Norfolk line. The Turkish artillery had not opened fire till three-quarters of an hour after " A " had started crossing. Their shells fell near the pontoons during " C's " passage, and some had fallen in the nullah on the right bank before " D " embarked. Casualties, however, were few. By 10.30 the battalion was only getting slowly forward through the enemy's works and dug-outs. By 12.20 they were under a heavy bombardment, directed on all the space north of the river. A few minutes later the ruins in front of them were taken and many Turks surrendered ; " D " was in reserve at this time. The line finally halted with its left just south of Shumran Fort and dug in for the night, no farther advance being practicable without reinforcements. The fort had been captured at the point of the bayonet, but evacuated owing to heavy losses from a cross fire of machine-guns. Lieutenant Lloyd, who had been responsible for the boat work, was now sent forward with a platoon to retake it, which he did under a heavy fire. For his conduct on this day he afterwards received the M.C. At 6 p.m. the Turks made an attempt to break through on the left, but were beaten off. " A " company, which had borne the brunt of the fighting, was then relieved by the 67th Punjabis, and went into reserve on the left of " D."

The casualties of the day had been by no means heavy, considering the circumstances. Six officers were wounded—Captains Blakiston, Shand (Adjutant), Lieutenant Berners, 2nd Lieutenants Lyus, Farmer, and Connors. Of other ranks, six killed, forty-one wounded, and three missing.

The night was so cold that no sleep was possible. At 6 a.m. on the 24th the advance on the Dahra ridge was resumed, Norfolk battalion in the centre, Gurkhas on right, 67th Punjabis on left, " D " and " C " companies of the Norfolk battalion being in front, " A " and " B " in support. After about 800 yards the 67th Punjabis were driven back, exposing the left flank of the Norfolk battalion. The latter and the Gurkhas reached their objective in three-quarters of an hour from the start, most of the casualties incurred being from machine-guns on the left, which flank was for three hours exposed to the risk of a counter-attack, owing to the repulse of the Punjabis. The advance was so rapid that the enemy's barrage was generally behind the British line.

The rest of the day was spent on the captured ridge, and at night the Norfolk battalion was relieved, and retired to the rear. On this day Lieutenant D. R. Carr was killed, and the following officers were wounded: Major de Grey; Captain Taylor; Lieutenants Chappel and Graham, 2nd Lieutenant Lloyd. Captain Hornor and Lieutenant F. Brown, slightly wounded, remained on duty. Of other ranks ten were killed, 112 wounded, and seven missing. During the advance on the ridge the battalion captured two 18-pounder guns.

On the 25th the march did not start till 3.45 p.m. as the 13th division was marching across the front, on the road to Baghdad, in pursuit of the Turks driven out of Kut by the 1st corps. When the 37th brigade, with the Norfolk battalion leading, did get off, five miles were covered on the road to Baghdad. Next day twenty more miles were marched at a considerable distance from the river, where much discomfort was suffered from want of water. The wreckage of the Turkish army strewed the road; four Krupp guns marked "1884" were passed on the 27th, and everywhere there was a litter of boots, shells, and everything cast away by the enemy in their hurried retreat. The effective strength of the battalion on February 28th was twenty officers and 721 other ranks.

By March 3rd it was at Azizieh close to the Tigris, and the 13th division was now behind when the 37th brigade had to halt for its supplies to catch up. On the 6th the Norfolk battalion was in sight of the great arch at Ctesiphon; on the 8th they passed over to the right bank. Next day they repassed the river to relieve the 36th brigade, and the advance guard of the Norfolk battalion was approaching the left bank of the Diala, where they supplied the outposts to the 37th brigade camp at Mismai ruins. Their piquets were on the left bank of the Diala on the 9th, facing the Turks beyond the river, where the sentries were seen to be particularly vigilant. On the 10th an Arab attack on the right piquet was easily driven off. Next day they were able to cross, thanks to the passage forced by the 13th division higher up. That day Baghdad was occupied and the Norfolk battalion, moving up the right bank of the Diala, found many Turks slain in the fight of the 13th division. Here they remained till the 17th, getting a plentiful supply of fish by bombing the river.

On the 18th and 19th there was a reconnaissance up the Diala, and about 200 Turks were buried.

Between the 20th and 23rd the battalion marched up the Diala to a point opposite Bakubah, about fifty miles from the mouth of the river, which place they took over from the 27th Punjabis on the 24th. Three days later the battalion was split up: "D" company was sent to Pul-i-Mikdar, "A" remained at Bakubah, and the other half battalion went to join the cavalry at Abdulla Effendi, where it was on outposts, with the 14th Hussars on the left, and the machine-gun squadron on the right. At 5 p.m. on the 29th half the Norfolk battalion followed the Hussars and machine-guns as they advanced, but next day was ordered to march to Deltawa to join the 13th division. On the way the half battalion was stopped and sent back to rejoin the rest at Bakubah. Here they remained till the 5th, when they supplied an escort for a number of motor-cars moving up the river. At Kizil Robat they came under heavy shell fire from Turks in the Hamrin range who had not been engaged in the events on the Tigris. Fourteen of the cars had to be abandoned, but the rest went on to Khanikin, where they met the advanced posts of Russians from Persia. The meeting of the allied forces at Kasr-i-Shirin was celebrated by a great welcome and entertainment given by the Russians.

On April 8th the escort was back at Bakubah, where nothing noticeable happened till the 18th, when "B" company was sent as escort to a "sotnia" of Cossacks going towards Zilla Robat, and, after seeing them off in the foothills of the Jebel Hamrin, returned, escorting some Russian generals, to Bakubah. There was no fighting and nothing to record, beyond the loss of one man killed by a wagon falling over a bridge.

During the months of May to September the battalion remained in garrison about Bakubah, which was the connecting link between the forces towards Baghdad and those on the upper Diala and in the Hamrin range. For most of the time the weather was excessively hot, tempered by dust storms and other unpleasantnesses. The duties were principally the furnishing of small escorts, fatigue parties, and training. Drafts of 200 men were received in June, which had had only six weeks' training in England and the same period at Belgaum. They required a good deal more training in local conditions.

On July 1st the effective strength of the battalion was nineteen officers and 599 other ranks. There was much sickness, the epidemic of diphtheria still prevailed, and many men had to be kept in a segregation camp at Karnabit. The low effective strength was largely due to leave to India.

On the 25th July Lieutenant-Colonel Jones Bateman died at Simla on leave and was succeeded in the command by Major Higson. By September 1st, thanks to improving health and the end of leave to India, the effective strength had risen to twenty-eight officers and 911 other ranks.

In October the season for active operations returned, and on the 10th–13th the battalion marched east to Beled Ruz Canal, where there was a regular entrenched camp. On the 15th orders were received for operations in the Hamrin range, having as their objective the control of the canal system on the left bank of the Diala. The special objective of the 37th brigade was to secure the crest of the range where the cart road crosses it.

On the 17th the battalion, with a strength of 774, was at the rendezvous two miles east of Beled Ruz, and at 9 p.m. marched towards Tel Kabba, which it reached at daybreak on the 18th. At 2 p.m. "A" and "B" companies, under the command of Major de Grey, went, as escort to the pioneers and sappers, to Chariz, where they were to improve the water supply. The rest followed, with the brigade, in the evening. Next day they started again to seize the Kizil Robat-Shahraban road where it crosses the easternmost ridge of the Jebel Hamrin. The cavalry covered the front and right flank. The first few miles were through the foothills in a strong wind, which died away as the Kizil Robat plain was reached. There were a few small cavalry skirmishes before the battalion was across the road at noon, but the infantry were not engaged.

At 8.15 a.m. on the 20th the Norfolk battalion marched in artillery formation, with the 7th cavalry brigade, for four miles towards Kizil Robat. At 11.30 they halted a mile short of that place, after being shelled by the Turks on the march. The enemy was found to have evacuated Kizil Robat and retired on Khanikin. In this neighbourhood, generally on the Kurdarrah River, the Norfolk battalion remained digging trenches, but without fighting, for the rest of October and up till November 20th, when they moved to the Ruz Canal, just north of the Talib bridge on the Shahraban-Kizil Robat road before it enters the hills. The remaining days of November were employed in trench digging, road-making, and practising attacks.

On December 1st the Norfolk battalion was back on the Kurdarrah River, piqueting Kizil Robat in order to prevent information leaking through to the enemy.

During the night of December 2nd–3rd the battalion marched to positions of deployment, at a bridge on the Diala one and a half miles from Kizil Robat on the Khanikin road. The bridge was broken and great difficulty was found in discovering a ford. At last one was found near the bridge, but there was a long, open stretch to be passed under the fire of the enemy beyond the river, which was sixty yards wide. At 7. 40 a.m. " A " company tried to pass under cover of a barrage, but the ford was so deep and the current so rapid that they were carried off their feet, and had to return. They did so without loss, thanks to a very efficient barrage which prevented the enemy opening fire. In this operation they had been aided by the 2/9th Gurkhas and 67th Punjabis moving along the opposite bank, with the cavalry on their outer flank.

By 9 a.m. four pontoons had come up, and an hour later the crossing had been effected and the ferry-head occupied. Owing to the paucity of pontoons, only three companies of the Norfolk battalion were over by 4 p.m. The enemy having retired, " A " and " B " companies moved forward to Tel Baradan, three miles west, " C " and " D " remaining at the ferry.

The object of the operations on this day had been to force the Diala, and to secure Tel Baradan and Tel Ahmadiat. The Norfolk battalion, apparently, had no casualties on this day, and by the 9th they were back at Beled Ruz, where they continued working and training till the end of the year. Their strength on December 31st was thirty-one officers and 1,013 other ranks.

1918

From January 1st till April 10th the battalion remained in the neighbourhood of Beled Ruz or Kurdarrah crossing, doing nothing requiring notice. On the latter date they moved to Mirjana, four miles above Kizil Robat, crossing to the right bank of the Diala on April 25th. and marching on the 26th–28th to Kifri, some forty-five miles north of Kizil Robat.

The Norfolk battalion had no fighting in the operations beginning on April 24th, which resulted in the Turks in this direction being driven into Kurdistan past Kifri, Tur Kharmati, and Kirkuk. The enemy, always threatened by turning movements in his rear, had evacuated Kifri before the battalion arrived there, and it did not move farther north in May or June, when it was generally in the neighbourhood of the Karra Tappa Canal. On June 25th the Lewis gun detachments of " A " and " C " companies were attached to some Kurdish irregulars commanded by Captain Dewing, D.S.O., M.C., with whom they had a lot of hard marching in very hot weather, but no fighting. The temperature varied from 110° to 120°, but there was no sickness. The detachments returned to the battalion at Mirjana on July 9th. At Mirjana the Norfolk battalion remained throughout August and September, chiefly employed on railway construction. They had no further fighting before the armistice in November, when they were at Imam Abbas. On December 31, 1918, when the period with which this history deals comes to an end, the battalion was at Shahraban.

When Lieutenant-General Sir R. G. Egerton relinquished command of the 3rd (Indian) corps on February 3, 1919, he issued the following order, which was communicated to and appreciated by the 2nd Norfolk battalion.

" On relinquishing command of the 3rd corps, it was my intention to offer a special message of farewell to the 14th division, which it was my proud privilege to command throughout the first eighteen months of its existence.

.   .   .   .   .

" The great feat of arms performed by you in the clearance of the DAHRA BEND was followed by the magnificent achievement at

SHUMRAN, when you forced the passage of the Tigris in full flood in the face of a determined enemy—a performance which will, I believe, live in history as unique in the annals of any army in the world. And in connexion with this I raise my hand to salute the gallant Norfolk Regiment in particular."

CHAPTER III

THE 3RD (SPECIAL RESERVE) BATTALION

THE head-quarters of this battalion, as well as the depôt of the regiment, were at Norwich at the commencement of the Great War. During peace head-quarters and the permanent staff occupied the depôt.

As special reserve officers only devoted a part of their time to soldiering, they were reinforced by a few regular officers and other ranks who administered the depôt. At the outbreak of war the 3rd battalion was commanded by Lieutenant-Colonel W. Corrie Tonge, D.S.O., the depôt by Major J. W. Carroll.

Directly war was declared it became the duty of the depôt and the 3rd battalion staff to call up, clothe, and equip all army reservists, and to dispatch all passed fit for general service to join the 1st battalion at Belfast. This work began early on the morning of August 5th and was completed by midnight on the 6th. It had been carried through without a moment's break and without a hitch of any kind. About 800 army reservists were called up, and of these about 700 were dispatched to Ireland in two large drafts.

On Saturday, August 8th, the 3rd (Special reserve) battalion was mobilized with a strength of 600 and was dispatched next day to Felixstowe, to take over and occupy their station as fixed under the plan of mobilization.

At Felixstowe the battalion formed part of the special reserve brigade for the defence of the neighbouring coast. The other units of the brigade were the 3rd Suffolk, 3rd Essex, 3rd Bedford, and 3rd Loyal North Lancashire battalions.

In addition to taking a hand in the defence of the Harwich coast defences against a possible invasion, the battalion had the duty of training and dispatching drafts overseas. This move to Felixstowe relieved various Territorial units which had been called out on August 4th and had been anticipating a hostile landing during the intervening days.

Fifteen years earlier, when it was still a militia unit, the 3rd battalion had volunteered for service in South Africa. Its services in that war have already been recorded. Since then its duties, as well as its title, had been greatly changed. It was now practically debarred from going abroad as a battalion, and the task demanded from it, as special reserve, was a far more weary and thankless one. It had to accept thousands upon thousands of recruits, to equip and train them, and then, as soon as the men showed promise of doing the battalion real credit, to draft them off to other regiments at the seat of war. Many of these men they were destined never to see again unless, returning maimed and worn out, they drifted back to Felixstowe, fit for " home service only " or for discharge. A large number, however, returned from overseas quite fit or only slightly wounded or sick. Several of them were sent back to the front three or four times.

It was heart-breaking work for the colonel and his staff. They could not feel that they were making history for their own battalion, though they might well consider that they justly shared in the history of the many Norfolk battalions or other units to which they contributed drafts.

The strength of the battalion during these momentous times was constantly varying; at times it was as high as a hundred officers and 3,000 other ranks.

Drafts for active service were constantly being dispatched, and the gaps thus left were immediately filled up, mostly by volunteer recruits, both officers and men. Some joined up late because they had at first failed to realize the urgent need for their services; others because they were too young at the beginning of the war, and were only able to pass muster as men with the lapse of time. There were also the conscripts of later times. Of these Colonel Jickling writes: "What struck me very strongly was that the spirit of the conscripts, after they had been a few weeks in training, was every bit as good as the voluntary men."

Colonel Tonge bears witness to the large number of Norfolk lads—thorough men in everything but years—who struggled to get themselves accepted as officers or men. "The spirit shown," he writes, "was very fine and conclusively proved that the race had not deteriorated in manly qualities. The history of the battalion during the prolonged period of the war is a monotonous one. It could be nothing else. It took men, trained men, and sent men out to the various theatres of war. And all the time, with its rapidly and constantly changing constitution, it had to maintain itself as a defensive fighting unit, in case the coast was invaded."

In connexion with this battalion the following matters may be mentioned:

On June 5, 1916, H.M. the King went specially to Felixstowe to inspect the brigade of which the battalion was a unit.

During the first great daylight raid on Felixstowe and the fleet in Harwich Harbour by seventeen German bombing aeroplanes the discipline of the battalion was very remarkable. When the attack commenced, at 7.30 a.m., the battalion was out at training, but each man at once went to the station allotted to him under such circumstances. Thanks to this prompt obedience to orders, the battalion avoided casualties such as were suffered by the other units in garrison and by the civil population. The battalion at this time was 2,500 strong.

A second and much worse raid occurred about ten days later, when the garrison suffered many more casualties. The 3rd battalion again escaped owing to the security of their trenches. The camp was hit and a hut set on fire.

During the Great War 724 officers passed through the 3rd battalion. It sent 242 drafts away as reinforcements to the various Expeditionary Forces. The total number of other ranks that passed through the battalion were:

13,029 as reinforcements to the several battalions of the Norfolk Regiment in the various theatres of war.

5,854 transferred to other units.

Total : 18,883 other ranks.

The principal details of each year were as follows :

In 1914 21 officers and 821 other ranks were sent as reinforcements to France.

In 1915 61 officers and 2,362 other ranks were sent as reinforcements and 1,119 other ranks were transferred to other units. The chief drafts sent away were :

> On June 23, 1915, 100 other ranks were transferred to the Essex Regiment.
>
> On July 24, 1915, 200 other ranks were transferred to the Essex Regiment.
>
> On September 10, 1915, 150 other ranks were transferred to the Essex Regiment.
>
> On September 29, 1915, six officers and 299 other ranks were sent away as a reinforcement to the 2nd battalion, but they were eventually attached to the 6th Battalion Royal Dublin Fusiliers. This draft, under Captain E. T. Horner, saw a good deal of fighting in the enemy offensive in 1915 and were in the retreat to the lines at Salonica.

721 other ranks were sent to the 7th Battalion.

250 other ranks were sent to the 2nd Battalion.

> On November 9, 1915, 350 other ranks were transferred to the 10th Border Regiment.

In 1916 129 officers passed through the 3rd Battalion. 3,652 other ranks went away as reinforcements, mostly to France ; but six officers and 568 other ranks were sent to the 2nd Battalion, and 153 other ranks to India. 1,840 other ranks were transferred to other units, including :—

> Five officers and 109 other ranks transferred to the M.G.C.
>
> 157 other ranks were transferred to the 2nd (H.S.) Garrison Battalion Suffolk Regiment.
>
> 150 other ranks were transferred to the 3rd Duke of Cornwall's Light Infantry.

100 other ranks were transferred to the Royal West Surrey Regiment.

In 1917 261 officers passed through the battalion. 3,809 other ranks went away as reinforcements, mostly to Norfolk battalions in France, but 300 went to Egypt in three drafts. 1,569 other ranks were transferred to other units, including 220 men to the M.G. Corps and 160 to the Labour Corps.

In 1918 252 officers passed through the battalion, including 50 officers who were sent to Egypt. 2,385 other ranks went as reinforcements to Norfolk battalions, all except 40 to France. 1,298 were transferred to other units.

The commanding officers of the 3rd Battalion during the war were Colonel W. Corrie Tonge, D.S.O., Colonel Sir Kenneth Kemp, Bart., C.B.E., and finally Lieutenant-Colonel C. M. Jickling, O.B.E., who held command from July, 1917, to July, 1919.

Though this history does not pretend to deal with events after 1918, it may be mentioned that, in March, 1919, the 3rd Battalion was moved to Ireland and quartered in Victoria Barracks, Belfast, where they were employed in keeping the peace between Orangemen and Catholics who at this period were very hostile to one another. Between March and July, 1919, the 3rd Battalion was gradually reforming itself into the 1st Battalion, and at the end of this time the staff of the 1st Battalion took over the headquarters of the 3rd Battalion, which returned to England for demobilization.

Colonel Tonge refers to the loss of 300 men, the best draft that ever left Felixstowe. These men volunteered to join the Essex Regiment and appear to have constituted the drafts of June 23, and July 24, 1915.

They were part of the reinforcements carried by the transport "Royal Edward" which was torpedoed and sunk in the Ægean Sea on August 14, 1915. She sank two and a half minutes after the torpedo struck her.

Of the 1,400 men she carried only 600 were saved, and the drowned included all but eighteen of the 300 Norfolk men. The men, who had had a route march just before leaving Alexandria, were waiting on deck for foot inspection about 9.20 a.m. Their lifebelts were down below, and when the ship was unexpectedly struck most of them ran below to fetch the belts. Owing to the ship's sudden heeling over and sinking, these never got up again. Those who escaped were picked up by a hospital ship which responded to the S.O.S. signal. To partly replace this sad loss another draft of 150 men to the Essex Regiment was dispatched on September 29, 1915.

Colonel Tonge also mentions that many officers commanding units overseas bore testimony to the excellent behaviour in action of drafts trained by the 3rd Battalion. In particular their proficiency in bayonet fighting was remarked on.

CHAPTER IV

THE 1/4TH AND 1/5TH BATTALIONS (TERRITORIAL)

(a) 1915 : GALLIPOLI—EGYPT

The history of the 1/4th and 1/5th Territorial Battalions in the Great War is so closely connected that it is possible and desirable to avoid repetition by dealing with both in the same section. They were together in the same brigade during the whole of the operations in which they took part in Gallipoli, Egypt, and Palestine, and even for a few days were amalgamated in a composite battalion.

The order for mobilization reached both battalions on the evening of August 4, 1914, a few hours before the formal declaration of war. Next morning the 1/4th Battalion assembled at the Drill Hall in Chapel Field, Norwich, and was billeted in the City of Norwich Schools on the Newmarket Road. The 1/5th Battalion mobilized at Dereham on the same day.

On August 11th, the 1/4th Battalion left by special train for Ingatestone in Essex, and on the 17th the 1/5th was transferred from Billericay, to which it had been sent after mobilization, to Colchester. Training for war was actively carried on in both battalions at their various stations in England.

The 1/4th were at Purleigh (Essex) on August 11th and at Colchester with the 1/5th on the 19th. There both battalions remained, training and practising route marches, till the spring of 1915, when the 1/5th proceeded, in March, to Bury St. Edmunds, and the 1/4th in April to the same place. At Bury St. Edmunds the officers of the 1/5th had a narrow escape when their hotel was set on fire by bombs dropped by German aeroplanes.

From May 21st both battalions became part of the 54th infantry division, and with the 1/5th Suffolk and 1/8th Hampshire constituted the 163rd infantry brigade. On the previous day the 1/4th Battalion had been sent to Watford, which it left by special train on July 29, 1915, for Liverpool, where it embarked on the S.S. "Aquitania" *en route* for the Dardanelles. It was commanded by the adjutant, Captain E. W. Montgomerie, owing to the illness of Colonel Harvey. On the same day the 1/5th Battalion embarked, also on the "Aquitania." It had been doing further training at Watford since early in May.

Each battalion had 1,000 other ranks and the officers originally with them were the following:—

4TH BATTALION	5TH BATTALION
Commanding Officer	*Commanding Officer*
Captain E. W. Montgomerie	Colonel Sir Horace G. P. Beauchamp, Bart., C.B.
Captains	*Majors*
C. W. W. Burrell	W. J. Barton
S. D. Page	T. W. Purdy
B. M. Hughes	
W. H. Jewson	*Captains*
J. H. K. Fisher	A. E. Ward (Adjutant)
B. Boswell	F. R. Beck
	A. D. Pattrick
Lieutenants	A. Wright, M.V.O.
T. W. Flatt	E. R. Cubitt
V. C. C. Corke	A. G. Coxon
W. V. Morgan	A. H. Mason
C. K. Bampton	E. R. Woodwark

4TH BATTALION—*contd.*

2nd Lieutenants
R. P. Caton
C. H. B. Elliott
H. J. Bradshaw
G. H. C. Culley
S. G. Steel
R. E. Burrell
R. B. C. M. T. de Poix
S. J. M. White
R. W. Thurgar
F. H. Collison
C. A. Wood
C. B. S. Spackman
J. H. Jewson

Quartermaster
R. W. Moore

Medical Officer
J. C. F. Hosken

5TH BATTALION—*contd.*

Lieutenants
T. Oliphant
E. A. Beck
G. W. Birkbeck
E. Gay
V. M. Cubitt
E. H. Cubitt
A. G. Culme-Seymour

2nd Lieutenants
R. Burroughes
M. B. G. Beauchamp
A. E. Beck
A. Beck
A. R. Pelly
M. F. Oliphant
R. Adams
W. G. S. Fawkes
W. C. James
M. B. Buxton

Quartermaster
Hon. Lieutenant Parker

Medical Officer
Capt. R. G. Laden

The "Aquitania" reached Mudros without adventure on August 5th, and the troops on board her were taken in smaller vessels, on the 9th, to Imbros, whence they proceeded, on the 10th, to the landing-place of the 54th division in Suvla Bay and bivouacked on the beach.

The country about the landing-place, as seen from the sea, is described by Colonel Harvey thus:

HISTORY OF THE NORFOLK REGIMENT

"On the left Suvla Point with Nebrunessi Point to the right formed a small bay, known as Suvla Bay, some mile and a half across. To the right of Nebrunessi Point a long, gently curving sandy beach, some four or five miles in extent, terminated where the Australian position at Anzac rose steeply to the Sari Bair range.

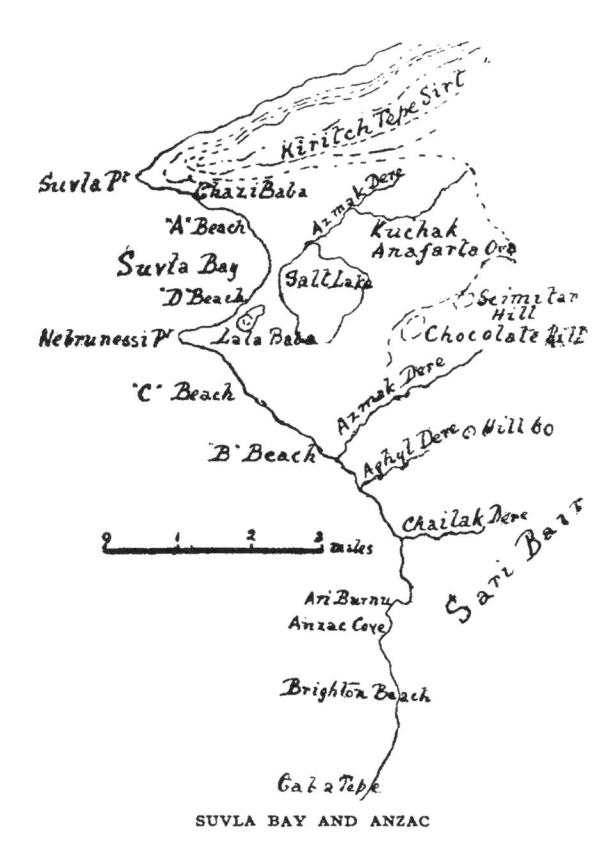

SUVLA BAY AND ANZAC

Inside and immediately in front was a large, flat, sandy plain covered with scrub, while the dry salt lake showed dazzlingly white in the hot morning sun. Immediately beyond was Chocolate Hill, and behind this lay the village of Anafarta some four miles from the shore. As a background the Anafarta ridge ran from the village practically parallel with the sea, where it gradually sloped down to the coast. Beyond the plain a number of stunted oaks, gradually becoming more dense farther inland, formed excellent cover for the enemy's snipers, a mode of warfare at which the Turk was very adept. Officers and men were continually shot down, not only by rifle fire from advanced posts of the enemy, but by men, and even women, behind our own firing line, especially in the previous attacks. The particular kind of tree in this part, a stunted oak, lends itself to concealment, being short with dense foliage. Here the sniper would lurk, with face painted green, and so well hidden as to defy detection. Others would crouch in the dense brushwood, where anyone passing could be shot with ease. When discovered, these snipers had in their possession enough food and water for a considerable period, as well as an ample supply of ammunition."

Want of water was one of the great difficulties of the British. They had suffered severely from it in the actions after the landing at Suvla on August 7th which had failed to gain possession of the Anafarta ridge.

The commander-in-chief, Sir Ian Hamilton, had now decided on another attempt to take that ridge with the aid of the 54th division, which was the last of his reinforcements landed.

Between the landing place and the Kuchak Anafarta Ova[1] lay a very difficult and intricate country in which it would be almost impossible to avoid intermixture of units and confusion before the final attack on the morning of the 13th. Accordingly, it was decided to send the 163rd brigade forward on the afternoon of the 12th to clear this area of any enemy detachments in it, and to establish itself about the Kuchak Anafarta Ova, thus enabling the main attacking force next morning to get so far on its way to the ridge without the confusion which must result from having to fight its way through a country of small fields surrounded by deep ditches and high hedges, with forest in the background. To add to the difficulties of the 163rd brigade, its orders were generally to clear the country, and no definite objective was assigned to each unit. The orders were to clear snipers out of the scrub, advance to the alignment of the 53rd division, and fill up the gap between it on the right

[1] Ova = plain.

and the 10th division on the left, and dig in for the night. Picks and shovels were issued before moving off.

Colonel Sir H. Beauchamp, commanding the 1/5th Norfolk, had been placed in local command of the brigade in the trenches occupied on the 11th and the early part of the 12th. The 1/4th Norfolk, who had been left on the beach to unload stores after the landing on the 10th, were presently moved up into the support trenches of the brigade, the front line of which, counting from right to left, consisted of the 5th Norfolk, 8th Hants, and 1/5th Suffolk Regiments. On the left of the 54th division was the 10th, the orders of the former being to link the latter up with the 53rd division, whose right flank rested on the Salt Lake and Azmak River. For this purpose the troops available were insufficient, with a front of only three battalions, and the same number in second line.

The advance on August 12th did not commence till 4.45 p.m., the naval bombardment covering it having started at 4 p.m. The order of the three leading battalions was as given above, the 4th Norfolk following in support behind the 5th Suffolk on the left. Directly the advance began the 1/5th Norfolk received an order to change direction half right, which they did. This order did not reach the 1/8th Hants, and consequently a gap was formed between the battalions, which continually increased as the advance proceeded.

As the brigade advanced it at once encountered serious resistance, and came under heavy machine-gun fire enfilading it from the left, and shrapnel on the right. The machine-gun fire was the more effective in stopping the British advance, and the 5th Norfolk battalion on the right began to get forward quicker than the left. Touch had been partially lost in the close country, and companies and battalions were much mixed up. What happened with the 5th Norfolk battalion is thus described in Sir Ian Hamilton's despatch of December 11, 1915, describing what he calls " a very mysterious thing."

> "The 1/5th Norfolk were on the right of the line and found themselves for a moment less strongly opposed than the rest of the brigade. Against the yielding forces of the enemy Colonel Sir H.

Beauchamp, a bold, self-confident officer, eagerly pressed forward, followed by the best part of the battalion. The fighting grew hotter, and the ground became more wooded and broken. At this stage many men were wounded, or grew exhausted with thirst. These found their way back to camp during the night. But the Colonel, with sixteen officers and 250 men, still kept pushing on, driving the enemy before them. . . . Nothing more was ever seen or heard of any of them. They charged into the forest and were lost to sight or sound. Not one of them ever came back."[1]

It was not till four years later that any trace was discovered of the fate of this body. Writing on September 23, 1919, the officer commanding the Graves Registration Unit in Gallipoli says :

"We have found the 5th Norfolks—there were 180 in all ; 122 Norfolk and a few Hants and Suffolks with 2/4th Cheshires. We could only identify two—Privates Barnaby and Cotter. They were scattered over an area of about one square mile, at a distance of at least 800 yards behind the Turkish front line. Many of them had evidently been killed in a farm, as a local Turk, who owns the place, told us that when he came back he found the farm covered with the decomposing bodies of British soldiers which he threw into a small ravine. The whole thing quite bears out the original theory that they did not go very far on, but got mopped up one by one, all except the ones who got into the farm."

The total casualties of the 5th Norfolk battalion are stated in their War Diary to have been twenty-two officers and about 350 men. The officers missing were—Colonel Sir Horace Proctor Beauchamp, C.B. ; Captain and Adjutant A. E. Ward ; Captains E. R. Cubitt, F. R. Beck (the King's estate agent commanding the Sandringham company), Pattrick, Mason, A. C. Coxon, Woodwark ; Lieutenants E. A. Beck, Gay, V. M. Cubitt, T. Oliphant ; 2nd Lieutenants Burroughs, Proctor,

[1] Sir Horace Beauchamp, Bart., C.B., had served in the Sudan, Suakim, and South African Campaigns, retired in 1904, and returned to serve in the war in 1914.

Beauchamp, Adams, Fawkes.[1] Major Purdy and 2nd Lieutenants M. Oliphant and A. R. Pelly were wounded but not missing.

The brigade had made some advance in face of very strong opposition, but was far from complete success. During the night the position gained was held in an irregular line, with three and a half battalions and two companies of the 1/4th Norfolk on a spur.

This account of the action of August 12th, taken from the naturally rather meagre entry in the War Diary, may be supplemented by the following rough pencil notes kept by Captain Montgomerie, who was commanding the 1/4th Battalion in the absence of Colonel Harvey:

" 12th August.—Had to meet guides from 5th Norfolk at 6 a.m. We started off at 5.40 for the mile walk, arrived at rendezvous, but no guide. Waited with battalion quarter of an hour, and then I left with adjutant to find 5th Norfolk. Eventually found them, only to find Sir H. Beauchamp had just left. Learned where I was expected to be, so sent for the battalion. Busy digging all morning. We were about to complete trenches when we were ordered to move and go in reserve to the brigade in an advance. The advance started 4 p.m. My orders were to follow on the left flank, as that one was unprotected. The three battalions advanced rapidly and all seemed well until I came to the top of a hill which overlooked the valley on the other side of which were Turkish trenches. I could see that they[2] were under shrapnel fire and seemed to be in trouble. I saw Captain Fisher just behind and sent him forward with " B " company. " A " company on left had already gone forward, and half " D " company also on extreme left; half " C " company on my right had wandered off to right and had gone to support of the Hampshires. Seeing that it was useless to send more troops into the valley, with no other troops coming up in rear, I halted there and prepared for all eventualities. It soon became

---

[1] Captain Coxon and 2nd Lieutenant Fawkes were both wounded and taken prisoners by the Turks. They were in captivity in Asia Minor till after the Armistice. The rest of the missing were all apparently killed.

[2] " They " evidently means the British.

apparent that the brigade was in difficulties. An officer of the 5th Suffolks came rushing back, asking for support and saying the enemy were surrounding him. He could not tell me anything definite. After he had cooled down a bit, he said that the enemy were getting round their right flank. It then appeared to me that the enemy must be retreating across the front of the Hampshires and 5th Norfolk. I sent him back with a few men and told him to let everyone know I was ready to help them from my hill. It was very difficult to absolutely locate their position. I sent a message telling the brigade head-quarters that I was going to hold the ridge overlooking the valley, but it was a long time before I could find them. I, later, saw the brigade major, who told me they were having an awful time in front, and would probably have to retire, and that I must be prepared to help them back. All through the night men were coming in who had lost their units, and I think I had 200 men with me next morning. I gave them water, of which they were in great need."

Captain Montgomerie's notes give the following account of the three succeeding days:

" 13th.—Next morning we learnt that the first line of the brigade were holding their own in a clump of trees about 1,500 yards to our right front. I held part of the ridge overlooking the valley with three platoons; the enemy being on my left flank, from where he sniped us day and night, but luckily with very little effect. I had a post on No. 2 and patrolled No. 1, but the snipers laid low. We dug in all day, but the men were very exhausted, and in want of food and water, and were not capable of much manual labour. The Essex brigade made an attack towards the Anafarta wells, but it had no effect.

" 14th.—Our men were now getting exhausted from hard work and lack of food. We sent up some food to them in the early morning. They were well off for water as they had four wells, but they ran considerable risk in getting it.

"15th.—It was decided that our first line should be relieved by the Essex brigade. I, from my ridge, was to give covering fire.

"The 1st Battalion Essex advanced well and lost few men. The other battalions, who had delayed, suffered more severely. All we could do was to keep down the fire of the snipers by shooting into the trees. Rumour has it that some of these snipers were tied to trees, with water and food within reach. Women snipers have been caught within our lines with their faces, arms, legs, and rifles painted green.

"After dark our men began to come in. Some came in well, but there were cases where the confusion was great. The last to come in were a party of 100–150 with Captains Hughes and Fisher. These officers had behaved magnificently throughout this show and they finished by leading the men back in very good order."

On the 16th both the Norfolk battalions were moved to a point near Kiretch Tepe Sirt on the ridge running north-east from Suvla Point, where the 31st brigade was. On the 17th the two battalions relieved the 6th Munster Fusiliers on Saddle Ridge near Jephson's Post.

Of this position Captain M. B. Buxton, M.C., writes:

"The line here stretched from the top of the ridge at Jephson's Post down to the sea. Jephson's Post was a strong post manned by machine-gunners, some from the brigade and some from the crew of a naval destroyer which stood about 400 yards off the shore. This post was able to command all the Turkish line down to the sea. The destroyer was able to render effectual help on several occasions; for if there was any movement in the Turkish lines, she at once opened fire with her guns.

"At night also her searchlight was directed on the Turkish line as it stretched up the hill, rendering the enemy's trenches clearly visible to our troops while our own were in darkness. The trenches here consisted, when the Norfolk battalions first reached the line, only of rifle pits, and the first thing that was done was to make a strong line of trenches and to build dug-outs. The gullies behind the line were generally deep and afforded excellent cover, but the country was so cut up by these gullies and so covered by scrub that it was extremely difficult to find the way about.

"During all this time the troops had been very short of water, often having only about a mugfull each day. The water was very scarce on the Peninsula and such wells as were dug in the plain were brackish.

"The 5th Battalion sank several small wells in the hope of finding water, but these produced nothing more than brackish and muddy puddles. Water, in these first weeks, was sent to the battalion in skins, and in the extreme heat a great deal of it evaporated. Later, when petrol tins were used they were found to be more satisfactory. All the water was brought in tank steamers from Egypt and pumped on to the Peninsula, where it was stored and distributed.

"As the left of the 5th Battalion rested on the sea, this was an excellent opportunity for bathing and washing, when things were quiet, which was taken much advantage of.

"While there the shortage of water and food and the hardships they had encountered much reduced the health of the battalion, and the majority were suffering from mild or severe forms of dysentery. This disease, and jaundice, and various fevers, from this time onwards, caused far more casualties than the Turks.

"The battalion was still only in fighting order, i.e. with haversacks only and no packs, and they were unable to get any blankets or change of underclothes till the end of August. While in the day it was extremely hot, at night it became very cold, so much so that it was almost impossible to get much sleep.

"The only officers with the battalion were Major Barton in command; Lieutenants Birkbeck, Beck, Cubitt; 2nd Lieutenants Buxton and James; and Lieutenant and Quartermaster Ford."

Captain Montgomerie's diary of events in the 1/4th Battalion whilst in the neighbourhood of Jephson's Post is as follows:

"16th.—I was relieved on the ridge by the 4th Essex early in the morning. The battalion joined up in trenches some 300 yards in rear of the ridge. We were busy digging trenches all day, and trying to collect the men to their various companies. In the late advance we had been in reserve, and three companies and one platoon had reinforced the first line, so they had become very scattered.

"In the afternoon the 10th division advanced along the ridge and cleared the whole hill of the enemy. Unfortunately we were unable to hold on to the extreme east of it. It was a fine sight to watch from the valley below.

"17th.—A quiet day improving trenches. Had a little shrapnel in the morning on the right. Bampton was killed by one of the shells. I was ordered to take over the lines held by the 8th Hampshires on ridge just to right of where I had been previously. This suited us well, as we would then have all four companies in that line. I had made all arrangements, and we were starting to move when I was sent for to brigade head-quarters, and told to take the battalion in support of 30th brigade on top of Kiretch Tepe. At this time I had also under me the remnants of the 5th Norfolk, which consisted of 150 men under one officer—Lieutenant Evelyn Beck. I sent out orders to collect the various companies and had to rapidly issue ammunition, water, and food. While preparing to move our men were heavily shelled with shrapnel and a few high explosives. We lost eight men. We started our movement up the hill at 7 p.m. It was a very tedious climb and as we were all heavily laden it was very slow. Anyhow, we managed to arrive at the brigade head-quarters at 12 midnight without any mishap. We were put right away into some trenches facing south on top of the ridge.

"18th.—Remained quiet, during the day. Orders were received in evening to relieve the 6th Munsters and Inniskillings in front line facing east. The Essex brigade was to relieve us. This relieving was muddled through all right. We had to do a lot of digging to make things safe.

"19th.—All quiet during day. Worked hard all night fetching food, water, etc., and improving the trenches.

"20th.—Were relieved of Jephson's Redoubt by Essex; so organized the line with two companies in firing line and two in support.

"21st.—Standing to arms at 3 p.m. as an attack was commenced on our right. There was no movement in our part of the battle-field. At night a party of Turks tried to make an advanced trench, but this was stopped by the torpedo boat on the left and the machine-guns.

"22nd.—A very quiet day; very little sniping. The enemy shelled us for the first time in this position, two shells fell very near. They are undoubtedly trying to hit the machine-guns near us. They shrapnelled the ridge farther along, and did a little damage to the Essex.

"23rd.—A quiet day. A little shelling in morning and evening. One shell hit head-quarters dug-out, but did no damage. These common shells do little damage. Sniping was bad in morning.

"24th.—Very quiet all day; very little sniping. The Turks tried to shell our trenches with H.E., but they all fell well short of our line. Orders received to be prepared to be relieved by the 162nd brigade to-morrow night. At about 6 p.m. this order was cancelled and we remained in our present place.

"25th.—All quiet."

Towards the end of August the Norfolk battalions were moved farther down the Gallipoli Peninsula, and Captain Montgomerie's diary gives the following account of the move and of events succeeding it:

"26th.—Quiet all day except for the sniping. Received orders to be prepared to be relieved by the 32nd brigade. They reckoned to be up to relieve us about 9.30 p.m. They arrived about 11.15 p.m., and then the head of the column had come wrong and had come to us instead of to the 5th Norfolk on the left. We had to get them clear, and then started putting them in our trenches. It was a long job, and, to add to our troubles, a gale sprang up with a certain amount of rain. A most uncomfortable night. We got back to the reserve trenches about a mile in rear about 4 a.m.

"27th.—A quiet day. Had a shave for the first time since landing. Prepared to move into reserve that night. Time of moving unknown.

"28th.—Started off to reserve about 1.15 a.m. It was only a short march but rather a fatiguing one. Men weak from dysentery and unable to keep up, but we eventually reached our new bivouac about 4 a.m. We were put down by the sea underneath the cliff. Little space, so we are very crowded. Not much cover if we are heavily shelled. Had a bread ration for the first time since leaving the 'Aquitania.' Battalion was put on duty. Each company on fatigue of some kind.

"29th.—A complete rest.

"30th.—Battalion ordered to go to "A" beach on fatigue duty until relieved. Sent the four companies under Captain Burrell—485 strong. Staff and sick remained behind. I went with brigade head-quarters to Anzac to see the trenches we were to occupy. Were met by brigade-major of New Zealand Mounted Brigade, and were taken to General Cox's head-quarters, where he explained situation to us. The New Zealanders had taken half Hill 60 and were at close quarters to the Turks. Very necessary that hill should be held. Later, went to communication trench behind, where we could see the whole situation. Both sides busy digging and throwing bombs.

"31st.—Companies on fatigue not relieved, and remained at "A" beach.

"September 1st.—Companies returned to Lala Baba. Orders received to be prepared to move to Anzac next day.

"2nd.—Move to Anzac postponed.

"3rd.—Moved to Anzac area. Left Lala Baba at 9.30, reached Anzac Kurja, about one mile from our destination, about 11 p.m. Guide from 5th Suffolks met us to show us the way. Got lost and had to find the way ourselves. Arrived at our destination 4 a.m.

"4th.—Remained in bivouac. Orders received to take over, on 5th, trenches now occupied by 5th Essex.

"5th.—Relieved 5th Essex at 8 p.m.

"6th.—All was quiet during the day, but we saw that the Turks were sapping up to us. Started taking steps to defeat them. At night a few bombs were thrown, and some shots fired. Nothing of importance.

"7th.—'A' and 'B' relieved by 'C' and 'D' about 4 a.m. Only just managed to get the relieving done in time.

"9th.—More or less quiet. We lose a few men every day, principally from a gun on our right flank which nearly enfilades us, and fires at a pretty close range. The fault lies chiefly with the men, who will not take proper care of themselves, nor make their dug-outs deep enough. Head-quarters moved up this evening to entrance of communication trench to front line. Colonel Harvey arrived, but went to command brigade."

Next day Colonel Harvey returned to the command of the battalion, which had been sadly reduced from an embarkation strength of twenty-six officers and 1,000 other ranks to thirteen officers and 580 men at the end of August. A month later its fighting strength was fourteen officers and 376 other ranks, with 218 in hospital. After the fighting in the middle of August, the struggle was more against disease and hardship than against Turkish guns and rifles. Dysentery caused havoc in all ranks, and in the middle of October there remained of the 1/4th Battalion only sixteen officers and 242 men fit for duty. Colonel Harvey himself fell a victim to dysentery almost immediately on his return, and by October 25th had to make over temporary command to Major C. R. Roberts-West, adjutant of the 7th Essex. When Colonel Harvey was sent home sick, on the 4th December, he left only ten officers and 170 men of the battalion fit for duty. In the 1/5th Norfolk battalion the circumstances were similar, except that, owing to its casualties on August 12th, the battalion had suffered more severely at the hands of the enemy. On September 22nd command of the remains of it was taken over by Lieutenant-Colonel H. J. Kinsman of the 4th Inniskilling.

The 1/4th Battalion was in various sectors of the trenches after September 10th, carrying on duties similar to those described in Captain Montgomerie's diary. It is needless to describe them further in detail. The Norfolk Yeomanry, afterwards the 12th (Yeomanry) Battalion Norfolk Regiment, shared these duties with the 1/4th in November.

The 1/5th Norfolk Regiment were at Aghyll Dere, north of Sari Bair, in the beginning of September, temporarily attached to the 162nd brigade at Gloucester Hill, where they were at times in the firing line. At the end of the month as many as seventy-one of their reduced numbers were sick, and on November 1st their numbers were so reduced that the battalion had to be reorganized in two companies. When, on November 5th, they were in the firing line at Aghyll Dere, Captain Balme was complimented by General Birdwood on a patrol which had been carried out by him on October 31st.

The following account of Captain Balme's exploit is given by Captain Buxton:

"The Turks had been in the habit of posting a listening post at night on a steep spur which led down from their line, but which could only be approached from our lines by climbing up, one at a time, a precipitous ridge which led up to it. Captain Balme of the 3rd Essex Regiment, who was attached to the 5th Norfolk, took out a small party one evening before dusk to attack this. They succeeded in climbing the steep sides of the ridge without attracting the attention of the Turks, and were able to get into the post before the Turkish outpost took up their position for the night. When the Turks put in an appearance they were most successfully ambushed, and Captain Balme was able to bring the whole of his party back without a casualty. For this he was awarded the M.C. Captain Balme was, later, invalided from Egypt, but rejoined his own regiment in France, where he was afterwards killed."

The evacuation of Anzac did not occur till December 18th-19th, but the 1/5th Norfolk battalion were embarked for Mudros on the 3rd.

Of the period after the move to the Anzac neighbourhood Major Buxton writes, from the point of view of the 5th Battalion:

"At the end of August the brigade was sent off to Anzac and attached to the 9th Corps, consisting of Australian and New Zealand troops. The 5th Battalion were attached to the 162nd brigade, consisting of the 10th and 11th London Regiment, 4th Northampton Regiment, and 5th Bedford Regiment. They held a line of trenches stretching along the brow of a ridge which rose above Aghyll Dere (or valley).

"The 5th manned the trenches alternately with the 10th London Regiment, each spell in the trenches consisting of about a week. After a week in the line the regiment went into rest on the other side of the ridge, only 200 yards from the trenches, and their time there was employed in fatigues, carrying parties, and digging trenches. It was possible from here to take bathing parties down the Aghyll Dere to the beach, which was about two and a half miles away. There were always a great number of men bathing, and at times the Turks used to shell with shrapnel, but fortunately never seemed to cause any casualties.

"About November the Suffolk Yeomanry were attached to the 5th Battalion for instruction in trench warfare, as they had only lately arrived, and they shared all the duties for about a fortnight.

"The Turkish line of trenches opposite the 5th Battalion were on the high slopes of the ridge connecting Khoja Chemen Tepe and Chunuk Bair, both of which were about 1,000 feet high. The Turks were able to get as much timber as they needed from the thickly wooded eastern slopes of the peninsula, and with this they constructed several lines of barbed wire entanglements, and were able to provide head cover to their trenches, and wood for strutting and dug-outs.

"On the western side the ridge was covered with scrub about three or four feet high, and there were a considerable number of olive trees in the valleys about twenty or thirty feet high. The

Australian troops were on our right, their line stretching from the southern branch of the Aghyll Dere to Anzac.

"Special mention must be made of the activities of the various Norfolk County Red Cross and Regimental and other associations, who were good enough to send out large consignments of cigarettes, tobacco, chocolate, fly-nets, and other luxuries, which were most welcome. Perhaps the most acceptable of all was a consignment of 2,000 or 3,000 sandbags made by various ladies in Norfolk which arrived early in September, at a time when sandbags in the front line were very scarce. This consignment was put to excellent use, and added not a little to the safety in the trenches and to the comfort of the men in the dug-outs.

"By about September, owing to the fact that great numbers of troops had been living in a small space, flies began to abound and became a perfect curse. It was impossible to prepare any food without it becoming covered with a horde of filthy black flies, and at all times of the day they were continually tormenting the troops and spreading disease.

"About the middle of October the rations greatly improved and, instead of bully beef and biscuits, rations of beef, bread, cheese, and all kinds of jam and marmalade were frequently sent up.

"The 5th Battalion were withdrawn from the trenches on November 30th. For about a week before this there had been a great blizzard, and the peninsula was covered with snow and the cold was intense. Later this turned to great storms of rain, and soon all the valleys which had been used as the chief means of communication for ration parties, etc., were changed into torrents. A great number of the barges and lighters which were used to bring the supplies and land the troops from the ships in the bay were wrecked on the shore.

"The 5th Battalion left the peninsula on the night of December 4th, and were embarked at Mudros. There were only two officers of the original 5th Battalion left with the battalion—Captain Eustace Cubitt, the adjutant, and Lieutenant Buxton. Captain Birkbeck, the only other remaining officer of the original 1/5th

Battalion who had left England in the 'Aquitania,' was detailed for duty as embarkation officer and remained, with Private Harrod, carrying out these duties on the peninsula till the final evacuation, and then rejoined the battalion."

The 1/4th, which was then at Reserve Gully, Anzac, went to Mudros on December 7th and 8th, its strength then being eleven officers and 199 other ranks.

On December 15th, the 1/4th embarked, with eleven officers and 237 other ranks, on the s.s. "Victorian" from Mudros for Alexandria, where it arrived on the 19th, and command was assumed by Lieutenant-Colonel W. A. Younden, T.D. The 1/5th who had gone to Mudros on December 4th, also went on the "Victorian" to Alexandria, where both battalions were, till the end of the year, at Sidi Bishr camp, and remained till the beginning of February, 1916.

(b) 1916 : EGYPT

Both battalions were transferred at the beginning of February, 1916, to Mena camp near Cairo. The camp was situated at the foot of the great Pyramid, and here the 54th division and other troops were busy for about six weeks training drafts from England and reorganizing. They were then sent to the defences of the Suez Canal.

The Turkish attacks on the Suez Canal had been beaten off a year before the two Norfolk battalions reached Egypt, but the line of defence on it was maintained, though practically never disturbed by the enemy. On this line of defence both remained at various posts till June, 1916. During all this period they were engaged in training, both for the original battalions and for the drafts they received from home. June and July were spent at Serapeum south and El Ferdan north of Ismailia supplying guards, outposts, and fatigues. The rest of the year 1916 was passed in much the same way and in the same neighbourhood.

Of this period Captain Buxton writes :

" From 1916 onwards the Suez Canal was defended by a series of fortified posts in the desert on the eastern side. These posts were about two to four miles apart. One line of them was at intervals on the bank of the canal. Farther east and connected by about four miles of light railway were the railhead posts, while about four or five miles farther east were the front line posts. These front line posts were situated on a range of sandhills about 300 to 400 feet high which afforded a good view of the surrounding country. Rations and water were brought up to these posts daily on camels from railhead. The posts were held by two companies. They were circular, about 150 to 200 yards in diameter. The camp was pitched outside the post, and the troops were employed daily in completing the defences of the posts by surrounding them with broad wire entanglements, digging fire trenches or communication trenches, or dug-outs. The trench digging was especially tedious ; for, owing to the soft sand continually falling in, it was often necessary to excavate to a width of about twenty feet, then to put in timber shuttering to give the ordinary width of the trench, and finally to shovel back a great deal of the sand against the shuttering. Should the enemy approach, the posts were occupied at once, and were to be held to the last, or till reinforcements were sent up."

(c) 1917 : PALESTINE

The year 1916 had been uneventful for both battalions ; 1917 saw them again engaged in active warfare in the operations towards Palestine. In February they were on the march across the north of the Sinai desert to the British front before Gaza.

Of this march Captain Buxton writes :

" In February, 1917, the 163rd brigade was ordered to march across the Sinai Desert, in order to assist in the attack on Palestine. Much of the march was along the ' wire road ' which had been laid. It consisted of four strips of ordinary rabbit wire netting which was laid and pegged on the sand, giving enough width for a battalion to march in column of fours. Marching was considerably easier on this than on the soft sand, into which often the men sank up to the ankles at every step.

"The general route was from Romani, by marches of about twelve miles a day, to El Arish. The brigade was led each day by the battalion which marched the best and in which the fewest men fell out. The 5th Norfolk battalion led the brigade the whole way across, without a man falling out, until the day before the brigade reached El Arish, when a machine-gunner got kicked off a refractory mule and injured his leg, so their place at the head was taken by the 5th Suffolk.

"Lieutenant-Colonel de Falbe of the Herts Yeomanry had been appointed officer commanding 5th Norfolk in January, 1916. In the middle of 1916 he was invalided home, and was succeeded by Lieutenant-Colonel Grissell, D.S.O., as commanding officer. Lieutenant-Colonel Grissell had been with the 2nd Battalion Norfolk Regiment for many years, and, being a very able and efficient soldier, soon brought the 5th Battalion up to a very high standard of efficiency. He was killed during the second attack on Gaza in April, 1917."

On March 6th the 163rd brigade relieved the 156th in the left sub-sector of the defences at El Arish, the 1/4th Norfolk taking over from the 8th Scottish Rifles at Mount Murray, and the 1/5th from the 4th Royal Scots at Mount Dobell, Bushy Knoll, and the Step. The 8th Hants relieved the 9th Scottish Rifles at Sea View, and the 5th Suffolk went into brigade reserve. In this neighbourhood the brigade remained till March 20th, when it set out for El Burj at 6 p.m., arriving there at 10 p.m. On the 25th the division was at Rafa and on the 26th marched, at 4 a.m., six miles to Beni Sela, where it spent the day concealed in orchards and groves. The march to In Seirat was continued at nightfall, but owing to the 163rd brigade losing its way in the dark, it only had two or three hours' rest before starting again at 4 a.m. for the first of Lieutenant-General Sir Charles Dobell's attacks on Gaza.

We can again quote Captain M. B. Buxton's account of the operations on this day, when he was acting as Brigade Intelligence Officer to Brigadier-General Ward, C.M.G., commanding the 163rd brigade. He writes:

".It was most unfortunate that there was a very thick fog on the morning of the 27th, for no one had any idea of the country

THE GAZA FRONT

between In Seirat and Gaza. There were several 'wadis' to be crossed and the R.E. had only made one or two crossings which were very difficult to find, and were usually crowded with columns of troops crossing. For this reason we must have lost about three hours, and it was not until 8 o'clock that we crossed the Wadi Ghuzze at Shekh Nebhan.

"The 53rd division was advancing along the coast, while the 54th was detailed to capture Sheikh Abbas Ridge, which was ground about 300 feet high overlooking Gaza. On our right was the Australian Mounted Infantry and New Zealand Light Horse. The 161st brigade was ordered to attack Ali-el-Muntar, a very steep hill at the S.E. corner of Gaza. The 162nd brigade were between them and our brigade.

"The brigade (163rd) marched the eight miles to Sheikh Abbas in artillery formation, arriving there about 10 o'clock without firing a shot, and took up their position along the ridge. All that day we remained there while the 53rd division and the 161st brigade were attacking Gaza from the south and the New Zealand and Australian cavalry were attacking from the N.E. The Turks had much larger forces in Gaza than we had expected, and large reinforcements were marched from Beersheba and other places round, and so the attack was not so successful as we had hoped.

"In the afternoon we received orders to take up a position during the night west of Sheikh Abbas on Mansura Ridge. The brigadier sent me down on my horse to find out the way, and I then came back and guided the columns to Mansura Ridge during the night.

"We passed the ration convoy coming up with our rations, but they had to be sent back to Wadi Ghuzze, as there was no time to issue rations; the men therefore got no rations or water that night. Directly it was light we saw a large force of Turks advancing on the ridge and they shelled us rather heavily. The 5th Norfolk were ordered to go forward and take up a line about 500 yards in front of the ridge. After a good deal of machine-gun and rifle fire the Turkish attack was broken up and they never got much nearer than 400 or 500 yards.

"The 5th Norfolk consolidated their position and remained there all day.

"The attack on Gaza was continued all day without much success."

The two Norfolk battalions were in the front line of the brigade all this day. During the morning Captain Wenn of the 1/5th Norfolk was killed.

By 4 p.m. it was clear that Turkish reinforcements were approaching from the east and were about to attack the front of the 53rd and 54th divisions in force. The attack materialized about dusk, but was broken up by artillery and machine-gun fire from the whole British line.

The 163rd brigade then received orders to cover the withdrawal of the 54th division to the west bank of the Wadi Ghuzze and to maintain communication with the 158th brigade, which was performing the same service for the 53rd division. This operation being successfully carried out, the brigade was back at In Seirat at 5.45 a.m. on the 29th. The losses of the Norfolk battalions on the 28th were :

1/4th. Two other ranks killed and seven wounded.
1/5th. One officer (Captain Wenn) killed and two other ranks wounded.

After the failure of this first attack on Gaza there ensued a period of preparation for the next. So vigorous and extensive were the preparations that Captain Buxton records that " every one expected that at the second attack we should take Gaza with comparative ease." There were constant reconnaissances by officers, and the infantry were kept busy making roads and crossings over the Wadi Ghuzze, which was in front of the line of hills on which was the British line of defence. The Wadi, then with few crossings, had been a serious obstacle and cause of delay in the first attack. Another work was the filling with water, brought up at night on camels, of the large cisterns at Umm Jerrar. The Wadi Ghuzze itself was used for ammunition dumps, which were protected from shell fire by the steep banks, often thirty or forty feet high. These also protected the pipe line, which was extended under them, and the water reservoirs which it filled. There was also some boring for water.

Up till April 16th the two Norfolk battalions were at In Seirat, taking their turn in the trenches of the defensive position, in support, or in reserve.

In the night of the 16th–17th the 163rd brigade moved to the assembly position at Sharta, with orders to again carry the Sheikh Abbas ridge at dawn. The general line of attack was now to face north-eastwards, with its left on the sea and its right on the Wadi running from Khirbet Sihan to El Azaferieh.

The capture of the Sheikh Abbas ridge on the 17th was effected without much difficulty by the 163rd brigade. The Turks only had a few outposts there and the 8th Hants and 8th Suffolk battalions, preceded by the two tanks, and supported by the two Norfolk battalions, established themselves on the ridge and consolidated the position. The Turkish main line was along the Gaza-Beersheba road. During the consolidation there was a good deal of shell fire, and " A " company of the 1/5th Norfolk, under Captain Birkbeck, received a good deal of the enemy's attentions, though fortunately there were few casualties.

The night of the 17th–18th and the whole of the 18th were spent in this position. The rest of the line had also attained its first objectives without serious difficulties.

Orders for the general attack on the 19th were issued so late on the 18th that they did not reach the men till nearly midnight, with the result that most of the night had to be spent in preparations for attack and distributing rations and water, all of which might well have been done during the day, had orders been issued earlier.

The orders contemplated the attack and capture of Gaza and the formation of a new line beyond it. There was to be a heavy bombardment from 5.30 a.m. for two hours before the infantry attack began.

The 163rd brigade was to attack about Khirbet-el-Bir with the 52nd division on its left. In front line were the 1/5th Norfolk on the right, the 1/4th Norfolk on the left, and the 8th Hants in support, with the 5th Suffolk in reserve.

The four battalions were ready at 5 a.m. for the advance, which was to commence at 7.30 after a heavy bombardment for two hours. To the bombardment the Turks had made little or no reply, but when the infantry moved forward it soon became apparent that the British artillery had done very little harm, and the attack was met by what Captain Buxton describes as " a perfect hell of artillery and machine-gun fire." The British artillery could not give them adequate support, as they had already fired away a great part of their ammunition, and, moreover, the range of 6,000 yards was excessive. Thus, with little support, the infantry had to cross some 1,700 yards of undulating country in full view of the Turks awaiting them in trenches and well-wired redoubts beyond the Gaza-Beersheba road.

At 7.30 the two Norfolk battalions advanced. Watching the first stages from brigade head-quarters, Captain Buxton writes that " it was a magnificent sight to see them going in extended order as if on a field day." Each battalion covered a front of about 900 yards. The right of the 1/5th Norfolk was directed on a Turkish redoubt which soon began to give trouble. The first low ridge was crossed by 8.30 and the second, about 500 yards farther on, was reached. The 8th Hants now moved with one tank against the redoubt on the right of the 1/5th Norfolk.

On the opposite flank, the left of the 1/4th Norfolk, the other tank advanced on another Turkish redoubt, but unfortunately was hit by a shell and put out of action. The 1/5th Norfolk battalion disappeared over the second ridge and communication between the battalions became very difficult.

The tank with the 1/5th and the 8th Hants was presently set on fire, but not before it had inflicted heavy damage on the enemy and sent back twenty prisoners taken in the capture of the redoubt, which was held by a party of the 1/5th Norfolk men and some of the Camel Corps. All this time the British had been suffering very heavy loss from the Turkish artillery, machine-gun, and rifle fire which the British artillery, at a range of 6,000 yards, was unable to keep down.

About 10 a.m. Lieutenant Buxton, who had gone out to get information for brigade head-quarters, telephoned what he had seen from a shell hole in which he had ensconced himself. In his own words :

" It was quite obvious what had happened. The advance had been held up just below the Turkish line, and one could see our men lying out in lines, killed or wounded. The 1/5th Norfolk ' B ' company, under Captain Blyth, had captured Tank redoubt and had held it for some time, till all ammunition was spent. No support came up, and so those who did not get away, sixty in all, were captured in the Turkish counter-attack. My second tank, under Captain Carr[1] had done very well in getting into the redoubt. The first tank had had a direct hit and was burning. It was obvious that our attack here had failed, and that most of our men had been killed. So I waited a bit longer, and when things were a shade quieter, got out of my shell-hole and ran back over the rise. There I came on about forty men of our brigade of all regiments. Major Marsh, who was O.C. 8th Hants, was there too, and Lieutenant Wharton of the 4th Norfolk. These men were just stragglers and all collected there. We decided it was no good going on then, so we started to dig ourselves in. This was all quite early in the morning—about 9. Marsh had a telephone line so I phoned back to Brigade H.Q. and gave them all the news.

"There were a lot of dead men and wounded all round us. Some of the latter we got behind our lines, in case the Turks tried a counter-attack. We were about forty men and one Lewis gun, and no one on our left or right for several hundred yards. The place we were holding was the top of a rounded hillock. The Turks kept us under pretty good machine-gun fire all day. Marsh and I lay in a rifle pit and ate dates and biscuits for a bit. We allowed no firing, as we wished to keep all our ammunition in case of a counter-attack.

"About 4 in the afternoon the 5th Suffolk were sent up to support us and to consolidate the position we had held. This was really a great relief. About seven the Brigadier came out after dusk and saw the place. He ordered us to retire during the night right back to our starting point, for it would not have been possible to hold this advanced position as long as there was no one on our flanks at all.

"During the day a few stragglers joined us, among them Corporal Burtenshaw and a private. He told me that Captain Birkbeck had been very badly wounded. I told the O.C. Suffolks whereabouts he was said to be. They promised to send out patrols to try and find him, but these did no good at all, as I afterwards heard.

[1] I.e. That with the 1/5th Norfolk attacking the redoubt on the right.

"We brought in a lot of wounded as we came back. The three attacking regiments of our brigade had all had very heavy losses. Each was reduced to about 150. The 5th Norfolk lost, killed or wounded, all the officers who went in, except one, and about 600 men."

Meanwhile the 5th Suffolk had been sent up to stiffen the line, which was entrenched about 500 yards from the Turkish trenches with the hill where Lieutenant Buxton was on its right.

About 2 p.m. the divisional commander had ordered the 161st brigade, less one battalion, to reinforce the 163rd, and the commander of the former at once placed two battalions at the disposal of the commander of the 163rd. At 2.23 p.m. a counter-attack was launched, with the 5th Suffolks on the right, the 6th Essex on the left, and all the artillery firing on the trenches. When this could make no progress, the 6th Essex were withdrawn behind the Sheikh Abbas ridge, whilst the remains of the Norfolk battalions and the 8th Hants dug themselves in in the positions they then occupied, and held on there till daybreak on the 20th. By 5.30 a.m. on that day they had retired to reserve, in left rear of the 5th Suffolks.

The casualties in this disastrous attack of the 19th were extremely heavy in the Norfolk battalions, as shown below:

	KILLED Offcrs.	KILLED Other ranks	WOUNDED Offcrs.	WOUNDED Other ranks	MISSING Offcrs.	MISSING Other ranks	TOTAL Offcrs.	TOTAL Other ranks
1/4th Norfolk ..	6[1]	49	11	312	1	99	18	460
1/5th Norfolk ..	6[2]	13	9	401	4	229	19	643

[1] Major W. H. T. Jewson; Captains W. V. Morgan, S. D. Page; R. W. Thurgar; Lieutenant F. J. Cole; Second-Lieutenant J. Levy.

[2] Captains A. E. Beck, G. W. Birkbeck, E. H. Cubitt; Lieutenants E. J. Gardiner, R. R. Plaistowe; Lieutenant-Colonel Grissell.

The 8th Hants had lost twenty-two officers and 546 other ranks. Every company commander of all three battalions was killed or wounded. Lieutenant-Colonel Younden of the 1/4th Norfolk was slightly wounded, and Lieutenant-Colonel Grissell of the 1/5th was wounded and missing.[1] With these terrible losses, aggregating well over the full strength of a battalion, it became necessary to amalgamate, for the time being, both Norfolk battalions in a single composite battalion, of which the 1st and 2nd companies were made up of the remains of the 1/4th, and the 3rd and 4th of the 1/5th. The command of this battalion was given to Lieutenant-Colonel Torkington of the Scottish Rifles.

From May 1st to 16th, when it was relieved by the 74th, the 163rd brigade was in reserve behind Sheikh Abbas. The Norfolk battalion then went into general reserve, with the 8th Hants and 5th Suffolk in front of it. On the 26th it went to Dorset House, and on the 29th to Regent's Park. On June 2nd the 5th Hants were made over to the 163rd brigade, pending the formation of the 233rd brigade, and were attached to the Norfolk battalion Head-quarters and one company to the 1/4th Norfolk, and six platoons to the 1/5th, all ranks of the 5th Hants being treated as reinforcements and split up amongst the several platoons of the two battalions. On June 1st the 1/4th and 1/5th had again become separate battalions, Colonel Torkington continuing to command the 1/4th and Major G. M. de L. Dayrell of the 5th Bedford being appointed to command the 1/5th. The 54th division, on June 12th–13th, relieved the 52nd in the left sector defences, the 163rd brigade taking over the left sub-sector from the 155th, in the space from the Gaza-Cairo road at Sniper's Post, across Samson's Ridge, to the sea at Sheikh Ajlin, and the 1/4th and 1/5th Norfolk being allotted to the right and centre of the brigade front. Here there was constant labour at digging trenches in heavy sand, where it was necessary to use sandbags everywhere, and to renew them frequently.

On June 26th the officers and other ranks of the 5th Hants were re-formed into separate platoons, one company being attached to the

[1] Afterwards found to have been killed. Lieutenant Buxton saw him and Lieutenant Eustace Cubitt about 7 or 8 a.m., and states both were killed about two hours later. The diary does not give names of wounded officers.

1/4th Norfolk and one to the 1/5th. During the month the 1/4th received reinforcements of two officers and 140 other ranks, the 1/5th of 242 other ranks. Casualties were small—two killed and four wounded between the two battalions. June and July were uneventful from the point of view of fighting, such few casualties as occurred being the result of shelling by the Turks. Further reinforcements of 175 men for the 1/4th and 245 for the 1/5th came out in July. Up till the 26th August there was the usual routine of trench warfare. Even then nothing noticeable occurred till the 163rd brigade was sent from the resting area into front line, with the 5th Suffolk, 1/4th, and 1/5th Norfolk in that order from right to left.

On September 3rd a raid by the Turks on the new trenches near the sea was stopped by artillery fire before it got within 300 yards of the trenches. There was a certain amount of bombardment by both sides, but the only other excitement was the capture of two Turks by the 1/4th in a fig grove, and the surrender to them of a Turkish deserter.

With the month of October began the more elaborate training for the coming offensive, now that the army had been reinforced and was commanded by General Allenby. Model trenches and practice attacks on them, with reorganization of companies on a platoon basis, i.e., riflemen section, Lewis gun section, etc., were the order of the day up till the 14th, when the 163rd brigade moved up to first line, where it had much difficult patrolling work to do. It relieved the 156th brigade in the left sub-sector, the 8th Hants being on the extreme left touching the sea, the 1/4th Norfolk in the centre from Hereford Ridge to Cairo Ridge, and the 1/5th on the right on Samson's Ridge.

During the last ten days of October working parties were supplied from the left and right battalions, but the 1/4th Norfolk were kept intact, ready to counter-attack in case of emergency.

On November 1st General Allenby was ready to renew the attack on the Gaza position, which had failed so disastrously in April. On that day the 163rd brigade began moving up from Marine View to the assembly positions, which were reached by all units by 2.30 p.m. The brigade took no part in the first phase of the operations, which consisted in a turning movement by Beersheba on the Turkish left, to be followed by an attack, on November 2nd, on their right near the sea, which, as was expected, confused them as to the real point of danger. During the rest of November 1st the Norfolk battalions were in trenches.

At 2.30 a.m. on November 2nd the 5th Suffolk, with "D" company of the 1/4th Norfolk attached for carrying purposes, formed up on the right outside the British wire, with the 8th Hants on their left. Between 2.30 and 3 a.m., both these assaulting battalions were advancing on Half-way House unmolested by a barrage, for the Turks believed them to be nothing more than a strong patrol.

At 3 a.m., having passed Half-way House, the 5th Suffolk got to hand-to-hand fighting without much loss on the way. The 8th Hants were not so fortunate. In the mist and the smoke of exploding shells their leading wave got split, part going towards El Arish, and part towards the Susan trench at El Burj. However, both battalions reached and occupied the objective trenches.

Meanwhile, the 1/4th Norfolk had formed in support at 2.15 a.m. on the rear of the 8th Hants, slightly to the right, with "B" company on the right, "C" on the left, and "A" in rear of "C," all in lines of sections in file. The machine-guns and light trench mortar were in rear of "C" under 2nd Lieutenant C. M. Collier, who was killed shortly after the advance began. As the battalion advanced at 3 a.m. it ran into the enemy's barrage, which had gone over the 8th Hants. They had heavy casualties from this, and, owing to the split in the 8th Hants, two companies ("B" and "C") of the 1/4th Norfolk followed the right of the 8th Hants towards Triangle trench, which was to the right of their proper direction. The orders were to follow the 8th Hants in touch with the 1/5th, which they were unable to find, though they were in touch with the 5th Suffolk on the right.

At 3.55 a.m., when they should have passed through the 8th Hants to attack their proper objective, the Crested Rock, they found themselves involved in hand-to-hand fighting in El Arish, and eventually occupied the trenches there. "A" company (it will be remembered that "D" was carrying for the 5th Suffolk), got into a trench still farther to the right. The duration of the fighting at El Arish upset all calculations, and rendered impossible the intended attack on Crested Rock. The

1/4th Norfolk appear to have got right into the area of the 5th Suffolk on the right, and found it impossible to locate themselves.

The 1/5th Norfolk had formed up at 2.50 a.m. on the left rear of the 8th Hants, who had already reached Half-way House. They, too, lost direction as they advanced at 3 a.m., lost touch with the 1/4th on their right, and arrived opposite the line Zowaid—El Burj, instead of that of Zowaid-Rafa. Here they had their right flank in the air, as was the left of the 1/4th. They were caught in the barrage at 3.30 a.m. when waiting to pass through, and it was too late to correct the direction. Some confusion resulted, but Captain Gardner, Lieutenants Cumberland, Catherell, and Pallett (all of whom became casualties) penetrated with small bodies of men to Island Wood, Gibraltar, and even to Crested Rock. Captain Gardner, at Island Wood with a small party, was forced by want of support to retire. Two officers with him did not return and were missing. The battalion took up the line Susan trench-Zowaid. The situation was obscure throughout, and the units were much mixed up. Eventually a line was consolidated as follows, counting from right to left:

- 5th Suffolk—Grace trench, Gertrude trench, Craig Post, Rook trench.
- 8th Hants, from El Burj towards Violet trench.
- 1/4th Norfolk, from Bertha trench to the junction of Grace and Violet trenches.
- 1/5th Norfolk, from El Burj to Zowaid.

The brigade had fallen considerably short of attaining its objective, a result due to the darkness and confusion.

The casualties of the Norfolk battalions were:

1/4th. *Killed*—2nd Lieutenants C. M. Collier and W. S. Giles,[1] and twenty-three other ranks.

Wounded—2nd Lieutenants Geldart, Lucas, and Jewell, and 102 other ranks.

Missing—Four other ranks.

1/5th. Unfortunately the casualties are not entered in the diary.

[1] Both of Royal Warwick attached to 1/4th Norfolk.

From the official list of officers killed it appears that 2nd Lieutenant W. H. Shaw was killed on this day. As above stated, Captain Gardner, Lieutenants Cumberland, Catherell and Pallett all became casualties, and two officers with Captain Gardner (names not mentioned) were missing at Island Wood. The casualties in other ranks were no doubt heavy as in the case of the 1/4th Battalion.

During the rest of November 2nd and all of the 3rd, the enemy's nervousness was shown by a heavy barrage and rifle fire which did no harm. On the 3rd the 1/5th Norfolk began a support trench, with communication trenches, eighty yards behind the captured line, which was consolidated. After dark the 1/4th were withdrawn to the rear, their trenches being taken over by the 5th Suffolk. Consolidation continued till the 7th, on the evening of which day the 163rd brigade concentrated at Marine View, leaving the pursuit of the now retreating enemy to be taken over by the 52nd division.

On the 8th the brigade (leaving the 1/4th Norfolk battalion behind) advanced to Sheikh Hassan.

On the 9th, when "D" company rejoined from the 5th Suffolk, the 1/4th marched to Sheikh Hassan, and by the 20th were on outpost duty on the high ground east of Bariyeh, between Jerusalem and Jaffa. On the 22nd they relieved the mounted division on outposts at Annabeh. From the 24th to the 27th the battalion was at Midieh, where, on the 24th at 8.40 a.m., an enemy cavalry patrol was seen entering Nalin. An hour later three patrols, each consisting of one platoon with a Lewis gun and signallers, were sent out to clear the place. 2nd Lieutenant Lewell, with one platoon of "B" company, went to occupy a hill east of Nalin; 2nd Lieutenant Wood took another platoon of "C" to another hill. On relief by a third platoon, Lewell and Wood were to go forward and clear Nalin, leaving the third platoon to cover their advance. Lewell, having cleared Midieh, moved down the ravine leading to Wadi Kureiha, where he had three men wounded by machine-gun fire, and took up a position. Wood also was fired on as he advanced, and had one non-commissioned officer wounded. He took post on a ridge 500 yards south of the third platoon.

It was now reported by two natives that there were 500 Turks in Nalin. This being confirmed by observation, the three patrols were ordered to keep their present positions till evening, and then retire to the outpost line. Two men, sent out by Wood to ascertain how many of the enemy were on the hill in front of him, were wounded by bombs. At 5 p.m. the three patrols returned, the casualties being one man believed killed, 2nd Lieutenant Lewell and five other ranks wounded.

On the 28th Shilta was occupied before daybreak by "B" company, as a company of the 1/5th had not turned up as promised. When it did arrive it took over Shilta.

At 3.30 p.m. the 1/4th received orders to assist the 155th brigade on the right in attack.

Shilta was now held by 2nd Lieutenant Gordon of the 1/5th, with his own men and some of the Royal Scots. Here he was attacked by 200 or 300 Turks with bombs and compelled to retire with the remains of his men to a hill 800 yards to the south-west. This exposed the right flank of the 1/4th, which had to be protected by moving up (at 7.30 p.m.) "B" company from support. At 1.30 a.m. on the 29th it was ascertained that 2nd Lieutenant Gordon (1/5th Norfolk) had fifty-three men and two Lewis guns, but very little ammunition. A supply was sent up to him. It was also ascertained that the 153rd brigade was arranging to take over from the 1/5th Norfolk and "B" company of the 1/4th.

The casualties of the Norfolk battalions in this affair were:

1/4th. Two other ranks wounded.
1/5th. One officer and twenty-seven other ranks missing, and six other ranks wounded.

The account in the brigade diary states that the company in Shilta was surprised and driven out. It made two counter attacks, both of which failed. After hanging on to the skirt of the village for some time, it retired south-west to the hill. The 155th brigade had been sent up to fill a gap on the right of the 163rd, which was to assist it as far as possible. All that was possible was to hold on to Shilta, and it was for this reason that the company of the 1/5th Norfolk was sent there.

The 163rd brigade, on December 1st, took over from the 162nd about Deir Turief, where it remained carrying out minor changes of position and patrols.

On December 9th Jerusalem surrendered to Sir E. Allenby, who entered it on the 11th, when the Norfolk battalions on the left of his line were engaged with the enemy. Early that morning a patrol of the 1/4th ascertained that the Turks were still holding the position known as Stone Heap Hill and the adjacent hills. At 5.30 a.m. another patrol came into collision with the enemy occupying Cistern Hill, and was ordered to retire as best it might, as the Turks were threatening an attack on Zephiziyeh Hill. They were shelling it, and " C " company of the 1/4th Norfolk who held it.

At 8 a.m. this company was in great peril, as a heavy attack on it was developing from the direction of Cistern Hill, directed specially on the north side of Zephiziyeh Hill from Et Tireh. By 9 a.m. the enemy, 300 or 400 strong, had got within bombing distance of " C 's " position and were working round its right flank. Some of them had succeeded in passing the " sangars " and had nearly reached the summit of the hill. Succour was now at hand in the shape of " B " company, which, at 8 a.m., had been sent forward to a supporting position on the rearward slope of the hill. It was now brought up into line, and, led by its commander, Captain Flatt, charged with the bayonet. Before them the Turks gave way at once, and were pursued over the " sangars " down the hill and towards Cistern Hill, where they were followed by machine-gun fire, causing them very heavy losses. In one place alone thirty of their dead were seen.

The 1/4th Norfolk also suffered severely. Captain T. E. A. Jennings and 2nd Lieutenant A. G. Wood were killed, with twelve other ranks. Captain N. M. Smith, Captain H. W. Flatt, and 2nd Lieutenant W. L. Gowing were wounded, the first and third of these afterwards dying of their wounds. Thirty-six other ranks were wounded, of whom five died later, and one man was wounded and missing. Special commendation for their conduct in this affair is given in the official account, to Sir T. Berney commanding on the hill, to 2nd Lieutenant Dean, who with part of " B " company drove the Turks from their lodgment on the south-east slope, and to Corporal Bindley, Lance-Corporal Painter, and Private Merryweather.

During December 13th and 14th preparations were made for an attack on Stone Heap Hill, in which the 1/4th Norfolk was in front, supported by " A " and " C " companies of the 1/5th.

Stone Heap Hill is described as a rocky feature overlooking the plain on the west, and flanked on the south-east by a similar hill known as Sanger's Hill. These two were joined by a rocky saddle 200 or 300 yards long. From the west point of Stone Heap Hill there ran, nearly due south, a spur stretching almost to the village of Deir Turief and ending in olive groves surrounding its foot. Between this spur and Sanger's Hill was a fairly deep depression, forming a watercourse which joined a Wadi at the edge of the olive groves.

The attack of the 1/4th began at 8 a.m. on December 15th, with " D " company on the right, " A " on the left, " C " in support, and " B " in reserve. It started from the point of assembly, in a cactus garden, about 1,600 yards south-west of Stone Heap Hill and on the north-west of Deir Turief. The left of the battalion was directed on the spur, the centre and right extending across the watercourse valley. It at once encountered heavy machine-gun fire from Stone Heap Hill, and from Sanger's Hill on its right flank.

It was necessary to hurry across the open space, and the crest of the objective was reached almost at charging pace. The supports, coming up behind the centre, enabled the right to swing round against the rocky saddle, from which the Turks were firing heavily on its right flank. The saddle was quickly cleared and, the 5th Suffolk having gained Sanger's Hill, the enemy was dislodged from the whole position and driven northwards.

Consolidation was at once commenced, but had to be kept behind the natural features to avoid heavy shrapnel fire from an enemy battery at short range. In the afternoon orders were received to storm a small round hill, 600 or 800 yards north of Stone Heap Hill, overlooking Et Tireh village. For this purpose two companies of the 1/5th Norfolk were sent up from brigade reserve. Of these, one company and two platoons advanced, with the other two platoons in reserve on Stone Heap

Hill. The way led along a narrow ridge connecting the two hills and exposed to fire from three sides. Thanks to a very efficient barrage, the objective was reached with a loss of only two killed and seven wounded, though a heavy shell fire was directed on the attackers, who held on to their capture without further loss till evening. The casualties of the 1/4th Norfolk were:

Killed—2nd Lieutenant B. T. W. Davenport and eleven other ranks.

Wounded—2nd Lieutenants Knowles, Hole, and another officer whose name is not given, and sixty-five other ranks.

These losses were out of six officers and 219 other ranks engaged in the actual attack.

Captain King is specially commended for cool leading. Sergeant S. Beale is mentioned as having captured a machine-gun single-handed and killed the two Turks working it; also for great courage in attending to the wounded under fire. Sergeant Wardropper and Privates Bates, King, and Andrews are also specially noticed.

The 1/5th Norfolk on this day lost two other ranks killed and seven wounded, all in the attack on the round hill.

(*d*) 1918 : PALESTINE

During the first five months of 1918 there is little or nothing to record regarding either battalion. The British line remained practically unchanged, running from a few miles north of Jericho, Jerusalem, and Jaffa to the sea. Training and preparation for the final battle on the Palestine front was actively going on all the time, but there was no fighting to mention, and both battalions were growing gradually in strength as they received reinforcements. There was the usual trench routine. In June matters were somewhat more lively, and the 1/4th Norfolk carried out a couple of rather extensive raids. On the night of the 8th–9th "C" and "D" companies started out at 7.30 p.m., under command of Captain Jewson, M.C., reaching their point of deployment at 9.10. Ten minutes later they advanced up the Bureid Ridge north-westwards, and swept along it without discovering any enemy or defences. They returned by the Wadi Haram, at 11 p.m., without loss.

On the night of the 18th–19th there was a " driving raid " by " A " company, under Captain Steel and 2nd Lieutenants Camilleri and Funnell. The party started at 7.45 p.m., reaching Wadi Rabah at 9.30. Three whistles sounded, and lights shown in the Turkish trenches on the slopes of Kayak Tepe, warned them that they were discovered. Nevertheless, though they heard an enemy patrol moving, they pressed on to the deployment point, where they faced due east and moved up the slopes of Kayak Tepe. There they were met by a heavy fire (including at least three automatic rifles) from Kayak Tepe and Jevis Tepe. Pushing on for the enemy's " sangars " they took the first lot, bayoneting fifteen Turks, of whom Lance-Corporal Duke claimed five to his own bayonet.

They now turned to the right against the next " sangar." Here they ran into wire which had to be cut with nippers. Only Sergeant Jobson succeeded in cutting a small gap.

The party was now under a heavy fire from the front, from machine-guns on Jevis Tepe, and from some Turks who had come up in the rear by the Wadi Rabah. 2nd Lieutenant Funnell, who was the only unwounded officer remaining, seeing the futility of waiting to cut the wire, began to move down the slope of Kayak Tepe. A party was organized by C.S.M. Covell to cover the retreat, and Sergeant Rickwood, M.M., with a small party, went out three times to gather up the wounded. He succeeded in bringing in all but two. 2nd Lieutenant Funnel had meanwhile called for a cover of artillery fire, which it was hoped had caused loss to the Turks.

The remains of the raiders got back with a good deal of useful information, but not without considerable losses.

Captain S. J. Steel and one man were killed at the wire; 2nd Lieutenant Camilleri was wounded early in the advance; fourteen other ranks were wounded, and two were missing, of whom one was known to be wounded.

On June 27th both the Norfolk battalions were moved to Ludd under orders to entrain for Kantara. The 1/4th were sent back to

Surafend before entraining, but the 1/5th had actually entrained and proceeded some distance before their orders were cancelled and they also were sent back to Surafend.

During these months the 1/5th had had even less excitement than the 1/4th. On the night of May 29th–30th an enemy patrol approached the post on the right held by " A " company, but was driven off by rifle fire and a Stokes mortar. The same thing occurred later in the night on the front held by " C ."

Nothing remarkable happened on the front of either battalion in July or August, or up till September 19th, when Allenby's final advance began.

For the great advance on September 19th the general idea for the 21st corps, to which the 163rd brigade now belonged, was to capture the enemy's defences between the foothills and the sea, and then to wheel to the right and advance eastwards into the hills. Rapid movement by the infantry was essential, and it was specially ordered that the main objective was to be adhered to, and there was to be no embarking on side shows. Commanding officers were expected to take risks in following up the general line of advance. The front of the corps, after the wheel, would be on a north and south line, from Wadi Deir Ballut to the Tul Keram-Messudieh road.

The 54th division had on its right the French battalions, which were now in the field on this front, in the centre the 163rd brigade, on the left the 162nd. The route of the 163rd was to be by Wadi Orwell and Ikba, so as to allow the French to use the Deben Wadi. On the left of the 54th was the Lahore division.

At 2 a.m. on the 19th the 1/5th Norfolk, who on this occasion were to head the attack (less " C " company) were ready, and the garrisons of the front trenches were withdrawn to allow the assaulting battalions to pass in front of the British wire, which they did at 3.45. The 163rd brigade had two battalions (1/5th Norfolk and 8th Hants) in first line and the other two (1/4th Norfolk and 5th Suffolk) behind. The companies were distributed under cover on the eastern slopes of Wadi Ikba.

At fifteen minutes after zero " C " company, which had been sent to support the 8th Hants, followed that battalion and received the benefit of the enemy barrage, which passed over it. It cost them a dozen casualties, of which half were due to a single shell. 2nd Lieutenant Wood received wounds of which he died next day.

Captain and Adjutant Walker was wounded as the battalion headquarters moved to a better protected position. So far the Turkish resistance, other than artillery fire, had not been strong. Presently a pause occurred, enabling the men to breakfast and the machine-gun detachment to come up.

At 11.45 the brigade was ordered to make good the high ground and Kh Sirisia. Captain James, with "A" company and two platoons of "D," was sent to do this, and was soon in action against about fifty Turks on a hill. 2nd Lieutenant Lovell had been pushed forward with a Lewis gun to a Wadi, whence he was endeavouring to keep down the enemy's fire. Working round the hill, he eventually occupied it, and, as Captain James had been wounded, he found himself in command of the company, which he brought up by the Wadi on to the ridge, from which the Turks retreated. The advance was now eastwards, with the French on the right and the 1/4th Norfolk on the left. It continued till stopped by darkness. The men were dead beat and suffering from thirst; nevertheless, Mesha was occupied before dawn by "B" and half of "D" companies under Captain Blyth, and held till they were relieved, at 3.10 a.m. on the 20th, by "C," who had been freshened up by a supply of water. At 4.15 p.m. that day the battalion was relieved and went back to the rear. The casualties in the 1/5th seem to have been limited to the two officers above mentioned, and about fourteen other ranks. The Turks had got away without waiting for the attack, and all the Norfolk casualties were due to artillery. The 1/4th Norfolk had none, though they helped in "a long and arduous pursuit over a most mountainous and difficult country."

With this early stage of Sir E. Allenby's Napoleonic battle fighting was at an end for the 1/4th and 1/5th Norfolk battalions. It is unnecessary to name the various places through which the battalions passed on their northward march. They were at Beirut in the first days of November, and remained in that neighbourhood till the 28th, when they embarked for Egypt. They disembarked, on the 30th, at Kantara, the

1/4th with twenty-three officers and 584 other ranks, and the 1/5th with thirty officers and 461 other ranks. From Kantara they entrained for Helmieh near Cairo, where, when we part from them on December 31, 1918, the 1/4th had an effective strength of forty officers and 923 other ranks, the 1/5th of thirty-three officers and 755 other ranks.

THE 2/4TH (RESERVE) BATTALION (LATER THE 11TH BATTALION)

For this battalion we cannot do better than quote the account of its doings in the Great War supplied by Brevet-Colonel Edward Mornement, C.B.E., T.D., late the Norfolk Regiment T.F. and Royal Engineers, who commanded it. He writes:

" In August, 1914, orders were issued to County Territorial Force Associations by Lord Kitchener to maintain the Territorial Force at home stations at the full strength of its establishment, by raising new units to replace the Territorial Units which volunteered for general service with the expeditionary forces.

" The rôle of the newly raised units was:

" (1) to supply drafts for overseas units.

" (2) to continue recruiting up to the establishment for home defence, the personnel being enlisted under two classifications, viz. for general service overseas, and for home defence only."

" 1914. The 4th (Reserve) Battalion the Norfolk Regiment T.F. was raised in September, 1914, by Major Edward Mornement, T.D., who was promoted Lieutenant-Colonel in October, 1914, and appointed to command the unit.

" The Drill Hall, Chapel Field, Norwich, was the head-quarters of the unit, which was chiefly recruited from South and East Norfolk and Norwich, in which city the men were billeted with subsistence on the inhabitants.

" During the months of August, September, and October, 1914, upwards of 700 rank and file, mostly ex-service men, enlisted from the National Reserve, and ex-Militia men were posted to the 4th Battalion the Norfolk Regiment.

"On the formation of the 2nd East Anglian Division T.F. under Major General W. F. Cavaye, the battalion, being the first to complete its establishment, moved to divisional head-quarters at Peterborough in November, 1914, and was billeted with subsistence on the inhabitants, uniform and equipment being issued.

"1915. The battalion was moved to Lowestoft in January, 1915, with orders to co-operate with the officer commanding the Naval Base (Captain A. A. Ellison), and shortly afterwards was renamed the 2/4th Battalion Norfolk Regiment T.F. An extensive system of fortification was carried out on the north, south, and west of the town, and hard field training proceeded with. Japanese .275 rifles were issued, and 80,000 rounds of ammunition. A battery of 12-pounder naval field guns was loaned to the battalion by the O.C. Naval Base, who also lent Petty-Officer Gunners R.N. who trained eighty rank and file of the battalion in gunnery. Very remarkable efficiency in sea-target practice was attained, and the guns always accompanied the battalion on night operations.

"By an ingenious method of constructing gun-pits and anti-recoil gear, the 12-pounder battery was adapted for high angle fire against aircraft. It is believed this is the first instance on record of guns (without high angle mountings) being used for this purpose.

"The same naval instructors also trained 200 non-commissioned officers and men in machine-gunnery with naval machine-guns. No Lewis guns had at this time been issued to territorial reserve training battalions.

"The battalion also provided the personnel for the naval searchlights, and for No. 2 armoured train, which operated on the railways of East Anglia.

"In July, 1915, the battalion was divided into :—

"(A) General Service category.

"(B) Home Service of lower medical categories.

"The former retained the name 2/4th Battalion the Norfolk

Regiment T.F. and moved to Bury St. Edmunds under command of Lieutenant-Colonel G. Woodwark, and the latter, having absorbed the low category men of the 5th Battalion Norfolk Regiment T.F., became the 61st provisional battalion T.F. under the command of Lieutenant-Colonel E. Mornement, T.D., and continued to garrison Lowestoft.

"During 1915 Lowestoft suffered severely from Zeppelin raids, and casualties occurred among the civilian inhabitants and the battalion. One boarding house in which twenty-eight men of the latter were billeted was demolished.

"In September, 1915, having completed the defences of Lowestoft, the 61st provisional battalion moved to the Bawdsey-Hollesley-Orford coast defence section, covering the northern defences of Harwich and Felixstowe, where extensive field fortifications were constructed. The head-quarters of the battalion was at Bawdsey Manor.

"At this period the battalion was brigaded with the 29th and 30th City of London Battalion T.F. under the command of Brigadier-General Westrope, with brigade head-quarters at Saxmundham, Suffolk, and formed part of the southern army under General the Rt. Hon. Sir A. H. Paget, G.C.B., K.C.V.O.

"During the winter 1915–1916 large numbers of category "B" recruits (late Derby groups) were posted to the battalion, and drafts of the Notts and Derby and North Staffords were attached for training, also many men, invalided from the various theatres of war, were transferred to the battalion, large drafts of category "A" men being posted to the overseas forces.

"1916. In March, 1916, the battalion was transferred to the northern army, under General Sir H. E. Smith-Dorrien, G.C.B., G.C.M.G., D.S.O., and moved to the Easton-Benacre-Kessington coast defence section with the head-quarters at Wrentham, Suffolk, and was again brought up to establishment with large drafts of category "B" and "C" recruits, mostly from the south and west of England.

"About November, 1916, the name of the battalion was changed to the 11th Battalion the Norfolk Regiment, T.F.

"In December, 1916, the battalion was transferred to the 212th brigade, 71st division, and moved to the Aldershot command. It was stationed at Guildford.

"1917. In March, 1917, the 71st division moved to Colchester and the 11th Norfolk occupied Sobraon Barracks and Meanee Barracks respectively. The few remaining category "A" and "B 1" men were transferred to over-seas units, and the battalion, being now composed of wounded, sick, and low category men generally, ceased to be a mobile field unit, and in the absence of further able-bodied recruits its function as a training reserve battalion ceased, and in consequence, by order of the Army Council, was disbanded in July, 1917. The personnel were discharged as medically unfit for further military service, or absorbed in garrison battalions, labour corps, or agricultural companies.

"It is worthy to be placed on record that as a training reserve and coastal defence unit the excellent service rendered by this battalion was highly commended by all the army, divisional, and brigade commanders under whom it served.

"A marked absence of crime and a high sense of discipline and esprit de corps, together with general efficiency, were characteristics of the battalion, which was most popular with the inhabitants of every town in which it was stationed.

"Some thousands of officers and men were transferred to units in the various theatres of war, and gained much distinction by their meritorious conduct, many of whom made the supreme sacrifice. It may be claimed that during its strenuous three years existence the battalion maintained the best traditions of the Norfolk Regiment."

THE 2/5TH BATTALION NORFOLK REGIMENT

By October, 1914, it became evident that the territorial army would have to be largely expanded. Recruits were coming in in large numbers, a very good class of men, but still only enlisted for home service. There were at this time about 400 or 500 men at the Depôt at East Dereham under the O.C. Depôt, who could, of course, not cope with this number with only one instructor permanent staff to assist him.

Captain (later Lieutenant-Colonel) G. Woodwark was appointed O.C. Depôt and two junior officers—2nd Lieutenants St. George and R. G. Cubitt—to assist him.

Major H. Ellis Rowell was gazetted Lieutenant-Colonel on October 3, 1914, and given command of the New 2/5th Battalion at East Dereham (then called the Reserve Battalion). This officer left the 1/5th Battalion at Colchester about the end of October for East Dereham, together with Lieutenant H. A. Durrant and 2nd Lieutenants C. Durrant, Blyth, Shakespeare, and Greenstreet, the last four having only just joined the 1/5th.

The men were immediately divided up into provisional companies and intensive training began in earnest. The troops were billeted in the town at the rate of 2/6 a day.

There were no rifles or equipment, and only a few N.C.O.'s were in uniform, but the zeal and enthusiasm of the men were extraordinary. No amount of work seemed too much, and the discipline was splendid, the O.C. rarely having a "crime." The fine band of the 1/5th, under Bandmaster Dines, was a great asset. Many officers were given commissions, including Lieutenants Ferrier, Hervey, L. Shutes, Partridge, Archdale, Hemsworth, and joined the battalion before it left for Peterborough. Sir Aylwin Fellows, the Chairman of the Norfolk T.F. Association (now Lord Aylwin), visited the head-quarters and gave leave for the O.C. to buy boots and what uniform could be procured for the troops; this was done and the association paid the bills. The only khaki that could be procured was second-hand, and this, together with overcoats (also part worn), had to do until the Government provided new ones later on. The association provided a full kit of underclothing, vests, pants, etc., etc., all very good and new.

On December 5, 1914, the battalion was ordered to proceed to Peterborough, where it came under the divisional command of Major-General Cavaye, the brigade commander being Brigadier-General Bodle, C.M.G. The men lived in billets. Early in January, 1915, a recruiting march was made through Norfolk, visiting the principal towns. The band and a picked company of men were under two or three officers and N.C.O.'s. This resulted in obtaining a great number of very fine recruits, who joined the battalion at Peterborough, bringing the battalion up to full strength. The O.C. was by special permission allowed to recruit 10 per cent over. It seemed a pity to stop recruiting, as another battalion could at that time have been raised, such was the patriotism. A great many junior officers joined here, and the battalion was thoroughly organized into four very strong companies under Captains T. B. Hall, G. Bracey, H. Smith, and H. A. Durrant.

On leaving East Dereham, Captain Woodwark resigned the post of O.C. Depôt and became the first adjutant of the 2/5th battalion. Lieutenant Adcock was quartermaster and Sergeant Crosbie regimental sergeant-major, with Lieutenant-Col. H. Ellis Rowell in command.

The battalion was quartered in Peterborough until May, 1915, when it proceeded to Cambridge. Here it remained until the end of July. It was during this time that all the home-service men were sent away, leaving the battalion with 800 Imperial-service men and all the officers. Major Woodwark also left to command the 2/4th Battalion. Captain Bracey became adjutant, and Captain H. A. Durrant assistant adjutant and instructor of musketry, this officer gaining a distinguished certificate at Hythe.

It should be mentioned that the battalion was suitably clothed and supplied with the Japanese rifle while in Peterborough, and the whole battalion was put through its musketry course at Grantham Range. At the end of July, 1915, the battalion marched to Bury St. Edmunds, stopping one night at Newmarket. After five days at Bury St. Edmunds they went into camp at Thetford.

After about a month in camp it proceeded to Brentwood in Essex for three weeks, and took part in the defensive scheme of London, digging trenches, etc. It then returned to Bury St. Edmunds for the winter.

It was at Brentwood that the first lot of junior officers left for Gallipoli to take the place of those lost in the 1/5th—2nd Lieutenants St. George, C. Durrant, C. G. S. Rowell, Hervey, Blyth, Shakespeare, Hemsworth, Hordle, L. Shutes, Partridge, Lyall, and Plaistowe.

When the first Zeppelin raid took place over London it was distinctly seen and heard at Brentwood.

In March, 1915, a bad raid took place over Bury St. Edmunds, when nine civilians and one soldier were killed, but there were no casualties in the 2/5th Norfolk.[1]

THE 3/5TH BATTALION NORFOLK REGIMENT

This battalion was formed in the early part of 1915 under the command of Colonel G. Cresswell, C.V.O., V.D., and was quartered at Dereham till August 1st, when it moved to Windsor and was encamped in the Great Park. In the first week of October, 1915, it moved to huts in the camp at Halton near Tring. Thence it sent out many drafts to the 1/5th in the East.

In February, 1916, Colonel Fletcher took over the command, and shortly afterwards the 3/4th and 3/5th Battalions were amalgamated and moved to Sussex.[2]

---

[1] The above account was supplied almost verbatim by Lieutenant-Colonel H. Ellis Rowell, T.D., commanding the battalion.

[2] Information supplied by Colonel Cresswell.

CHAPTER V

THE 1/6TH AND 2/6TH (TERRITORIAL) BATTALIONS NORFOLK REGIMENT

THE following account of the 6th Battalion Norfolk Regiment was kindly contributed by Colonel B. H. L. Prior, D.S.O., who commanded the battalion before the war and on its mobilization in 1914. Later (1916) Colonel Prior joined and assumed command of the 9th Battalion the Norfolk Regiment. During the war he was four times wounded, and gained the Distinguished Service Order and Bar:

"Under the scheme of Home Defence prevailing in 1914, the observation and patrol of the British coast was entrusted to certain cycle and mounted corps of the Territorial Army. The 6th Battalion was one of the cyclist battalions entrusted with the patrol and observation for the whole of the Norfolk coast, from Wells in the north to Gorleston in the south.

"1914. On mobilization in 1914 the various companies of the 6th Battalion paraded at their peace stations and proceeded by road to their war stations. All war stations were occupied on the night of mobilization, a fact which emphasizes the efficiency of the battalion. When the battalion was mobilized it was nearly at its established strength, the deficiencies being made up almost entirely by the rush of ex-members of the corps to re-enlist.

"During the first few months of the war there appeared every probability of the enemy attempting a raid on the Norfolk coast. The concentration of troops in the Eastern Counties was heavy, and the 6th Battalion acted as eyes and ears to a very considerable force.

"When volunteers for service overseas were called for, the battalion made a splendid response, all the officers and over 90 per cent of the other ranks signing on for active service. Towards the end of 1914 a second battalion was formed, being raised almost entirely by the recruiting efforts of the 1/6th Battalion. The 2/6th Battalion was almost immediately sent to Bridlington, where it undertook similar coast defence duties on the Yorkshire coast.

"1915. During 1915 the 1/6th Battalion was composed entirely of foreign service "A 1" men, who offered to go abroad as cyclists, infantry, pioneers, or in any other capacity; but they were officially informed that the coast defence duties entrusted to them were too important for them to be spared. Towards the end of 1915, however, the 1/6th Battalion was relieved of the greater part of the coast defence duties, and retired a few miles inland as a mobile reserve, and thereafter undertook more consistent training in infantry drill and trench warfare than had hitherto been possible.

"Both the 1/6th and 2/6th Battalions supplied from the ranks an excellent stamp of men for commissioned service with the regular and new armies in the field, the first battalion furnishing some 150 non-commissioned officers and men for this purpose, many of whom did exceptionally well. For example, a lance-corporal who obtained his commission ended up in the war as a brigade-major, having won the D.S.O., M.C., and a foreign decoration.

"1916. In 1915 a small draft had been sent away from the 1/6th Battalion to the divisional cyclists, and this was followed in the spring of 1916 by a draft of six officers and 120 men for service with the Gloucester Regiment. In July, 1916, practically the whole of the remainder of the original 1/6th Battalion, and a very large proportion of the 2/6th Battalion were drafted out to oversea units. The majority of the 1/6th Battalion were posted to the 8th Battalion the Norfolk Regiment, and most of the 2/6th Battalion were sent to the 1st Battalion the Norfolk Regiment. The others were distributed to the various units in France.

"From this date the identity of both the 1st and 2/6th Battalions as a Norfolk unit practically ceased to exist. Both

HISTORY OF THE NORFOLK REGIMENT

battalions were filled up with low category men and became draft-finding units with home defence duties. The 1/6th Battalion was subsequently transferred to Ireland, and the 2/6th Battalion remained in Yorkshire.

"During the period, August, 1914–July, 1916, neither battalion had actual contact with the enemy other than occasional shots at the Zeppelin raiders. Nevertheless, their patrol work, especially that of the 1st Battalion during the winter, 1914, was exceptionally hard. Some notable feats of endurance were performed, of which one example may be cited. In the early part of 1916 the 1/6th Battalion was ordered to furnish a platoon to take over from the London Cyclists at Kessingland in Suffolk. On relief, this platoon (comprising men recruited at Thetford), under the command of Lieutenant Fison, rode back from Kessingland to North Walsham, a distance of fully fifty miles, in the teeth of a heavy snowstorm and over roads in a shocking condition. They accomplished the complete journey at a uniform pace of seven miles per hour, and with only one casualty. The magnitude of this feat will be apparent to all those who know the Norfolk coast roads and the effect of snow and a north-easterly head wind. When it is remembered that each man carried a rifle with a full complement of equipment and ammunition, besides pack and great coat, it speaks volumes for the condition and state of efficiency the battalion had attained as military cyclists.

"It will always remain the deep and lasting regret of all ranks of the original 6th Battalion that they were not permitted to take part in the Great War as a unit.

"The splendid feats of many individual members of the battalion, coupled with the magnificent reputation earned by each draft, and the splendid esprit de corps shown by all ranks, would have earned for it a splendid reputation on the field of battle."

There appears to have been also a 3/6th Battalion formed at Norwich, and commanded at first by Lieutenant-Colonel Barnham, but no information regarding it has been furnished.

CHAPTER VI

THE 7TH (SERVICE) BATTALION IN FRANCE

(a) 1914–1915 : ORGANIZATION—ST. ELOI—GIVENCHY

THE 7th (Service) Battalion was the first of the "Kitchener" battalions of the regiment to be formed—at Shorncliffe. By August 22, 1914, it was at full strength of about 1,000 men. The composition of the battalion was somewhat mixed. "D" company and half of "C" consisted of London men, who, in the press of work, had been sent down to Norwich to be attested. There were also men from Lancashire and elsewhere, so that it may be said that about half the battalion only were Norfolk men. As with other battalions, there was at first a great shortage of equipment available. For months the men had no rifles; many were short of boots and uniform. The formation of the battalion had been assisted by sending to it a few non-commissioned officers from the first battalion and Depôt, under the command of Lieutenant-Colonel J. W. V. Carroll, and the adjutant, Captain R. T. H. Reynolds, both from the Depôt.

At Shorncliffe the battalion was quartered in barracks with the 7th Suffolk Regiment; but, as the accommodation was short, two companies had to be kept under canvas on Sir John Moore's Plain till January 1, 1915. The weather being then very bad, the battalion was moved into billets at New Romney and Littlestone-on-Sea, with the exception of "B" company, which occupied Dymchurch and the redoubt.

On February 15th the battalion was equipped with the new leather

American equipment in place of the web one. The march to Aldershot, starting on February 23rd, via Ashford, Maidstone, Sevenoaks, Redhill, Leatherhead, and Woking, ended at Aldershot on March 1st, after a very trying time of very bad weather, borne most creditably by all ranks. At Leatherhead the battalion on the march passed Lord Kitchener. At Aldershot the battalion was quartered in the Malplaquet Barracks, which they shared with the 5th Royal Berkshire Regiment.

The training of the battalion in musketry and an advanced course was continued, though much hampered by an epidemic of measles and by shortage of rifles. The men were sometimes at Aldershot, sometimes in billets at Wokingham, till they were reviewed by Lord Kitchener with other battalions of the new army. They had had a longer period of training than some other battalions, and were impatient to be off to the front, when, at last, on May 30, 1915, they entrained for Folkestone. There they embarked on the "Invicta" for Boulogne, whence, on the 31st, they entrained for Lumbres via St. Omer. Their strength was thirty officers and 954 other ranks, besides transport. The officers were:

Lieutenant-Colonel J. W. V. Carroll.

Majors J. C. Atkinson and F. E. Walter.

Captains R. Otter, A. R. Fellows, P. C. Preston, M. J. Tuck, G. B. Johnson, J. Hammond, R. Gethen, J. M. Howlett, J. Tilley.

Lieutenants F. G. Keppel, H. L. F. A. Gielgud, C. E. Proctor, O. C. Harvey, A. P. Green, H. R. G. Montgomery, T. A. Buckland.

2nd Lieutenants A. N. Charlton, L. C. Borthwick, L. C. Drenon, J. A. G. Wharton, H. V. Franklin, H. S. Curwen, J. K. Digby, H. V. Carley.

Adjutant, Captain R. T. H. Reynolds.

Quartermaster, Hon. Lieutenant F. W. Frost.

The battalion still found it had a good deal of training to do—practice in trench digging, instruction in trench warfare, and other things which could be learnt better at the front than in England. It belonged to the 35th brigade (commanded by Brigadier-General C. H. C. van Straubenzee) of the 12th division (commanded by Major-General

Wing),[1] the other battalions of the brigade being the 7th Suffolk, 9th Essex, and 5th Royal Berkshire Regiments.

The Norfolk Regiment was represented on the staff of the 35th brigade by Major S. J. P. Scobell, a regular officer holding the appointment of brigade-major, and by Captain A. Scott-Murray, who, from 2nd Lieutenant in the 7th Battalion, was promoted to staff captain.

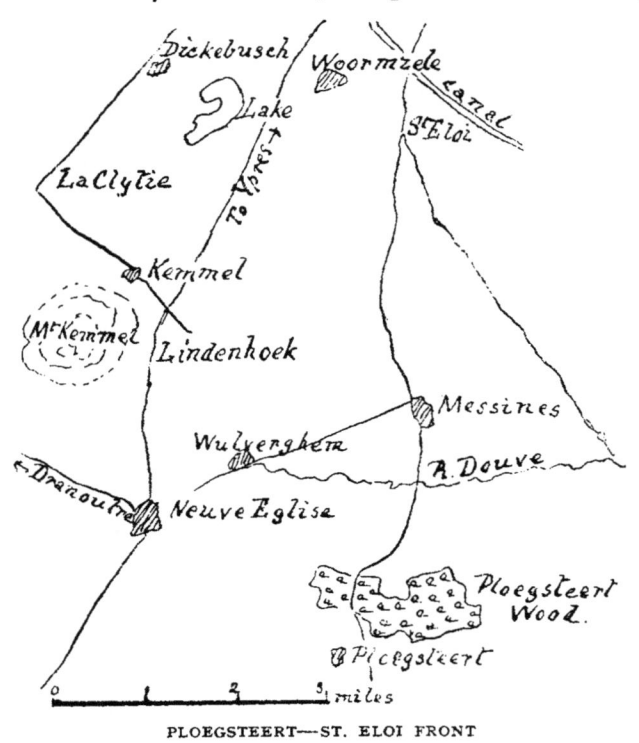

PLOEGSTEERT—ST. ELOI FRONT

After being at various places the 7th Norfolk battalion at last found themselves at the front, where they took over trenches Nos. 113–120 from the Royal West Kent Regiment at Ploegsteert Wood on July 4, 1915. The Royal Canadians were on their left, and there was some mining and shelling and a great deal of very destructive sniping going on. For the rest of the month the Norfolk battalion were alternately

[1] The division had been commanded for a short time at Shorncliffe by Major-General Spens.

relieving and being relieved by the 5th Royal Berks in the same trenches. Their casualties during the month were five men killed, one officer (Lieutenant G. E. Proctor), and twenty-two other ranks wounded.

On August 4th 2nd Lieutenant Digby was killed in throwing a bomb with a trench catapult. August was much the same as July, with plenty of hard work in trench making and wiring. The casualties of the month were two officers and five other ranks killed; twenty other ranks wounded, of whom twelve were due to heavy bombardment on the 16th. Lieutenant-Colonel Carroll having been promoted to command a brigade, Major J. C. Atkinson temporarily commanded the battalion till it was taken over, on October 8th, by Major F. E. Walter. On September 20th the battalion bombers successfully stopped the work of a German party, and on the 26th the trenches were given over to the 3rd Canadians, when the 35th brigade marched for the neighbourhood of Loos. There, on the 30th, the Norfolk battalion occupied some shallow and disconnected trenches at Philosophe, on the left of the French, "D" company holding a chalk pit. The early days of October saw much heavy German shelling. Between the 1st and 4th the battalion lost by this eleven men killed and fifty-seven wounded, and on the 8th Lieutenant A. P. Green and twelve men of "D" company were wounded by a single long range shell. On the 12th the Norfolk battalion moved from billets to take over the line in front of the quarries near St. Elie, then held by the Coldstream Guards. The line held was roughly semi-circular, the left extremity, on St. Elie Avenue, being close up to a German trench forming the chord.

Next day the 35th brigade was told off to attack. The attack was to be made under cover of a smoke cloud, and the part assigned to the 7th Norfolk Regiment was to close in along the German trench from either end of their semicircle, thus straightening out their line on the chord. The left of the battalion would also bomb along a communication trench running back opposite to it from the German front trench.

Before the attack of the 13th Major-General Wing had been killed, along with his A.D.C., by a shell, and was succeeded in command of the 12th division by Major-General A. B. Scott, C.B., D.S.O.

The British bombardment began at noon, and by 1.45 was intensive, but the smoke screen went wrong, and by some error was stopped at 1.40 p.m. The left of the Norfolk battalion had begun bombing with the object of meeting the bombers from the right, and also of clearing the German communication trench. The 6th Buffs were now on the right and the Suffolk battalion on the left of the 7th Norfolk. Owing to the failure of the smoke screen, the Germans could be clearly seen manning their trenches when the attack was launched at 2 p.m. The Norfolk battalion soon began to suffer severely from a German machine gun opposite their right, enfilading their attack, which our trench mortars were unable to knock out. Its fire almost annihilated one squad as it tried to get through. On the left fifty men succeeded in taking 200 yards of the enemy trench and held on there till the exhaustion of their supply of bombs forced them to retire till reinforced by " A " company and half of the Royal Berkshire.

Meanwhile, bombers under 2nd Lieutenant Franklin had penetrated some distance along both the main trench and the communication trench and had blocked both. " B " company, endeavouring to follow the Berkshire battalion, were impeded by the confusion in the trench and by the Berkshire bombers being held up. Further reinforcements it was impossible to send, as they were mown down by the machine gun in the first twenty yards. The casualties in this, the battalion's first serious fight, had been very heavy. Five officers were killed or died of wounds, and six were wounded. Of other ranks sixty-six were killed, 196 wounded, and 160 missing.

The officer casualties were :
Killed—Captain Preston ; Lieutenants Buckland and Tucker ; 2nd Lieutenants Carley and Curwen.
Wounded—Captains Tuck, Gethen, Howlett and Otter; Lieutenant Green and 2nd Lieutenant Wharton.

On the 14th the Norfolk battalion was withdrawn to the old British line, from Fosse Way to Hulluch Road, where they were shelled all day. Drafts of 263 men between the 15th and 17th replaced in part the losses of the 13th, and on the 19th the battalion stood to, but was not called up to repulse a German counter-attack on the quarries taken on the previous day by the brigade bombers. They went back to billets in

Béthune on the 20th, where they were inspected by Major-General Scott, who congratulated them on their exploits of the 13th.

Their next move was on the 26th to Vermelles, which was now in the back area near the Béthune-Lens road. They moved into front line on the 31st and spent all November at various places in the neighbourhood, or at Béthune. At the end of the month their strength was twenty-four officers and 863 other ranks. They seem to have moved about more than some battalions in December, on the 15th of which month they took over the front line from the 6th Royal West Kent Regiment on the left of Givenchy Church. They stood to during the gas attack of the 2nd Division on the 21st December, but were not called up to fight, and on the 27th they were in front of Festubert, where they ended the year with a strength of twenty-eight officers and 963 other ranks. Brigadier-General A. Solly Flood now commanded the brigade in succession to Brigadier-General van Straubenzee, and held the post for a long time. He took over the command some time after the attack of October 13th.

(b) 1916: HOHENZOLLERN REDOUBT—THE SOMME—OVILLERS—RIDGE TRENCH—BAYONET TRENCH

January and February, 1916, were passed in the usual routine of trench warfare till, on February 29th, the battalion relieved the 9th Essex in the quarries on the right of the brigade front a little south of the famous Hohenzollern redoubt, where, on March 2nd, the 36th brigade, on the left of the 35th, after firing three mines, attacked across the open. During this the Norfolk trenches were considerably damaged by German shells, which continued heavily on the 3rd. A thaw set in on the 5th after a period of snow and frost.

On February 18th, the Hohenzollern Redoubt, then held by the 37th brigade, was counter-attacked by the enemy. At 6.18 p.m. the Norfolk battalion was ordered to stand to, and a few minutes later was placed under the orders of the 37th brigade and posted in Lancashire trenches. Next day they relieved the 6th Buffs in front line, where "B" company held three important craters on the left of the battalion front, with " A " on its right, and " D " and " C " respectively in right and left support. A company of the Suffolk Regiment, under Major Henty, was attached to the Norfolk battalion and placed on the right of " A " company. There was much work to be done on trenches, and German snipers were very active; one of them wounded Captain Reynolds in the head. The corps commander at this time had an elephant gun,[1] which was lent for use on German loopholes, with excellent results.

Nothing very remarkable happened up till April 24th, when the 12th division being relieved in the neighbourhood of the Hohenzollern redoubt, entrained for Lillers, after twelve days in the trenches, which had resulted in two officers being wounded, and of other ranks seven killed and twenty wounded. From Lillers the battalion went to Cauchy, where, on the 27th, it stood to on an alarm of a German gas attack, which was beaten off with heavy loss to the enemy without the Norfolk battalion having to take part.

During May, Colonel F. E. Walter, now commanding the battalion, received the D.S.O., and Lieutenant Franklin received the M.C. for his bombing exploits of October 13th. The first sixteen days of June passed uneventfully in the neighbourhood of Béthune, Annequin, and Noyelles, the battalion being a good deal split up at times for working parties.

At midnight of the 16th-17th the 7th Norfolk battalion entrained at Fouquereuil for the neighbourhood of Amiens, through which they marched next morning to Vignecourt, where they spent the next nine days in practising attacks in preparation for the great offensive on the Somme, which was at first fixed for the 29th, but was postponed till July 1st, on account of wet weather.

On July 1st the 7th Norfolk battalion marched to Hennencourt Wood. At 6.50 p.m. they started again, under orders to occupy the intermediate line of trenches south-west of Albert, ready for an attack on Martinpuich next day, provided the 8th and 34th divisions had got through the German front line system. After an hour's march the plans

[1] This elephant gun, the property of General Hubert Gough, was much cherished, so much so that C.O.'s looked upon its handing over clean and in good order as almost as important as handing over trenches.

were changed. The 8th division had failed to take the villages of Ovillers north and La Boisselle south of the Albert–Bapaume road, and the 12th division would now have to try its hand on them. The 23rd brigade made over its line in front of Ovillers to the 35th, which stood, with the Berkshire, Suffolk, and Essex battalions in front, and the 7th Norfolk in reserve, behind the embankment of the Albert–Arras railway. There they remained till 11.15 p.m. on July 2nd, when they moved into trenches for the attack on Ovillers. La Boisselle had been taken that evening by the 19th division.

At 2 a.m. on July 3rd the 12th division was in position for the attack, which was ordered for 3.15 a.m. The 35th brigade was on the right, the 37th on the left, and the 36th in reserve. In the 35th brigade the Berkshire battalion was in front on the right, the Suffolk on the left, the Essex in support, and the Norfolk in reserve.

As the other battalions advanced in darkness and mist, the 7th Norfolk followed through communication trenches, where they encountered very heavy artillery fire, losing one officer (Captain Tilley) wounded and about one hundred killed or wounded of other ranks. When they wanted bombs the whole of a party bringing them up was wiped out by machine-gun fire. The attack of the leading battalions having failed, the 7th Norfolk battalion was not allowed to attack, but took over the whole brigade front from the other three battalions, which were withdrawn to support for reorganization. These three battalions had suffered fearful casualties—310 in the Berkshire, 356 in the Essex, and 505 in the Suffolk. Holding the line from Dorset Road on the right to Barrow Road on the left the battalion was badly shelled. Colonel Walter was hit by a piece of shell about noon, but remained on duty. During the rest of the day it was quiet on the Ovillers side whilst the 19th division on the right, having been driven from La Boisselle, were again attacking it.

During the night of the 3rd–4th Captain Lucas (R.A.M.C.) disappeared whilst getting in the wounded from between the lines. He appears to have wandered accidentally into the German trenches.

At 10 a.m. on the 4th, and again at 3.30 p.m., a heavy German barrage fell on the trenches, but the Norfolk casualties were only about eight in the twenty-four hours ending at noon on the 4th. At 4 p.m. Colonel Walter's place in the trenches was taken by Captain Ogilby, his second in command. The rest of the day was quiet; more wounded were brought in in the ensuing night, and some work was done in improving the fire trenches.

The 5th was another day of shelling, consequent on a fresh attempt by the 19th division on the rear of Ovillers, and the night of the 5th–6th was employed like the preceding one.

At 3 a.m. the shelling began again; one shell, landing in the bay in which were the head-quarters of "D" company, killed Lieutenant Green and wounded 2nd Lieutenants Allen and O'Donnell. At 2 p.m. on the 6th, on relief by the 36th brigade, the battalion went into intermediate trenches on the Bazincourt–Albert line.

The operations against Ovillers had caused casualties in it as follows:

Killed—Lieutenant A. P. Green and eleven other ranks.

Wounded—Lieutenant-Colonel Walter; Captain Tilley; 2nd Lieutenants Allen and O'Donnell, and eighty-seven other ranks.

Missing—Twenty other ranks.

After this the battalion moved successively to Albert, Varennes, Warincourt Wood, and Authie, at which latter place it was attached to the 4th division for work behind their line, rejoining the 35th brigade when it took over from the 12th brigade of the 4th division at Bertrancourt.

On July 22nd–25th it was in reserve to the front line facing the German position at Beaumont Hamel, where, and at Varennes or Bouzincourt, it passed the rest of the month and the first days of August, chiefly in training.

On August 7th it took over Ovillers, which had been taken during its absence, from the 11th Middlesex of the 36th brigade. "A" and "B" companies were in Ovillers itself, and "C" and "D" behind them, north-east of Albert. The 35th brigade was now holding the line in this sector with the 7th Suffolk and 5th Berkshire battalions in front line, the 7th Norfolk in support, and the 9th Essex in reserve.

On the 8th the Suffolk battalion and the Australians failed in an attack on a German strong point, which they carried next day, after which the Norfolk battalion relieved the Suffolk in the front line. On this day Lieutenant-Colonel Prior of the 1/6th (Cyclist) battalion temporarily joined the 7th.

The line was now facing north-west in and behind 5th Avenue, a trench running south-west from the Pozières trench, which ran north-west from Pozières. "B" company held 5th Avenue, with "C" behind it in the parallel 4th Avenue, "D" in 3rd Avenue, and "A" in Ovillers. The German front line was in 6th Avenue, and their strong point, which had just been taken, was in 8th Street, a communication trench connecting 3rd and 4th Avenues.

There was heavy German shelling on the 10th and 11th, 2nd Lieutenant F. M. B. Case being killed on the former day. The lines were thinned out as far as was safe, but on the 11th 2nd Lieutenants Summerskill and Manners were wounded, and of other ranks thirteen were killed, seventy-six wounded, and three missing between the 9th and the 13th. This was the heaviest shelling the battalion had yet experienced.

Preparations were now being made for an assault on 6th Avenue and trenches on its right. This position is described in the brigade diary as Ridge Trench.

At 10.30 p.m. on the night of August 12th–13th the 12th division, and the 4th Australian Division on its right, attacked on a front of about one mile. The 7th Norfolk was the right battalion of the 12th division, separated by the Pozières trench from the left of the Australians. The 9th Essex were on their left, and their objective was 6th Avenue.

"A" and "D" companies were in front line, "B" and "C" behind, and each company formed two waves of attack. A tape on which to form had been laid in front of 5th Avenue, otherwise known as Ration trench. At zero hour (10.30 p.m.) the advance began under cover of a strong barrage on 6th Avenue. As it lifted the Norfolk battalion pushed on into the German trench, in which, the enemy having been surprised, they encountered no very serious resistance. They captured twenty out of the thirty Germans in it. They at once proceeded to bomb the dug-outs, to consolidate the captured position, and to make strong points. There were few casualties in the actual attack, but several afterwards from German shells in the captured trench. The 9th Essex had been checked at first, but eventually got into the trench in touch with the left company of the Norfolk battalion. By midnight the Norfolk battalion was in communication with the Australians, who had successfully stormed their section; but the 37th brigade, on the left of the 35th, was held up by machine-gun fire and had made little progress. Patrols were sent out but generally stopped by the British barrage. However, one of the Norfolk men and one of the Essex penetrated the German trenches, each of them bringing back three prisoners.

By dawn all the men had been withdrawn from 6th Avenue, except the garrisons of the strong points, in each of which one Lewis gun, one machine gun, and forty men were left. Eighteen Germans of the 29th Regiment had been taken in the attack by the Norfolk battalion, whose casualties were:

Officers: Missing, believed killed—2nd Lieutenant A. A. Goosens.
Wounded: Captain Bennet; 2nd Lieutenants Woodham, Bright-Betton, Potter, and Jackson.

Other ranks: Eight killed, 102 wounded, eighteen missing.

The following order of the day was issued by the brigadier to the officers commanding the 7th Norfolk and 9th Essex battalions:

" Please convey to all ranks of the battalion under your command the brigadier's high appreciation of the way they have comported themselves in the recent operations. Whilst it may be said that the task set was not a hard one, and that the actual infantry fighting was but little, the fact of being able to form up for and execute an assault after the severe shelling they had endured for a night and two days points to soldierly qualities of the highest order."

On August 13th the 12th division was relieved by the 48th and marched for Arras where, on the 16th, it came under the orders of the 6th corps of the 3rd army. Here it relieved the 11th division and stood with all three brigades in line, the 35th on the left with the Suffolk and Berkshire battalions in front, the 7th Norfolk in brigade reserve, and the Essex in divisional reserve. The Norfolk battalion had their head-quarters with " A " and " B " companies in Arras, " C " in Ronville, and " D " in Achicourt. Matters were fairly quiet here, and on the 31st the Norfolk battalion took the place of the Suffolk on the right of the brigade front line.

The total casualties of the Norfolk battalion in August had been— Officers, two killed and seven wounded; other ranks, twenty-one killed, 186 wounded, twenty-one missing. Nothing unusual happened in the first eight days of September, though the casualties during work on trenches amounted to one man died of wounds and twelve wounded. At 2 a.m. on September 9th 2nd Lieutenant Ketteringham went out with eighteen men of " C " company to raid the German trenches. Whilst cutting the wire they came upon five Germans, all of whom they killed. They then went on into the German trench, where they had not much time to spare, owing to the delay in wire cutting. They accounted for a few Germans and brought back some caps and papers, but the Germans were not wearing shoulder-straps. The party got back at 2.30 without any casualties. On a previous patrol, on the night of August 31st–September 1st, 2nd Lieutenant Ketteringham had met six Germans, who attacked his party with bombs, badly wounding two of his men, one of whom he carried in on his back. For these services he received the M.C. On September 27th, Colonel Walter having gone to command the brigade and Colonel Prior to command the 9th Norfolk battalion, Captain Gielgud succeeded to the command of the battalion for the time being. The September casualties were only two other ranks died of wounds and ten wounded.

On October 2nd the 7th Norfolk battalion marched to Bernafay Wood, south-west of Longueval and just east of Montauban, the 36th and 37th brigades being in front facing Gueudecourt. On the 10th the 35th brigade relieved the 36th, the 7th Norfolk and 7th Suffolk battalions holding the front trenches, with the 9th Essex in support and the 5th Berkshire in reserve. The 7th Suffolk, of the 37th brigade, were on the right, the 41st division on the left of the brigade front.

An attack on the Germans in what was known as Bayonet trench was arranged for the 12th, and the assembly positions were reached by 5 a.m. on that day. The assault was made at 2.5 p.m., with all four companies disposed in depth on a front of one platoon each, in the order "D," "C," "B," "A," from right to left. On the right of the 7th Norfolk battalion was the 7th Suffolk, on the left a battalion of the Royal Scots Fusiliers of the 30th division. The objectives were (1) to capture Bayonet and Scabbard trenches, (2) to go on later to Luisenhof Farm and establish the line beyond it.

When the battalion had got forward fifty yards under cover of the barrage, it ran into a heavy German machine-gun fire from both flanks. The advance continued, but before the objective trench was reached it encountered uncut wire, which, combined with the machine-gun fire, brought it to a standstill and compelled the men to seek shelter in shell holes, from which they fired at the Germans standing up in their trenches to fire, causing them many casualties. The left company of the Suffolk battalion succeeded in entering the trench where there was no wire, but was bombed out. The left of the Norfolk battalion got within about 100 to 120 yards of Scabbard trench, a distance which lengthened to 200 yards at the junction of Scabbard and Bayonet trenches, and again closed in to twenty yards on the right, opposite the unwired part of Bayonet trench. After dark another attempt was made to cut the wire, but it was too strong, and the survivors of the attack crawled back to the trenches from which they had started, where they and the 7th Suffolk battalion were relieved by the 9th Essex and retired to reserve near Flers. The casualties in the Norfolk battalion on this day were:

Officers: Killed—2nd Lieutenants C. Shepherd, S. R. Mitchley, and C. Sizeland. Wounded—Captain Howlett, Lieutenant Montgomery, 2nd Lieutenants Thorn and W. J. Jones. Missing, believed killed—2nd Lieutenants H. Smith and A. Shaw.

Other ranks: Killed—Thirty-six, wounded 125, missing fifty-one.

There were left in trenches only eight officers and 350 men in all. After the Essex on the 18th, and the Berkshire battalion on the 19th, had failed in attacks on Bayonet trench, whilst the 88th brigade on the right had got into it, the 12th division was relieved by the 29th, and retired to Mametz Wood. On the 21st the battalion was thanked by the brigadier for its efforts in the recent attacks.

Next day it "embussed" at Dernancourt for Lattre St. Quentin, whence it marched to Montenescourt.

On the 25th it was back near Arras, in the positions it had occupied in August.

The total casualties during the last tour in the Anglo-French offensive had been:

Officers: Killed or died of wounds—five, wounded five, missing, believed killed, two.

Other ranks—Killed or died of wounds—fifty-four, wounded 130, missing fifty.

For the rest of October, all November, and the first five days of December, 1916, the battalion was in the same neighbourhood, with nothing particular to be recorded, except the death, while inspecting wire, of Captain J. Tilley, who had previously been wounded at the Somme.

At 3 a.m. on December 6th about fifty Germans were seen advancing north and south of the Achicourt–Beaurains road against trenches H. 30 and 31. In front of the latter they were stopped by machine-gun fire before reaching the British wire. In front of H. 30 some of them got into the wire, where they were fired on by the Norfolk sentry post. One officer and one man were killed and another, badly wounded, died soon after being brought into the British trench. Another German officer fell into the trench, saying in English, "I'm wounded," and, on being questioned before he died at the dressing station, said his party had been one hundred strong. Yet another German was knocked down in the trench by a bomb of which the safety pin had not been drawn. The raiders had blackened faces, and most of them carried automatic pistols. The Norfolk battalion was congratulated on its repulse of this raid by the divisional general. There was a curious sequel to this affair. Next day five fish-tailed bombs were dropped just where the German officer had fallen. None of them exploded, and it was found that the following rather pathetic note was attached in duplicate to two of them: "Comrade,—On the night of the 5th–6th Lieutenant Schulter and three men fell into your hands. He is my greatest and only friend. Does he still live, or where is he buried? If you have ever had a friend in danger, send me an answer by a 'little mine' to Lieutenant Muller." It was addressed "English Comrade." A Verey light had been fired just before the bombs came over. A reply was sent, by order of the brigadier, as requested, stating that all who had fallen into the hands of the battalion were dead. Two or three days later the Germans threw over name-plates for their graves, one for the officer and another for the three men, on the assumption that the latter would be buried in one grave.

The rest of the year passed quietly, the battalion moving on December 19th to Wanquentin, and on the 20th to billets at Gouey en Ternois in "B" area. The diary records the receipt of many Christmas presents, each man getting at least three. Thanks to drafts the battalion had regained a fighting strength, on December 31, 1916, of nineteen officers and 894 other ranks.

(c) 1917 : ARRAS—CAMBRAI

During January, 1917, the 7th Norfolk battalion was a few days at Gouey en Ternois, whence it went by motor bus to Auxi-le-Château. There is nothing to record during this month, which was spent in training, varied by inspections and football. February was equally uneventful save for an inspection on the 2nd by the commander-in-chief (Sir Douglas Haig), who congratulated Colonel Walter and the battalion on its services and on a demonstration of methods of conveying messages given before him. This demonstration was a very big affair. About 200 generals and staff officers were specially brought up in buses and other conveyances to witness it. Trench mortars, etc., were used, and there were two or three casualties due to accidents. Had a German aeroplane happened to fly over it might have made a very important "bag." The principal object of the demonstration was to show how to combine trench mortars, bombs, rifle grenades, and the bayonet in an attack.

On the 8th the 7th Norfolk battalion moved to Noyelette in buses and on the 24th to Lattre St. Quentin.

On the 3rd March they moved to I. 2 sub-sector of the Arras trenches, where they had plenty of hard work for over a fortnight in trench digging, with occasional bombardments. On the 23rd a raid by the 9th Essex was well supported by the flanking fire of the Norfolk machine guns. The enemy barrage did little havoc, but later in the day 2nd Lieutenant Dawson was wounded, and a gas shell which hit the battalion bomb store blew it up and gassed five men. Next day some small balloons were sent over by the Germans carrying incitements to the population against the British.

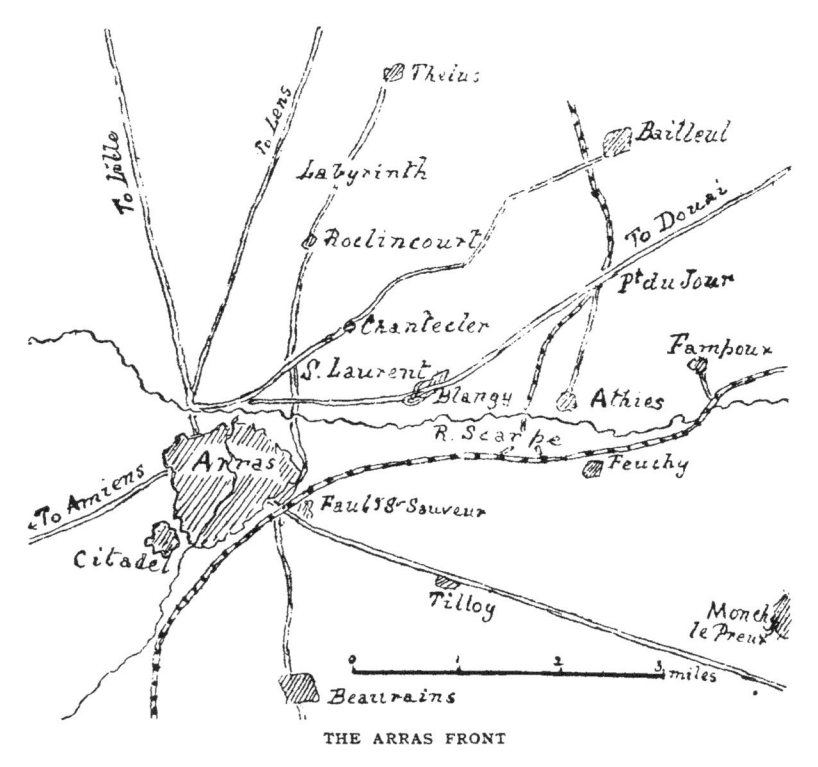

THE ARRAS FRONT

On the 26th the battalion went via Arras to Talavera Camp at Agnez-les-Duisans and next day to Legnereuil in the Beaufort training area.

April 5th saw it back at Agnez-les-Duisans, and the 6th at Arras, after leaving six officers and 108 other ranks at the former place. Early in April command of the brigade was taken by Brigadier-General Berkeley Vincent.

An attack on the German trenches was being prepared for the 9th, and on the 7th the C.O. and company commanders reconnoitred the route from the cellars of the Museum, where they were quartered, by underground passages to the front trenches.

On the 9th the battalion moved at 3 a.m. from the cellars through a passage which brought it out at the Broad Walk, where "C" and "D" companies went to the reserve line, "A" and "B" to the duplicate reserve line. The objective of the battalion in the forthcoming attack was the gun-pits and trenches just east of Tilloy Lane, Cambrai Road, and Maison Rouge, the general objective of the brigade being the Feuchy-Wancourt line about Feuchy Chapel, on the right bank of the Scarpe a couple of miles east of Arras.

As the troops in front vacated the front trenches the 7th Norfolk battalion moved into them. So far they had only lost two men wounded.

At 10.5 a.m. orders were received to be ready to advance from the blue line objective to the further attack. As they moved towards this line the Norfolk men found that it had not yet been completely taken, and the brigade had to deploy 400 yards west of it; in this advance the Norfolk battalion suffered several casualties from gun and rifle fire, especially from the ruins of Tilloy on their right. Here 2nd Lieutenant J. W. C. Bolland was killed. At eight minutes after noon the attack was launched, the Norfolk men going forward with great dash and quickly silencing the machine guns and snipers from whose attentions they had been suffering. The Germans began to surrender freely; in Tilloy Quarry ninety of them stood with hands up and were taken. Here touch was established with the 3rd division on the right. The first objective had been captured almost without fighting. In a "camouflage" trench, running north from the Cambrai road, fifteen Germans and three machine guns were taken, and here the battalion head-quarters were established. Some delay had been caused by taking prisoners. Maison Rouge was taken and between 1 p.m. and 1.30 p.m. the Norfolk Suffolk, and Berkshire battalions were suffering some losses from British "shorts." Without pausing at the first offensive, the Norfolk battalion pressed on and captured the second without opposition, gathering in prisoners as they went, including some German artillery officers in a gunpit. The 7th Suffolk and 9th Essex now passed through the Norfolk battalion to attack Feuchy Chapel. A platoon of the Norfolk battalion followed to " mop up," and later all who could be collected went up to assist the Suffolk and Essex battalions. So far the 7th Norfolk had captured at least 250 Germans, seven 77 m.m. guns, and six machine guns. Their casualties were :

Officers : Killed—2nd Lieutenants G. F. Barton and J. W. C. Bolland. Wounded—Captain Paget Crosby ; 2nd Lieutenants Popham, and J. W. L. White.

Other ranks : Killed twenty-one, wounded 135, missing six.

The situation now was that the British held Feuchy Chapel redoubt, but had not yet succeeded in taking the brown objective line along the Feuchy-Wancourt road.

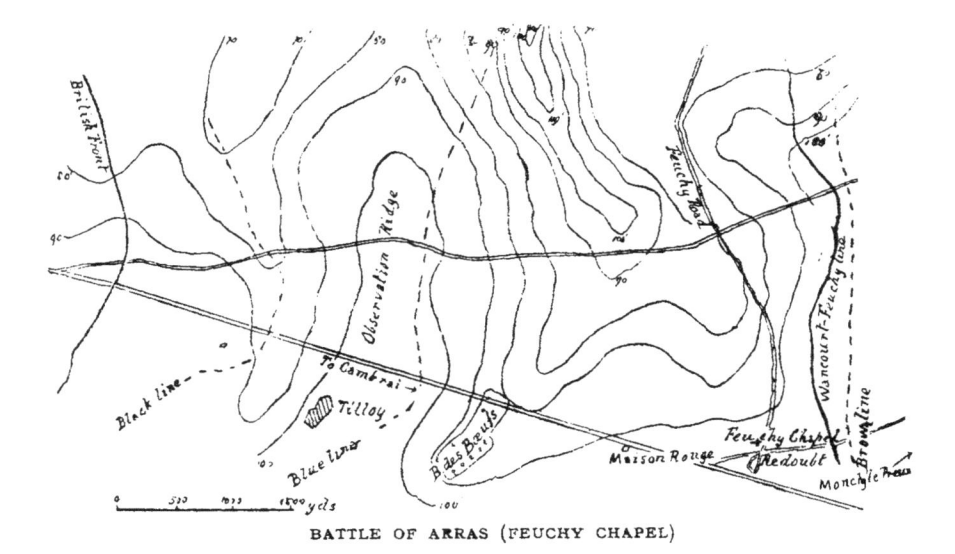

BATTLE OF ARRAS (FEUCHY CHAPEL)

The Suffolk and Essex battalions were respectively north and south of the Cambrai road at Feuchy, each of them being reinforced by a company of the 7th Norfolk. The Essex held the whole of the Chapel redoubt. The Suffolk were in touch with them, but had failed to take the church redoubt, on account of wire and machine-gun fire. Two companies of the Queen's, from the 37th brigade and the rest of the Norfolk battalion were ordered to support the Essex and Suffolk. The

Germans were retiring east of Feuchy Chapel, but trickled back at night into the brown line.

Orders for the 10th required the 35th brigade to take this brown line by assault, with the aid of two companies of the Queen's, and six companies from the 36th brigade.

At 8.15 a.m. the 7th Norfolk battalion, with two machine guns attached, assembled along the Chapel road on either side of Tilloy Lane, with the 9th Essex on their right and 7th Suffolk on the left. They were to attack the brown line to the right of the Cambrai road. This attack was to be aided by a turning movement on the left, to be executed by the 5th Berkshire and the six companies from the 36th brigade. These were to cross the brown line on the left, where it had already been opened by the 15th division, and then to turn southwards on the eastern side of it.

Whilst the battalion was taking up position it was much troubled by a German sniper, who caused at least thirty casualties, chiefly N.C.O.'s.[1] The attack was now postponed till 12.30 p.m., and even then, if uncut wire was encountered, the attack was to be turned into a demonstration, in order to assist the turning movement. As the wire was found to be untouched this course was pursued, and a bombing attack was pushed up Tilloy Lane by the Norfolk battalion. The Germans on the brown line, finding it turned, evacuated it, leaving in it only a few men, who were taken.

The 37th brigade now passed through to the attack on Monchy-le-Preux and the green line objective, whilst the consolidation of the brown line was completed, the 7th Norfolk battalion occupying the outpost line from Orange Hill south-east of Feuchy village to a point 800 yards south of the Cambrai road.

On the 11th the 36th brigade relieved the 35th on the brown line, but had hardly done so when the 35th were again sent back, as the

[1] This sniper was certainly one of fifteen Germans taken shortly afterwards by the Essex men, who had suffered even more severely from his rifle. His captors were anxious to identify this brave enemy, but his companions, apparently fearing he would be shot, refused to say which he was. Naturally any idea of punishing him for gallantly doing his duty was far from the thoughts of the British, but German ideas were evidently different.

36th was required to relieve the 37th at Monchy-le-Preux. The 7th Norfolk battalion was in support at Maison Rouge, where they found themselves, in wet or snowy weather, in inferior dug-outs, the best having already been occupied by the gunners.

On April 13th the battalion, on relief, returned to Arras and other places farther back for a period of training and reorganization, after which it returned, on the 25th, to trenches at Monchy Wood, where "A" and "B" companies were in front line, with "C" and "D" in support. Here, next day, Lieutenant Humphrey and 2nd Lieutenant Haig-Smellie, with nine other ranks, were wounded and two men killed, most of them by snipers or machine-gun fire. Here the Norfolk battalion was in front of the Germans in Rifle trench, on which an attack was projected for the 28th. The objectives of the attack on the 28th were:

(1) The capture of Rifle and Bayonet trenches, and
(2) The consolidation of a line in advance of these.

Zero hour was 4.25 a.m. on the 28th. At fifty minutes after it the four companies, together with the 5th Berkshire, were to carry the first objective. The attack was not successful. "A" and "B" went over the top before getting into touch with "C" and "D," whom it was found difficult to locate even at 2 p.m. Both attacks were soon held up by machine-gun fire, and the men of "A" and "B" with their flanks exposed, were lying in shell holes near the German trench, whilst "C" and "D," having run into uncut wire, never got up to it. For the whole day the entire battalion was in the shell holes, suffering from the fire of snipers and machine guns. At night such as were able crawled back to the British trenches, whilst stretcher parties went out to collect the wounded under a fire which, with the aid of Verey lights, was so heavy and accurate that many of the wounded could not be brought in. The casualties were specially heavy in "C" and "D" companies.

A further attack was ordered for the 29th, when the 9th Essex were to make a frontal attack on Rifle trench, supported by attacks on the flanks with bombs, rifle grenades, and Stokes mortars, and by a heavy bombardment of the trench all day. At 3 a.m. on the 30th the 9th Essex took the trench, but were driven out by two counter-attacks with bombs.

The casualties of the Norfolk battalion between April 25th and 30th, amounted to twelve officers and 223 men, but, unfortunately, details are not given in the war diary. Colonel Walter has given us the following names which he can remember:

Killed: Captain D. C. Graham, 2nd Lieutenants H. F. Manners, W. Dover, and R. Lancaster.

Wounded: Lieutenants Jackson and Potter.

On May 1st the 7th Norfolk battalion was sent for a rest in the old German trenches at the Railway Triangle, west of Feuchy, whence they moved into divisional reserve on the Wancourt–Feuchy line, between the railway and the Cambrai road.

At 9 p.m. on the 4th, on the failure of an attack by the 36th and 37th brigades, the 35th relieved the latter in first line, with the Norfolk battalion in front, the Essex in support, and the 7th Suffolk and 5th Berkshire in reserve. The Norfolk battalion was in Rifle and Monchy trenches, which had been captured in their absence. Here there was a good deal to be done in repairing the trenches under the usual daily bombardments, by which, or by rifle fire Lieutenant English, Lieutenant Potter, and Major Gielgud were wounded, and about eight other ranks killed and twenty wounded.

On May 24th the 12th division was relieved by the 29th and was presently transferred (less its artillery) to the 18th corps. After three weeks' rest and training in back areas it was again at Arras on June 17th, whence, next day, the Norfolk battalion was sent into the old "brown line," the objective of the attack of April 9th astride the Arras–Cambrai road, whence they moved farther north on the same line. During this tour of trenches nothing remarkable happened till the end of June, when the 12th division, on relief by the 4th, returned to Arras, where it was again transferred to the 17th corps. Nothing requiring special notice occurred till the night of July 11th–12th, when the 7th Norfolk battalion relieved the 7th Suffolk in the front trenches, where, just before the relief, the 9th Essex had been heavily attacked and had lost one of their trenches.

On the 12th Captain Archdale was wounded by a machine gun from a low-flying German aeroplane. This aeroplane made a practice of flying up and down every morning about 9 o'clock. Everybody, from the C.O.

downwards, shot at it, but apparently without seriously damaging it. There were a few casualties from bombardments during neighbouring attacks in which the 7th Norfolk were not engaged, and low-flying aeroplanes continued to give trouble; but there is nothing to be noted till August 1st, when the Norfolk battalion relieved the 7th Royal Sussex in the left sub-sector of the right sector of the divisional front. Here " D " company was in Tool trench on the right, " C " in Hook trench on the left (with one platoon in Saddle Support trench), and " A " and " B " in Pick Cave and Saddle Support trenches.

The night of the 2nd–3rd witnessed a very heavy German attack on these trenches, which was launched at 9 p.m. on a signal by horn. The Norfolk rifles and machine guns at once opened fire and the attack hesitated. Then the horn was sounded again and the attackers pressed on in three waves. " D " company, holding the centre of the position, finding its position untenable owing to damage to part of the trench from trench mortars, moved 150 yards to the right, down the trench, leaving only one post occupied. Into this sector the enemy broke and pushed 120 yards down the Pick Avenue communication trench. On the right and left the Norfolk line had repulsed the enemy with heavy loss. On the left 2nd Lieutenant M. R. W. Allen (" C " company) moved his men out of the trench and met the enemy with the bayonet, thus preventing him from getting into the trench with a single man. Acting with great coolness and gallantry Allen met his death from a bullet through the head. Of the two remaining officers of " C," 2nd Lieutenant Ferguson went down the trench to try and get into touch with " D," and was taken by the Germans who had got into the centre.

Lieutenant Hogarth-Swann, now left in command of " C," promptly constructed a bombing block on the right of his trench, as a protection against the portion captured. On the right of this captured portion 2nd Lieutenant W. H. Benn had been killed early in the action, and 2nd Lieutenant Haylock was in command of " D." He also, assisted by Sergeant J. S. Johnson, constructed a protective bombing block in Tool trench. The German barrage ceased about 10 p.m.

Meanwhile, two platoons had been sent up to support the front from Saddle Support trench, their place being taken by two other platoons from Pick Cave. The two sent up to the front had orders to bomb the enemy out of the central part into which he had broken. " C " and " D " companies had independently arranged to bomb inwards towards one another against the German flanks until they met. The C.O. arranged that, as " C " and " D " met, lights were to be sent up as a signal to " B " to attack up Pick Avenue, which it was hoped might end in the death or capture of all the intruding Germans. Captain Haward, with " B," finding that " C " was held up, started his attack up Pick Avenue, and about 8.30 a.m. had joined up with " D " in Tool trench. By that time, the few surviving Germans having fled, connexion was quickly established with " C " and the whole line was recovered. In Hook trench, on its recapture, much material was found, showing that the Germans had meant to hold, and not merely to raid it. A table had been set, apparently for the German officers' mess, with a bottle of champagne. The latter was consumed with due appreciation by some of the Norfolk men. The casualties were :

Officers : Killed—2nd Lieutenants M. R. W. Allen and W. H. Benn. Wounded—Captain Ketteringham ; 2nd Lieutenants Adams and Dawkins. Wounded and missing—2nd Lieutenant Ferguson.

Other ranks : About ninety killed, wounded and missing.

The work of 2nd Lieutenant Hogarth-Swann is noted in the diary as particularly good ; also that of 2nd Lieutenant Woolsey, who dug out a buried trench mortar at Saddle Support and himself served it. The latter also, on patrol, found two German light machine guns in the side of an old communication trench and brought them in single handed under heavy rifle fire. For these services he was awarded the M.C. During the next two days 2nd Lieutenant Tarrant was wounded, and 2nd Lieutenant Norwack was blown down a dug-out stairs by a bomb. On August 7th the Norfolk battalion, on relief by the 7th Suffolk, went back to the line of April 9th, 700 yards south of the Cambrai road. This tour of the trenches had cost them altogether :

Officers : Killed two, wounded and missing one, wounded five.

Other ranks : Eight killed, sixty-seven wounded, five gassed, ten missing (of whom three known to be killed), four died of wounds.

It was afterwards learned, from German prisoners, that the Germans had suffered very heavily, one regiment having to be withdrawn with one company practically annihilated.

In a successful but costly raid on the 9th by the Suffolk battalion the 7th Norfolk only took part to the extent of sending " D " company to escort German prisoners.

From the 12th to the 18th the brigade was training in the back area near Arras, and its time after that, in the Monchy sector, to the end of August was uneventful. September was passed in the same neighbourhood, the period being notable only for heavy German bombardments during the battalion's service in trenches from the 17th to the 24th. 2nd Lieutenant Robartes was wounded, and the casualties in other ranks were fifteen killed or died of wounds and forty-nine wounded.

Early in October Lieutenant-Colonel Walter went sick and was invalided home. Major Gethen took over from him, and was in command during the raid of October 13th, about to be described. Shortly afterwards he gave over the command to Major Gielgud, who in due course was promoted Lieutenant-Colonel to command the battalion.

During the early part of October the battalion was practising for a raid to be made from Pick Cave, where it relieved the 7th Suffolk on the 13th. The raiders formed up an hour before zero and went over promptly to time, covered by a heavy barrage. Following it closely, they broke into the enemy trench, which was full of Germans, who, apparently being surprised, either ran or surrendered freely. The men appear to have been particularly exasperated by a long series of trench mortar bombardments at this time, for little quarter was given, and it was estimated that, whilst only thirty prisoners were brought in, at least 200 Germans were killed by the raiders, besides many found dead from the bombardment. The raiders returned within half an hour of their start, after destroying the trenches and dug-outs and bringing back a light machine gun and a "fish-tail" bomb mortar. The casualties in officers killed were extraordinarily heavy, which may account partly for the exasperation of the men. There were killed 2nd Lieutenants C. A. Ireland, M.C., F. L. Kerkham, W. D. Bonham, and W. J. Jones (died of wounds); wounded, Captain Tayler (taken prisoner) and

2nd Lieutenant D. G. White. Of other ranks eighteen were killed or died of wounds, thirty-seven wounded, and eleven missing. About this time Major Gielgud took over command temporarily from Major Gethen.

After this the battalion went back to Arras on the 18th, and into training for the rest of the month two marches west of Arras. The 12th division was relieved by the 4th after the 22nd, and remained in the training area till November 16th, when the Norfolk battalion entrained for Péronne and moved through it to huts at Moislans. On the 18th they took over front line trenches, ready for the coming great attack towards Cambrai on the 20th. In this the 12th division was on the extreme right of the infantry, just south of the road from Gouzeaucourt by Lateau Wood to Masnières and Cambrai. It was the right division of the 3rd corps, and had the 20th division on its left, north of the road. The attack started at 6.20 a.m., the 35th brigade having a front of two battalions, the 5th Berkshire on the right and the 9th Essex on the left. The 7th Suffolk, in support, were to " leapfrog " the leading battalions for the attack on the main Hindenburg line, whilst the 7th Norfolk acted as brigade reserve, except " C " company, which appears to have been sent forward. The battalion, as is evidenced by its casualties, did not take any very prominent part in this day's fighting. It lost Captain C. W. Archdale, killed; 2nd Lieutenants Hogarth-Swann and R. T. Hedges wounded; six other ranks killed, twenty-four wounded, and six missing.

From the 21st to the 28th, after the successful attack, matters were very quiet on the front of the 3rd corps. The Norfolk battalion was moved up into the front line, where they were to have their day of trial on the 30th.

At 6.30 a.m. on that day a tremendous German bombardment opened on Villers Guislain, which presently spread to the whole divisional front, and those of the divisions to the right and left. An hour later the infantry attack was launched in great force. Gonnelieu was taken, and at 7.35 the attack from that place on the left, and Banteux on the right, fell upon the Norfolk battalion in front and right flank in overwhelming force. By sheer weight of numbers the battalion was forced back on its head-quarters and a strong point of its left front. Many men were surrounded and compelled to surrender, but the fight was continued with the greatest courage, and heavy losses were inflicted on the enemy. By 10 a.m. 2nd Lieutenant Maddison was the only officer left with the battalion, and he, with the remaining men, attached himself to the 9th Royal Fusiliers. The whole 35th brigade was almost surrounded and forced to retire hurriedly from Villers Guislain across the open plain to

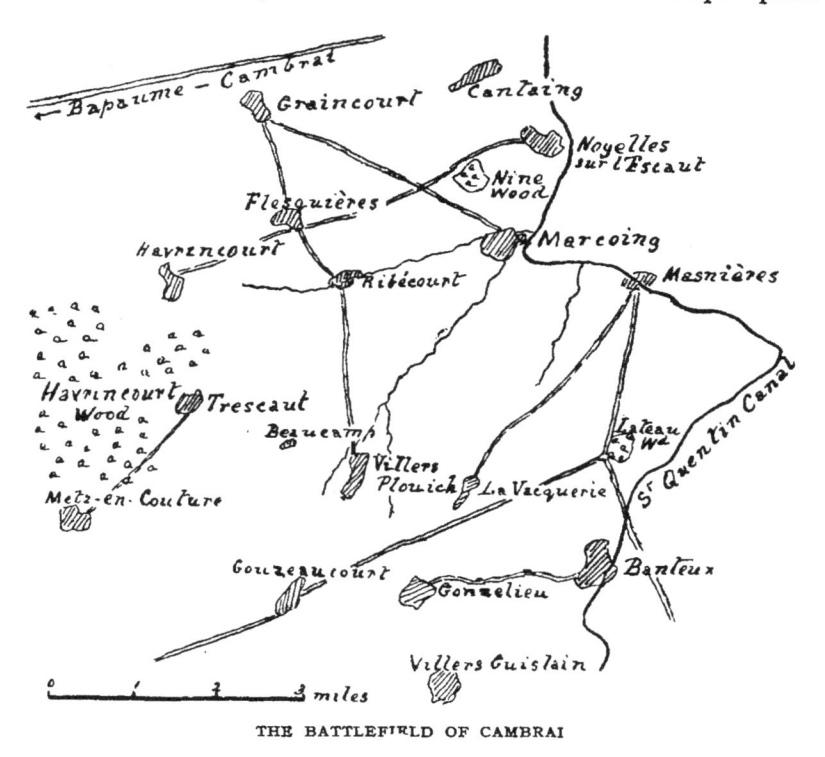

THE BATTLEFIELD OF CAMBRAI

Gouzeaucourt. It had been attacked not only on its right flank, but also in front, from the direction of Lateau Wood. The machine guns endeavoured to stem the tide, but the brigade, almost surrounded, was compelled to fall gradually back, inflicting heavy losses on the enemy. The retreat was in the direction of La Vacquerie, north of Gonnelieu, and a rear-guard action was fought by the artillery and other troops from Villers Guislain, including perhaps the remains of the Norfolk battalion, which succeeded in holding up the German advance, whilst the arrival of the cavalry and tanks on the right, as well as the Guards from Havrincourt Wood, enabled a counter-attack to still further stem the tide. At nightfall the remnants of the 35th brigade were holding La Vacquerie, and Gouzeaucourt was again in the possession of the Guards division.

The battle, which was undoubtedly a complete surprise for the British, was very confused, and neither the Norfolk battalion war diary nor that of the 35th brigade gives a very clear account of what happened in their direction. The battalion diary was destroyed to save it from the enemy, and the existing one is only a compilation from information collected. How heavily the battalion was engaged is clear from the casualty list:

Officers: Killed—Lieutenant-Colonel H. L. F. A. Gielgud, M.C.; Captain and Adjutant A. N. Charlton, M.C.; Lieutenant M. L. Chaland, M.C.; 2nd Lieutenant Payne. Wounded seven—Captain Haward; 2nd Lieutenants A. R. Brown, Kontill, E. C. Page, Stubbs, Pratley, and Anable. Wounded and missing four—Captain Potter, Lieutenant W. G. Collins, 2nd Lieutenants Parish and Summers. Missing—2nd Lieutenant Goddard. Shell shock (hospital)—2nd Lieutenant Kemp. Altogether eighteen officer casualties.

Other ranks: Killed twenty-seven, wounded eighty-nine, missing 204, wounded and missing 13.—Total, 333.

Lieutenant-Colonel Gielgud was succeeded by Lieutenant-Colonel E. T. Rees in command of the battalion.

A fresh attack on December 1st forced them back to the south of the Cambrai road, whence, on relief, they retired to the reserve line. On December 3rd and 4th they were at Heudicourt picking up stragglers and being rejoined by some details who had been in huts at Manancourt under Major Gethen, and had apparently not been in the battles of November 20th and 30th.

The battalion, after its recent experiences, required a long period of rest, reorganization, and refitment. It was moved to various places in the rear until it found itself, towards the end of December, 1917, training at Merville, south-east of Hazebrouck.

(*d*) 1918 : ON THE LYS—THE ANCRE—THE FINAL ADVANCE

From Merville the 7th Norfolk battalion went, on January 15, 1918, to Sailly, in the reserve area of the right of the divisional front on the Lys. Most of this month also was spent in training. On February 6th the battalion received a draft of five officers and eighty-four men from the 8th Norfolk battalion, which had just been disbanded and distributed to the other battalions in France, which were in great need of reinforcements. This was a complete company of the disbanded battalion.

During February, too, there was generally nothing beyond the usual trench routine about Sailly and Fleurbaix, except on the 20th, when the Germans attempted a " silent " raid on a post on the Norfolk battalion's left front. Only one German succeeded in entering the trench, where he wounded two men with a stick bomb, but was killed himself. The rest of the party retreated. On the 24th training began for a projected attack on the enemy's post at Erquinghem, on the right bank of the Lys, of which a model had been prepared at the training ground.

The battalion diary for March was unfortunately destroyed by shell fire, and the existing one is a reconstruction—never so satisfactory as an original.

On March 1st 2nd Lieutenant A. E. Knights had, on a reconnaissance, discovered a narrow gap in the enemy's wire between two of his posts. It was decided to attempt a small raid by this at 10 p.m. that night. Captain Nash, with 2nd Lieutenant Brackley and thirty men of " C " company, was to enter the German trench by the gap in the wire, and then to attack the posts to the right and left. A covering party of twenty men was to remain at the point of entry, as near as possible to the enemy's trench. There was to be an artillery barrage for one minute at 10 p.m., to be then converted into a " box " barrage.

At 9.45 the raiders assembled in " No Man's Land " ; at ten the barrage began punctually, and a minute later the raiders entered the trench. The Germans, though surprised, put up a stout resistance. Eight or ten of them were killed, the concrete shelters were bombed, and the raiders, carrying one prisoner with them, got back with a loss of only two wounded.

On the 9th, when in billets at Sailly, "B" company's billet was hit by a shell which killed six and wounded nine men.

During the next three days, when the battalion was again in the trenches, there were alarms of German attacks which ended in nothing more serious than an attempt to cut wire which was driven off by rifle fire.

On the other hand, on the 12th, 2nd Lieutenants Izard and Ingram went in search of two suspected German posts; they found one, but neither it nor the trench near it had been occupied for some time. The two officers returned safely.

For some days before the 18th there had been considerable artillery activity on the enemy's side. That night he attempted a raid on a Norfolk post. After a short bombardment the Germans entered the trench to the right of the post, which they were unable to take. They were driven out without the necessity of a counter-attack by a platoon which was sent up for the purpose. One wounded German was found lying under the parapet.

Next night a determined attack was made on another Norfolk post and the adjoining one in the Essex trenches. After a bombardment by trench mortars, the enemy entered to the left of the Norfolk post and moved towards the support line. Being discovered, the Germans opened fire on the post from its left rear. Sergeant Pollington, in command of the post, moved his men into the communication trench leading to it, so as to face the enemy, who rushed the trench, but were driven out of it, carrying off the sergeant as a prisoner. When they were half-way across "No Man's Land," he hit his guards in the face with his steel helmet and succeeded in escaping. 2nd Lieutenant J. R. Holland, leading a patrol down the communication trench was shot dead, as well as the man behind him.

This was the time of the great German offensive in the spring of 1918, and on the 24th the 35th brigade was sent south to the Albert neighbourhood. The 7th Norfolk battalion arrived by bus near Senlis, on the Doullens-Albert road, at 10 a.m. on the 25th. At 5 p.m. they were ordered to Fricourt to support the 36th and 37th brigades on the line Contalmaison-Mametz; on the way they were diverted to come under the orders of the 35th division beyond Maricourt, and finally they were sent back to Albert.

Next day the battalion was sent at 9 a.m. to a line on the Ancre, between the north of Albert and the south of Aveluy, with outposts on the river and the main body on the Arras railway. " A," " B," and " D " companies were in line, " C " on outposts. Later, they were ordered to withdraw outposts, demolish bridges, and make inundations in their front. " C " company passed into support. Later, a gap was formed by the Suffolk battalion's movements between their left and the Norfolk battalion's right, in which the enemy established himself in a house, thereby necessitating a slight withdrawal of the line on the right. At dusk the Germans attacked the right of the Norfolk battalion and their defensive flank. They gained a footing in the advanced positions, but were ejected by a counter-attack with the loss of one of their light machine-guns. As the Norfolk battalion was hard pressed, they were reinforced by one company of the Essex and one of the Northamptonshire. The former was placed in reserve to " A " and " C " companies, whilst the latter dug itself in at a factory.

On the morning of the 27th the battalion received heavy shell and machine-gun fire, and the right flank had to retire, but the attack was not pressed by the Germans and their fire slackened. The right flank was now in the air, and there was no news of the position of the Suffolk battalion in that direction. The line had been re-established by Lieutenant Colonel Rees, with forty men, but was much harassed by a machine gun in a low flying aeroplane. A Lewis gun, sent out a hundred yards to the right, was unable to maintain itself against artillery fire, and the same fate attended another party sent out in the same direction. At last, Captain Weaver and R.S.M. Golder succeeded in establishing a post 400 yards to the right.

At 11 a.m. the Germans were advancing in strength on Aveluy, where both flanks of the Norfolk battalion were in the air. Colonel Rees then ordered the battalion, as well as the reinforcing companies of the Essex and Northamptonshire regiments, to fall back in three waves to the crest in rear, with their left on the Bouzincourt-Aveluy road. The operation was executed with great difficulty under artillery and machine-gun fire, but Colonel Rees, Captain Tapply, and 2nd Lieutenant Brumbley, two machine-gun officers with Vickers guns, and about 150 men finally established themselves in a forked sunken road just south of the Aveluy-Bouzincourt road. Later, a few reinforcements, under Captain Weaver, with 2nd Lieutenants Lark and Phipps, kept in touch with this post. In the afternoon the position became precarious, as the enemy were enfilading the road with machine-guns, and working round by the left. Captain Tapply, going back for instructions to brigade head-quarters, was told to hold the position if possible and three Vickers guns were ordered to support it, but never arrived. At dusk the enemy had almost surrounded the post, which they rushed. Colonel Rees was wounded and taken prisoner, as well as Captain Soames (R.A.M.C.), but most of the garrison succeeded in escaping. Captain Tapply had reached the line held by the Northamptonshire company in rear of the post, and hearing that it was hard pressed, took up two platoons to support it. On the way he met the retiring garrison, which he placed on the exposed right flank of the Northamptonshire company. Early on the 28th the brigade was relieved by the 190th, and returned to Hennencourt. At Bouzincourt the Norfolk battalion was met by Major West of the Suffolk Regiment, who had collected some 200 of the Norfolk battalion, and had been deputed to command the battalion, owing to the capture of Lieutenant-Colonel Rees. The casualties of the Norfolk battalion in this heavy fighting were :

Officers : Killed five—Captain C. F. W. Nash, M.C.; 2nd Lieutenants G. H. Scolding, Wallis, T. Hewitt, W. S. Brumbley, M.C. Wounded five—Lieutenant Heselton; 2nd Lieutenants Blake, Phelps, Havers, and Hurt. Missing nine—Lieutenant-Colonel Rees, M.C. (wounded); 2nd Lieutenants Haylock, Barter, Senior, Ingram, Hopton, Clarke, Hill, and Captain Soames (R.A.M.C.). Total officer casualties nineteen.

Other ranks : Killed six, wounded and missing two, wounded seventy-two, missing 202. Total 282.

On April 1st command of the battalion was assumed by Lieutenant-

Colonel F. S. Cooper, D.S.O., of the Suffolk Regiment, who was succeeded by Lieutenant-Colonel Ashley Scarlett, D.S.O. On April 2nd the 12th division again went into the line, relieving the 17th, with the 35th brigade on the right, the 36th on the left, and the 37th in reserve at Hennencourt. The Norfolk battalion was in the support line of the 35th, disposed in two lines of short, disconnected trenches, where movement was only possible at night; battalion head-quarters Millencourt.

After two quiet days on the 3rd and 4th, a heavy bombardment was opened at 7.10 a.m. on the whole valley of the Ancre, from the front line back to Millencourt, followed by an attack on the Suffolk battalion on the right front, which had gained nothing by 11.15. The attack extended to the left of the Australians, on the right of the Suffolk battalion, with no greater success. At dusk " B " company moved up to relieve the Suffolk battalion, and a platoon of " A " to reinforce their supports. The Australians had now fallen back 1,000 yards, which necessitated the use of " C " company to form a defensive flank on that side. The officer in command, finding some Australians still there, left one platoon in touch with them, and posted two across the Albert-Millencourt road.

At 10.20 p.m., owing to the position on the right, the front battalions of the brigade were ordered back. The 7th Norfolk advanced 200 or 300 yards and the Suffolk battalion retired through them. The losses on this day were only eight wounded.

The 6th was a quiet day, as were the next three, save for bombardments and gas shells. The men were much exhausted by the general bad conditions. On the 10th the battalion went back, on relief, to Hennencourt, and was kept training and working at local defences in the neighbourhood till they started back for the front on the 23rd, on which date Major Gethen took over command of the battalion. They were now at Mailly, a little north of their recent position, and facing the Beaumont Hamel position, which was once more in German hands.

At the end of the month, when " C " company was moving off to work at the trenches, two German shells exploded amongst them, wounding 2nd Lieutenant Bell, killing six men, and wounding twenty-three. Another shell, next day (29th) wounded six men of " B " company.

The great German offensive towards Amiens had been held up, and during the first twenty days of May there is nothing to note, the Norfolk battalion alternately relieving and being relieved by the 9th Essex. The divisional front was now held by two instead of, as heretofore, by three brigades. Of each brigade two battalions were in front and one in close support. On May 21st Major Gethen reverted to second in command, on the arrival of Major H. Ashley Scarlett.

On the 25th–26th the battalion went back for rest and training at Acheux Wood and Arquêves, where it stayed till June 16th, when the 12th division was attached to the 5th corps, and relieved the 35th division about Forceville and Senlis. During June there is nothing noticeable except the death of Captain J. G. Miles on the 26th, whilst reconnoitring in front, and an outbreak of influenza so severe that, on the 29th, only 180 men could be supplied for digging.

On July 7th 2nd Lieutenant Fowell went out with a party to try to bring in a prisoner. They got into a German post which was empty, and stayed there for the enemy to return. Presently they were discovered, and the machine-gun fire was so hot that they had to return, which they did without loss. Next day some of the German naval division were lured out of their trenches and then brought into ours at the point of the revolver.

On the 9th another post, rushed by 2nd Lieutenant Dilworth and four men, was found empty.

The 12th division being now relieved by the 17th, the 7th Norfolk battalion went into the back areas for training till the end of the month, when Major Scarlett returned to the command from sick leave, and the 35th brigade again went up, at the beginning of August, this time to the front at Treux on the lower Ancre.

In the night of August 5th–6th the Norfolk battalion relieved part of the 1st battalion 132nd American Infantry in the front system. On the 6th the enemy succeeded in penetrating to the supports of the division on the right of the Norfolk battalion, which necessitated the formation of a defensive flank. In this operation " B " company did good work in opening communications with the battalion on the right, who expressed their appreciation of its co-operation. The situation on the right, facing Morlancourt, was partly restored on the 7th by a counter-attack. On the 8th an attack was made on the German trenches. The assembly points were reached about 3 a.m., zero hour being at 4.20. " A " and " B " companies were in position at that time under a moderate but accurate retaliatory fire, from which " B " had, by 5.40, suffered heavy casualties. At 6.15 a tank which had lost direction came up, and five minutes later the attack was launched in a thick mist, which, while it facilitated the surprise of the enemy, made it very difficult for the British to maintain their direction. On the right of the Norfolk battalion was " B " company in front, with " A " in support ; on the left " D " supported by " C." The two latter had had several casualties by 7.25 as they advanced. At 8 a.m. " A " was reported to have taken the first objective trench, and to be advancing on the second. A gap which had formed between the left of " A " and the right of the 9th Essex was filled by a platoon from " C." By 9 a.m. all objectives had been gained, and two light machine guns taken, but there were some gaps in the line and some mixing of units, due to the mist. By 12.40 p.m. " B " company had been forced to evacuate its final objective trench by trench-mortar fire, and was in a shallow trench behind it, which was commanded by the enemy on a hill. The right flank of the battalion was exposed, but no enemy could be seen, except those retreating over the sky line in front.

The position on the right was now cleared by an attack by the Cambridgeshire battalion, in which 300 prisoners were taken, and work was at once commenced on consolidating the captured trenches, patrols being sent forward to Morlancourt.

Next day there were few signs of the enemy, who now held only the north-east edge of Morlancourt. One of their machine-gun positions, being located, was rushed by 2nd Lieutenant Bradley and a party, who killed several Germans in it.

There is nothing much to be said of the period from August 10th to the 21st. Command of the brigade was assumed by Brigadier-General Beckwith, C.M.G., D.S.O., on the 11th, and on the 12th the battalion was represented at the King's inspection by 2nd Lieutenant Natusch and seven other ranks. There were some gas bombardments at night, and on the 21st, in anticipation of a fresh advance, the Norfolk battalion relieved the 9th Essex in front.

As the enemy was believed to be expecting the attack, a fire of Lewis guns was kept up all night to prevent his hearing the arrival of tanks.

The 35th brigade was to lead the attack, with the 36th on its left, and the 47th division on its right. The first objective was to be taken by the Norfolk battalion with the 1/1st Cambridgeshire on their right. The 9th Essex and 5th Buffs (attached to the 35th brigade) would then pass through to take the second objective, the Norfolk and Cambridgeshire battalions following them later. The Norfolk battalion quickly got possession of their part of the first trench, but the Essex and Cambridgeshire were not entirely successful. The position was rather obscure, but the C.O. succeeded in reorganizing the battalion on the correct line.

The corps cavalry now passed forward, but were unable to do much, and came back at 9 a.m. In the attack the Norfolk battalion's casualties had been:

Officers: Killed—Lieutenant J. A. W. Peyton. Wounded—2nd Lieutenants King, Cuthbertson, Palmer, Fowell, and Pratley.

Other ranks: C.S.M. Jackson badly wounded, and about a hundred other casualties.

The battalion was in touch with the Essex on the left, but the 47th division on the right had not been so successful, and the position there was uncertain.

Next day the enemy counter-attacked the 47th division, and, as two of its battalions gave ground, the 35th brigade had to form a defensive flank, which was done by the Buffs, facing north, whilst the 9th Essex and 7th Norfolk battalions faced east. Later, the Australians, on the right, counter-attacked and restored the position.

The next attack, on the 24th, fell to the 37th brigade. As the Norfolk outposts were being withdrawn Captain T. Rolfe was killed. The battalion moved back to the old British line. It was now reorganized, owing to its losses, in three companies, of which No. 1 consisted of the old "B" less one platoon; No. 2 of "C" and "D," and No. 3 of one platoon of "A" and one of "B."

On the 25th the brigade advanced in support of the 36th and 37th.

At 3 p.m. it was learned that the enemy were holding the Mametz ridge, and the 7th Norfolk battalion advanced with the Cambridgeshire on their right. Of the former, when the advance started at 4.20 p.m., No. 2 company was in front, No. 1 in support, and No. 3 in reserve. At first no opposition was encountered, but presently the advance was held up by machine-gun fire. After dark a machine-gun post in the Pommiers redoubt was stormed by Sergeant Everitt with a party. Many Germans were killed or taken, along with two machine guns.

Next day the 36th brigade passed forward, and, as a counter-attack was expected on the 27th from the direction of Trônes Wood, the 7th Norfolk battalion formed a defensive flank facing north-east.

On the 28th Maltz Horn Ridge was stormed by the 9th Essex and 1/1st Cambridgeshire and a hundred prisoners were captured. That evening the Norfolk battalion took over the outposts, and, in the heavy shelling, 2nd Lieutenant G. Maddison was killed. On the 29th the 37th brigade went through to a line east of Maurepas, and the 7th Norfolk battalion took up a line west of it, with the 9th Essex on the left extending to the famous Falfemont Farm. Thence on the 30th, as the 47th division passed forward, the Norfolk battalion retired for rest north of Favières Wood.

During the month they had advanced eleven miles and had taken thirteen machine guns, three trench mortars, one " granatenwerfer," and sixty prisoners.

It is a little difficult to distribute the August casualties between the various actions; but the total casualties of the month are stated in the diary :

Officers : Killed three—Captain T. Rolfe, Lieutenant J. A. W. Peyton, 2nd Lieutenant G. Maddison. Wounded or gassed nine—Lieutenants Dawkins and Pratley ; 2nd Lieutenants Dilworth, Bradley, King, Cuthbertson, Fowell, Palmer, Hogarth-Swann.

Other ranks : Killed or died of wounds forty-seven, wounded or gassed 313.

In the first three days of September the Norfolk battalion was reorganizing at Montauban. On the 5th the 12th division relieved the

18th at Vaux Wood on the Somme, and at 6.45 a.m. the battalion advanced through the wood with great difficulty, as parts of it were held by the enemy, and there was gas hanging about in others. Nevertheless, it got forward to its final objective, a trench just west of Nurlu. The casualties were:

Officers: Killed—Lieutenant W. P. Markwick. Wounded—Captains Shutes and Ferrier (gassed), Lieutenant Lloyd, and 2nd Lieutenant Birrell.

Other ranks: Eighty-four killed or wounded.

On the 6th the battalion supported an attack by the 1/1st Cambridgeshire and 9th Essex north of Nurlu, and in the evening went with the brigade into divisional reserve, where they remained training till the 17th, when they returned to Ville Wood, a mile south of Nurlu. On the 18th they attacked north-eastwards at 5.20 a.m. with Room trench as their final objective. The attack was in four waves, over a distance of 1,700 yards in all to the trench on the north-east of Epéhy.

The first wave gained its objective without difficulty, but the second wave, passing through it in the dark, got too far to the right and came under heavy artillery and machine-gun fire, especially on the railway embankment due south of Epéhy. The battalion was somewhat disorganized, but was reorganized at the embankment and got forward another 200 yards, where it held on for the rest of the day. Many Germans were killed, and about fifty taken, with two machine guns.

The Norfolk casualties were about 120 on this day, the officers being:

Killed—Lieutenants G. B. H. Plant, M.C., and K. C. Kirby.

Wounded—Captain Dillon, Lieutenant Forster, 2nd Lieutenants Lawrence, Lee, Davie, and Nixon.

The attack was continued at 11 a.m. on the 19th, the 1/1st Cambridgeshire and 5th Northamptonshire passing through the Norfolk battalion, but not getting very far. They eventually reached Ockenden and Room trenches, which were their objectives. The latter trench was occupied next day by the Norfolk battalion in relief of the 5th Berkshire.

On the 24th Lieutenant Spencer was killed and nine men were wounded by the German barrage for an unsuccessful attack on the troops on the Norfolk left, and at night they went, on relief by American troops, into support of the 9th Essex. They were not again engaged in that month.

During September they had taken sixty prisoners, twenty-five machine guns and one trench mortar. Their casualties were in all fifteen officers and 270 men.

The fighting career of the 7th Norfolk battalion had now almost ended. The diary for October is meagre, but only mentions one more action, on the 10th, when it is stated that the battalion occupied a sunken road 800 yards from the Quéant-Drocourt line, after some resistance. Two days before they had occupied the Fresnes-Rouvroy line, north of the Scarpe, on the road to Douai. On Armistice day they had been left far in rear of the British front and were at Landas, whence they marched forward as far as one march beyond St. Amand, where they arrived on the 26th November and stayed till the end of the year.

CHAPTER VII

THE 8TH (SERVICE) BATTALION IN FRANCE AND BELGIUM

(a) 1914–1915 : ORGANIZATION AND EARLY DAYS ON THE ANCRE

THE 8th Battalion Norfolk Regiment dated from September 4, 1914, when sufficient men had volunteered in reply to Lord Kitchener's call to warrant a commencement being made with its organization. Like the 7th Battalion, it was organized at Shorncliffe, the staff originally consisting of one regular officer of the regiment, one quartermaster-sergeant, R.G.A., and one ex-colour-sergeant of the 1st Battalion.

For the early history of the battalion we cannot do better than quote the following passage from an account furnished by Major H. P. Berney-Ficklin, M.C., who saw much service with it, part of it as adjutant. Much of what he says about the difficulties and circumstances of organization applies equally to the other service battalions. He writes :

> "The conditions in England at this time were practically indescribable. Men appeared in thousands . . . all in civilian dress . . . and had to be found accommodation, food, cooking utensils, and boots ; and had at the same time to be taught the first principles of soldiering. England owes a very large debt to those ex-non-commissioned officers who came forward immediately, some of them after ten or fifteen years civilian life, and placed their experience (rusty perhaps, but albeit of the utmost value) at the service of their country.

"On the evening of September 4th the first batch of recruits arrived on St. Martin's Plain—some 250, under Captain the Hon. W. F. North, a retired cavalry officer, who assumed temporary command of the battalion.

"By September 15th the battalion had reached a total of 1,200 men. Brevet-Colonel F. C. Briggs, a retired officer of the Devonshire Regiment, had assumed command, and about twenty officers had been appointed. The officers varied from those who had recently quitted the Regular Army and had been placed on the reserve of officers, to those who had only two or three days' experience of soldiering, and who had obtained their commissions by importuning Whitehall day and night without cessation.

"By September 20th the battalion had grown to some twenty officers and 1,300 men; later on arrangements were made to increase the number of officers.

"Some idea of the difficulties experienced in these early days may be gleaned from the fact that there were sixteen men to a tent, and that there was an average of two plates and at the most half a dozen knives and forks to each sixteen men, that tobacco tins had to be used as cups, and that there was a shortage of ablution places and washing materials. The latter were compensated for by taking the whole battalion down to the sea at 5 a.m. every morning and making every man bathe. It was impossible to prevent new recruits coming. A company would start a route march 300 strong and return with 310, and no one knew or could find out who were the new men. Costumes were of the weirdest. A gigantic sailor in blue sweater and trousers jostled a campanion in a grey suit and straw hat round which were the colours of a well-known Cambridge college. A swallow-tailed coat, striped trousers and spats concealed a future signal-sergeant. Some had no boots, others practically no clothes; whilst some brought suit cases and trunks, and yet all were fired with the same enthusiasm. Men shared everything together. The keenness to learn was extraordinary, and deputations for more and longer parades (the battalion was then working twelve hours a day) were frequent. Of crime there was practically none, and such as there was received such severe (and unauthorized) punishment at the hands of the men, long before the offender was brought before his commanding officer, that few strayed from the paths of righteousness. Of the difficulties of supplies, postings, promotions, records, etc., little need be said. They can best be imagined by those who have been similarly situated.

"Parades started at 5 a.m. and continued almost without interruption until 2 p.m., and there were frequent night operations. Furthermore, since every man desired to attend every parade, and since the proportionate number of officers was such that every one had to be on parade continuously, such things as company commanders' conferences from 10 p.m. to 4 a.m. were frequent; men were sometimes paid at midnight.

"About September 24th, Field-Marshal Lord Kitchener visited the battalion. He stayed about an hour, but in that time took everything in, and left the battalion well satisfied with his few words of congratulation. He tore away the bindings of red tape and authorized by word of mouth the private purchase of boots, forks, knives, spoons, and basins out of public funds (the battalion bought 1,000 pairs of boots that afternoon); he also told the battalion that they were now regarded as a unit to be equipped and trained.

"On October 3rd the battalion left Shorncliffe for Meeanee Barracks, Colchester. Officers and about one per cent of the N.C.O.'s were in khaki; the remainder still retained their heterogeneous apparel. The men swung up the streets of Colchester in even columns of fours, heads held high, and with a feeling of superiority to the mere civilians whose gibes at their appearance fell on barren ground. The spirit was there—knowledge could not fail to come. THE BATTALION WAS IN BEING.

"The winter of 1914–15 found the battalion training hard at Colchester. Civilian clothes had given way to postman's blue, which in its turn was gradually being superseded by khaki. Rifles for drill purposes were available in small quantities; some officers had horses; transport was appearing, very slowly it is true, but nevertheless coming, and training went on continuously. Esprit de corps reigned high, and was fostered by the publication in battalion orders of every mention of the 1st and 2nd Battalions that occurred in the newspapers. The battalion was the senior unit in the 53rd infantry brigade and in the 18th division, consisting of Eastern County regiments. Especially in one way this period of training at Colchester was of the greatest help. It provided an understanding between officers and other ranks that can rarely have been exceeded. More than ninety per cent of the officers and men came from Norfolk. The consequences were that men lived, ate, slept, and worked in their sections and platoons in which they were to fight in France. The officers not only knew their men by sight and by name, and by their military proficiency, but knew many of the details of their private life. On this foundation was the morale and esprit de corps of the battalion built up. In April, 1915, the battalion was transferred to Codford, some seven miles from Salisbury. Here during the fine summer of that year training was continued on the same intensive scale. By this time the battalion was fit in every sense of the word, and in the middle of June was almost fully equipped, and then orders came round for every man to have four days' leave. It was realized that this meant that the period in England was drawing to a close, and when equipment was finally complete to the minutest detail the battalion, together with the remainder of the division, was personally inspected by His Majesty King George. Rumours of the Dardanelles, Mesopotamia, and Salonika spread like wildfire, and it was only when entraining forms and states for use in France were received that head-quarters became aware of their ultimate destination.

"On July 20th the whole battalion was assembled and reminded that before them lay the task of worthily upholding the good name of the regiment, and on July 25, 1915, thirty-four officers and 997 other ranks embarked at Folkestone to join the British Expeditionary Force.

"The officers who originally accompanied the battalion are shown in the following list, with a list of deaths and honours won.

This list does not include any officer who subsequently joined the battalion, and no casualties apart from deaths are shown:

Nominal Roll of Officers of the 8th (Service) Battalion the Norfolk Regiment who Proceeded to France on July 25, 1915

" Brevet-Colonel	F. C. Briggs	Died 1916.
Major	H. G. de L. Ferguson, D.S.O.	Commanded battalion November, 1915, to March, 1918. Bar to D.S.O. Brevet rank of Lieutenant-Colonel
Do.	L. Fletcher	——
Captain and Adjutant	H. P. Berney Ficklin, M.C.	Brevet rank of Major on promotion. M.C.
Captain	C. F. Ashdown	M.C.
Do.	W. C. Gardiner	——
Do.	Hon. W. F. North	——
Do.	S. J. Paget	Killed 1918.
Do.	R. H. R. Nevill	——
Do.	J. H. Hall	——
Lieutenant	C. Shelton	M.C. Missing 1917
Do.	B. P. Ayre	Killed 1916
Do.	A. T. Berney Ficklin	M.C.
Do.	L. F. St. J. Davies	M.C. Died 1918
Do.	F. J. Morgan	D.S.O., M.C.
Do.	H. V. Hughes	——
Do.	J. F. Evans	——
Do.	R. E. Beckerson	M.C. and Bar
Do.	H. J. Impson	O.B.E., M.C.
2nd Lieutenant	A. J. H. Patten	M.C. and Bar
Do.	F. A. H. Owen Lewis	——
Do.	W. C. Morgan	Killed 1916
Do.	R. H. S. Fox	M.C.

2nd Lieutenant	E. E. M. Neilson	-	——
Do.	R. Grand	-	M.C.
Do.	G. W. S. Spencer	-	Died of wounds 1916
Do.	S. N. Cozens-Hardy	-	——
Do.	G. E. Miall Smith	-	M.C. Killed 1917
Do.	H. F. Hayes	-	——
Do.	H. M. MacNicol	-	Killed 1916
Do.	E. J. Pryor	-	——
Do.	F. Wright	-	——
Lieutenant and Quartermaster	F. W. L. Gleed	-	Died 1917
Captain	W. A. Todd, R.A.M.C."		

The 53rd brigade of the 18th infantry division consisted on landing in France of the 8th Norfolk, 10th Essex, 6th Royal Berkshire, and 8th Suffolk Regiments, and was thus mainly an Eastern Counties brigade. The brigade was commanded by Brigadier-General Hickie, the 18th division by Major-General Maxse.

Landing at Boulogne on July 26, 1915, the battalion entrained, at 10 a.m. on the 27th for Mollien-aux-Bois, north of Amiens, where it remained till August 3rd, when it moved to Lavieville, three miles west of Albert. There it was employed in digging trenches in the second line behind Aveluy, and receiving instruction in local war conditions till August 24th, when it moved to Bray, and on September 4th relieved the 8th Suffolk in trenches near the Mametz-Carnoy road.

This part of the line was taken over next day by the 5th division (in which was the 1st Norfolk battalion) and the 8th Battalion was in billets at Albert from the 18th to 26th, when it relieved the 6th Berkshire in trenches close up to the La Boisselle area on the Albert-Bapaume road. Here it was subjected to a good deal of bombardment by aerial torpedoes and other annoyances of trench warfare.

There is nothing particular to note till October 12th, when the battalion was inspected by Sir C. Munro, K.C.B., commanding the 3rd army of which the 10th corps (in which the 18th division then was) formed part. The following army order was issued :

"The Army Commander was very pleased with the appearance of the 8th Battalion Norfolk Regiment when he inspected them yesterday. The battalion looked smart, drilled well, and its turn out was most creditable. The Army Commander was particularly struck with the first line transport of the battalion. Will you please convey the Army Commander's appreciation to all concerned?"

On October 14th command of the battalion passed from Colonel Briggs to Major H. G. de L. Ferguson, D.S.O., who held it almost to the end of the battalion's existence in 1918. Nothing unusual beyond the ordinary routine of trench warfare occurred in October, the casualties during the month from bombardments and snipers being two officers wounded, five other ranks killed, and thirteen wounded.

So, too, during the first two-thirds of November the battalion was backwards and forwards between Buire on the Ancre and the front line trenches.

On November 22nd, the enemy fired a large mine at the junction of the Norfolk and the Essex lines, following it up by heavy fire but not making any infantry attack—not even occupying his own lip of the crater, which was a hundred yards long by fifty broad, with a depth of forty feet. This was the only remarkable occurrence in November, during which month the Norfolk casualties were three other ranks killed and eleven wounded. December passed equally uneventfully. On the 21st the battalion was taken back to Bussy-les-Daours to practise attacks on a model of the German trenches.

(b) 1916: THE SOMME FRONT—MONTAUBAN—DELVILLE WOOD—THIÉPVAL—SCHWABEN REDOUBT

During January, 1916, the 8th Norfolk battalion was still in the neighbourhood of Albert taking alternate turns in the trenches with the 8th Suffolk. The casualties of this month are not stated, but in February, when the same routine continued, they were four other ranks killed or died of wounds and eleven wounded.

In March the 8th Norfolk battalion was successively at Albert, La Houssoye, Bray-sur-Somme, and in the Maricourt defences (on the 17th), after which they went into rest billets at Etinehem from the 21st to the 28th, when they were again in trenches in the Z. 1 sector. The quietude of this month is shown by the casualties, which were only four other ranks wounded.

April was spent between the Z. 1 sector, the Maricourt defences, and rest at Etinehem till the 30th, when the 17th King's Liverpool relieved the Norfolk battalion, who went back, on May 1st, to La Houssoye, and on to Vaux en Amienois, where they had three weeks of steady training for the great Anglo-French offensive on the Somme. This battalion had been kept, with the rest of the division, for this great adventure, and it is this which largely accounts for its comparatively uneventful history prior to that. So much was this the case that when it did go into action in the Somme battle it still had twenty-six out of the thirty-four original officers, and about 600 out of the original 997 men, a very unusually large percentage for a battalion which had been eleven months in France. As the battalion was disbanded in February, 1918, its whole fighting history is crowded into the comparatively short period from July, 1916, to the beginning of 1918. It was none the less glorious for that. It had been intended in September, 1915, to be used to exploit, on the Amiens front, the successes expected from the battle of Loos; but, as has been already said, it was not called on.

On May 25th it was again at Bray, and for the rest of the month was busy digging in at Billon Wood, south of Carnoy. Up to June 24th Bray, the sub-sector of the defences north of Carnoy, and Billon Wood were alternately the positions of the 8th Norfolk battalion. Only in the position north of Carnoy was there much shelling to be borne. The great preparatory bombardment of the German trenches began on June 24th and continued until the general advance began on July 1st.

On June 26th the 8th Norfolk battalion had gone to Carnoy, from which village it was to share in the offensive, which at this point was directed due north.

On the morning of July 1, 1916, the 8th Norfolk battalion had on their right the 7th Queen's of the 55th brigade, on their left the

6th Berkshire of the 53rd, beyond which was the 54th. On the right of the 18th division the 30th and on the left the 7th were attacking. The 8th Norfolk battalion was in position in the assembly trench in the early hours, which were comparatively quiet and allowed of the men having some tea at 5.30 a.m. The assembly trench was just north of Carnoy, the objective being the enemy's trenches south-west of Montauban. At 7.20 a.m. the intensive bombardment began and was promptly followed

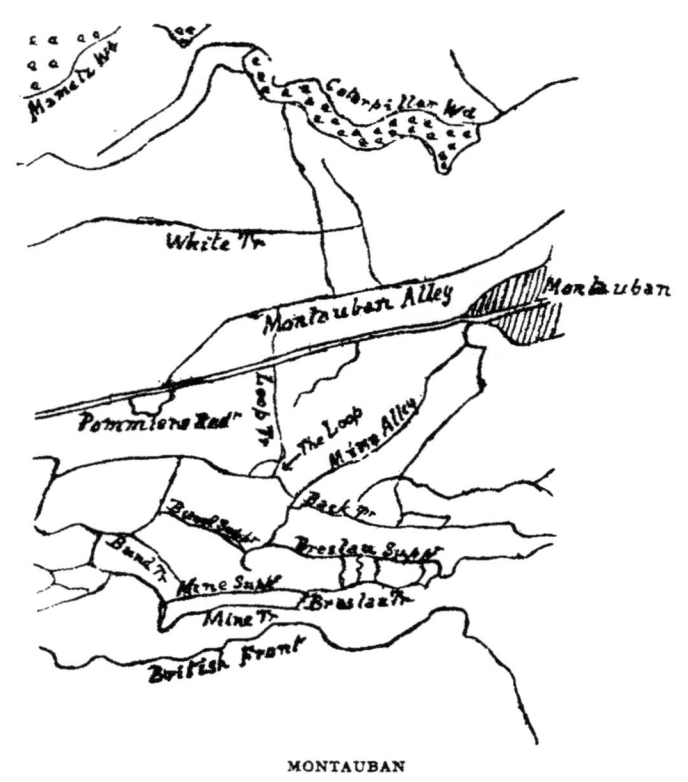

MONTAUBAN

by the enemy's retaliation. Seven minutes later the Germans fired a mine on the Norfolk front which did no damage. At the same time the first wave of the battalion's attack, consisting of part of "C" and "D" companies, deployed and lay out thirty yards in front of the assembly trench. This was effected without loss, and immediately after the assault went forward, the two companies moving each in four waves, which left the assembly trench successively. The German trench, known as Mine trench, was reached by the two companies practically without opposition or loss. Those Germans who still remained alive in it after the British barrage had passed were thoroughly cowed and surrendered at once. By 7.40 a.m. Mine Support trench had been taken, the wire in front of it having been wiped out by the artillery. "C" company, on the right, had taken thirty prisoners from the west edge of the Mine crater. So far the casualties had been very few.

By 8.40 Bund Support trench had been taken without difficulty and a halt was made.

The continued advance was not so easy, for as the companies left Bund Support trench they came under a very heavy machine-gun enfilade fire from Breslau support and Back trenches. Officers and men fell in large numbers. "D" company, on the left, had been reduced to about ninety men and was commanded by C.S.M. Raven, as every officer was *hors de combat*. "C" had only two subalterns left, and not more than a hundred men. About 10.30 a.m. Pommiers trench, the first objective, was reached and taken in part by "D," a part of "C" also getting into it. The rest of "C" on the right, however, was stopped by machine-gun fire, and by a German strong point at the junctions of Boche and Back trenches with Mine Alley.

"C" was now reinforced by a platoon of "B" its supporting company, under 2nd Lieutenant Miall-Smith, and by the battalion bombers with Sergeant West. With this help the strong point was taken, and about 150 Bavarians, with two officers, were captured. This success enabled the right of "C" to push forward into the hitherto untaken portion of Pommiers trench.

Meanwhile, "A" company, in reserve, had advanced at 7.45 a.m. in artillery formation and consolidated in Mine Support trench. It then went forward to Bund Support trench and consolidated there. "B," the support company, having, as already stated, sent one platoon to "C," followed with the other three to Pommiers trench. The Pommier redoubt had been taken by the 54th brigade by 9.30 a.m.

At 3 p.m. "D" company had taken the Loop, and it, with "C," advanced on Montauban Alley the final objective of the battalion.

Owing to the heavy machine-gun fire from this line, and from northwest of Montauban, " D " again suffered very severely, whilst " C," on the right, led by 2nd Lieutenant Attenborough, failed in repeated attempts to reach the Alley. At last a bombing party commanded by 2nd Lieutenant Gundry-White gained an entrance by bombing up Loop trench on the left. Both 2nd Lieutenant Attenborough and R.S.M. Coe were killed just before the success. Montauban Alley was now taken, and the battalion was in touch with the 7th Queen's, of the 55th brigade on the right, and the 6th Royal Berkshire on the left.

At 6 p.m. consolidation of the captured position was begun and patrols went out to reconnoitre along Caterpillar and East trenches. " C " company, with its reinforcement of a platoon of " B," could only muster one officer and seventy or eighty men between them. " A " company was therefore brought up from Pommiers trench, and sent forward to hold the advanced position known as Green Lane, where, about 8.p.m., it began constructing strong points and sending out patrols towards Caterpillar Wood.

The enemy continued a heavy bombardment, with 5·9 in. and a few 77 mm. guns, on the west end of Montauban Alley, especially on its point of junction with Loop trench.

The 8th Battalion's first big battle had cost it terribly heavily. Of officers there were killed or died of wounds Captain B. P. Ayre and 2nd Lieutenants J. H. Attenborough and S. A. Wharton; wounded Captain and Adjutant Berney-Ficklin, M.C., Captain Hall, 2nd Lieutenants Hampson, Blackborn, Padfield, Ironmonger, Cozens-Hardy, and MacLean. Of other ranks 102 were killed, 219 wounded, and thirteen missing. Total casualties—eleven officers, 334 other ranks. To the congratulations of the commander of the 13th corps General Maxse added his to his division : " Well done. It's what I expected. Now hold on to what you have gained so splendidly."

The next day was one of bombardments of varying intensity by the enemy, in which 2nd Lieutenants Vos and Piper and twenty-six others were wounded. The casualties from the same cause were twelve on the 3rd, on the evening of which day the battalion was relieved by the 8th Suffolk battalion, and returned to bivouac at Carnoy, where it remained till the 7th, when it went back to training near Grovetown Camp on the Albert-Bray road.

There their losses were partly recouped by a draft of ten officers and 240 men from the 1st, 7th, and 10th Battalions. By the 18th they were in bivouac in the Talus Boisé salient just east of Carnoy.

On the 19th the 8th Norfolk battalion was ordered up to the valley north-east of Carnoy to be ready for a counter-attack on Delville Wood. Reaching the valley at 4.30 a.m. they were ordered to be in position to attack at 6.15 a.m.

The brigade orders required the battalion to take the whole southern portion of Delville Wood as far as Princes Street, the central ride, from east to west through the wood.[1] During this attack a barrage would be maintained on the wood north of Princes Street. Directly the southern portion of the wood had been cleared, the 10th Essex and 6th Berkshire battalions were to form up just south of Princes Street, and the 8th Suffolk in Longueval village.

The 8th Norfolk would then take over the whole wood and hold it with sixteen strong points round the edge. The battalion orders placed " A " company on the right in front line, " B " on the left, " C " in support, " D " in reserve. " C " was to be responsible for dropping posts along Princes Street from west to east as the attack progressed. The attack was to be from the south-west.

At 5.30 a.m. " A " and " B " moved off from the valley. Just before reaching the south-west corner of the wood, " A " deployed and " B " came up on its left for the same purpose; but heavy machine-gun fire from just north of Princes Street forced it to come round and deploy on the right of " A," which, at the same time, eased off leftwards as far as the west end of Princes Street, so as to make room for " B " on its right. This delayed the deployment, and no attack was possible before 7.15 a.m. up to which hour the brigade artillery was requested to keep the barrage on the south portion of the wood.

It was known that the South Africans were holding the line north-west along Buchanan Street, and thence west along Princes Street and the southern portion of Longueval.

[1] See sketch at p. 25.

The attack launched at 7.15 a.m. went well on the right, and "B" got forward to Campbell Street by 7.45; but "A" was held up by machine-gun fire from north of Princes Street. As the British barrage was now on that portion of the wood, it was not possible for bombing parties to deal with these machine guns. The left two platoons of this company suffered particularly severely, losing both their officers (2nd Lieutenants MacNicol and Benn) killed. The position at 8.15 a.m. was this: "B" was on the line of Campbell Street as far as the centre of it; on its left was "A" in a diagonal line running north-west to the north end of Buchanan Street, having with it 2nd Lieutenant Gundry-White and his bombers. The line of Princes Street west of Buchanan Street was held by a platoon of the reserve company "D" and a few posts from "C."

At 9 a.m. "B," on the right, had advanced half-way through the wood from Campbell Street towards King Street, but was held up here and suffered rather heavily from machine-gun fire. One platoon was sent up by "C" from support, under Lieutenant Hughes, which took a machine gun at the south end of King Street and killed all its crew.

At the same time "A" pushed on to the line of Campbell Street, whilst "C" dropped more posts on the line of Princes Street, from its junction with Buchanan Street to that with Campbell Street, and Lieutenant Gundry-White's bombers drove off a German machine gun which had been causing loss from just north-west of the northern end of Buchanan Street.

At 11.30 the battalion was holding the line of King Street and Princes Street, the latter being occupied by "C" (less one platoon sent to "B"). Here there was a delay till the British barrage lifted from the extreme eastern edge of the wood, when "B" again pushed forward and occupied the south-eastern edge, and the eastern as far north as Rotten Row. "A" was held up by a machine gun posted at the eastern extremity of Princes Street till 2nd Lieutenant Gundry-White and his bombers finally succeeded in driving it back, when "A" got into touch with "B" at the east end of Rotten Row, from which point its line extended across the wood diagonally to the north end of King Street.

At 12.40 the other three battalions of the 53rd brigade were sent forward to take the part of the wood north of Princes Street, whilst the 8th Norfolk battalion made strong points on the east, south-east, and south edges of the wood south of it.

The afternoon was fairly quiet in the wood, but German shells rained incessantly on the south-east part of Longueval.

The attacks of the other battalions in Longueval and the northern part of Delville Wood could make but little progress, and they had to dig themselves in, as had the Norfolk men in the southern portion. Here, from the afternoon of the 19th till the early morning of the 22nd, when it was relieved, the 53rd brigade had to hold on to the captured portion of the wood against a tremendous bombardment, a perpetual fire from snipers, and innumerable attacks by small bodies of Germans in the tangled undergrowth and amongst the ruined trees.

Again the 8th Norfolk battalion had suffered fearful casualties. Of officers, 2nd Lieutenants W. C. Morgan, H. M. MacNicol, and B. W. Benn were killed. The wounded were Lieutenants Evans and Cozens-Hardy, 2nd Lieutenants Miall-Smith, MacLean, Llewellyn, Laker, Wadley. Lieutenant F. St. J. Davies was also wounded but able to remain at duty. In other ranks the losses were seventy-eight killed or died of wounds, 174 wounded, thirty missing. Total casualties, eleven officers and 282 other ranks.

On relief by the 1st Gordon Highlanders on the 22nd, the 8th Norfolk battalion went to Grovetown, thence by train to Longpré-les-Corps-Saints on the 23rd, to Arques by train on the 26th, and thence by march to Godewaersvelde, which they reached on the 29th. Here they were training and reorganizing till August 5th, when they proceeded by stages to the 18th divisional training camp south of Bailleul, reaching it on the 12th, and being inspected by H.M. the King on the 14th. After twelve days spent here in training of all sorts and route marching, the battalion went by train to Diéval, and on by march for more training in the area Herlin-le-Vert–Chelers–Magnicourt, and from September 1st to 8th in the Monchy-Breton area.

By September 18th the 8th Norfolk battalion was at Forceville camp, whence, on the 25th, they proceeded in fighting order to Wood

Post in Authuille Wood for the attack next day on Thiépval and the high ground north of it.

In this assault the leading battalions of the 53rd brigade were the Suffolk on the right and the Essex on the left. The 8th Norfolk were in brigade support, the Berkshire in reserve. The only part the Norfolk battalion played in the advance on Thiépval was the supply of a party

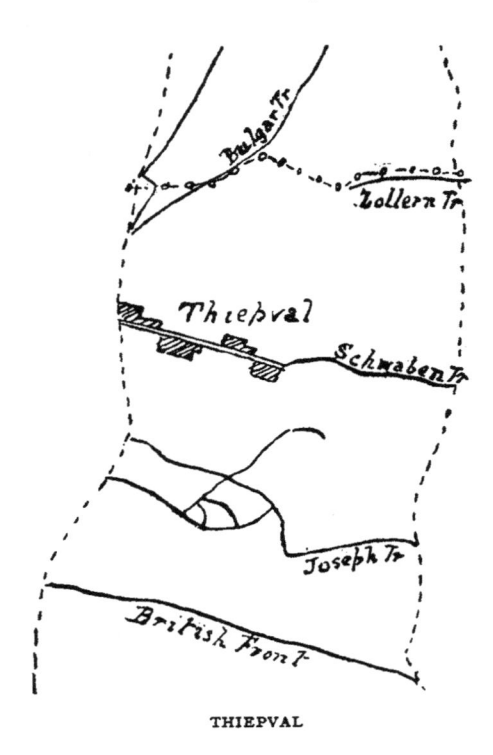

THIEPVAL

of "C" company and one platoon of "B" to follow the leading battalions and "mop up." "A" and "D," with battalion head-quarters, remained at Wood Post.

The attack began at 12.35 p.m. and progressed splendidly, the Suffolk and Essex battalions reaching Thiépval with little difficulty, whilst the "moppers up" completely cleared the village and the trenches south of it within the brigade areas. That is the account in the battalion diary, which is naturally not concerned to deal fully with others than its own battalion. From the records of the division, however, the severity of the fighting is clear. Its casualties amounted to 1,456; even those of the " moppers up " of the Norfolk battalion were thirty-nine in all, though only two men were killed.

" A " and " D " companies moved up to the old British front line, and later to the first assembly trench of the attackers. Here they came under the German barrage, which, however, fell chiefly on the 2nd assembly trench.

On the 27th the " mopping up " party, which had dug in northeast of Thiépval, returned to the battalion. The German shelling still continued.

At 1 p.m. the 8th Suffolk battalion and the 7th Queen's (55th brigade) on their left attacked respectively the trench on the right of Schwaben redoubt and the redoubt itself, the 8th Norfolk being again in support of the 7th Queen's. "D" company "mopped up" for the Queen's, whilst two other platoons did so for the Suffolk battalion. Here again the leading battalions, as at Thiépval, had the severest fighting, and for several days after were engaged in constant combats to maintain themselves against the frequent counter-attacks on a position of which the value was fully appreciated by the enemy. A full account of these days is given in the history of the 18th division.

On the morning of the 29th, after leaving " A " company as a reserve for the Queen's, the Norfolk battalion fell back to their position of the 27th, and the same evening the battalion was withdrawn to Forceville, except " B " company, left at Crucifix Corner to carry the dead for burial, an occupation on which they were still engaged on the 30th. The casualties of the battalion at Thiépval were:

26th and 27th—2nd Lieutenant Jeary wounded, with two other ranks killed, thirty-three wounded, and eight missing.

28th to 30th—2nd Lieutenant Wright wounded. Other ranks, five killed, eighty-three wounded, of whom eighteen remained at duty.

Total casualties, September 26th–30th—Officers, two wounded. Other ranks, seven killed, 116 wounded, eight missing—in all 133.

On October 2nd the battalion replaced the 7th Queen's at North Bluff, north of Authuille, where they were in dug-outs.

An attack on the Schwaben redoubt, where there had been furious fighting ever since September 28th, was planned for October 4th, but the attack across the open had to be postponed, and the officer commanding the Norfolk battalion decided on a large and carefully organized bombing

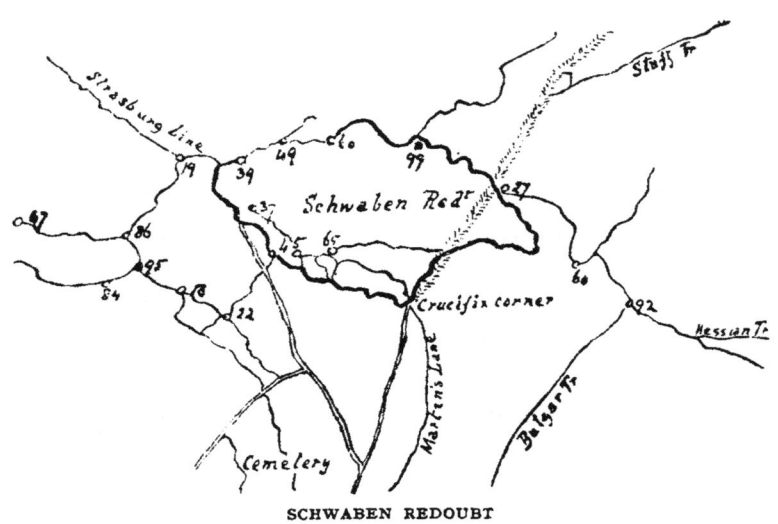

SCHWABEN REDOUBT

attack, to be made on the morning of the 5th by the battalion bombing officer, who was to take with him the battalion and company bombers, the Lewis gunners, and the battalion snipers. The plan was to attack from both flanks. Support parties were told off in rear to replace casualties, and side parties were selected for each trench which branched off from the main lines attacked. The idea was to work down these side trenches and form blocks immediately junctions were reached. A barrage was arranged to cover all German trenches to the west of the line marked by points 86 and 19, a line running nearly south to north just outside the western end of the redoubt, as well as the German communication trenches on the north of it.

The attack was arranged for 6 a.m., and, owing to the trenches being knee-deep in mud, assembly was begun as early as 2 a.m. Even that was not early enough, and the attack had to be postponed till 7.30 a.m.

The left and right attacks must be described separately.

Left attack.—On this side there were three parties attacking along three parallel trenches. At first all went well, and the centre and right parties joined hands at point 39 in the north-west corner of the redoubt, on its farther side. The left party was more strongly opposed and was unable to reach its objective, point 19 in the Strasburg trench, just outside the north-west corner of the redoubt. They were counter-attacked by a strong working party across the open, and by bombers along the trenches. The attack across the open was repulsed by the Lewis guns, but with the bombers it was different; for the mud in the trenches made it very difficult to get up sufficient supplies of bombs whilst the Germans on the defensive had theirs close at hand. The left party was therefore forced back to its starting-place, point 45 in the south-west margin of the redoubt. About the same time another counter-attack across the open towards point 65, on the rear of the right party, was practically annihilated by Lieutenant Gundry-White with Lewis gun and rifle fire.

The *right attack*, meeting with strong opposition from the start, was at first driven back to point 27 on the north-east edge of the redoubt. In the very strenuous fighting along this line 2nd Lieutenant Whitty was killed, and many other casualties occurred. But the British were not to be denied, and pressed steadily forward along the northern margin of the redoubt till they found themselves fifty yards to the west of point 99. Here, at 2.30 p.m., orders were received to consolidate in anticipation of the relief of the 18th division by the 39th. The 18th division had taken, with a loss of nearly 2,000 casualties, the whole of the Schwaben redoubt, except a small strip on the north-west about points 19, 39, 49, and 69. The casualties of the 8th Norfolk battalion on October 5th were:

Officers: Killed—2nd Lieutenant T. Whitty, M.C. Wounded—Lieutenant L. F. St. J. Davies, 2nd Lieutenant Inch.

Other ranks: Ten killed, forty-nine wounded, twenty-nine missing.

After its severe trials in this great achievement the 18th division went back into training and rest in the neighbourhood of Candas.

It returned to Albert on the 16th, when Colonel Ferguson resumed command of the 8th Norfolk battalion on relinquishing temporary command of the brigade. Here the battalion was employed in and out of trenches and furnishing diggers till the 21st, when it again went into front line for the projected attack on Regina trench.

This was a long trench running from the sunken road to Grandcourt, some 1,100 yards east of the Schwaben redoubt, eastwards as far as the Courcellette-Miraumont road, a length of about 3,000 yards. The objective of the attack was the capture of the Regina trench from a point 150 yards west of the Miraumont road leftwards, establishing strong points at the junctions with Courcellette trench, Twenty-three Road, and Left trench.

The Norfolk battalion was to have the 10th Essex on its right, and the 11th Lancashire Fusiliers (74th brigade) on its left. The battalion was thus disposed:

" C " company on the right, with its objective from the point 150 yards from the Miraumont road to the junction of Kinora trench. " B " continued to the left as far as Left trench. " D " in support, would go forward as far as Regina trench, help in consolidating, and then return by Kinora trench to the starting-point in Hessian trench. " A " was in reserve.

The strength of the battalion for this attack was eighteen officers and 540 men.

" C " and " B " formed up in Hessian trench for attack in two waves, and in Vancouver trench for a one-wave advance. " D " was in Sudbury trench, " A " in Zollern trench, with orders to move up to Vancouver trench at zero.

At zero (12.6 p.m.) " C," " B," and " D " went over, and six minutes later were in Regina trench. The Germans on the front of " C " surrendered freely, but those opposed to " B " put up a stout resistance, which ended in their being all taken or killed. The resistance was specially strong in the gap of a hundred yards between the left of " B " and the right of the Lancashire Fusiliers. Of this part the history of the 18th Division gives the following account:

" A party of Landwehr put up a good fight, however, against

the company of 8th Norfolks that was led by Captain Morgan, D.S.O. Only most aggressive bombing caused them to give in. Afterwards Captain Morgan took sixteen prisoners in very easy fashion. He was superintending the clearing up of the trench, when he noticed a waterproof sheet hanging from the parapet. Lifting it, he found that it screened the entrance to a dug-out eight steps deep. On each step sat a couple of Germans, their backs to the entrance. When Captain Morgan called to them to come out, they came unarmed. When the Norfolk and Essex were in full possession of Regina, a dozen Germans who had lost themselves descended into the trench, not knowing it had changed hands. They did not seem unduly depressed when they found themselves prisoners."

This first phase of the operations ended at 2 p.m. on October 21st.

The second phase was from 2 p.m. to 6 p.m. on the same day. On account of the casualties incurred, and the large amount of consolidation required, " D " company was now ordered to remain in Regina trench. " A " in Hessian trench, was to be ready to help " D " if called upon, in which event its place would be taken by one company of the 6th Berkshire.

At 6 p.m. " B," " C," and " D " were in Regina trench, in touch with the battalions on their right and left; " A " was in Vancouver trench, with two posts in Hessian trench.

From 6 p.m. on the 21st to 6 p.m. on the 22nd the battalion held its position under the usual heavy shelling by the Germans. During the night of the 22nd–23rd " A " took its place with " C " in Regina, whilst " B " and " D " returned respectively to Hessian and Vancouver trenches. " D " had done very good work in opening up Kinora trench.

There was a thick mist up to 11 a.m. on the 23rd. Consolidation was continued under intermittent shelling till nightfall, after which the battalion was relieved by the 11th Royal Fusiliers (54th brigade). The Norfolk casualties in these operations were:

Officers: Killed—2nd Lieutenants J. W. Case, and H. V. Marsh (died of wounds). Wounded—Captain Shelton, M.C. (missing), 2nd Lieutenant Barrington, M.C.

Other ranks: Twenty-seven killed, ninety-four wounded, fifteen missing. Total 136.

The rest of October and the early days of November were spent uneventfully at Albert, and in the trenches north of Pozières.

From November 5th to 8th, the Norfolk battalion was at Warloy, where General Maxse, commanding the 18th division, presented decorations and medals gained for Montauban, Delville Wood, Thiépval, Schwaben redoubt, and Regina trench, viz. one D.S.O., six M.C.'s, six D.C.M.'s, thirty-one M.M.'s, thirty-seven parchment certificates. The weather about this time was very wet and the trenches full of mud.

On the 13th all preparations were made for exploiting the results of an attack about St. Pierre Divion by the 19th division; but, as part of the attack on the left was held up, the Norfolk battalion was not called into action, and returned, from the trenches north of Pozières, to Ovillers. There is nothing special to note in November till the 19th, when the battalion began to move to the Forest of l'Abbaye near Abbeville for training, where they remained till the end of December.

(c) 1917–1918: THE ANCRE—IRLES—YPRES—POELCAPPELLE—DISBANDMENT

At the end of January, 1917, the 8th Norfolk battalion went forward from the training grounds to the front line near Miraumont, where they were in trenches in the right sector of the brigade front, following the ordinary routine of trench warfare till February 15th, when they moved into the front trenches for the attack, on the 17th, down the slope of the valley on the left bank of the Ancre below Miraumont. By this time General Maxse had been promoted to command the 18th corps, and had been succeeded in the 18th division by Major-General R. P. Lee.

There had been five weeks of intense frost on this front which at last broke on the very morning of the attack when, " the hard surface of the ground turned first into one big slide, and then became a sea of mud, in which rifles and machine guns got clogged, and through which the infantry pressed a slow, floundering, stamina-testing way."[1]

On this day the 54th brigade was on the right of the 18th division, with its right touching the 2nd division, and its left touching the right of the 53rd brigade, about a hundred yards west of the part of Boom Ravine leading down like the stem of a T, the head of which was formed by its branches to the right and left. Thus the 53rd brigade would not

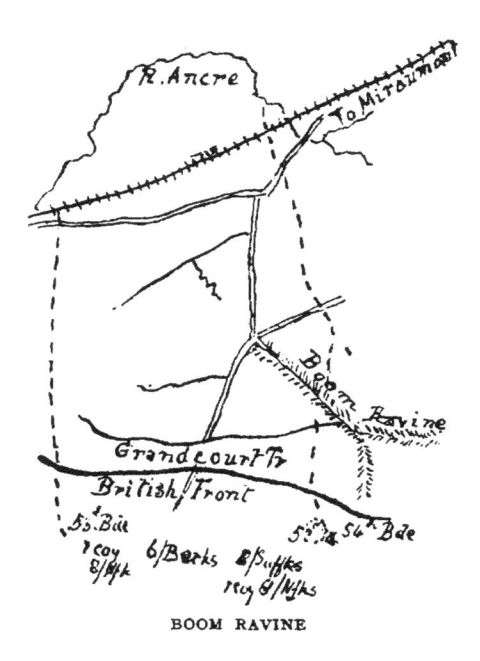

BOOM RAVINE

touch the stem of the T, and only its right would come on the crosspiece. For the attack the 8th Suffolk battalion was to be on the right, touching the left of the 11th Royal Fusiliers of the 54th brigade. On their left the 6th Berkshire took up the line, of which the extreme left was " A " company of the Norfolk battalion. " B " was attached to the 6th Berkshire, " D " to the 8th Suffolk, and " C " was to carry bombs and ammunition. The companies were thus much divided up and the fortunes of each must be followed separately.

[1] " History of 18th Division," p. 140.

Till midnight of the 16th–17th the whole battalion was kept in Thiépval in the gravel pits. By 4 a.m. it had moved to the assembly points south of the long Grandcourt trench.

To the eternal shame of two deserters from another division, the hour of attack had been given away to the enemy and the chance of surprise ruined.

Consequently the formation, at 5.30 a.m., was carried out with the greatest difficulty under a tremendous German barrage. The difficulty was enhanced by the darkness and the slippery ground. The casualties in this preliminary were one officer and fifteen other ranks in " A " company alone.

At zero (5.45 a.m.) " A," to which were attached four bombing sections of " C " and two Lewis guns from head-quarters, advanced close up to the British barrage, from which a few " shorts " were received on the left. It was still dark and difficult to distinguish on the left the British barrage from the bursting of the German shells. The dazzling effects of shell bursts and gun flashes added to this difficulty, and the two left sections of the first and second waves lost direction, as did part of the third. These troops which had so lost direction began advancing with the Grandcourt road on their right, instead of on their left as was intended. Captain Ashdown, commanding " A ", rapidly collected his men and led them back to the intermediate objective, Grandcourt trench, which had been reached without great difficulty, thanks to a very efficient Stokes mortar bombardment. There he got into touch with the left of the 6th Berkshire, which had kept exact direction.

This first objective was reached by 6 a.m. An hour later the final objective, on the railway line in the Ancre valley, had been attained, and, under severe sniping fire, " A " company set about the construction of two strong posts, one near their junction with the 6th Berkshire, the other farther to the left. Here it remained under heavy shell fire, which was directed especially on the area south of the Grandcourt-Miraumont road, till it was relieved, on February 19th, by the 10th Essex. " B " company had formed up at zero on the 17th under an intense German barrage from Loupart Wood. At 8.30 it moved forward into Grandcourt trench, where it remained, suffering some casualties, till withdrawn to

Hessian trench at 4.30 a.m. on the 19th. " C " also formed up at zero, and was hard at work all day, till 6 p.m. on the 17th, carrying up bombs, R.E. material, and other supplies to the forward dumps. The going was bad, and got worse as the thaw took effect. The right party had about seven casualties as soon as they came under shell fire; the left, on the Grandcourt road, suffered less, but in the slippery going several men were incapacitated by sprained ankles or accidents. This party was in St. Pierre Divion by 6 p.m., the right not till midnight. All the 18th " C " was busy carrying. So great was the difficulty that the left party of thirty men took two and a half hours to cover 200 yards with a load of one box S.A.A. and two boxes Mills' grenades to two men. Early on February 19th the company was back in the gravel pits, very much exhausted after thirty-six hours of this heart-breaking work, for their conduct of which 2nd Lieutenants Bartley and Sherlock are commended in the diary. " D " was lying under a bank very heavily shelled up to noon on the 17th, when two platoons were withdrawn to Regina trench, and small carrying parties were supplied to the 8th Suffolk battalion. On the 18th, at 9 a.m., the two remaining platoons were sent back to Regina trench; by 3 p.m. all were back in the gravel pits, and by 3 a.m. on the 19th in dug-outs in Hessian trench. The casualties on these days were:

Officers: Wounded—2nd Lieutenant Peyton.

Other ranks: Seventeen killed, fifty-seven wounded, and eighteen missing. Total ninety-two, of which thirty-five were in " A " and twenty-three in " B."

On the 22nd the battalion relieved the 10th Essex in front, for the day only, and then went back to the rear till March 4th, when it again moved up to the front, and on the 10th was again employed in the attack on Grevillers trench and the village of Irles, a little to the east of Miraumont.

The Grevillers trench extended south by east from the rear and centre of Irles, which was strongly held by the enemy, and was covered on the east by Resurrection trench to the north and Below trench to the south of the Miraumont road. Resurrection trench had been taken by the 8th Suffolk battalion on March 6th. It is true that when Irles was attacked on the 10th the Germans were about to evacuate it, but their intended evacuation was turned by the attack into a flight from it.

The attack on this occasion was to be a converging one by the 10th Essex from Resurrection trench due eastwards, whilst the Norfolk battalion was to advance on Grevillers trench north-eastwards, then to wheel to their left and join the Essex east of the village.

The Norfolk battalion orders were to capture Grevillers trench and push out certain strong points. "D" was to take the trench farthest to

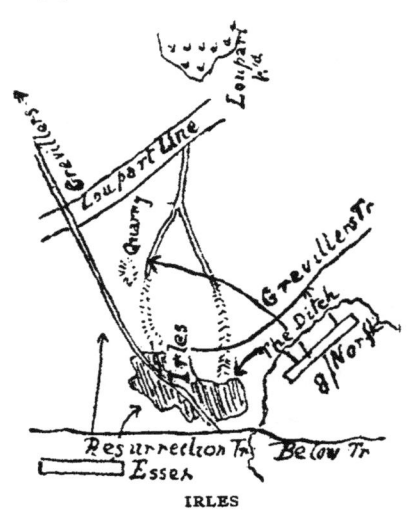

IRLES

the right and establish two strong points. "B" would act likewise on the left of "D" whilst "C" cleared the south-east of Irles, and also established two strong points. "A" would remain as reserve in Below trench. Again the action of the several companies is, for clearness' sake, described separately.

"D," getting off punctually at zero, reached and got into its portion of the trench at 5.21 a.m., and at once sent out a platoon to make the strong point. At 6 a.m. it was in touch with the 2nd division on the right, and with "B" on the left. It had taken thirty prisoners and two machine guns, a third being reported later. During the day "D" dug itself in safely in Grevillers trench, which had been practically wiped out before it was reached. Only a few posts were found and one strong point, in which eighteen Germans held out till they were eventually captured by two non-commissioned officers of " B " and " C." At 4 a.m. on the 11th " D " was relieved and sent back to Mouquet Farm.

" B " meanwhile also advanced at zero, leaving one platoon behind till 5.35, when it halted to put on respirators on account of an alarm of gas, which proved to be false. Five minutes later Captain Morgan realized that he had overrun Grevillers trench, which was now an unrecognizable network of shell holes. It afterwards transpired that the company had, in the thick mist and darkness, swung three-quarters right instead of half right, and so had missed the guidance of the Irles-Loupart road.

Captain Morgan now sent out 2nd Lieutenant V. M. Harrison with some men to the point where he thought the strong point should be made, and instructed him to dig in there. The rest of the company then returned south-westwards and immediately struck the Irles-Loupart road. It was getting light, but the mist still lay heavily.

" C " advanced in artillery formation, with two sections left in rear with the object of swinging into Irles and clearing the south and east of the village. At 5.20 the company came on uncut wire ten feet deep which could not be passed. The two leading platoons, which had extended after passing the Irles-Loupart road, now pushed on to construct the two strong points, whilst the supporting platoon began consolidating on the site of Grevillers trench. Lieutenant Dillon, seeing nothing of " B " on his right, moved in that direction along the line of Grevillers trench with a Lewis gun. Some men running, whom he believed to be " B," turned out to be Germans, who fired on him. He was now at a point where the trench was only two feet deep, and was under heavy rifle fire. At 5.45, as this fire slackened, he saw a large body advancing towards him astride the Irles-Loupart road, which turned out to be " B " returning after overrunning its objective. The Germans who had fired on him were now trapped between him and " B." A few of them were killed and the rest surrendered. They were much astonished at being attacked in rear, since they had neither seen nor heard the passage of " B " over the line of the trench. " B " now got into touch with " D " on the right, and had one platoon out in its strong point.

As there was a gap between the left of " B " and the right of " C," Captain Morgan filled it with the platoon he had left behind. Consolidation was begun by " B " at 8.30. 2nd Lieutenant Harrison had consolidated his strong point when he found himself in the midst of German snipers lying in the surrounding shell holes, where twelve of them were killed in the course of the day. The rest of the day was uneventful for " B," which was relieved at 4.30 a.m. on the 11th, and sent back to the gravel pits.

We must now return to the doings of " C " after Lieutenant Dillon had established his communications with " B." Before that he had already sent out 2nd Lieutenant Piper with No. 9 platoon, with orders to construct a strong point. Piper reached the point indicated to him at 6.10 a.m. The map was found to be wrong in marking a quarry, on the north of which the point was to be, larger than it really was. Piper's strong point was designated as No. 3. No. 10 platoon (2nd Lieutenant A. St. J. Banks) had also reached the site of its strong point at 6.32.

At 6.30 Lieutenant Dillon was at Piper's post, where he got into communication with the 10th Essex about the Irles-Grevillers road, which they had reached by the north side of Irles.

At 7.15 2nd Lieutenant Banks was consolidating a shell hole, in which he had found a badly wounded German officer and seven men, when he saw two German officers and thirty men moving north-east up the valley from Irles and firing on Piper's strong point and his own. Who these were will be shown presently.

Meanwhile 2nd Lieutenant Sherlock with the two sections of " C " left in rear had entered Irles from the ditch on its south-west side and begun clearing the village. A troublesome machine gun, quite close, was taken on by a lance-corporal and five men, until it was captured by a party of the Essex from the other side of the village. The Germans in the village, who were mostly taken in batches of three or four, stated that Irles had been nearly empty till early in the morning, when a hundred men were sent in again to meet an attack which was expected from Resurrection trench, and not from the ditch on the south side of Irles.

At 7.10 a large party of Germans, caught in flank, refused to surrender and began retreating north-east along the valley from Irles. It was this party which was seen by Banks and Piper five minutes later. Sherlock, realizing that these Germans would run right up against Piper's point, followed them, and the Germans found themselves between the fire of Sherlock's and Piper's men. They fought well till they had lost about ten men, when the officers came forward and surrendered. Sherlock now returned to the clearing of Irles, and, as the German line of retreat was clearly by Piper's point, he extended his men in the south of the village and beat it up towards Piper.

By noon the village had been cleared, and, according to the battalion diary, about 130 prisoners had been taken, though the history of the division claims only sixty-eight. Sixteen machine guns were taken, as well as a number of eight-inch brass cartridge cases stacked ready for removal. "C" continued its consolidation till relieved at 3 a.m. on the 11th.

The casualties in this affair were not heavy. Only one officer (2nd Lieutenant Scott) was slightly wounded. In the actual attack there were six men killed, fourteen wounded, and four missing; later six more were wounded and three missing. Total casualties thirty-four of all ranks.

After this very successful affair the battalion went back into training areas till the end of the month.

During the first eighteen days of April the training was specially for semi-open and open warfare in the neighbourhood of Béthune. On the evening of the 25th, when in billets at Bully Grenay and Les Brebis, the Norfolk battalion was unlucky enough to be hit by a heavy shell which killed seven and wounded four men.

On the 28th they were moved by rail to Arras, and bivouacked in a field just west of the ruins of Beaurains on the road to Bapaume. At the end of the month the strength of the battalion was forty-nine officers and 953 other ranks.

On May 3rd occurred the attack of the 18th division on Chérisy which ended disastrously in failure. It is fully described in the history of the 18th division, but it is beyond our scope; for the brigades engaged were the 54th and 55th. The 53rd was kept in reserve about Neuville

Vitasse, and was not called up at all. All the same, it appears probable the Norfolk battalion got some of the "overs" from the battle in front, since their casualties in May were 2nd Lieutenant Howlett wounded, eighteen other ranks killed, forty-five wounded, and one missing. Of these sixty-four casualties, twenty-one occurred in a raid on the 21st on a new trench under construction by the Germans. It was empty, but the raiders, for no result, suffered these casualties.

From the Chérisy area the division went to the support camp at Henin-sur-Cojeul in the beginning of June, the whole of which month was spent in resting and training. The 8th Norfolk battalion had forty-six officers and 956 men on the 30th. July 3rd saw the division on its way to a new field, the Ypres area, where it was training till the 27th for the approaching third battle of Ypres, for which the 31st was fixed as Z day. On Y day (the 30th) the 8th Norfolk battalion, who had reached Canal Reserve camp the previous day, moved into the assembly trenches.

The 18th division was again part of the 2nd corps, now in the fifth army. On this occasion the 30th division was to lead the advance, between the 24th on its right and the 8th on its left. Behind the 30th came the 18th, which was to "leap-frog" it when it had succeeded in taking the final objective, known as the "black line," which passed through the centre of Glencorse Wood, southwards, outside the western boundary of Inverness Copse, to the divisional boundary some 300 yards east of the southern end of Dumbarton Lakes. The first objective of the 30th division was the blue line, running parallel to the black line, some 600 or 700 yards short of it.

The 53rd brigade was on the left of the 18th division and was to "leap-frog" the left of the 30th as those troops got into Glencorse Wood.

In the advance of the 30th division a most unfortunate mistake occurred; for the infantry of its left wheeled leftwards over the divisional boundary and attacked Château Wood instead of Glencorse Wood. Nevertheless, a message came back that the 30th division had Glencorse Wood, and that mistake induced the 53rd brigade to move forward into the gap now left to the south-west of Glencorse Wood, towards Surbiton Villas and Clapham Junction. Consequently, the Suffolk and Berkshire battalions at the head of the brigade came, at a time when the barrage had passed forward, on strong German positions which were believed to be in British hands, and suffered severely from machine guns in strong points about Clapham Junction and Surbiton Villas.

During the first phase of the battle " A " and " D " companies of the Norfolk battalion started in the railway dug-outs, " B " and " C " were at the Zillebeke Bund.

At 8.50 a.m. " C " advanced to the R.E. dump at Zillebeke, the other companies following at ten-minute intervals into the Ritz Street area. At 10.10 a.m. news came in that the 30th division had failed to gain the first objective, and orders were received by " A," " B," and " D " companies to get under cover where they were, which they did, and remained till 5 p.m., when they were withdrawn to the assembly positions of the morning.

The interest for this day centres round " C," which had advanced at 10 a.m. according to time-table, before orders similar to those for the other companies could reach it. Moving forward through a fairly heavy barrage, Captain Patten with " C " was on the blue line by 10.55. Here he met a brigade intelligence officer, who informed him that the 8th division on the left was held up. He therefore continued straight along the boundary line, between the left of the 18th and the right of the 8th division, till he came under heavy rifle fire from the north-west corner of Glencorse Wood. Extending the three platoons with him, he went forward to reconnoitre. Here he met Captain Hudson commanding the very weak left company of the 6th Berkshire battalion. It was then seen that the enemy was advancing in extended order east of Stirling Castle, and in artillery formation behind the north-east corner of Glencorse Wood. Patten, seeing that the Berkshire had suffered very heavy casualties, and that the 2nd Lincoln of the 8th division had been forced, apparently by the fire from Glencorse Wood, to a distance of 350 yards from the divisional boundary, decided to bring up his company. The machine-gun fire prevented him from getting into touch with the right of the Lincoln battalion. " C " therefore moved, inclining to the left, to a position slightly in left rear of the left company of the Berkshire. This left incline was rendered necessary by the fact that previously the company had been masked by the left of the Berkshire in shell holes, and also by the existence of the gap between the Berkshire and the Lincoln battalions.

As soon as this move was completed, " C " opened fire with all its rifles and three Lewis guns on Glencorse Wood, and on the Germans advancing from the east of Stirling Castle. About 12.30 2nd Lieutenant Bentley, who had been left in rear with one platoon of " C," brought it up and was placed on the left, thus enabling " C " to fill practically the whole of the gap between the Berkshire and the Lincoln battalions. For the whole afternoon " C " kept up a heavy and harassing fire on Glencorse Wood from the shell holes in which it was established. It was suffering all the time from artillery fire. By 3.30 the left company of the 6th Berkshire had lost all its officers, and had only twenty-one other ranks left. Patten, therefore, took over this remnant, as well as a platoon of the King's Liverpool, and some " moppers up " of the Essex who were in the neighbourhood. " C's " casualties had been very serious.

At dark Patten, after reconnoitring the position in his front, disposed his force in four strong points divided thus : (1) The left company 6th Berkshire, (2) right half of " C," (3) the other half of " C," (4) the platoon of King's Liverpool, with a section R.E. and the composite platoon of infantry attached to it. The Essex " moppers up " were divided between the right and left rear of this line of strong points. Here he continued consolidating till 3.30 a.m., when his little force was relieved and retired to the west Bund of Zillebeke pond.

The casualties of the day, apparently all in " C," were :

Officers: Wounded—2nd Lieutenants Fishwick, A. E. Harrison, and Petrie.

Other ranks: Killed five, wounded twenty-nine (three of them remaining at duty), and six missing. Total casualties forty-three all ranks.

During the first nine days of August the 8th Norfolk battalion was in rear about Zillebeke Lake, Cornwall camp, and canal Reserve camp.

On the morning of the 10th they were warned that they were to advance again to Château Segard, and possibly to the trenches in front of Inverness Copse, to take part in an attack, at 7 p.m., on the north-west corner of that wood, which the 55th brigade had failed to take. At 8.30 a.m. they moved to Château Segard, and after remaining there till 2 p.m. were sent on to the Ritz Street area and placed under orders of the 54th brigade. At 5.30 p.m. they and the 6th Berkshire were ordered to take over the front line of the 54th brigade. In this relief there was a good deal of confusion, but fortunately the enemy did not attack till 4.30 a.m. on the 11th. Even then part of the line was still held by parts of the 11th Royal Fusiliers and 7th Bedford battalion, of the 54th brigade.

The Norfolk battalion had been on the move for the last twenty-two hours, and had only just got into their new position, when a strong German raid fell upon a strong point held by some of them and some of the 7th Bedford battalion, whom they were relieving. The strong point was lost, and the enemy also broke through the part of the line (between " A " and " D " companies) which was still held by some of the 11th Royal Fusiliers. " B " was ordered to be ready to counter-attack at once when a message was received that, though the right platoon of " A " had been forced back, the left was still holding. " C " was then ordered to counter-attack at once, to retake the strong point, and any part of the Switch trench north-east of it which the enemy had occupied. As the Germans now held the strong point with four machine guns, Colonel Ferguson decided to make a converging attack on it with " C " in front and " B " from the right.

Under the covering fire of Lewis guns and snipers, and with the assistance of a platoon of the 6th Berkshire, the attack went forward in sectional rushes. The strong point was re-captured, with nine German prisoners, the two machine guns which had been lost with it, and those Norfolk and Bedford men who had been taken in it.

This attack, which was led by Captain Morgan, was over 600 yards of difficult country overlooked by the strong point itself, and swept by machine-gun and rifle fire from higher ground occupied by the enemy. It was without a barrage. After it was launched the enemy's fire slackened somewhat, and " B " was able to strongly support " C " by enfilading the enemy in the open, and to form up between the strong point and Inverness Copse. The attack started at 5.25 a.m. and the position had been recovered by 6 a.m. At 8.30 the battalion was reorganized in line. " A " company was in the line on the left of the strong point, which was held by " C," whilst " B " was in the trench on its right, and " D " in reserve about Surbiton Villas. During the evening of the 11th the enemy made several attempts on the strong point, but it had now been well consolidated and wired, and they were driven off. Of the attack to recover the strong point Brigadier-General Higginson wrote:

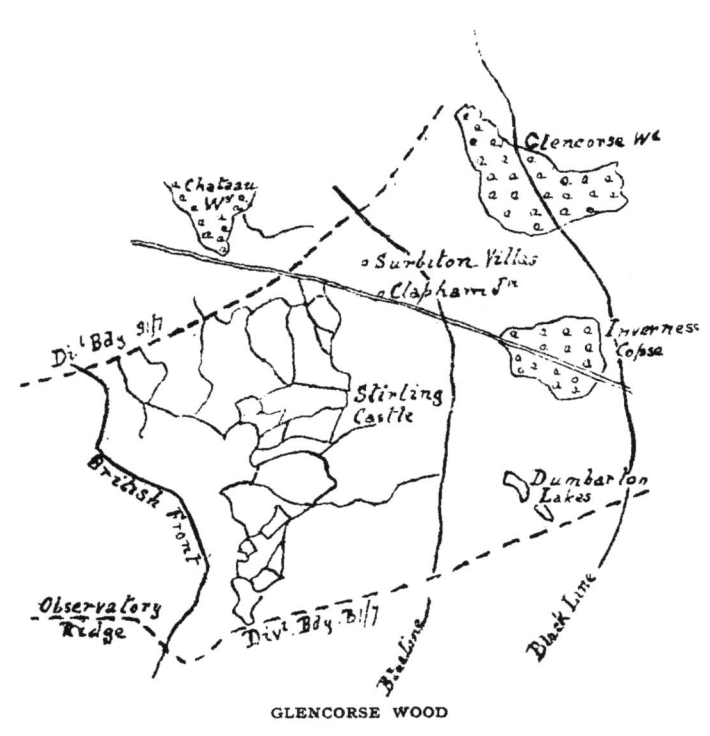

GLENCORSE WOOD

" Captain J. D. Crosthwaite, Brigade-Major, was an eye-witness of the attack, which he describes as having been carried out in a most dashing and gallant manner. It was carried out without any artillery preparation, and entirely on the initiative of the commanders on the spot. The assaulting troops advanced by rushes, under the cover of fire from Lewis guns and rifles. The enemy losses were heavy; I myself saw a considerable number of dead Huns when I visited the strong point afterwards. I desire to record my appreciation of the able manner in which Lieutenant-Colonel H. de L. Ferguson, D.S.O., O.C. 8th Norfolk Regiment handled the situation, and the splendid manner in which the assault was carried out. The leadership of the officers and non-commissioned officers and the gallantry of all ranks in the assaulting companies are worthy of the highest praise."

The situation remained unchanged during the 12th, and in the ensuing night the battalion, on relief by the 9th London and 8th Suffolk, returned to Railway dug-outs. The 13th-14th was a bad night, especially for " C " company. The enemy was bombarding the neighbourhood of Railway dug-outs with gas, and about 12.30 a.m. on the 14th, a 5.9 inch phosgene gas shell penetrated the roof of the dug-out occupied by the officers of " C," exploded inside, and completely blocked the entrance. The seven officers in it were unable to get out, and, in the confusion and amongst the debris, were unable to get on their masks. 2nd Lieutenant Chapman escaped through the hole in the roof made by the shell, and succeeded in rescuing the others, including 2nd Lieutenant Bentley, who had been wounded by the explosion. Some gas got into the head-quarters shelter and affected the C.O. and other officers. The results of this gas bombardment were, seven officers seriously and four, with twelve other ranks, slightly affected.

At 8 p.m. on the 14th the battalion moved to Crab Crawl, which must have been one of the most terrible shelters imaginable, a place in which anyone with the slightest inclination to claustrophobia must have gone mad. It is described as a long, oval tunnel in Observatory Ridge, from which, in places, there led out T heads and recesses for troops. There were eight or nine entrances by passages six feet high and one foot broad, so that a man had to move sideways in them; hence no doubt the name given to this horrible place. The T heads were ventilated, after a fashion, by blow holes leading to the hillside, but many of these had been blocked up by the shells which were constantly falling on the neighbourhood. There were ventilating pumps, but they had broken down. In some of the recesses the air was so foul that a candle could not be kept alight.

When the Norfolk battalion reached Crab Crawl, they found it already occupied by two companies of the 6th Berkshire, and a number of machine-gunners and others. There was no staying outside in the pitiless rain of shells, and the only remedy possible was some relief of the congestion by sending back half the battalion to Railway dug-outs. Even then Crab Crawl must have been a second edition of the Black Hole of Calcutta.

The Norfolk battalion did not play a very leading part in the attack of August 16th on Inverness Copse. " A " and " B " companies were employed in finding carrying parties, under the orders of the staff-captain of the brigade. " D " was put under the 79th Field Company R.E. to assist in consolidating the strong point at the north-west corner of the copse when it should be taken. " B " was in reserve, and " C " remained in Crab Crawl, ready to take the place of the reserve company of the 12th Middlesex, in the event of that company being called up.

In the evening, when it appeared that the strong point had not been taken, " D " was sent back to Crab Crawl. Later, " B " was sent to support the 7th Bedford battalion, and " D " to Menin Road tunnel. " A " and " C " were at Dormy house, and then back in Railway dug-outs, where they were rejoined in the morning of the 17th by " B " and " D," returned from the line.

The following table shows the casualties from the 10th to the 16th:

	Killed		Died of Wounds		Wounded	
	Officers	Other Ranks	Officers	Other Ranks	Officers	Other Ranks
Noon 10th to morning 11th	1	42	—	3	7	87
,, 11th ,, 12th	—	2	—	—	—	12
,, 12th ,, 13th	—	—	—	—	—	1
,, 13th ,, 14th	—	—	4 gas	—	4 gas	12 gas
,, 14th ,, 15th	—	1	—	—	—	—
,, 15th ,, 16th	—	—	—	—	1	18
Total	1	45	4	3	12	130

The officers were :

Killed—Captain W. Bunting, M.C.

Wounded—Major Ashdown, M.C.; Captains Morgan, D.S.O., M.C., and Lightfoot; Lieutenants Lampard, Abbott, M.C., Blackborn, Cuttrill.

Died of Gas—Lieutenants J. A. Lewton-Brain, D. A. Leamon, W. R. Williamson, M.C.; 2nd Lieutenant G. Allen.

Affected by Gas—Lieutenant Banks; 2nd Lieutenants Bartley, Sherlock, M.C., and B. E. Chapman.

On the 18th the battalion went by train to the Rubrouck training area to recover and train.

At Rubrouck it remained till September 23rd, when it went by rail and march to Poperinghe, and on to Road camp, where nothing remarkable occurred, except the award of honours for the Ypres operations of July 31st and August 11th to 16th. These were Military Crosses, 5; D.C.M.'s, 2; Bars to Military Medal, 1; Military Medals, 9.

The first three weeks of October were spent on the west bank of the Yser Canal, and partly in training for the attack of October 22nd in the Poelcappelle neighbourhood. On the 8th Lieutenant-Colonel Ferguson, after commanding the battalion almost continuously for three years, proceeded on six months' special leave to England, and was succeeded by Major E. N. Snepp. The only other notable event was on the 15th, when the German bombardment was specially severe, causing several casualties. One shell made a direct hit on a " pill-box " in which was the regimental aid post. The medical officer was wounded, two men were killed, and one wounded. On the 20th the battalion was in Cane trench ready for the coming attack.

Hitherto the fragments of the village of Poelcappelle had defied all British efforts to complete their capture. Of the village there was practically nothing left, hardly a brick remained upon a brick, and only here and there, where the church or a larger house had stood, was the site marked by a larger heap of rubbish, amongst which " pill-boxes " had been planted by the enemy. Everywhere the whole area was pitted with shell holes, and even the metalled road to Langemarck, passing through the length of the village from south-west to north-east, was practically unrecognizable. The attacks hitherto had been from the south; this time it was decided to attack from the north, at the same time deceiving the enemy by a " Chinese " attack towards the south, which consisted in drawing the German fire by the use of dummy figures.

The British front line on October 22nd ran due north and south through the centre of the long village, which had extended along the road

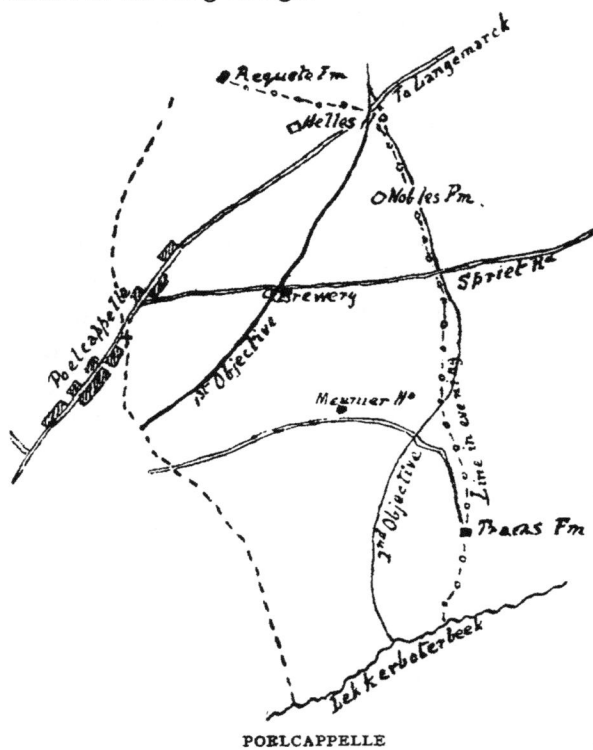

POELCAPPELLE

from south-west to north-east. It passed right through the site of the church. Here the British were holding on against constant counter-attacks, with varying success. The whole country was waterlogged, as the result of persistent rain in an area always liable to this fate. The final capture of the village and beyond was reserved for two battalions of the 53rd brigade, the 8th Norfolk and the 10th Essex.

The Norfolk battalion formed up at 2 a.m. on the 22nd, on tapes which had to be punctuated at short intervals with aluminium discs to prevent their being lost in the mud. Such protection as the men had been able to dig for themselves had been limited by the water level to a depth of two or three feet. "C" company was in an absolute swamp, and had to be moved forward a hundred yards before zero hour to harder ground. Though there was heavy German artillery fire, the casualties in forming up were few.

For the attack the Norfolk battalion was to lead off. The Essex would follow later, when the 8th Norfolk were on the first objective, a line running, from a point on the left divisional boundary 800 yards forward, south-west to rejoin the starting line 300 or 400 yards south of the church. In the capture of the second objective, a line from the same point in the left boundary to one on the right boundary 350 yards in front of the starting line, the Essex were to play the leading part by "leap-frogging" the Norfolk battalion. The latter were to attack on a front of all four companies. Beyond the left, the 14th corps was also attacking.

At 5.35 the 53rd brigade barrage opened, three minutes after that of the 30th division on the left.

The Norfolk battalion had "C" company on the right, then "D," "A," and "B" to the left, the last-named passing through Requête Farm on the extreme left. As they dashed forward after the barrage, "B" encountered some opposition at Requête Farm which they overcame, and then inclined rather too much to their right. Lieutenant Symonds was killed by a shell as he was correcting this direction. The company then pushed on to Helles house and the concrete emplacements north-east of it. The house was taken, but a strong resistance from two light machine guns and a bombing party was met with at the emplacements. This, too, was crushed and an officer was captured, with twenty-five men. Later, eleven wounded Germans were found in the emplacement. Throughout the advance "pill-boxes" had been a source of trouble, but the Norfolk men were so quick that the boxes were surrounded before the garrisons could get out, and all were taken or killed inside.

Meanwhile "D" had got rapidly forward and was in possession of the stronghold of the Brewery by 6.50 a.m. The 18-pounder barrage had lifted properly, but near the Brewery a stationary 4.5 inch howitzer barrage failed to lift as the 18-pounder passed, and the centre companies suffered some losses from it.

"Mopping up" was done quickly, and, as the first objective was reached, posts were pushed on to clear the way for the Essex to pass through. When they had passed, soon after 7.30 a.m., "D" took over "C's" front on the right, and the latter company passed over to a position west of Requête Farm, in support of "B." There it suffered from enemy shells; it had left its former post with thirty-six men, who were very soon reduced to fourteen.

At 10.30 a.m. the C.O. 10th Essex requested the 8th Norfolk battalion to take over his line in front of Helles Farm and Noble's Farm to Spriet Road as, owing to casualties, he required more men to hold his front south of Spriet Road, where, after taking the whole line of the second objective, his right had passed forward as far as Tracas Farm, which it had occupied.

This request was complied with at 3 p.m., though the brigade orders had only required the farther advance of the Norfolks to be at dusk. "B," "C," and "D" took over this line.

The rest of the day was passed under a heavy German bombardment, directed by aeroplanes flying at a height of 500 feet which found no British planes opposing them.

That night the Norfolk and Essex battalions were relieved in the area they had so gloriously won, and the former returned to Cane Trench and its neighbourhood.

Says the history of the 18th division: "The triumphant Essex and Norfolks . . . tramped back to hear the whole division—and General Maxse—singing their praise." They had indeed triumphed, but, as was to be expected, the Norfolk losses were heavy.

Of officers there were killed Lieutenant R. S. M. Inch, M.C., and 2nd Lieutenant F. F. G. Symonds. Wounded—2nd Lieutenants Thornley, Platten, and G. P. Brown, and Captain Todd (R.A.M.C.).

Of other ranks, thirty-two killed, 153 wounded, thirty-nine missing. Total 224.

This was destined to be the battalion's last great action before its dissolution. We quoted Major Berney-Ficklin at the beginning of this section, and it is fitting that he also should sing the swan-song of the battalion with which he had done so much strenuous service and which, for a short period, he had himself commanded. He writes:

"On November the 5th Lieutenant-Colonel E. N. Snepp was seriously wounded by long range gun fire, when the battalion was resting in huts some considerable distance from the firing line. On November 22nd Lieutenant-Colonel J. D. Crosthwaite, M.C. (London Regiment), assumed command. During November and December the battalion held the line in the vicinity of Poelcappelle, resting usually in the Herzeele area, and quitting trenches for the last time about the middle of December.

"January, 1918, found the battalion in brigade reserve near Elverdinghe and it was here, on the 29th, that it learned of its coming disbandment. Rumour had been current in December, but the knowledge that the brigadier and divisional commander were both fighting for the battalion to be retained had led them to hope that it would escape the drastic cutting down which had become necessary in the interests of the army as a whole, But it was not to be, and on January 29th the battalion paraded for the last time, and was addressed by the brigadier. Only one officer and a very small proportion of those who were with the battalion on St. Martin's Plain were present.

"The brigadier told the parade of his sorrow at losing the Battalion. Comparisons were naturally impossible, but he had always felt that, when he had asked the 8th Battalion Norfolk Regiment to do a thing, that thing was done.

"And so the battalion returned to billets to think of the happy comradeship of the past, and to speculate on what the future held in store.

"On February the 6th, fifteen officers and 300 other ranks proceeded to join the 9th Service Battalion of the regiment, whilst five officers and one-hundred other ranks went to the 7th Service Battalion.

"On February the 20th the remainder were drafted to corps reinforcement camps and entrenching battalions, and, to quote the last entry in the war diary : ' The 8th Service Battalion the Norfolk Regiment ceased to exist from to-day '.

"But it is not so. The battalion will live for ever in the minds of those who were privileged to serve with it. All ranks had striven to uphold the fine tradition of the gallant regiment of which it formed a part, and the message it received from the colonel of the regiment had told them that their endeavours had resulted in all that was desired—the approbation of the regular battalions.

"The comradeship and harmony can never be forgotten, and the constant meeting of old friends of whatever rank is still, and always will be, one of the happiest occurrences to which one can look forward.

"As for the some 770 of our comrades who will not return, to them is due the greatest of all debts ; and though their bodies may sanctify those hallowed spots of British ground which are to be found throughout the length of France, yet ' their name liveth for evermore.' "

CHAPTER VIII

THE 9TH (SERVICE) BATTALION IN FRANCE.

(a) 1914—15. RAISING. THE QUARRIES NEAR HULLUCH.

The 9th Battalion was first formed at Norwich on September 9, 1914, and three days later proceeded to Shoreham with a strength of about 900 under the command of Major E. Orams. We need not follow it through the course of its training and organization at Shoreham, which did not differ in form or difficulty from those of the other service battalions of the regiment. In June, 1915, it moved to Blackdown Camp, near Aldershot, where its more advanced training was continued and its equipment completed. In August it was reviewed by Lord Kitchener, and on the 30th of that month it passed over to Boulogne to commence its active service on the Western front. The officer commanding at this time was Colonel Mansel Shewen, who proceeded with the battalion on August 31st to Montcavrel, where it remained training till September 21st, when, in consequence of Colonel Shewen's promotion to the command of a brigade, the battalion was taken over by Lieutenant-Colonel E. Stracey on September 21st.

The officers at this time were:—
Lieutenant-Colonel E. Stracey, Commanding Officer.
Major E. Orams, 2nd in Command.

Major J. E. Cooke.	Lieutenant W. V. Coates.
Captain H. E. M. Turner.	2nd Lieutenant J. E. Hill,
do. A. H. Stracey.	do. J. E. Crosse,
do. J. R. W. Blake,	do. V. H. Goodman,

Captain	H. J. Buxton,	2nd Lieutenant	E. B. Walker,
do.	C. S. Robinson,	do.	C. Upcher,
do.	D. C. Graham,	do.	W. H. G. Meire,
do.	A. Finch,	do.	J. F. Fox,
do.	W. Cadge,	do.	S. Hallam,
Lieutenant	F. W. A. Kendall,	do.	G. E. Glanfield,
do.	N. Robertson,	do.	W. W. Everitt,
do.	T. Frederick,	Lieutenant	W. G. Helsby, R.A.M.C. Medical Officer.
do.	W. J. Spurrell,		
do.	W. P. Lightbody,	2nd Lieutenant	C. W. M. White.
Lieutenant and Quartermaster E. Smith.			

Of all these officers Lieutenant (now Captain) and Quartermaster E. Smith alone came out of the war with the battalion. He appears not to have been wounded, though he had a mention in despatches to his credit.

Other ranks numbered 987.

From Montcavrel the battalion marched, on September 21st, reaching Béthune on the 25th. The marches were severe and the first two especially tried the men heavily. From Béthune it went on the same day, to Lonely Tree Hill south of the La Bassée Canal. At this time the 71st brigade, of which the 9th Norfolk battalion was a unit, was part of the 24th division, to which, by its numbering, it would naturally belong. The other battalions of it were the 8th Bedford, 9th Suffolk, and 11th Essex.

At Lonely Tree Hill the 9th Norfolk formed for attack in support of the 11th Essex, but was not engaged. On the 26th, at 3.30 a.m., orders were received to assist the 20th brigade in its attack on the quarries west of Hulluch, the objective of the 71st brigade being Vendin-le-Vieil. At 5.30 they were in what, before the British advance of the previous day, had been the German front trenches. The attack was launched at 6.45 a.m. and the battalion made a gallant effort to advance on the quarries. So heavy, however, was the fire they met, especially from the numerous German snipers, that they could make little or no progress and were compelled, after suffering very heavy casualties, to again seek cover in the trenches. The trial had been very severe, and the battalion certainly had rather bad luck in being sent into a big battle almost the moment it arrived on the fighting front, and before it had got accustomed to its conditions.[1] At 4 p.m. the 2nd Worcester passed through to the attack of the quarries, which had so far failed.

At 7 p.m. the enemy, sending up flares, opened a tremendous rifle fire on the Norfolk trenches, of which the reverse slope was occupied to await a German attack. So hot was the fire that the Norfolk men presently had to fall back to trenches in rear to get cover. They were then relieved in these trenches by the Grenadier Guards, and marched back to Lonely Tree Hill. The trenches were being already occupied by other troops, the 9th Norfolk battalion received orders to concentrate at Vermelles, which was done at 6 a.m. on the 27th.

How heavy had been the enemy's fire on the 26th is evidenced by the battalion's casualties, which were :

Officers : Killed, five—Captain W. Cadge ; Lieutenants W. P. Lightbody and B. H. Goodman, 2nd Lieutenants C. W. M. White and W. H. G. Meire.

Officers : Wounded, nine—Captains A. H. Stracey, Finch, and Graham ; Lieutenants : Frederick and J. E. Hill ; 2nd Lieutenants Upcher, Crosse, E. B. Walker and J. F. Fox.

Of other ranks there were thirty-nine killed, 122 wounded, thirty-four missing. Total 209, officers included.

When the battalion reached Ham in wet weather on September 29th, it had only sixteen officers and 555 other ranks. After being in camp in several places in the neighbourhood of Proven, the 71st brigade was transferred to the 6th division, with which it remained till the end of its service. It changed places with the 17th Brigade, transferred from the 6th to the 24th division. The constitution of the brigade was now altered. The first Leicester battalion joined it from the 16th brigade, and the 2nd Sherwood Foresters from the 18th, whilst the 8th Bedford took the place of the 1st Leicester and the 11th Essex that of the Sherwood Foresters.

---

[1] Unfortunately, we have been unable to obtain any detailed account of the battalion's movements on this day. The War Diaries give little assistance.

On October 15th the Norfolk battalion was at Poperinghe with a strength of twenty-four officers and 1,014 other ranks.

For the rest of 1915 there is little to be told. During November the battalion was in and out of trenches in the neighbourhood of Ypres, going through the usual monotonous routine of such service in the winter. On November 11th 2nd Lieutenant G. Glanfield was killed by a shell. December passed in the same way. An extra heavy bombardment on the 19th led to the expectation of a German attack which did not materialize. At this time the Norfolk battalion was in trenches near St. Jean.

(b) 1916. THE SOMME FRONT—THE QUADRILATERAL—MILD TRENCH.

January, 1916, saw the battalion still in the St. Jean direction, sometimes in one sector of the defences, sometimes in another, alternating in reliefs with the 9th Suffolk or the 1st Leicester, and there was no change in February. On the 12th of that month, when the Norfolk battalion was just being relieved by the Suffolk, there was another threat of an infantry attack, and German smoke delayed the relief, but nothing came of it. On that day 2nd Lieutenant H. F. Barton was killed by a shell and 2nd Lieutenant Cumberland wounded.

At the beginning of March the battalion was on the south side of the Ypres salient, about La Bassée Canal, and the month was ushered in by heavy bombardments on both sides. Then there was a period of snow followed by thaw, rendering the trenches more than ever miserable. At the end of the month the Norfolk battalion had moved back into the training area near Wormhoudt. From April 5th they were training near Calais, whither they had proceeded by train. Between the 15th and 19th they were marching back to Wormhoudt, and on the 23rd they found themselves again in the trenches on the canal bank, where, on the 30th, Captain E. E. C. Wellesley was killed by a shell. The same routine continued throughout May, the alternation of reliefs being then generally with the 2nd Sherwood Foresters. Casualties occurred on most days from shell fire, varying in amount.

On June 7th Captain Frederick, who had received the Military

Cross only two days before, was wounded by a rifle bullet. June was not much more interesting, save for a patrol by a mixed force of Norfolkmen, Sherwood Foresters, and others under Captain Smith, R.N.V.R., Lieutenant Failes, and 2nd Lieutenant Sprott of the Norfolk battalion, in which seven men of the battalion were wounded.

On the 29th the corps commander 14th corps stated that, at his recent inspection, he found " it was evident that great trouble had been taken by the C.O. and company officers to bring the battalion to such an efficient state, and the corps commander considers that the result of the inspection reflects great credit on all concerned."

July again was a month without much interest—training and trenches, at Merckeghem and on the canal bank.

On August 2nd the battalion entrained for the Somme front, reaching Villers Candas on the morning of the 3rd and marching with the rest of the brigade (2nd Sherwood Foresters, 1st Leicester, and 9th Suffolk battalions) to Beauval, Léalvillers, and Mailly-Maillet, where they relieved the 2nd Royal Irish Rifles on the 5th. On the 14th the Norfolk battalion relieved the Coldstream Guards in trenches in the left sector, where there was some shelling by which 2nd Lieutenant Fox was wounded. They were at Mailly-Maillet again on the 20th till the 26th, on the 27th at Louvancourt, 28th Beauval, and from the 29th to September 5th at Flesselles practising for the coming attack. By the 8th they were in the "Sandpit Area," about half way between Albert and Bray, on the south side of the main road. The night of the 11th was passed in shell holes south of Trônes wood, where the men had to construct shelters to live in. In the heavy shelling of the 13th there were wounded Major Turner, Captain C. S. Robinson (died of his wounds), and 2nd Lieutenant Garnham. At 1 a.m. on the 15th the Norfolk battalion took up a line on the road from Ginchy to Leuze Wood for an attack on the "Quadrilateral."

The general scheme was an attack by the fourth army on the enemy's defences, from Combles Ravine on the right to Martinpuich on the left, designed to seize Morval, Lesbœufs, Gueudecourt, and Flers, and break through, the French following a similar course on the right, and the reserve army to the north.

The 71st brigade orders of the 14th required the 9th Norfolk battalion on the right, and 1st Leicester on the left to form up along the general line of the sunken road running due south from Ginchy. Each battalion was to be on a front of 250 yards, with two companies in front line and two in support, each company having a front of one platoon. The left of the Leicester battalion would be close up to Ginchy and the right of the Norfolk on the sunken road where it is crossed by the railway.

On the right of the 71st would be the 16th brigade, with the 18th in divisional reserve. The Norfolk battalion would direct, with their right on the railway.

When the Norfolk and Leicester battalions were waiting in formation at 5.50 a.m. a tank[1] passed forward through them, and at 6.20 the 9th Norfolk and Leicester battalions passed through the Suffolk and Sherwood Foresters in front of them for the attack on the first objective.

The German position is thus described in General Marden's short history of the 6th division:

> On September 9th a successful attack had given us Ginchy and Leuze Wood, but the Germans were holding very strongly the high ground which lies in the form of a horseshoe between the above-named points, and which dominates the country for some distance to the south. The trenches followed the slope of the spur roughly at the back end of the horseshoe, and covered access was given to them by a sunken road leading back to the deep valley which

[1] This was the first occasion on which tanks were used.
It may interest the reader to know the origin of the term "tanks." The author can vouch for the correctness of the following. During the development of the idea of an armoured "land-ship" capable of crossing trenches, the greatest secrecy was kept, considering the number who were in it. The question arose as to how the new weapon was to be spoken of, so as not to disclose its nature. At that time water for the troops was generally supplied in the continental armies by means of wheeled water-carriers or "tanks," whilst the British favoured underground pipes. The question of adopting the continental practice was under discussion, and it was suggested by a member of one of the committees on "land-ships" that they should be written or spoken of as "tanks." It might be hoped that the use of the term would induce the enemy to believe that they were only some new form of water-supply. The term was at once adopted, and is likely to stick to the new arm permanently.

runs north from Combles. At the top of the spur just south of the railway was a four-sided trench in the form of a parallelogram of some 300 yards by 150 yards, called by us the 'Quadrilateral'."

At 7 a.m. the O.C. 9th Norfolk battalion reported that the first tank had reached the German front line, and that his leading companies were out of sight.

As the Norfolkmen advanced up the glacis-like slope with insufficient artillery support, due to the barrage having a gap of 200 yards just in front of the Quadrilateral to allow of the advance of the tanks, they

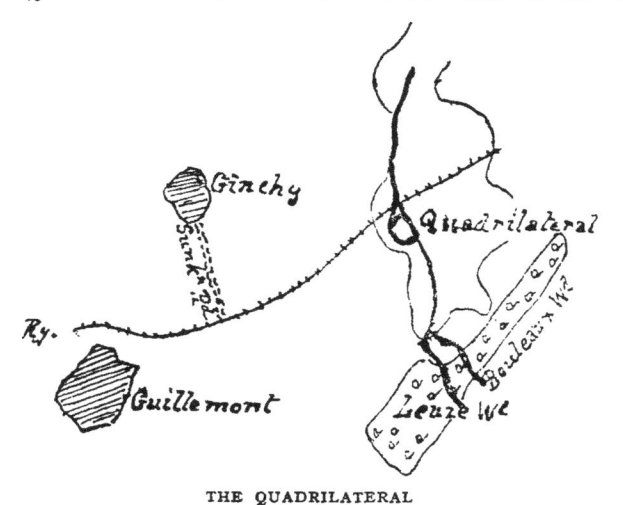

THE QUADRILATERAL

encountered uncut wire through which they were unable to get forward. The same fate had met the Leicester battalion on the left, who were not in touch with the 9th Norfolk on their right or the Guards on their left. By 11.45 the 9th Norfolk had Major Bradshaw and about forty men close up to the enemy's wire in front of the Quadrilateral. The rest were scattered in shell holes between them and Ginchy road. The Suffolk battalion, holding the Ginchy-Leuze Wood road, were more or less mixed up with them. Of the three tanks allotted to the division two had never got off, and the third had been disabled.

At 12.55 orders issued that the 71st brigade was not to attack the Quadrilateral, but was to endeavour to improve its position by working round the flanks, with a view to a subsequent attack on it by the 18th brigade. There was no change in the position up till 6.30, when the 14th Durham Light Infantry was placed at the disposal of the brigadier, who ordered one company along the railway to support the 9th Norfolk, the rest to remain in reserve in trenches south of Guillemont. An hour later the 14th Durham Light Infantry attacked the trench running north from the Quadrilateral, but, as they were not in touch either with the Leicesters or the Sherwood Foresters, they could get no help from those battalions, and the attack produced no results, as the trench was found not to lead into the strong point.

After midnight the Norfolk and Suffolk battalions, being relieved by part of the 18th brigade, moved back into trenches south of Guillemont, where the day was spent in collecting the men, and in the evening the 9th Norfolk went back to trenches near Trônes Wood.

The casualties of the 9th Norfolk in this unfortunate action amounted to 431 other ranks, the details of which are not stated in the diary. Of officers there were :—

Killed, four—Captains W. T. de Caux and E. J. Jephson ; Lieutenant J. L. Goddard ; 2nd Lieutenant J. F. C. Bashforth.

Wounded, twelve—Captains Spurrell and O'Reilly; Lieutenants Failes and Crosse ; 2nd Lieutenants Cumberland, Morgan, Anthony, Glover, Garnham, Jackson, Forster and Sprott.

Missing—Lieutenant Phelps.[1]

After such serious losses the battalion naturally required a considerable period of recuperation and refitting. On the 19th it went to billets at Ville sur Ancre, on the 24th to bivouac north of Carnoy, and next day to Bernafay Wood, where the 71st brigade was in reserve to the 6th division. From the 26th to the 30th it was in shelter trenches north-east of Ginchy, and next day, on relief, went back to north of Carnoy.

Lieutenant-Colonel Prior, who took over command of the battalion on October 1st, 1916, says that he found it composed almost entirely of

[1] Afterwards found to have been killed.

fresh drafts, with only a very small percentage of experienced non-commissioned officers and men left. There were only three officers left with it who had taken part in the Quadrilateral battle. It was commanded by Major Lewis of the 2nd Leicester battalion, who had been appointed second in command. The new colonel had a difficult job in reforming and finding company commanders for his battalion, which he knew was very shortly to go into action again.

On October 16th it was again in front trenches, with the 2nd Leicester in support.

The front of the battalion was in Shine trench, on the gentle slope towards the enemy from a ridge east of Gueudecourt, facing Le Transloy. The battalion head-quarters were on the reverse slope, with no proper communication trench with the front.

There was a heavy bombardment to be borne on the 17th, and on the 18th the attack was to begin on Mild trench. The general attack was by the fourth army, in conjunction with the French on the right. On the left of the 9th Norfolk was the 12th division. Their first objective was Mild trench, the second was the continuation of Cloudy trench, from its junction with Mild trench as far as the right of the 12th division. The attack was to be in the dark, a very difficult job always, and especially so with the inexperienced men who formed so large a proportion of the battalion at this moment. The difficulties were greatly added to by the wet weather, which turned the ground almost into a quagmire, and made the parapets so slippery that there was the greatest difficulty in going over at all. Moreover, the Norfolk left flank was at first exposed, and would remain so until the troops on their left got forward into alignment. This necessitated flank protection for some time. A heavy and very accurate bombardment was kept up by the enemy continuously throughout the night.

When the attack commenced, at 3.40 a.m., there was some delay in getting over, not from want of goodwill, but from the physical difficulty of mounting the greasy parapets. Even where slots had been cut in them, as often as not a man would slip back into the trench. In consequence of this delay, much of the protection of the British barrage was lost, and the battalion got an undue share of the German barrage.

Colonel Prior's scheme of attack was for " A " and " B " companies to lead, with " C " in support ready to come through them and exploit any initial success, whilst " D " was detailed to protect the exposed left flank. The night was a very dark one, and as " A " and " B " rushed forward to Mild trench it is not very surprising that each lost direction and moved towards its outer flank, thus leaving a gap between them which " C " was not near enough to fill. The course of the fight was throughout obscure, but it appears that the left of " B " company succeeded in its attack on Mild Trench, established itself there under Lieutenant Cubitt, and blocked the trench towards its right. The right of this company failed to get into the trench. As for " A," it diverged, as has already been said, to its right, and a party was seen in front of the 9th Suffolk, the battalion on the right. It had missed and overrun its objective and was never seen again. Another party which had got into the middle of Mild trench was all killed or taken. Two companies of the 1st Leicester, which had been attached to the Norfolk battalion were not got up into the fighting line.

The above account, which is mainly taken from the brigade diary (that of the battalion being of the briefest), may be supplemented by the following extracts from an account by Colonel Prior of what he himself saw :—

" I determined to go up the line and see for myself what had happened. Just as I was starting I met a runner from 2nd Lieutenant Cubitt, of " B " company, with a report that he had gained his objective, and, though counter-attacked, had driven the Bosche out of the trench and had been holding it since. . . . I saw Blackwell (" D " company) . . . and told him to organize a party from his company, reinforce Cubitt, and take command of the position. I then went on along the line, and here the news was not so good. The right of " B " and " A " companies had apparently failed. There were stragglers of both companies who had got back to our original front line, but they could say very little beyond the fact that, in the darkness, they had missed their direction, got caught in the Bosche barrage, and those who were not killed or wounded had eventually got back to their own line. . . . I then retraced my steps and went over to the H.Q. of the 9th Suffolk Regiment, who were on my right, to inquire whether they knew anything. Colonel Latham said he had a report that at dawn fully a platoon of " A " company was seen well beyond their objective and much to the right of it—in fact, in front of his battalion line, and still advancing."

Colonel Prior then went, via battalion H.Q., again to the left to see that the captured position there was consolidated.

" There the garrison holding the trench, despite a good many casualties, were in the best of spirits. They had been heavily shelled, sniped at, and machine-gunned, and at least once counter-attacked, but they had had a success, they had taken their trench, and before I left I felt quite satisfied they would die to a man rather than lose it. Blackwell was the life and soul of the party and had carried out his work admirably. He had put in a block on his right flank. On his left was the Gueudecourt road, on the other side of which were the Hampshires."

Colonel Prior's story may well be supplemented by the following account of the taking of the trench from a private letter from 2nd Lieutenant A. T. K. Cubitt, who was afterwards killed on August 22nd, 1918.

" Precisely to the minute the great British barrage opened, the whole earth shook, the noise was deafening, and the sky was lit up with the flash of guns. I clambered over the top and walked slowly forward till I fell into a shell hole. I crawled out of the shell hole, then walked blindly forward again until I came to the Bosche trench, shattered and with many dead. . . . There was one live German in that trench, a few yards from me, with a bomb in his hand; but when our boys came over the parados and leaped into the trench, up went his hands and he shouted ' Camerade ! Camerade.' . . . I felt exceedingly tired and would have liked to have slept, but we'd got that trench and I wasn't keen on losing it.

" The Bosches were coming down the communication trench towards us, but my little party of bombers—only seven strong—bombed them back, three being killed in doing it. That left me with one lance-corporal and seven men to hold the trench. Picking up captured German rifles (our own being caked with mud and it raining in torrents) we sniped over the parapet. I called for a volunteer to take a message back to Head-quarters for reinforcements. Within five minutes one was on his way. We recommended him for the Military Medal. . . . I saw an officer and four men crawling towards me under heavy fire ; two of the party were killed, but the officer (Lieutenant Blackwell) got there with the other men. He took over, and I went to sleep in the mud! Subsequently others came to our assistance and for forty-eight hours, with water up to our knees, soaked to the skin, practically no water to drink, and dead beat, those splendid boys ' stood to,' fought, and bombed, and held on. It was glorious to see how when one man was killed another took his place, and, when he fell, a third man. They were all heroes.

"Time after time we were shelled, but took no harm ; then the Bosche snipers got busy and quickly picked off three of our men. Blackwell put up his periscope to have a look and got a bullet through it. Turning it upside down he put it up again, only to have the other end smashed.

"Then we put up a Bosche steel helmet, a bullet came through that and ricochetted into a sergeant's eye, or rather his cheek just below the eye. The helmet was his joke, so he smiled through it.

"At last we got some water in petrol cans. Under cover of night I elbowed myself along a communication trench with mud a foot deep for about 100 yards, and got into a little dug-out in the support line. Here I had some bread and butter and a mixture of lemon squash and whiskey! I thought it was great. Towards midnight 19th—20th we were relieved in more senses than one. Never was I more pleased to hand over a trench or ditch than I was that one, never more grateful to God for having helped me through."

This letter, which is too long to quote in full, not only fills a gap in the story of Mild Trench but is a noble tribute to the spirit of the Norfolk men, including the writer himself, who was then only just twenty-one. For his conduct in this action he was awarded the Military Cross.

The casualties were again very heavy, 239 other ranks, of which details are not given. The officer casualties were:—

Killed—2nd Lieutenant T. S. Page.

Wounded—Captain Rowell; 2nd Lieutenants Beesley, J. W. Clarke, Henshall, Cowles, and Gravestock.

Missing—2nd Lieutenants J. C. Page and Badcock.[1]

The D.S.O. for Lieutenant Blackwell, M.C. for 2nd Lieutenant Cubitt, and a D.C.M. for Sergeant Gould were awarded for the success on the left. Colonel Prior adds: " The equally grand work of the platoon of ' A ' company, who fought the Bosche to a finish, remains but an incident hitherto unrecorded and unsung."

On October 19, after digging a communication trench to the captured part of the Mild Trench, the battalion was relieved, and proceeded, partly by march and partly by rail, to Annezin near Béthune, where it remained training and refitting till November 24th, when it was attached, till December 4th, to the 24th division for work, chiefly in tunnelling with the Royal Engineers.

On December 5th it rejoined the 71st brigade, and three days later relieved the 9th Suffolk battalion at Cuinchy, in the right sub-sector of the defences.

In December, 1916, a draft of 140 men reached the battalion and is described in the diary as " the best we have had for months." Though the men had not yet had any training at the front, fifty per cent. of them had over two years' service. On December 10th Colonel Prior, returning from a reconnaissance for a proposed raid, was shot through the right forearm by a German sniper, a wound which necessitated his absence from the battalion for more than three months. The command was taken over on the 15th, by Lieutenant-Colonel R. S. Dyer-Bennett of the 1st Leicester Regiment.

[1] Both ascertained to have been killed.

(c) 1917. TRENCH RAIDS—SUBURBS OF LENS—HILL 70—
BATTLES OF CAMBRAI.

On January 2nd a patrol of eight Germans got into an unoccupied part of the 9th Norfolk trenches in the quarries of the right sub-sector. One of them lost his way and was killed by "B" company; three were killed by "D" company; the remaining four had captured a Lewis gunner. They were just conveying another prisoner across "No Man's Land" when Corporal Hare rushed to the rescue, and, with the help of the prisoners, disposed of the remains of the enemy patrol.

On the 27th command of the battalion was taken by Lieutenant-Colonel J. B. O. Trimble. The whole month was spent in and out of trenches near Vermelles, generally relieving or being relieved by the 9th Suffolk. February was spent between Mazingarbe and Béthune, and in the beginning of March the battalion was again in the quarry trenches. On the 10th Colonel Stracey took command till the 24th, when Colonel Prior returned, more or less recovered from his wound. The casualties in February were ten other ranks killed and nine wounded (one of them accidentally). On March 2nd Lieutenant Mutimer was slightly wounded, seven men were killed or died of wounds (one) or gas (three), twenty-two were wounded, seventeen gassed, and four accidentally injured.

Most of the gas cases occurred on the 3rd; the wound casualties were chiefly on the 24th and 25th, when there were heavy bombardments as a prelude to German raids, in the second of which they left behind one dead man and one prisoner. The Norfolk loss in this affair, chiefly from the bombardment, was one killed and seven wounded. As usual, however, the sufferings of the troops in winter trench warfare were greater from the conditions of service than from the enemy, and the Germans themselves seem to have suffered in the same way. Of trench conditions Colonel Prior writes:

"I very much doubt whether anyone who was not actually serving in the trenches in the winter of 1916—17 can conceive the terrible time our troops went through. It is only those who have been there, who know the effect of a cold thaw on the liquid mud of Flanders, and its paralysing effects, who know what it is to stand silent and motionless for their tour of duty, legs and arms completely numbed, and with no chance to restore the circulation, It is only those who have actually suffered who can have a real conception of what misery our sentry groups went through nightly. On relief from sentry duty the man was but little better off, his sole chance of restoring circulation being to try and clean his trench of some of the liquid mud. Finally, when the whole group came off duty one hour after daylight they had to turn into a dark, muddy dugout, sodden with wet, caked with mud, and exhausted with cold and exposure, and sleep, if they could, just as they were. And that went on night after night for the whole tour of duty, varied only by sudden death in the shape of a hostile shell, a patrol into the unknown dangers of ' No Man's Land,' or a hostile attack."

The first eight days of April spent in the trenches of the St. Elie sector near Loos were succeeded by six of training and refitting at Philosophe, when the battalion again went into front line, with the 2nd Sherwood Foresters on their left, the 9th Suffolk in brigade reserve, and the 1st Leicester in divisional reserve at Philosophe.

On the 23rd, at 4.10 a.m., there was a German raid of about twenty men on the Norfolk trenches. Four of them got unobserved through the wire, but under Lewis-gun fire the whole raiding party was driven off, leaving two dead in the wire. Next night a raid of about the same strength managed to pass through a gap between " B " company on the right and " C " in the centre, under cover of a barrage which cost the Norfolk battalion two men killed and three wounded. The raiders appear to have penetrated about 500 yards behind the front, and were only observed when they were withdrawing. At this time the 71st brigade was holding a line of 4,500 yards, with three battalions in front and one in support. With such an extensive front the line was really one of outposts, and it was impossible to prevent patrols slipping unobserved through gaps between them. The positions of the outposts companies were governed by the tunnel system, a nodal point with three rays spreading forwards. At the nodal point was the reserve company, with the others at the ends of the rays, having their platoons arranged generally to guard a tunnel exit each. Colonel Prior tells the following of this period:

"The Bosche made a very determined night raid, broke into the trenches of the Sherwood Foresters on our right, and part of the enemy, led by a sergeant-major, swinging round, came up between the front and support lines of my right company. They got into the dug-out of the front line platoon, and captured the sergeant who was portioning out the rations, and at the moment unarmed. They brought him up to the trench and ordered him to get out, which he promptly obeyed, kicking his nearest captor in the mouth as he did so, and bolted to the front line, yelling to the men to line the parados as the Bosches were behind them. Although, in making his escape, he was severely wounded, his prompt action saved the situation. The majority of the enemy doubled back, leaving the sergeant-major (badly wounded) and one unwounded prisoner in our hands, and several dead in our lines and in ' No Man's Land.' "

On April 25th the 9th Norfolk battalion was moved to opposite Hill 70, where they were placed under orders of the 16th brigade. They arrived very tired at Maroc at 4 a.m., and, just as they were leaving it at 2 p.m. to take post in the Loos sector, the place was heavily shelled, with the result that 2nd Lieutenant G. E. Hall was killed, two other ranks killed, and five wounded. This is Colonel Prior's account of the new position:

"The front allotted to us was a bestial place. On our right were the remains of the mining village of Cité St. Laurent, which was partially held by the 46th division and partially by the enemy, and from there, after crossing the railway line, ran along a Bosche communication trench. The 9th Suffolks, on our left, carried on this line until they struck the old ' No Man's Land,' across which a new trench had been dug, and so joined up with the old divisional front line. In front of us was the famous Hill 70, which afforded the Bosche fine observation, and which he was determined to hang on to at all costs. The enemy had only been driven out of this line by dint of hard fighting, and at the time we took over there was little possibility of making further advance until the 46th division on our right were able to push farther through the masses of broken masonry and machinery of the Cité. As it was, our right flank was some distance in front of the general line held by the 46th Division and caused me considerable anxiety. The enemy was fighting very fiercely; he had altogether the best of the ground, he knew exactly where every dug-out was placed, and altogether had every means at his disposal to give us a most unpleasant time. He certainly succeeded."

At midnight of the 27th—28th the battalion suffered from a retaliatory fire consequent on the firing of gas projectors by the 16th and 18th brigades. The morning was devoted by the enemy to heavy fire on the British front trenches, whilst in the afternoon he turned an intense bombardment on the support trenches. Under cover of this, at 5 p.m., the Germans seized an advanced post of the 9th Norfolk. This was promptly recovered by a counter-attack in which 2nd Lieutenant H. E. Dodson was killed.

At 11 p.m. a platoon under 2nd Lieutenant Campbell went out to raid the enemy north of the dynamite magazine. A portion of the platoon rushed the trench junction, but most of it was driven back by a cross fire of machine guns. The bombers, who, under the command of a corporal, got into the trench, being unaware of the repulse of the rest, dispersed some of the enemy and bombed along the trench and five dug-outs without any casualties. The main body of the raiders lost one killed and one wounded. The chief result was the discovery that the enemy held his front line in force, at any rate at night. On the 29th there was more retaliatory fire and gas shells causing heavy loss. Altogether, between noon on the 28th and midnight of the 29th, the battalion lost 2nd Lieutenant H. E. Dodson, killed; Captain Crosse, 2nd Lieutenant Coleman, and six other ranks gassed ; thirteen other ranks killed or died of wounds, and thirty-one wounded.

During the night of the 30th-31st " A " and " B " companies, which had been much shaken by the heavy bombardment, were relieved in front line by " C " and " D " from support. The Norfolk battalion was on this front from April 24th to May 1st in trenches which, though dry, were wide and had been so badly battered as to afford poor protection from shell fire. The total casualties of the period bear testimony to its trying nature :

Officers : Killed—2nd Lieutenants G. E. Hall and H. E. Dodson.
Gassed—Captain Crosse and 2nd Lieutenant Coleman.
Wounded—2nd Lieutenants Cooke and Bennett.

Other ranks : Twenty-eight killed (two died of wounds), ninety-nine wounded or gassed. Total all ranks 133 in eight days.

The most tragic event was on the last day of the tour. Between 11 a.m. and noon, in the course of a German bombardment with 8 inch armour-piercing shells and lighter stuff, a dug-out occupied by a platoon of " C " company was hit direct and blown in. Of the tenants, one officer and thirty-six other ranks, twenty men were killed, the officer and fourteen others were wounded, and only two men escaped without injury.

In the night of May 1st the 71st brigade, being relieved by the 18th and 138th, went into brigade reserve in the neighbourhood of Verquin and Vaudricourt. The brigade front was then on a line northwards from the Vermelles-Hulluch road, with the 16th brigade on its right and the 199th on the left. The brigade front was held by two battalions, and the full tour of service was eight days each in front line, brigade reserve, again in front, and in divisional reserve.

After 10 days' training the battalion relieved the 9th Suffolk in the right sub-sector. This was generally a quiet tour, for the enemy shells were usually directed over the 9th Norfolk's heads on brigade headquarters. It was believed the enemy was about to fall back on the Drocourt-Quéant line, and he certainly gave little trouble in front. Colonel Prior even sent two volunteers out who moved for a long way down outside the German wire, until bombs were thrown at them from a small post in the wire itself. Covered by Lewis-gun and rifle fire, and directed by Sergeant-Major Neale from the parapet, the two volunteers got safely back. The enemy was clearly not in a provocative mood, and did not use rifle or machine-gun fire. Colonel Prior opines that this may have been due to the fact that the opposing German division was just being relieved, and did not want to end up by provoking retaliatory measures. Their successors were much more active. Colonel Prior tells the following of the new division's early days:

"The new Bosche division was not yet acquainted with their new line, and this led to an amusing incident. The sentry group of 'D' company one afternoon saw a Bosche dodging along the enemy's front line, which was in parts shallow and in poor repair. He soon reached the craters, and, to the intense surprise of Sergeant Parlett, who was on duty, slipped over the top of the crater and slithered down to the bottom. He was promptly covered by the sergeant, ordered to 'hands up,' and brought down as a prisoner. He turned out to be a German sergeant-major doing his final tour in the line before going back for an officer's course and a commission. In his zeal to carry out his work well, he had gone round the whole line, and, not finding the sentry post at the crater as expected, thought it must be on the other side. This mistake he paid for by being captured; but one must admit one felt rather sorry for the man. He was a fine, soldierly looking fellow, and felt his position most keenly. The 9th battalion signalized this capture by posting two notices in 'No Man's Land' informing the enemy that their sergeant-major was now getting rest and decent food, and inviting others to join him."

After a week out of them, the 9th Norfolk battalion was again in the front trenches near St. Elie from May 27th to the 31st. During this period a number of small balloons, with blank strips of paper attached, drifted over from the German lines. The battalion diary supposes them to have come from British agents behind the enemy lines, but there is nothing to show what they really were.

The casualties of May were two officers (2nd Lieutenants Willoughby and C. D. Smith) wounded, twenty-six other ranks killed or died of wounds, and forty-seven wounded. Of these seventy-five casualties, thirty-five occurred in the dug-out of " C " company on the 1st.

Nothing remarkable happened in June till the 12th, when a raid was carried out by an officer and thirty-five other ranks of " B " company at 11.30 p.m. As the wire had already been cut, there was no necessity for a preliminary bombardment. The party attempted to rush the gap, but were fired on and incurred several casualties, including 2nd Lieutenant Campbell wounded, one man killed, and four wounded. The withdrawal was covered by artillery fire.

During the remainder of the month the battalion was in and out of trenches at Vermelles, Verquin, Mazingarbe, and in corps reserve at Bully Grenay.

Captain Blackwell was slightly wounded, and altogether the casualties in June were five killed and twenty-five wounded. " B " company, thanks to its raid and the fact that it got an undue share of the German retaliatory fire, lost all these, except eight wounded. The object during a great part of the month was to deceive the enemy as to the direction of the impending attack by the 46th division on the right.

By 2 a.m. on July 1st the Norfolk battalion was in billets in Cité St. Pierre, a suburb on the north-west of Lens. Three-quarters of an hour later the 46th division attacked on a three brigade front, the 139th brigade being on the left, with the 9th Norfolk as its reserve, and having two companies of the Sherwood Foresters under its orders for the assault. The assault was successful and all objectives were reached, but, owing to insufficiency of numbers for so difficult a task, the ground passed over was not properly cleared of the Germans lurking in the houses and dug-outs between the starting-point and the final objective. The position is thus described by Colonel Prior:

" The Cités are all suburbs of Lens composed of the ordinary class of modern suburban houses. There was a certain amount of open ground between the Cités, but for the most part suburb ran into suburb and made it a most difficult fighting area. The feature of the French domestic architecture is that every house, however small, is provided with a cellar, and naturally the cellars in this sort of fighting played an important part. The cellars, even without preparation, gave a certain amount of protection from shell fire, and, when well shored up and covered with rubble and cement, made excellent dug-outs. With cellars and the walls of houses to screen their movements, it was difficult to know where the enemy was and what his strength was, and altogether it seemed a risky undertaking for one weak and very highly tried division, with no troops to back them. So weak were the Sherwood Territorial Brigade (139th) that the 2nd Sherwood Foresters were at once tacked on to them and thrown into the attack, leaving the 9th Norfolk as the sole support."

At 7 a.m. the enemy made a strong counter-attack on the 139th brigade, in which the lurkers in houses and cellars joined. The 9th Norfolk, however, were not called up to assist in this fight, which caused heavy losses to the 139th brigade and the 2nd Sherwood Foresters. The position was generally very obscure, and it was specially doubtful how far the 137th brigade (on the right of the 139th) had got forward. Colonel Prior was ordered to provide two companies to assist the 2nd Sherwood Foresters in an attack next morning. He felt considerable doubt as to the expediency of the movement, but the question was solved by the failure to arrive of the guides who had been promised. Consequently the attack, for which " A " and " B " companies were held ready, failed to come off in the morning, was postponed till the afternoon, and finally cancelled.

During July 2nd " A " and " B " companies, under orders of Colonel Bradshaw of the 2nd Sherwood Foresters, were in Cité Jeanne d'Arc, south of St. Pierre, with battalion head-quarters 300 or 400 yards behind, whilst " C " and " D " were still in Cité St. Pierre. In the evening all were re-united under Colonel Prior at Bully Grenay. On the night of the 3rd-4th they were relieved by the 27th Canadians, and re-joined the 71st brigade in support and reserve trenches opposite St. Elie. On the

10th they took the place of the 9th Suffolk in the right sub-sector with the 1st Leicester on their left.

On the 16th a considerable raid on the German trenches was attempted. No preliminary bombardment was ordered, and no precise zero hour fixed. The barrage was to commence in response to signals by Verèy lights from the raiders. The party, consisting of two officers and thirty-six other ranks, began crawling forward at 2.46 a.m. Owing to some mistake, the smoke barrage began whilst they were still crawling over, and the light from the shells gave them away. All hope of a surprise was gone. To add to their difficulties, a British machine gun was firing on the gap in the German wire intended to be used, and another had to be sought. All this disorganized the party, and it is doubtful if they all reached the trench. Some of them, led by the two officers, did reach it, formed a block, and proceeded to work leftwards, bombing what was apparently a mine shaft as they passed. Then they encountered resistance from about twenty Germans. The officers used their revolvers, and some of the men, getting out of the trench, bombed the enemy in it from a flank. Having failed to overcome this resistance, or to drive the enemy out, the raiders had to withdraw without prisoners or any real success beyond the killing of four Germans, and total casualties inflicted on the enemy estimated at fifteen. The raiders had only one man slightly wounded and one missing.

The moral drawn from this affair was the danger of relying on light signals. Brigadier-General Feetham, commanding 71st brigade, wrote:

" The young officers and inexperienced troops, who predominate now in infantry battalions, lack the training, or only exceptionally have the quick perception necessary to enable them to adapt themselves at once to unexpected situations."

On the 18th 2nd Lieutenant F. H. Randall was killed by a shell. Nothing else of note happened till the 30th, when after being inspected by the brigadier-general, the 9th Norfolk and 1st Leicester battalions were sent off on loan to the 57th brigade between Laventie and Armentières. They were agreeably surprised to find this really meant an easy time, as their business was only to facilitate certain movements in the

170th and 171st brigades. During the whole of this tour, up to August 25th, the only casualty in the battalion was one man killed, " through sheer bad luck," as Colonel Prior says. That officer found plenty of time for training of all sorts, especially in attacks and other schemes, by which he aimed at making both officers and men think out situations for themselves. There were changes in the divisional and brigade commands; General Ross made over the 6th division to General Marden, whilst Brigadier-General Feetham, promoted to a division, was succeeded in command of the 71st brigade by Brigadier-General Brown of the Gordons.

On August 26th the Norfolk battalion was in divisional reserve at Noeux-les-Mines, the 6th division having now taken over Hill 70. In this neighbourhood they remained till the end of September, taking the usual turns of front line, support, and reserve, and undergoing the usual enemy shelling in varying degree. The casualties in September were 2nd Lieutenants Walsha and Peddie wounded, and of other ranks eight killed or died of wounds and sixty-two wounded. Nearly half of these occurred under circumstances thus described by Colonel Prior:

"A working party was waiting to move off, and lying down by the side of a road, when an instantaneous fused shell landed and killed or wounded an officer and thirty other ranks."

October was a continuance of the situation of September, with little variation. The trenches were very wet, and there was such difficulty in communication that the battalion diary records that it took an orderly five hours to go out from battalion head-quarters to the front companies and back again. The weak point in the line was a gap of 200 yards between the left of the 6th division and the right of the 46th, which was partially defended by " D " company in support trenches. There was some use of gas on the British side, and unfortunately two of our gas cylinders were hit by the enemy and resulted in a spread of our own gas in the British lines. During October the casualties were 2nd Lieutenants Jarvis and Bullen wounded; other ranks, fourteen killed or died of wounds and thirty wounded. The strength of the battalion on October 31st was forty-three officers and 818 other ranks.

The battalion was now about to play its part in General Byng's great success towards Cambrai, and in the subsequent German riposte. It was hard at work training at Longuereuil on models of the Hindenburg Line in the neighbourhood to be attacked, though, needless to say, the name of the locality of the attack was kept secret, since surprise was of the essence of the forthcoming operations. Co-operation of infantry with tanks received special attention. Even commanding officers of battalions were not told till well on in November that there was to be an attack at all, or where it was to be.

At 6.15 a.m. on November 15th the 9th Norfolk left Longuereuil and, partly by march, partly by rail, reached Péronne twelve hours later. Thence, marching by Mt. St. Quentin, they went into hutments at Manancourt, a village which, like all in the neighbourhood, had been destroyed by the Germans in a way which, to quote the diary, formed "a standing monument to the military thoroughness of the enemy." The 16th was spent in hutments at Dessart Wood, half way to Gouzeaucourt, the utmost care being exercised to conceal the arrival of fresh troops by suppressing lights at night and other means. On the 17th the 9th Norfolk relieved a battalion of the Rifle Brigade in front line south of Ribécourt, but the latter left thirty men in the front trenches to mask the fact that a new battalion had arrived. None of the Norfolk men were allowed into these forward trenches. On the 19th the outpost line was pushed forward into "No Man's Land" to prevent the enemy from hearing the assembly of troops and tanks. Lieutenant Cubitt wrote that, though aerial observation was almost impossible owing to mist, "it seems remarkable that the great movement of troops, guns, munitions, cavalry, etc., did not attract the ever-vigilant Bosche airman, or the O.P. of their gunners."

The general plan was to capture the Hindenburg Line on a wide front by surprise. Reconnaissances by land and air had shown that it was very heavily wired, but it was a characteristic of the coming operations that there was to be no preliminary bombardment or wire cutting by the artillery. All reliance was placed on the operation of tanks flattening out the wire on widths sufficient to allow the infantry to pass freely.

The tasks set for the 71st brigade, to which the 11th Essex was now attached, were as follows:

The 1st Leicester were to furnish the first wave of the attack, preceded by three sections of tanks, to occupy and "mop up" the enemy's outpost trench (Plush[1] trench) and the first Hindenburg system known

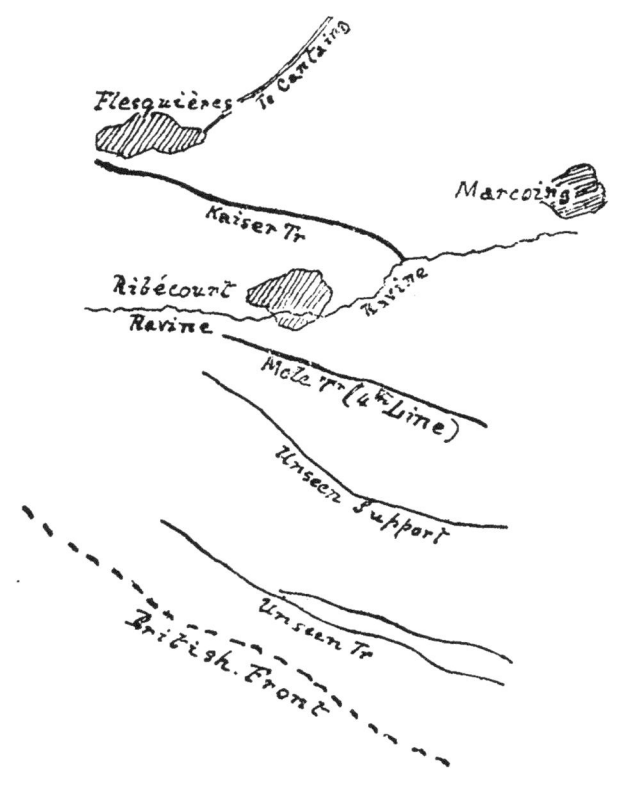

FIRST BATTLE OF CAMBRIA—ATTACK OF 9TH BATTALION

as Unseen trench and Unseen support, from the fact that they were sited on the reverse slope of the ridge and not visible from the British side. The right section of tanks was to go with the 1st Leicester, the left to go through Ribécourt village in advance of "A" company of the Norfolk battalion.

[1] The name is curious and looks as if it was a corruption of the name Villers Plouich, which was not far off, just behind the British front.

Moving off immediately after the first wave was to come another section of tanks, followed by the 9th Norfolk, passing through Ribécourt, and "leap-frogging" the 1st Leicester on the way. Behind this second wave there would be a third section of tanks and the 11th Essex, whose objective was the Hindenburg support system (Kaiser and Kaiser support trenches). In the night of November 19th–20th "C" company was in the outpost line, "A," "B," and "D" each divided equally between front line and supports.

Ten minutes before zero hour (6.20 a.m. on the 20th) the tanks moved off from Beaucamp reserve line, and at zero the barrage opened upon Plush trench. The movement of the tanks being slow and variable, some companies of the Leicester battalion got in front of them. The Norfolk battalion advanced with "D" company on the right, "B" centre, and "A" left, all passing, as they came up, through "C," which followed them in support.

The enemy barrage did not open till eight minutes after the British, and it is then described as being "ragged," and directed on fixed areas which it was not difficult to distinguish and avoid. The section commanders were very skilful in doing this, and in resuming proper direction after passing the fire-swept areas.

As Colonel Prior has furnished a full account of this battle it seems best to let him speak for his battalion by quoting the material parts of his description :

"I had arranged that, if everything went well, I would establish battalion head-quarters in the enemy fourth line, i.e. about half way between Unseen support and Ribécourt village. As nothing could be seen of the advance after the battalion had crossed the ridge in front of us, I settled to go over with the battalion, accompanied by Lieutenant Dye, my intelligence officer, and a couple of orderlies. . . . It was still fairly dark and Dye and I wandered well out across 'No Man's Land,' but there was no sign of either friend or foe. Everything was very peaceful and still, and there was no indication of the inferno that was shortly to be set loose. . . . The guns had opened before we got half way down the line, and the leading line of tanks, followed by the Leicesters, were crossing our trenches and starting across ' No Man's Land "—a wonderful spectacle in the half light of the early morning. Ponderous, grunting, groaning, wobbling, these engines of war crawled and lurched their way toward the enemy lines, followed by groups of men in file. Overhead our shells were pouring over. The barrage lifted from the enemy's outpost trench to the other side of the hill, where we knew that the Unseen trench was getting it hot ; but the slowness of those tanks ! It is at these moments that one itches for quickness and rapidity, and the slow, deliberate action of these monsters was exasperating. Neither tanks nor Leicesters were clear of our lines when we reached ' A ' company. I have never seen men in better fighting spirit. They all stood up and cheered when I reached them. . . . Our barrage had brought a reply from the enemy's guns, and a spasmodic barrage was put down by him, causing the Leicesters and ourselves some casualties. . . . The light was still very hazy, and the smoke and dust caused by the enemy's shell-bursts made it very difficult to distinguish whether each little column of attackers were our men or the Leicesters. I was, however, anxious to get on and over the hill, so as to be able to get a view of the Promised Land, and then be able to control the fight. In the advance we came across Blackwell with ' D ' company. He told me that both Cuthbert and Cubitt had been wounded, and that he himself was hit but could carry on. That was the last I saw of him, for he was killed later on. When the doctor examined his body he found that the first wound was a terrible one ; despite which he continued to lead his company, crossed the Hindenburg Line, and initiated the attack against the final objective before being shot dead. . . . Dye and I pushed on and successfully crossed the enemy outpost line and over the hill top."

After describing the gigantic size of the Hindenburg wire defences, and how, in the heavy fire which greeted them during their passage, Lieutenant Dye was mortally wounded, Colonel Prior describes his arrival in Unseen trench, which the Leicester battalion had not yet finished clearing, and continues :

"I then pushed along the communication trench and reached Unseen support. Here I found a number of 'C' company who were evidently not quite sure what their next action was, for I heard one man say, 'Well, what do we do now?' I shouted out, 'Now, my lads, you'll take the ruddy village,' at which they laughed and clambered out of the trench with me. I then found that Failes and the greater part of his company ('C') were already in front of me, and that they had reached the fourth line, in which I had decided to form battalion battle head-quarters. By some means or another, in the advance to this point, 'C' company had outstripped the other three companies, to say nothing of the tanks, and, instead of being in support, they now found themselves the front line company. Ribécourt was immediately in front of us, and I could see parties of the enemy running through the streets. Our artillery was putting down a smoke barrage on the farther side of the village, and several houses were on fire and blazing merrily. The question I had to decide was whether to hang on in our present position and wait for the arrival of the tanks and the three other companies, or push 'C' company in. The enemy already showed signs of recovering from the initial surprise. We were now being shelled pretty persistently and accurately, as well as machine-gunned. I determined to take immediate action, and directed Failes to push forward at once, take the part of the village lying on this side of the ravine, and hold the bridge crossing it. 'C' company swept on and effected this in brilliant fashion, securing a large bag of prisoners. In the meantime the tanks had negotiated the formidable obstacle of the Hindenburg trench, and were making much more rapid progress on the down hill slope towards Ribécourt."

From the battalion diary it appears that, as "C" opened fire and advanced, seventy Germans came forward with hands up and surrendered. "C" was then able to seize the near part of the village and two bridges over the ravine passing through it. The clearing of the village beyond the ravine fell to the lot of "D" on the right and "A" on the left, with "B", which passed through "C" at the ravine, in the centre. "C" dug in at the ravine. Colonel Prior says that he was almost alone in the fourth line (Mole trench) till joined by some trench mortar men.

> "'B' company had then gone through and were in the village. 'A' company was a little later on the left, and I saw them make a beautiful attack on the line of houses on the left of the village, supported by a male tank whose gun was in action. 'A' company was attacking by sectional rushes, covering the advance by rifle fire, and I could not help feeling that my efforts at open warfare training whilst at Tinques had not been wasted. I could not, however, see or hear anything of 'D" company and was rather anxious about them. Cheering messages from 'A,' 'B,' and 'C' companies, reporting complete success, began to come in, the runners arriving with broad grins and puffing German cigars. . . . At last a message from Beezly of 'D' company reporting complete success."

"A" and "D" had met with strong opposition and had had much hand-to-hand fighting in clearing the village. On the left two particularly troublesome machine guns were knocked out at close quarters, and their crews killed or wounded by a party under Lieutenant Hancock and C.S.M. Neale. Other machine guns were disposed of by Lewis-gun or rifle fire. It was estimated that the action of the 9th Norfolk cost the enemy some eighty casualties in killed and wounded and about 600 prisoners.

The battalion's attack ended with the capture of Ribécourt, when the 11th Essex passed through to take the Kaiser front and support trenches. For the rest of the day the 9th Norfolk battalion was busy consolidating at Ribécourt, with outposts north of it. In the evening they took over, from the 11th Essex, the Kaiser trenches, where the accommodation was bad, "A" and "D" companies in the front Kaiser trench having no dug-outs.

One more quotation may be given from Colonel Prior:

> "It would be impossible to set out all the extraordinary incidents of that glorious day: how Hancock and his sergeant-major rushed an enemy machine-gun position and settled a bet as to who would kill

most Boches. This was won by Hancock, but sergeant-major Neale always contends that he was unduly handicapped by having to use his bayonet, whilst Hancock had a revolver. How a runner of 'D' company, without assistance, took over seventy men prisoners, including a staff officer. How Worn, wounded in the first hundred yards of the advance, carried on with his platoon until he reached his final objective, the railway station, and consolidated his position. How Thompson of 'B' company, who in the darkness of the night prior to the attack had fallen down and very badly sprained his ankle, deliberately refused to go sick, and, with the aid of his servant, limped over in front of his platoon, and carried on until the objective was reached. How one man of 'A' company, having very daringly and very foolishly penetrated an enemy dug-out, leaving his rifle outside, knocked down the Bosche who thrust a pistol at his head, seized the pistol and harried his opponent by a vigorous application of the butt end. Some of these things are written down in the records of gallantry which have earned awards; many more and equally gallant actions never will be recorded, and some are recorded only in the memory of those, and, alas! their number has been sadly reduced, who took part in that glorious first day of the first battle of Cambrai."

Colonel Prior speaks very highly of the conduct of non-commissioned officers called on to take over platoons whose officers had been killed or wounded. He specially mentions Sergeant Playford, who took command of Lieutenant Jones's platoon when that officer was killed.

The casualties of the battalion were perhaps not so heavy as might have been expected on a day like this. They were:

Officers: Killed—Captain S. F. B. Blackwell; Lieutenants C. G. Jones, and G. H. G. Dye. Wounded—Captain Crosse; Lieutenant Cubitt; 2nd Lieutenants Worn and Cuthbert.

Other ranks: Killed twenty-nine, wounded fifty-eight.

For the next five days the battalion was engaged in wiring and consolidating its new positions. On the 26th it relieved the 8th Bedford in front line to the left of Noyelles-sur-l'Escant, "C" and "D" companies being in front, "A" and "B" in support. Next day the battalion changed places with the 9th Suffolk in support.

On the 30th came the great German counter-attack, in reply to the battle of the 20th, at a time when the 9th Norfolk battalion was in Nine Wood, south-west of Noyelles. The German attacks were on the flanks of the great salient created by the battle of the 20th, and the 6th division, being in the head of the salient, was in great danger of being cut off, though it was not actually engaged. Of course it came in for its share of shelling, and part of its transport at Gouzeaucourt narrowly escaped capture.

December 1st was a day of heavy shelling and air attacks. An attack on Cantaing failed, but in this the 9th Norfolk appears not to have been engaged, and in the evening they relieved the 9th Suffolk in front line. The shelling continued heavily on December 2nd, and on the 3rd the brigade position was altered so as to hold Noyelles only lightly, and to form a defensive flank towards Marcoing. That evening the front was withdrawn to the Hindenburg support line (Kaiser trenches), a withdrawal which rendered the position less anxious and less dependent on what might happen on the flanks. The shelling was continued, but no infantry attack took place before the division was withdrawn for rest.

Whilst in the Hindenburg support line the disposition of the battalion was one company in outpost line, three in front and support trenches, each of these three being partly in the front and partly in the support trench To the left company was assigned the rôle of counter-attack if required. The outpost company was changed each night.

From December 14th to 31st the 9th battalion was training and attending lectures at Bailleuval in the Lens area. The weather was very cold, and the good Christmas dinner, which the battalion diary specially mentions, was no doubt very welcome.

(d) 1918 : THE GERMAN OFFENSIVE OF MARCH AND APRIL—THE FINAL BRITISH ADVANCE BY LE CÂTEAU—THE MARCH TO THE RHINE

January, 1918, opened for the 9th Norfolk battalion with sixteen days of training. still in very cold weather, at Courcelle, whence they moved, with the brigade, via Bapaume to Frémicourt, taking over from the 6th Gordon Highlanders (152nd brigade) at Le Bucquière on the Bapaume-Cambrai railway.

From the 21st to the 26th they were in trenches in front of Dénicourt, where, on the 22nd, there was a heavy bombardment from 8 to 10 p.m. At first it was not realized that gas shells were being used, and, though no one was very badly gassed, eight officers (including Colonel Prior) and ninety others had to be evacuated to field ambulances before the end of the month.

From the 26th to the 31st the battalion was in divisional reserve at Frémicourt, but the demand for working parties was so heavy as to prevent training. It was about this time that brigades were reduced to three battalions of infantry. In the 71st brigade it was the 9th Suffolk who had to be disbanded. It will be remembered that the 8th Norfolk suffered the same fate at the same period.

The January casualties were remarkable—nine officers and ninety-two other ranks gassed, and only one killed and two wounded by fire. In the beginning of February the battalion was reinforced by fifteen officers and 300 other ranks from the 8th Battalion, which was being disbanded. On the 13th the 6th division was relieved in the Dénicourt area by the 51st and transferred to the Quéant-Pronville sector, in which it remained till the great German offensive of March 21st. The position is thus described by General Marden in his history of the 6th division:

" The front held by the division was generally on a forward slope opposite the villages of Quéant and Pronville. ' No Man's Land ' averaged three-quarters of a mile in width. The whole area was down hill and very suitable for the action of tanks. The position lay astride a succession of well-defined broad spurs and narrow valleys (like the fingers of a partially opened hand), merging into the broad transverse valley which separated the British line from the two villages above mentioned. All the advantages of the ground lay with the defence, and it seemed as if no attack could succeed, unless by the aid of tanks. A large portion of the front line—notably the valleys—was sown with 2-inch trench mortar bombs with instantaneous fuzes, which would detonate under the pressure of a wagon, but not of a man's foot. In addition, five anti-tank 18-pounder guns were placed in positions of vantage. The wire was very broad and thick. The position would, indeed, have been almost impregnable had there been sufficient time to complete it, and had there been separate troops for counter-attack.

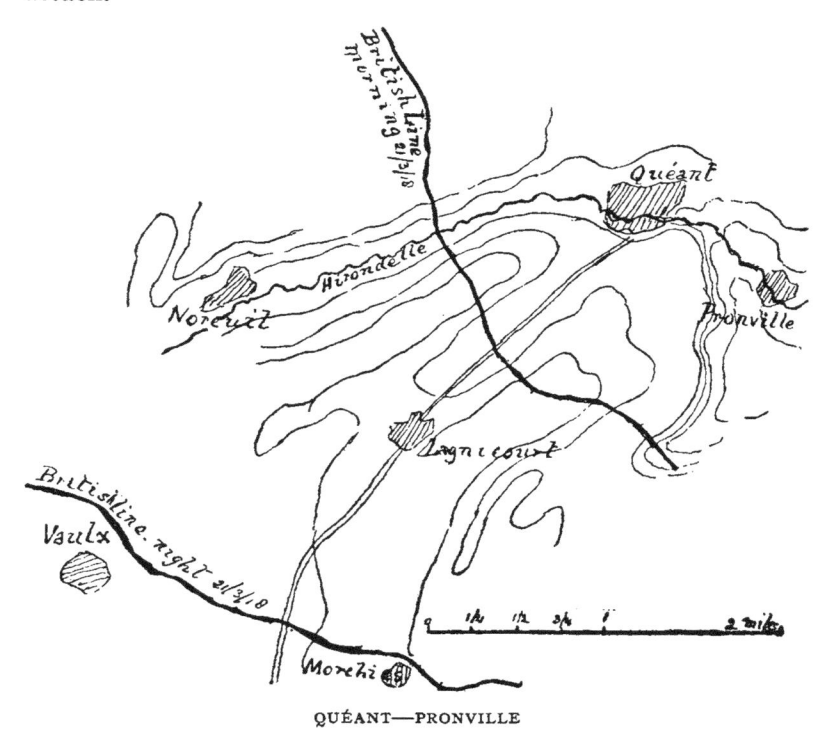

QUÉANT—PRONVILLE

"The ground was a portion of that wrested from the enemy in the Cambrai offensive of November-December, 1917, but had only improvized trenches. A month's hard frost in January had militated against digging, and, though there were a complete front trench and reserve trench, the support trenches hardly existed, and dug-outs were noticeable by their absence. The front was 4,500 yards in extent, the three brigades in line—18th on right, 71st in centre,

16th on left—on approximately equal frontages. The depth from front or outpost zone to reserve or battle zone was about 2,000 yards. With only three battalions in a brigade, there was no option but to assign one battalion in each brigade to the defence of the outpost zones, and keep two battalions in depth in the battle zone. With battalions at just over half strength, and with the undulating nature of the ground, the defence resolved itself everywhere into a succession of posts with a very limited field of fire.

"A good corps line called the Vaux-Morchies line had been dug, the nearest portion a mile behind the reserve line, and this was held by the Pioneers and Royal Engineers, owing to scarcity of numbers."

When Colonel Prior returned to the command of the battalion he found it in the Lagnicourt trenches. There were frequent alarms and rumours of impending attacks which he recognized were not mere cries of "Wolf." The history of the 6th division equally shows that the approaching storm was far from being unexpected. It broke on the morning of March 21st with terrible violence. At this time "B" and "D" companies were in front line, "C" in support, "A" in reserve in the sunken road at Lagnicourt near battalion head-quarters. Of the other two infantry battalions of the brigade, the 2nd Sherwood Foresters were in the front line on the left of the Norfolk battalion, the 1st Leicester in reserve.

Of what happened on that memorable day we shall quote freely the account given by Colonel Prior himself:

"I spent the whole night in going round the front line posts with Cutbill of 'B' company and Sprott of 'D.' It took me a very long time, as I had to make a good number of alterations, and it was very near dawn when I got back to battalion head-quarters. During the course of my tour I went some way out into 'No Man's Land,' and obtained the impression that this was no longer a false alarm. I don't quite know what gave me this impression. In the Bosche lines there was a stillness which, at the same time, was not a complete silence, just as if a large number of men were already in position, waiting in intense excitement, and speaking to each other in whispers. So much so that, on my return to battalion head-quarters, I told Lieutenant Tyce, the officer on duty, that I felt convinced that the attack would be made, and that I therefore should not turn in until daylight. A few minutes later the crash came.

" All over the front the sky was lit by the flash of the enemy guns, and shells began to drop. Rushing out of battalion head-quarters a whiff told me that our line was being searched with gas shells. The men were turning out and getting into their gas masks as they ran to their posts. . . . Having seen that everything was in readiness, so far as ' A ' company and battalion head-quarters were concerned, I went out to the right, where I could see more of our front. It was getting much lighter, and the bombardment over the whole of our front was terrific. Shells were bursting everywhere, and the noise was frightful. . . . The gas shelling had stopped, and had been replaced by heavy shells."

At this time Colonel Prior heard from Captain Failes, commanding " C " (support) company, that, though the bombardment was still intense, he had seen no sign of an enemy advance.

A runner from " B " company came in presently, the first of several sent who had succeeded in getting through. That company was in sore straits—2nd Lieutenant Williams had been killed, Captain Cutbill dangerously wounded, and 2nd Lieutenant Percival, who sent the message, begged for trench mortar support, which it was difficult to arrange.

The bombardment, says General Marden, had at first been with gas and high explosives on the back areas to cut communications and dis-organize reinforcements, and then, between 7 and 8 a.m., had been turned on to the front areas with such violence as to annihilate the garrisons of the forward trenches, from which few survivors came back to the reserve lines. " So intense was the bombardment that four out of five concealed anti-tank guns were knocked out by direct hits." The German infantry attacks were principally by the three valleys, leading respectively to Noreuil on the left, Lagnicourt in the centre, and Morchies on the right.

To the two front battalions of the 71st brigade (the 9th Norfolk and 2nd Sherwood Foresters) alone does the divisional history attribute a repulse of the first attacks. Towards 11 a.m. the enemy had driven back the 59th division, on the left of the 6th, had forced back the 16th brigade nearly to Noreuil, had taken Lagnicourt, and driven in the left of the Sherwood Foresters in the valley, and were close up to their head-quarters. The front line of the Norfolk battalion was reported to have been occupied by the enemy, as well as that of the close supports.

To return to Colonel Prior's narrative

"This threatened the whole of our battle position, and I therefore saw Hancock, explained the position to him, and directed him to take his company over in a counter-attack against the enemy threatening the Sherwood Foresters. I also sent an urgent message to brigade for reinforcements, as, when 'A' company had left, I should only have a few men in hand. In the meantime both 'A' company and head-quarters had been suffering from the continuous shell fire. Whilst I was actually settling matters with Hancock and pointing out the line of his advance, three out of his four subalterns were wounded. I watched 'A' company's advance over the shell-swept ground with very mixed feelings—pride at the gallant, unfaltering advance, and dread of the cost that would have to be paid. The wounded of all companies were coming in at an appalling rate, and from these I learnt that our casualties in the front had been very heavy. A wounded man from 'A' brought me back a cheery message from Hancock that he had reached the Sherwood Foresters' head-quarters, and was giving his men a breather before charging with the bayonet. Almost at the same time Failes ('C' company) rang up on the 'phone and reported that the enemy had attacked his position in great force, had been completely routed, and that he could hold his trenches easily against a frontal attack. Having reported this to brigade, and received from the brigadier the assurance that he had dispatched me two companies of the Leicester Regiment, I felt considerably elated and ran up to tell the battalion H.Q. the news of 'C' company's success. I was just reaching the left of our trenches, when, to my surprise and consternation, I saw a party of the enemy coming over the brow of the hill not fifty yards away from us. I got a machine gun on to this party at once and they fled back. The position was, however, most alarming. It was obvious that the enemy had broken quite through the defences on our left flank, the promised reinforcements had not arrived, and I had only about sixty men left with me. Still more serious was the fact, that, should the enemy attack and succeed in driving us out, the whole line held by the Sherwood Foresters, ' C ' company, and the brigade on the right of ' C ' company would be in deadly peril. All the men I could collect I got into position to resist the new danger, gave orders for the destruction of all maps, papers, and orders, and telephoned the position of affairs to the brigade. The brigadier, to whom I spoke, said that the Leicesters should have been up with me long before this, and I must hang on at all costs.

"Shortly afterwards the first company of Leicesters came up and I detailed Captain Shelton, in command, his orders. It was a great relief to me to have a good, strong company to reinforce my small force, especially as the enemy were now very close to us and pressing in on the north of the sunken road. Having got the Leicesters into position, I again reported to the brigade and was told by the brigadier that the enemy had taken the Report centre, and that I was to try and withdraw my head-quarters to the Vaux-Morchies line, a new line of defence that had been recently dug. As the Report centre was located in a sunken road immediately behind battalion H.Q., and on my direct line of retirement, I did not think there was the faintest hope of getting back, and our whole position appeared quite untenable.

" It is difficult to explain on paper the extraordinary position we were in. ' C ' company, with a few remnants of ' B ' and ' D,' were holding the original battle position, with the remains of the Sherwood Foresters on their left. The remains of ' A ' company, after a most desperate fight, had dropped back and formed the first stage of the protective flank. With a large interval between them, this was carried on by the two Leicester companies, and on their left flank, as I moved back to the Morchies—Vaudricourt line, I dropped out small flanking parties from battalion H.Q. and such stragglers from 'D' company and the Sherwood Foresters as I could pick up. In result the battalion was holding its original battle position on a front of less than 500 yards, with a long, protective flank of close upon two miles curling quite round on to its line of retirement. How I reached the new line safely will always remain a mystery, as we had to pass within less than a hundred yards of the enemy holding the Report centre sunken road. In the Morchies line I found a support company of the 1st Leicester Regiment, as well as a company of the Leicester Pioneers."

After explaining why he gave up the idea of a counter-attack on the Report centre, Colonel Prior continues:

"The day was rapidly closing in and I began to be very nervous as to the safe withdrawal of the troops, the more so since the brigade on our right were effecting their withdrawal and I learnt from them that their battle position was now evacuated. Withdrawal orders had long since been dispatched, and it was now dusk. At last I could stand the suspense no longer and determined to go forward and superintend the withdrawal myself. I had only got about 200 yards on my way when to my delight I met Failes returning with the remnants of his splendid company. All day long had they fought the oncoming enemy hordes, and each attack had withered and broken down before their fire. Failes himself estimated that his company alone had accounted for upwards of 2,000 of the enemy. They had fought until their rifles were too hot to hold and their Lewis guns had to be cooled down before they would fire another magazine. Finally, when ordered to withdraw, they had come out bringing all their casualties. The remnants of the Sherwood Foresters and the flank guards were similarly brought in."

In the Morchies line the men of the intermingled Norfolk, Sherwood Foresters, and Leicester battalions were sorted out.

The remains of the 9th Norfolk were a mere handful. All the officers of " B " and " D " companies were casualties, only one lieutenant remained of " A," and of " C " Captain Failes and one subaltern alone were not *hors de combat*. The casualties were :

Officers : Killed, ten—Captains M. W. C. Sprott, M.C., J. E. Hancock, D.S.O., C. M. Coller, B. Cutbill, and J. E. Hill ; 2nd Lieutenants Setchell, W. J. Faulke, C. A. Williams, F. S. Lewington and W. S. Wright. Wounded, five—Lieutenant Barker ; 2nd Lieutenants M. J. Cooke, J. R. C. Lane, Thornley and Greatorex. Taken prisoner, 2nd Lieutenants Burton and Percival.

Other ranks : Killed thirty, wounded 147, missing 170. Total seventeen officers and 347 others.

It will be remembered that, according to General Marden, battalions were " at just over half strength."

In addition to the quotations from Colonel Prior, we may perhaps give the entry in the battalion war diary :

" Owing to the heroic resistance of our men the enemy had only penetrated our front and close support line up to 12 noon. This was due to the overwhelming numbers of the enemy and the obliteration of our system of defence. Our support company (' C ') did very gallant work in Skipton Reserve, holding on until 5 o'clock ; then, when both flanks had gone, and not until then, did they retire. Previous to this there had been a very gallant counter-attack by the company in reserve going forward from the sunken road at Lagnicourt to Skipton reserve. This, and the persistent efforts of the men in Skipton reserve, entirely baffled the enemy, as attacks were given up, and he confined his attacks to Lagnicourt and the flanks. This being successful, our men in Skipton had to retire, owing to their part of the line being exposed to great danger."

When Colonel Prior, as senior officer present, had sorted out the remnants of the three battalions as far as possible, orders were received for the Leicester battalion to hold the line, whilst the 9th Norfolk and Sherwood Foresters went into support behind Morchies Wood.

The shelling continued steadily, but so exhausted were the men that they were heedless of it. Colonel Prior even saw a shell explode in a shelter where some of " C " company were sleeping. Fortunately, on going there, he found that no one had been hurt, and that many of the men had not even waked, though part of the wall had been blown away and the place was full of smoke and fumes. Colonel Prior continues :

" Captain Byon of the Foresters then came to me for orders, and, as I had heard nothing from the brigade, I thought the only thing to be done was to select a defensive position where we were. Captain Byon had only about a hundred men left as representing his battalion, and when, shortly after, I got my own men out, the full extent of the fearful casualties became apparent. To the best of my recollection, there were less than eighty men left of the splendid battalion I had commanded thirty hours previously. From what I could learn from the few survivors of ' B ' and ' D ' companies, the front and close support line had been literally blown to pieces with shell and trench mortar fire, and fearful casualties had been sustained before the actual attack took place. As a result the actual resistance was confined to small groups of survivors, and these were speedily overrun and surrounded. It subsequently transpired that the actual number of unwounded prisoners taken was very small, the greater proportion of ' missing ' being either killed or badly wounded. ' C ' company, augmented by such few survivors of ' B ' and ' D ' as joined them, also received a fearful shelling, but escaped the trench mortar fire, and were able to make a resistance that must remain for ever a bright passage in the history of the Norfolk Regiment. Remembering the partiality of the enemy to attack through a valley, Captain Failes had moved part of his command well down to the right and covered the valley. Here the enemy met with tremendous losses at ranges varying from forty to 400 yards. It was not merely a frontal attack that ' C ' company had to meet but, as has already been detailed, the enemy broke through the Sherwood Foresters and seriously threatened, not merely to wipe out that battalion, but to turn ' C ' company's line as well. The enemy did in fact reach the left of ' C ' company's trench, and it was only by repeated and most heroic bombing attacks that he was kept at bay and the line remained untaken. In every attack and counter-attack Captain Failes proved himself to be a resolute and skilful leader. His company backed him most nobly, and absolutely and completely stopped the enemy onrush. I have recounted the initial advance of ' A ' company, and, never having heard the full and complete story of their counter-attack, I must leave this to others more competent to tell. This I know, for I got it from the Sherwood Foresters that night, that their dashing advance and intervention in the fight came at a most crucial moment, and saved a situation which looked most ugly. They suffered most fearful punishment, losing their gallant commander, Captain Hancock, one of the bravest officers who ever put on His Majesty's uniform, but their attack brought the enemy's advance at this point to a standstill and placed him on the defensive. It is not too much to say that the enemy must have suffered at least six casualties for every one inflicted on the battalion, and the small gain of ground had cost him very dearly."

During most of the 22nd Colonel Prior, at the request of Colonel Latham of the Leicester battalion, held a covering position outside Morchies Wood. A counter-attack on the right by the 25th division having failed, the Germans again attacked in great force, and the 9th Norfolk, fighting in the rear-guard action, fell slowly back on Beugny. Just as the retirement commenced Colonel Prior was badly wounded and compelled to hand over the command to Captain Failes. What remained of the 9th Norfolk, with the Leicesters on their right, and Sherwood Foresters on their left, still held the high ground 500 yards north of Beugny, where they were relieved, in the night of the 22nd-23rd, by the 123rd brigade and retired via Frémicourt and Bapaume to Bihucourt. Thence on the 24th they went by train, via Doullens, Etaples, Boulogne, and Calais, to billets at St. Sixte near Proven on the 26th, and into the Winzerlee area on the 27th to refit.

On the 30th they were inspected by General Plumer, who expressed his satisfaction at the turn out.

Of the praise of General Byng, conveyed in a farewell order to the 6th division on its leaving the 3rd Army, the 9th Norfolk can claim a very large share. He wrote:

"I cannot allow the 6th division to leave the third army without expressing my appreciation of their splendid conduct during the first stages of the great battle now in progress. By their devotion and courage they have broken up overwhelming attacks and prevented the enemy gaining his object, namely, a decisive victory.

"I wish them every possible good luck."

On April 1st the Norfolk battalion was again moved to the front, this time to the Ypres salient, where they went into the left sub-sector of the defences at Polybecke, with head-quarters in the remains of Polygon Wood, where they were relieved on the 7th by the Sherwood Foresters. A threatened attack on the 11th did not materialize, and on the 14th the battalion went to Dranoutre. Next day "D" and "A" companies were in front line, "C" in support at Crucifix Hill, and "B" in reserve. Arrangements had been made for "C" to counter-attack if necessary, but its losses, due to a continuous bombardment commencing at noon on the 15th, necessitated "B" taking its place as the counter-attacking force. Lieutenant-Colonel F. R. Day was now in command. At 2.30 p.m. on the 15th the enemy advanced, and by 3 o'clock had obtained a footing in the front trenches. From these he was again driven by "B's" counter-attack. "B" now held the line, and also formed a defensive flank on the right, where its flank was exposed by the capture of the front line there. Presently "B" was forced to retire before the great strength of infantry and machine guns brought up by the Germans.

Line was then formed along the railway, with the left of the battalion in touch with the 1st Leicester at Clapham Junction. At 10.30 p.m. the 71st brigade was ordered into divisional reserve behind Mt. Kemmel. Here half the Norfolk battalion were dug in east of

Locre, the other half on the road leading north-west from Kemmel. Here they remained till 8 a.m. on the 17th, when they went into dugouts under heavy shell fire. After moving up, on the 18th, into close support of the 1st Leicester, they were relieved in the night of the 19th-20th, by the 11th company 83rd French Infantry, and went back to Westoutre and on to Ouderdom. The 25th was the day of the loss of Mt. Kemmel by the French. Though the 9th Norfolk stood to on that day they were not called up. The total casualties of the battalion in April were:

Officers: Killed—(on the 15th) Captains H. V. E. Byrne, M.C. and G. Failes; 2nd Lieutenant W. T. Nancarrow. Wounded—Major Spurrell; Lieutenants Beezley and F. Jackson; 2nd Lieutenants B. A. Smith, Orchard, Webber, Finnigan, Middleton and A. J. N. Jones.

Other ranks: Killed fourteen, wounded 156, missing 254.

All but three wounded occurred on the 15th. The trench strength of the battalion on the 16th was only six officers and 150 men.

At the end of April they were holding strong points near Goldfish Château west of Ypres. Here they remained working on defences till May 12th, when they moved to the Ypres Canal south of the city.

On the 28th-29th, the French, on the right of the 6th division, were attacked and driven back, which necessitated the formation of a defensive flank by "D" company on the right. The casualties in May were:

Officers: Wounded—Captains R. A. Jones, E. D. Selfe; 2nd Lieutenants Elliott, Croxford, and Bullen.

Other ranks: Killed sixteen, wounded fifty-three, gassed twenty-three.

Captain Failes received the D.S.O. he had so well earned in March.

During June and July the battalion remained in the same neighbourhood without fighting, the casualties in June being only seven men wounded, including accidents. In July the officer casualties were heavier—2nd Lieutenant Simpson was killed; 2nd Lieutenants J. L. Murphy, Garbutt, Dye, Fothergill, and Miller wounded, the two last named remaining on duty. Seven other ranks were killed and twenty-seven wounded.

Colonel Prior returned to command the battalion on July 28th, when its two halves were awkwardly separated by the Dickebusch Lake. But he was not really fit for active service, having been much shattered by wounds and gas, and less than a month later was compelled, by the verdict of a medical board, to leave the battalion again under the command of Colonel Day, who retained it for the rest of the war.

August was also uneventful. During this month an American platoon was attached to each first line company. The casualties of the month were :

Officers : Killed—Captain E. D. Selfe. Wounded—2nd Lieutenants Elliott and Crow.

Other ranks : Killed three. Wounded twenty-three.

The final offensive of the Allies was now in full swing when the 9th Norfolk marched, on September 1st, to St. Omer, where they entrained, reached Corbie east of Amiens at 2 a.m. on the 2nd, and went into billets at La Houssoye. There they were training till the 14th, when they went by march and bus to Monchy Lagache, on the extreme right of the British line. Orders on the 17th were for attack on the following morning. At midnight the battalion moved forward by the south side of Holnon Wood into a quarry. Owing to lateness of the start, a heavy barrage, and rain, only three companies had reached the quarry by zero hour (5.30 a.m.). These three left it at 6 a.m. ; the fourth was found later and sent to the point of assembly. To reach that point the battalion had to march parallel to the front under a barrage in the rain, and the three companies lost direction and got scattered. Only one company and two platoons of the others reached the assembly point, which was on the east side of Holnon Wood. That wood, with bad tracks and drenched with gas, was almost unpassable, and for this reason the 71st brigade had had to go round by its south side, the 16th by the north.

The 6th division front was practically coextensive with the eastern side of the wood, and the advance was to be up 3,000 yards of slope to the heights overlooking St. Quentin. About the centre was another Quadrilateral, recalling unpleasant memories of the one in the Somme battle. The 71st brigade was to attack on the right, the 16th on the left. The left on the 71st included the Quadrilateral in its objective.

At 9 a.m. the six platoons of the Norfolk battalion advanced, but, under the heavy barrage and machine-gun fire from the Quadrilateral, were compelled to edge off to the right, where they remained in action. The remaining companies and battalion head-quarters were assembled in a sunken road at 3 p.m. and presently the battalion was reorganized in three companies, of which one was engaged against the Quadrilateral and two were held in reserve in the sunken road. The difficulties of the attack were enhanced by the failure of the French to take Round and Manchester Hills on the right.

Little or no progress having been made on the 18th, orders issued at 1.45 a.m. on the 19th, for a renewal of the attack at 4 a.m., with the object of capturing North Alley, in conjunction with the rest of the 71st brigade on the right and the 16th brigade on the left.

Owing to the failure of the troops on the right to attack, and to the 16th brigade being held up by the Quadrilateral on the left, two companies of the Norfolk battalion, who had got forward as far as midway between Douai trench and North Alley, were compelled to retire to the former, where they remained in action for the rest of the day. "A" company and two platoons were withdrawn to reserve in the sunken road. There had been hard fighting and great losses on the two days, and it was decided to defer further attack, pending more complete preparation for what was recognized to be much more than the rearguard action which the Germans were at first believed to be fighting.

On the 20th the battalion was again reorganized in only two companies, distributed between Douai and Valley trenches, with reserve in a quarry.

On the 22nd it was relieved, and occupied New and Valley trenches. On the 24th it again went back, on relief by the 11th Essex, and was once more reorganized in three companies. On the 29th, on being relieved by the French 11th Chasseurs, it went still farther back, without taking part in the capture of the Quadrilateral by the 16th and 18th brigades on the 25th.

The severe casualties during these operations were mostly suffered on the 18th. They were:

Officers: Killed—Captain S. F. Lane; Lieutenant A. A. Walsha; 2nd Lieutenant R. L. Norton. Wounded—Captains

Cozens-Hardy and F. W. Lee; Lieutenant L. S. Martin (on the 19th); 2nd Lieutenants Brand, Connor, Fothergill, and Elliott (on the 29th).

Other ranks: Killed or died of wounds twenty-six, wounded, 150, missing, five.

On October 1st, at Tertry, the battalion received a draft of 150 men and were able to resume a four-company organization. On the 4th it went by bus to the Magny la Fosse training area till the 6th, when it relieved the 1st Buffs in trenches, ready for another attack on the 8th.

St. Quentin had now been passed, and the Hindenburg Line carried by the Americans and the 46th division. These were now to be relieved by the 6th division, as they were exhausted. The French on the right had followed the Germans through St. Quentin, but had made little progress beyond, so that the 46th division, and the 30th American division on its left, formed a considerable salient towards Bohain. The attack was directed slightly north of east, and the front line of the 71st brigade consisted of the 2nd Sherwood Foresters on the right and the 9th Norfolk on the left, with the 1st Leicester in reserve. No tanks went with the attack, but a battalion of " whippets " was to follow it. On the left of the 9th Norfolk were the 118th American Infantry Regiment. " C " company on the left and " D " on the right were the first line, with " B " in support and " A " in reserve.

At 5.10 a.m. the advance commenced, and the Norfolk battalion steadily pushed on till, at 9.23, they were on a line south of Brancourt station. At 11.56 they were still on this line, in a sunken road leading from Brancourt to Fresnoy le Grand, in touch with the Americans on the left and the Sherwood Foresters on the right. A company of the Leicester battalion had been lent to the 9th Norfolk as reserve. Brancourt was still untaken, and the Norfolk battalion was warned that, if the Americans took it, a counter-attack was to be expected, and the defenders must be aided by Lewis-gun and machine-gun fire by the 9th Norfolk.

The advance was still scarcely up to the first objective. At 3 p.m., the Americans being reported nearly up to the objective, the 9th Norfolk were ordered forward, but found themselves held up by machine guns at Brancourt on their left and Jonnecourt on the right. Their losses had again been so great at to necessitate organization in two companies, for which purpose they were withdrawn to their original line at 6.20 p.m. The officer casualties on the 8th were:

Killed or died of Wounds—Captains R. Brunger and W. W. Everett, and 2nd Lieutenant Burford.

Wounded—Lieutenant Mutimer and 2nd Lieutenants Hopegood, Middleton and Reed.

The casualties in other ranks are not stated separately for each day, but for the whole of October they were: killed seventy-one, wounded 484, missing seven.

At 8.30 p.m. it was announced that the 71st brigade would probably attack the high ground towards Bohain on the 9th. The 1st Leicester battalion were to relieve the Sherwood Foresters and part of the 9th Norfolk, who were to establish posts connecting up with the Americans at Brancourt Farm. At 2.30 a.m. on the 9th the Norfolk battalion received orders to take part in the attack on the high ground, relieving part of the American right.

The assembly was effected only with very great difficulty, owing to the darkness in an unknown country, but was safely accomplished and the 9th Norfolk advanced behind a strong barrage. No great opposition was encountered till the railway west of Bohain was reached. Here it became more strenuous, but the Norfolk battalion, working round by the north, turned the German right and pushed after the retreating enemy through Bohain, to the east of which they established posts. Vast quantities of material were captured in Bohain. That night the Norfolk battalion held the east of Bohain, with the Leicester on their right. There were no officer casualties on this day, and, as stated above, casualties is other ranks are only given for the whole month.

For the 10th the order was for the Sherwood Foresters and Leicester battalion to pass through the 9th Norfolk, who were to go into brigade reserve west of Bohain. In the attack of that day the Leicester battalion did not get on as far as was intended, owing to the 46th division on the right being held up.

On the 11th it appeared likely that, as the brigade front extended, it might be necessary to form a defensive flank on the right. The Americans on the left had got well forward, and the object of the day was to bring the 71st brigade, and the 46th division on the right, up into line with them. Accordingly, the Norfolk battalion was brought forward in the centre of the brigade, with the Leicester battalion on the right and the Sherwood Foresters on the left.

The brigade diary states that the opposition on this day was much more strenuous than on the preceeding two. The Leicester battalion was not able to get on as far as was proposed; the Sherwood Foresters made repeated attempts to push on to the high ground known as Bellevue Ridge.

Starting at 5.30 a.m. the 9th Norfolk fought their way forward till 6.40, when they were somewhat in advance of, but in touch with the battalions on either side. In consequence of their advanced position their flanks suffered severely from machine-gun fire, and they had to stop. Artillery fire was then turned on to the machine-gun nests in a copse, and at 12.50 the battalion endeavoured to push forward, in conjunction with another attack by the Sherwood Foresters on the Bellevue ridge from the north-west. A protective barrage was arranged for this advance. Ten minutes later two tanks went forward against the machine-gun nests in the copse, and with them went the 9th Norfolk. This operation was successfully carried out and the copse occupied; but owing to the British artillery fire being short, the Norfolk battalion had to withdraw from it and consolidate on the line from which they had started. The officer casualties on the 11th were: Wounded—2nd Lieutenants S. W. Clark, R. F. Harrison, and Myson. For the four days, 8th to 11th, the total casualties are given as ten officers and 266 other ranks.[1] In the same period the 9th Norfolk took 390 prisoners, and one anti-tank gun.

[1] In the list of casualties for October in the battalion War Diary the following officers are shown as having been wounded on the 15th: 2nd Lieutenants Webber, Bird, Hawksley, Major, and Emmerson. There seems to be some mistake here, as neither this diary nor that of the brigade, nor the history of the 6th division show the 9th Norfolk as having been engaged on that day. 2nd Lieutenants Larkman and Pike are shown as wounded on the 21st, another day not recorded as one of fighting; but of course the wounds may have been from shelling in back areas.

That night the Norfolk battalion was relieved, and went into billets south of Bohain to rest, but to be ready to counter-attack.

On the 14th they relieved the 3rd Battalion 107th American Infantry on the left of the 2nd Sherwood Foresters, returning to billets at Bohain on the 16th. After training there on the 18th and 19th they went, partly by bus, to St. Souplet, where they relieved the 108th Americans, and next day, thanks to a draft of 260 men, were again able to form four companies. The 71st brigade had now taken the place of the 75th (British) brigade (25th division) and the 54th (American) brigade 27th (American) division, and was to continue the attack on the 23rd.

The brigade formed up in the early part of the night of the 22nd—23rd, zero hour being at 1.20 a.m.

The line of assembly was on the light railway from Câtillon to Le Câteau, whence the attack was directed north-eastwards towards the Bois de l'Evêque. The battalions were the 9th Norfolk on the right, 1st Leicester left, 2nd Sherwood Foresters reserve. The two leading battalions were to carry the attack through to the objective, which was marked on the map by a red line 300 or 400 yards beyond the south-west edge of the Bois de l'Evêque.

There had been very heavy shelling of the starting line during the night, and a thick mist in the morning made the assembly very difficult; but the battalions were in position up to time and had a good start.

The first check occurred very soon, when many wired hedges and fences, in a close country of small fields, were met with and found to be almost unpassable. By 5.30 a.m. brigade head-quarters received a report from the 9th Norfolk that the attack had been held up from the first by this cause, and by a very severe machine-gun fire. Half an hour later it had been definitely held up, and the barrage had been lost as it moved ahead. The Norfolk battalion was unable to get more than 400 yards from the assembly line, and was stopped short of the Bois de l'Evêque, though some small scattered parties were farther on.

The 1st Leicester battalion was on the same line, except their left company, which had been able to push forward. A section of tanks had got on to the red line, but finding the infantry were not following, and being under fire from a 77 mm. gun, had returned.

At 7 a.m. the Sherwood Foresters (reserve) were digging in on the starting line with three companies, the fourth in reserve.

The two tanks were now ordered to report to the O.C. 9th Norfolk and to clear up the machine-gun nests obstructing the advance.

At 11 a.m. the situation was reported to be that the remnants of the four companies of the Leicesrer battalion were holding the red line on the left. Thence the line ran back south-east through the Bois de l'Evêque. The Leicester were in touch with the 20th Manchester of the brigade on their left, but there was no contact between the right of the 71st brigade and the left of the 18th. To fill the gap the Sherwood Foresters were pushing up a company.

After 1 p.m., as there was a distinct slackening of the vigour of the enemy's defence, it was decided to move the Sherwood Foresters north-eastwards, whilst the 9th Norfolk, who had now been reorganized, would work round through the area of the 25th division on the left, and, forming up on the road from Bazuel to the north, would push through the Bois de l'Evêque south-eastwards. The attack in this direction was expected to be easier, as it was parallel to the paths and drives in the wood, whilst the original line of attack had been directed at right angles to them through thick undergrowth. Before this could be completed, however, darkness stopped the fight. The 71st brigade ended the day about half way through the wood. The operation was considered a success, as it had broken the enemy's resistance and facilitated the clearing of the Bois de l'Evêque next day by the 16th brigade. The casualties of the Norfolk battalion on this day were:

Officers: Killed—2nd Lieutenants C. D. Smith and R. B. Bray.
Wounded—Lieutenant H. G. Palmer; 2nd Lieutenants A. Miller, Coates, B. Campbell, Teal, and J. H. Clarke.
Other ranks: seven killed, sixty-one wounded, sixty missing.
The battalion took thirty prisoners.

At 6 p.m. the Norfolk battalion was withdrawn from the front, and later in the night the 71st brigade was relieved by the 16th, which continued the attack next day.

This was the 9th battalion's last battle; for, though they took their turn in front line, they had no more active fighting till the 6th division was relieved in the night of October 30th—31st, and went back to billets in the Fresnoy le Grand area.

On Armistice Day the battalion was at Bohain, where the news was, as with other battalions, received with calm satisfaction. On the 14th it started on its march to the Rhine, being the only battalion of the Norfolk Regiment which was to have the satisfaction of entering German territory and forming part of the Army of Occupation. We need not follow the march in detail. Passing through Dinan, reminiscent of the early German brutalities of August, 1914, it reached the frontier of Germany on December 13th, and crossed it. The day was one toward which all ranks had looked eagerly forward. Malmédy, now Belgian, was the first halting-place in Germany. Thence the route passed through places unknown to fame till Brühl, a few miles south of Cologne, was reached on December 23rd, where Christmas was spent, for the first time since that of 1913, at peace. Of the march their commanding officer wrote in May, 1919, after describing it in detail:

" The march was very trying at periods, but all ranks enjoyed it. The battalion received many congratulations on their marching. It was a splendid performance, as the majority of the men had not been taught to march like the old army, but nevertheless they were a credit to the old regiment. As typical of the British soldier, he made himself at home with all sorts and conditions of people, and he treated his conquered enemy in characteristic British style. It is certain that the conduct of the battalion taught the Hun a lesson."

10TH BATTALION (SERVICE) NORFOLK REGIMENT.

The 10th Service Battalion was formed on October 21st, 1914, but in March, 1915, it was turned into a reserve battalion to find drafts for the 7th, 8th, and 9th Service Battalions. It was then called the 10th (2nd Reserve) Battalion Norfolk Regiment. Subsequently it became a training battalion and remained so until the end of the war.

11TH BATTALION NORFOLK REGIMENT (T.F.)

For this battalion see account of the 2/4th Battalion above, under 1916.

CHAPTER IX

THE 12TH (YEOMANRY) BATTALION IN GALLIPOLI, EGYPT, PALESTINE AND FRANCE

(a) 1915—1916: GALLIPOLI—EGYPT—SOLLUM

The history of this battalion in the Great War differs from that of all others of the Norfolk Regiment, in that it was originally the Norfolk Yeomanry Regiment. As such it went to Gallipoli as a unit in the 1st Eastern Mounted Division, and was only made into the 12th (Yeomanry) Battalion of the Norfolk Regiment in February, 1917. It was always distinguished from the regular, territorial, and service battalions by being described as the " 12th (Yeomanry) Battalion." Though its history in the war does not strictly belong to the History of the Norfolk Regiment until it became the 12th Battalion, it is desirable to recount briefly its doings previous to that date.

The Yeomanry Regiment sailed from Liverpool for Gallipoli on September 25th, 1915, under the command of Lieutenant-Colonel A. F. Morse, with the following officers :

Majors—A. R. Buxton, J. F. Barclay, M. E. Barclay.

Captains—H. A. Birkbeck, E. C. Ruggles-Brice, J. D. Paul, N. A. C. Flower.

Lieutenants—Sir J. F. Ramsden, Bt., T. F. Preston, G. Fenwick Owen, L. S. Hill.

2nd Lieutenants—J. G. Frere, F. G. L. Worster, M. C. Bonsor, J. Harbord, A. C. Cannan, A. T. Gimson, J. H. Michell, C. P. Wyatt, T. R. Swift, J. S. Goslett.

Adjutant—Captain J. T. McMurrough Kavanagh, 7th Hussars.
Quartermaster—J. A. Sayer.
Medical Officer—B. N. Ash.

The voyage in the "Olympic" through the bay of Biscay was very rough and unpleasant, but the only incident of note which occurred was on September 30th, in the Mediterranean, when the crew of a French collier was picked up in open boats. Their ship had just been sunk by a submarine, and there was some risk in the "Olympic's" stopping to pick them up. The same day a periscope, probably belonging to the submarine which had sunk the French ship, was seen and fired at. The submarine dived and the "Olympic," after a good deal of zig-zagging in her course, got safely away. She reached Mudros without further adventure on October 2nd, and the regiment remained on board till the 8th, when it transhipped into a smaller ship, the "Abbasieh," for the Gallipoli Peninsula. When Anzac Bay was reached on the evening of the 8th a storm blew up, rendering it impossible to land the men. The transport went to Imbros for two days, and on the evening of the 10th it was found possible to land at Walker's Pier, Anzac, during the night of the 10th—11th. Thence the regiment marched, on the morning of the 11th, to Dixon's Gully, about three miles from the landing-place. The day was spent in digging in. On the 14th two squadrons were sent up to learn the work in the trenches. Though they came under shell fire at once, there were no casualties.

The regiment was attached to the 54th East Anglian division, temporarily commanded by Brigadier-General Hodgson. It had arrived too late for any active fighting on the peninsula, and was doomed to spend its time there in irksome and monotonous trench warfare, in which, like the 4th Battalion, it suffered many more losses from disease than from the enemy's fire. By October 16th it had already lost seventeen men from its effective strength, chiefly by dysentery. At this time it was attached for instruction in trench work partly to the 1/4th Essex and partly to the 1/8th Hampshire Regiment. The men off duty lived in the gullies at the top of which were the trenches.

On October 21st two squadrons took over Norfolk Street trenches from the 1/6th Essex, and the regiment was attached to the 163rd brigade.

Two days later its losses of fighting strength from disease were one officer and thirty-five other ranks. It was at this time that the yeomanry regiment came into contact with the 1/4th Norfolk Regiment, by which it was relieved in trenches on the 26th, and sent to the rest camp, a term which described a state of strenuous work, with constant fatigues of all sorts, and no complete immunity from shelling.

The trenches which the regiment continued to occupy, alternating with the 1/4th Norfolk battalion, were situated just on the right of the Hill 60, which overlooked the Suvla plain and the Salt Lake, From Hill 60 in the left they stretched across the Kaiajak Dere or watercourse and about one hundred yards up the southern bank of it. The trench across the watercourse was sunk five or six feet below its bed, and when wet weather filled the stream the trench was, of course, flooded. The drainage of this part of the trench was a great difficulty and was never really successfully overcome.

During November and the first days of December the Norfolk Yeomanry took turns in these trenches, first with the 1/4th Norfolk battalion, and then with the Suffolk Yeomanry. The 1/4th left the peninsula on December 7th—8th. On the 11th Lieutenant Harbord was hit by a Turkish sniper through the neck, and was lucky to escape with his life. The casualties from enemy fire continued small, only one man being killed in November and two wounded, but it was otherwise with diseases, of which dysentery was the most serious. The regiment had embarked at Liverpool with twenty-six officers and 504 men ; by November 27th it had fit for duty only fourteen officers and 301 other ranks.

From December 6th it was reorganized in two wings, instead of as hitherto in three squadrons. These two wings relieved one another in trenches, and the Suffolk Yeomanry made a similar arrangement. Before that these two regiments had relieved one another.

The great blizzard of the end of November had given the regiment a very bad time in the trenches, and the position in the watercourse had been particularly troublesome. When working at it on the night of December 6th—7th, one man was killed and another very badly wounded.

The dead man, who was very heavy, was brought to the rear with great courage and exertion by a comrade, an ex-policeman. The 4th and 5th Battalions had both left the peninsula before the real evacuation began; the 12th remained there till the last moment.

This very difficult operation was, as is well known, carried out with complete success, almost without loss. Commanding officers of regiments only began to suspect that some unexpected move was on foot from the orders which they began to receive regarding supplies just before December 13th. It was only on that date that they were told, in the strictest confidence, what was on foot. Even then they had to allay the suspicions of others by stories of their regiments being withdrawn to Lemnos and having to send an advance party of forty men in the case of the Norfolk Yeomanry. So well was the secret kept that the men never guessed what was coming, though the officers may have had suspicions. The latter were only told two days before the evacuation, and even then it was said the evacuation was not to be till the 23rd. The advance party, and a very little luggage, was sent off, and of course it included the weakest of the men. From the 13th onwards various bodies of troops with stores had been shipped at night both from Anzac and Suvla. The main evacuation was carried out in two nights. On the first some 10,000 men left Anzac, including only a small party of the Norfolk Yeomanry. On the next night the regiment was divided into three parties. The smallest of twenty-one picked men, remained in the trenches, firing as if they were fully manned. The other two parties were embarked, but the small one held on in the trenches till 1.40 a.m. on December 20th. Even then they made for the shore in three sections at five minutes intervals and got safely off. That night was fine, but almost immediately afterwards it began to blow hard. The evacuation from Suvla and Anzac had been completed in the very nick of time; a few hours later its continuance would have been impossible, and might well have ended in disaster if it had been only partially effected and a force too weak to resist the Turks had found itself isolated in the trenches.

From Mudros, where it was landed, the regiment embarked for Egypt with only thirteen officers and 221 other ranks fit for duty.

The casualties from enemy action had been insignificant, only about six killed and twenty wounded between October 11th and December 20th; the deadly enemies had been dysentery and other diseases, and the terrible trials from exposure, especially in the blizzard at the end of November. The voyage was uneventful and Alexandria was reached at 8 a.m. on Christmas Day.

Disembarking, the regiment marched through Alexandria and went by tram to a temporary camp about five miles out, at Sidi Bishr, removing next day to the permanent camp.

Here it spent the whole of January as a unit of the 1/1st Eastern Mounted Brigade, which had not yet been assigned to any division. Re-equipment, delayed by shortage of ordnance stores, was not completed till February; even then no transport or saddlery was available.

On the 22nd the 1/1st Eastern and 1/1st South-eastern Mounted Brigades were amalgamated to form the 3rd Dismounted Brigade, under Brigadier-General H. W. Hodgson, C.V.O. The brigade, with a total strength of 149 officers and 2,398 other ranks, comprised the East Kent, Suffolk, West Kent, Norfolk, and Sussex Yeomanry, the Welsh Horse, a signal troop, and machine-gun section made up from the several regiments.

The first half of March was devoted to training the dismounted units, of which the Norfolk and Sussex Yeomanry were the weakest in numbers. On the 14th the brigade was attached to the 42nd division and dispatched on the 16th to El Kubri, near Suez, where it arrived on the 17th.

The Norfolk Yeomanry were sent, on March 21st, to work at the defences of Crewe's Post, an advanced post beyond the Suez Canal in the desert. Want of water was a trouble here. The regiment was now on the outpost line of the Suez Canal defences. The only serious attack on the canal had been defeated long ago, and there was no fighting and very little sign of the enemy.

The work at Crewe's Post being completed, the regiment went to Suez in April and back to El Kubri in May. Here they remained working on canal defences, training, route marching, and practising musketry, with occasional variations in the form of sports, etc. On April 20th

Lieutenant-Colonel Morse and Major J. F. Barclay were gazetted substantive in those ranks, having previously been temporary.

At the end of June the regiment removed to El Ferdan, where they were similarly employed, and on July 27th they went by train back to Sidi Bishr camp. They were now destined to go to Sollum on the Mediterranean coast, some 250 miles west of Alexandria, where they were to form part of the Western Coastal Force watching the Senussi. The regiment, sailing on the 29th, reached Sollum on July 31st. It had now been reinforced by drafts to a strength of twenty-three officers and 424 other ranks. Colonel Morse, who had been on leave to England, rejoined them here on August 25th.

Sollum was very different from the desert in which they had recently been. From the beach the hills rose 600 or 800 feet, with the desert stretching away southwards from there towards the Siwa Oasis 150 miles off, the head-quarters of the Senussi. The hills ran down to the sea with gullies ending in charming little bays, whilst at Sollum itself there was a considerable open beach on which the main body of the Coastal Force was encamped. On the hills facing the desert was a semicircle of posts and forts, forming an entrenched camp. The regiment, as a unit of the garrison, alternately occupied part of these posts or was quartered on the shore with the main garrison. Beyond the perimeter the armoured cars scoured the desert for a considerable distance south. Of the enemy nothing was seen during the regiment's stay at Sollum.

Life at Sollum was decidedly pleasant. The climate was generally good; the men were kept happy and in good health with frequent sports and games. As for the officers, they had a little indifferent shooting and plenty of quite good sailing, besides sports and games. They even did a little fox hunting of sorts. As there were no hounds, this consisted in those taking part spreading out in line and drawing the scrub, and, as soon as a fox was viewed away, galloping after him until someone could get near enough to knock him over with a stick, or he got to ground or was lost in the scrub. Anyhow, it served to while away the time. Moreover, officers occasionally got a chance of leave to Alexandria or Cairo. Of course there was a good deal of training and musketry to be done, as well as work in wiring and improving the defences of the camp.

All August and September the regiment was in garrison at Sollum, or on outpost duty. In October, from the 10th to the 24th the regiment was training for the mobile force. In the early part of the month it had been in the outpost line, and after the 24th " B " and " C " squadrons formed the reserve to that line. From November 7th the battalion had another turn of outpost duty, and on the 12th an order issued that all dismounted yeomanry were to be trained in infantry drill and tactics under regimental arrangements. At first a good deal of difficulty was found in this, owing to scarcity of qualified instructors.

The duties continued as before, alternately in and out of the outpost line.

On December 26th orders were received from the Coastal Section Western Force that the brigade was to be reformed as an infantry brigade. The Norfolk yeomanry were to form one battalion, to be known as the Yeomanry Battalion of the Norfolk Regiment. It was decided to convert each of the three squadrons into a company under the existing squadron commanders. For the 4th (" D ") Company, one troop was to be taken complete from each squadron—This company to be commanded by Captain J. Dawson Paul, who had now returned after being invalided from Gallipoli.

1917

(a) PALESTINE—GAZA—BEERSHEBA—SHERIA—JERUSALEM

On January 14th what had hitherto been known as the 3rd dismounted brigade was converted into the 230th Infantry Brigade, and on February 11th the name of the battalion was changed to the 12th (Yeomanry) Battalion Norfolk Regiment. The brigade was now, with the 229th and 231st, part of the 74th Infantry Division.

In addition to the 12th Norfolk, the brigade comprised the 10th Buffs, 15th Suffolk, and 16th Royal Sussex Yeomanry Battalions.

On March 7th and 9th the battalion was sent by sea to Alexandria, where it received two large drafts aggregating five officers and 563 other ranks. At Sidi Bishr camp it was kept at infantry training. From February 21st command of the brigade was taken by Brigadier-General McNeill, and on March 20th Major-General E. S. Girdwood became commander of the 74th division, a post which he retained as long as the 12th Norfolk battalion was with it.

By April 10th the battalion counted thirty-eight officers and 972 other ranks when it entrained for El Kantara, where, next day, it crossed to the eastern side of the canal and again entrained for railhead on the road to Palestine.

On the 12th it was in bivouac at railhead at Deir-el-Belah, near the coast south-west of Gaza.

On the 15th it was sent into the line of outposts east of Wadi Ghuzze with the Suffolk battalion. Here it had one man wounded. On the 16th, when it had returned to camp, orders issued for the coming attack on Gaza, for which the 74th division was to be in reserve.

At 1 a.m. on the 17th the battalion marched out to entrench itself in the Wadi Ghuzze near Raspberry Hill. It took no part in the battle of this day. In the attack of the 19th the battalion, being in reserve, followed the attacking force, but though it was able to see a good deal of the battle, it had no fighting. Its only casualty was one man wounded by a shell. After the failure of this attack the 74th division was moved farther to the right, and the 12th Norfolk battalion entrenched near Tel-el-Jemmi, east of the Wadi. Here it was in reserve on the right flank of the army. This march, in the morning of the 20th, was particularly trying. It was all through sandy " wadis," and as transport was very short the men had to carry a great deal on their backs. They were done up at the end of it, and water was short.

On the 28th the battalion again marched up the Wadi Guzze to the entrenched position on the British right about Tel-el-Fara, where " A " and " C " companies held the crossings of the Wadi, whilst " B " and " D " were in a line of redoubts a mile and a half behind the right. Here they were kept busy digging and wiring trenches and redoubts till, on May 12th, they were relieved by the 15th (Yeomanry) Suffolk Regiment and went into reserve about Sheikh Nuran. On the 16th they again went into the new battle line, where they occupied and completed redoubts 1 to 13.

On May 27th—28th the 54th division took the place of the 74th, which marched to Wadi Man. Here they remained all June, their training hindered by numerous fatigues of different sorts. It was at this time that the supply of Lewis guns was raised to eight per company. Though the health of the battalion was good on the whole, there were a good many cases of septic sores and septic throats, and one case each of scarlet fever and diphtheria, due to the foulness of the ground taken over from another regiment, which had suffered in the same way. On June 28th command of the army in Palestine was taken over by General Sir Edmund Allenby, G.C.B., G.C.M.G., who at once drew up his plan of operations.

On July 9th the battalion moved into the dug-outs occupied by the 4th R.S. Fusiliers in the second line of defence. Here they were hard at work training when, on the 19th, Sir P. Chetwode inspected them and expressed his satisfaction at their appearance and turn-out. By the end of the month the battalion had 177 fully trained Lewis gunners, eighty-eight bombers fully trained, 118 partly so, and forty-three snipers. Health was better in July, and men were sent in batches to the rest camp at Rafa or the " change of air " camp at El Arish. At this time the band instruments were brought up and practised, and some new ones were bought. The band was found most useful in cheering the men on some of the very trying marches they afterwards had to do in the advance. The strength of the battalion on July 31st was thirty-three officers and 900 other ranks. On August 7th the battalion was back again near the sea, after being relieved in the Apsley House area by the 1/4th Norfolk Regiment. They were now about one and a half miles south-west of Deir-el-Belah.

On September 1st, 1917, Colonel Morse was evacuated sick and was temporarily succeeded by Major M. E. Barclay. The battalion was then in the Regent's Park area, close to the sea. Colonel Morse was not able to rejoin till the battalion was in France in 1918.

On October 1st Major J. F. Barclay, on return from leave, took over the command. Training went on as usual till the 13th, when the battalion was inspected in fighting order by the G.O.C. 74th division. For months past the troops had gone through a very strenuous time,

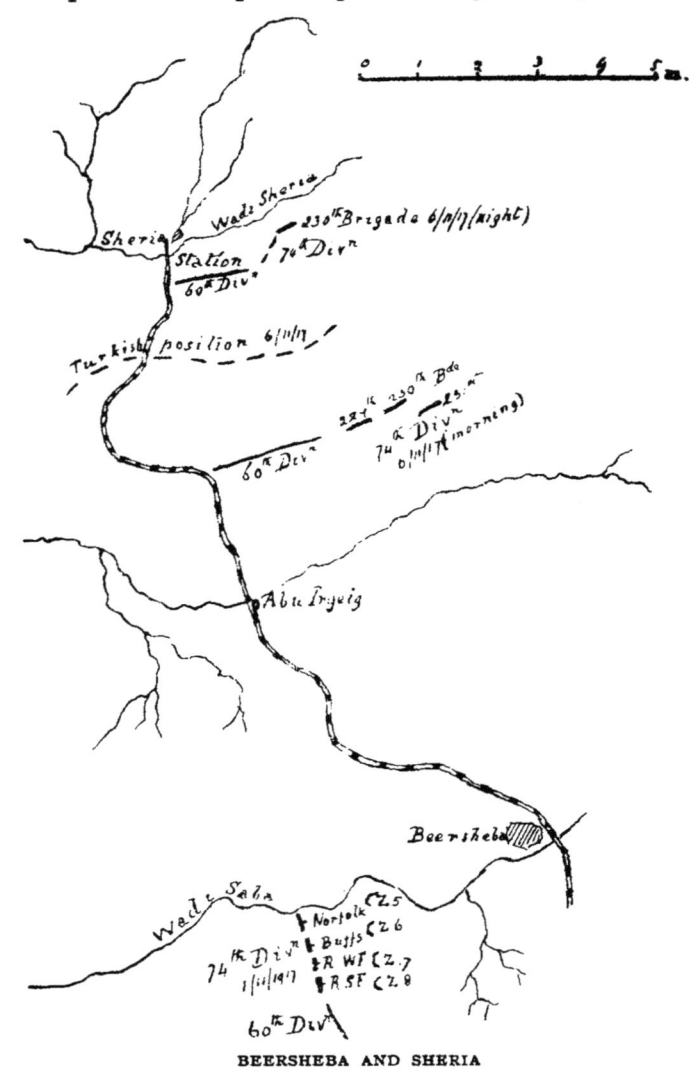

BEERSHEBA AND SHERIA

practising many operations, among them smoke screens to cover wire cutting operations, attacks, night marches, etc. The work at digging trenches had been particularly trying in great heat, tempered by dust storms, and with constant shortage of water. In September and October senior officers who were going to command their battalions went on three reconnaissances in front of Beersheba, the attack on which with a powerful force of six divisions was to be General Allenby's first operation. The object of these reconnaissances was to enable officers to fix their places of deployment and where to conceal their battalions previous to deployment. They were covered by screens of cavalry pushed out in front. One of the greatest difficulties was the supply of water, of which very strict limitations had to be fixed and rigidly adhered to, as the very limited supply had to be carried on camels.

The 74th division was moved from the neighbourhood of the sea up the Wadi Ghuzze to El Gamli, whence it marched on the night of October 29th—30th to Khasif, some six miles due east, where, during the 30th, it lay concealed and covered by the 229th brigade. That they succeeded in evading discovery was perhaps due mainly to the superiority at this time held by the British in the air. Anyhow, it is clear that the enemy had no inkling of the approaching attack on Beersheba. Their view was afterwards ascertained to be that " an outflanking attack on Beersheba with about one infantry and one cavalry division is indicated, but the main attack, as before, must be expected on the Gaza front." They believed there were six infantry divisions in the Gaza sector, whereas the six were really destined for Beersheba, whilst a good deal of camouflage, in the shape of standing camps occupied by details, concealed the weakness of the force left before Gaza.

The battalion was to be led in this attack by Major M. E. Barclay, as long acquaintance with the ground had given him a knowledge of it which Major J. F. Barclay had not had time to acquire.

On the night of October 30th—31st the 230th brigade, including the 12th Norfolk battalion, marched to its assigned positions—a march which entailed crossing the stone-strewn Wadi Saba, running through Beersheba from the north-east to eventually join the Wadi Ghuzze.

That night was spent, very uncomfortably, in getting into the Wadi Sussex, a tributary on the left bank of the Wadi Saba. The enemy had not apparently heard all the unavoidable noise of crossing the stony Wadi Saba. The Sussex Yeomanry were on outposts that night.

The objectives of the 230th brigade in the attack of next day were :

(1) A Turkish work known as Z6, part of which was to be taken by the Buffs, the right battalion of the 230th brigade.

(2) Another work, Z5, to the left of Z6. During the assault on Z6 this work was to be masked by a Norfolk company. When Z6 had fallen the battalion would wheel to the left against Z5, which was the most northerly of the Turkish redoubts and was just above the south bank of the Wadi Saba. On the right of the 230th was the 231st brigade, and beyond it the 60th division. The attack was to begin from the right and be taken up towards the left as the right attack succeeded. Its general direction was eastwards towards Beersheba, with its left flank on the Wadi Saba. The 12th Norfolk battalion sent forward its first wave of attack about daybreak, passing through the Sussex outposts and encountering heavy shell fire as it moved over the open and across a Wadi. The Turk had only now realized that the attack was coming.

Beyond the Wadi the battalion was delayed on the ridge, waiting for the troops on the right to get forward. These troops on the right of the 230th brigade had edged somewhat to their right, leaving a gap which had to be filled by the reserve company of the Buffs. On the left of the 230th was the 229th brigade, covering the crossing of the Wadi Saba against attack from the North. Once the Norfolk battalion got going again the first objective was quickly taken, the works to the right of it having already fallen to the troops in that direction. Here the regiment wheeled to its left against Z5. In it a certain number of prisoners were taken ; but most of the Turks had already escaped, leaving behind only a few snipers and machine guns to cover their retreat.

North of the Wadi Saba some Turkish cavalry had been seen coming up ; they turned out not to be reinforcements, but merely troops covering the Turkish evacuation of their position in that direction.

The positions taken were strong and well wired, and their capture, in an action which worked like clockwork throughout, was a most satisfactory achievement.

The Norfolk battalion had taken the north (left) end of Z 6 between 11 a.m. and noon, the attack all along the line having been hurried up by nearly an hour, as it was seen that the Turks were wavering. The battalion did its duty splendidly throughout.

On November 3rd the Norfolk battalion started northwards to march, under trying conditions with a "Khamsin" wind blowing, to the Wadi Irgeig, where it spent a night on outpost duty.

On the afternoon of the 4th Major M. E. Barclay went forward almost alone to reconnoitre northwards towards Sheria, the capture of which with its water supply was very desirable. Captain Birkbeck had instructions to bring on the battalion after dark. The march was a difficult one, owing to want of a map for the latter half of the march. Thanks to the intelligence officer, who had seen one at brigade head-quarters, the exact spot desired was reached. This was largely due to Lieutenant Stokes, the intelligence officer, who displayed great determination in refusing to allow his judgment, based on the map he had seen, to be influenced by criticisms or suggestions of error. On the 5th Major J. F. Barclay rejoined the battalion, with some men who had been left behind at El Gamli before the attack on Beersheba, but Major M. E. Barclay continued to lead the battalion. Major J. F. Barclay had only got back to it late on the 5th. Lieutenant H. E. Dodd was wounded in this action and Major M. E. Barclay was also slightly wounded, but remained on duty.

The attack on Sheria was to be led by the Sussex and Suffolk battalions, with the 12th Norfolk in support. Unlike the attack on Beersheba, this one was made with little previous reconnoitring, and no practice attacks. It started at daybreak with the 230th brigade on the right, the 229th on the left, and the 231st in support of the right. The leading battalions of the 230th, though they met with a stubborn resistance, carried the work in front of them, south-east of Sheria, and by 8.30 a.m. the 229th had carried five more works. Then a halt was made to rearrange intermingled battalions, which were lying out in the open under a heavy shell fire. When they had taken their final objective, the Norfolk battalion had been pushed forward to fill a gap which had formed in the line. The maps were again inaccurate, and, when Major M. E. Barclay at last found his head-quarters after the fight, they were not in the place intended, and were taking shelter in a watercourse under a very heavy shelling. In the evening the battalion was ordered to support the Buffs in an outpost line; but, as the Buffs were scattered all over the place, this was no easy matter, especially as, owing apparently to the bad maps the outpost line which was supposed to be occupied was really well behind the Turkish front. The final halting place was near the Wadi Sheria, above (east of) Sheria itself. At dawn on the 7th the 60th division, on the left of the 74th, started to attack Sheria railway station. At first the 12th Norfolk battalion conformed to the movement of the 60th division, but was soon stopped, as Sheria had been taken by 6.30 a.m. Presently the Yeomanry Mounted Division passed through in pursuit. The sight of mounted yeomanry, when they themselves were acting as infantry, naturally aroused regrets in the 12th battalion. The casualties of the battalion on these two days were one officer (Major H. A. Birkbeck) severely wounded; other ranks, two killed and eighteen wounded.

At 4 p.m. on November 9th the 74th division began marching back south to Irgeig, and on the 10th to Gozel Basal north-west of Khasif, where it arrived, after a trying march with little water and a "Khamsin" wind blowing. There was a distribution of military medals on the 11th, also four N.C.O.'s were promoted to 2nd Lieutenants in the field, viz. Company Sergeant-Major C. W. Spalding, Company Quarter-Master Sergeant F. R. Watts, Sergeant W. Stone, M.M., and Sergeant R. T. Heading; and on the 17th Captain Birkbeck received the M.C.

The battalion was now in rear of the fighting front and on the march westwards via Sheik Nakhrur, where Captain Fenwick Owen and Lieutenant H. G. Cobon received the M.C.

The reason for bringing back the 74th division was that its transport was required for the cavalry and the 60th division pursuing the Turks.

On November 18th the division was again on the sea coast, at St. James's Park opposite Gaza, near the mouth of the Wadi Ghuzze.

On the 25th it was just east of Gaza, beginning its march by the Gaza-Jerusalem road to join the army near the latter. The marches were generally long and trying, and it was here that the band was found a valuable asset. Another thing which served to amuse the soldiers and keep up their spirits in these weary marches was the regimental mascot

"Abdul," a small donkey which had been found at El Gamli beside its dead mother at the beginning of May. It soon became a pet, and after surviving a diet ranging from tea to soapy water, and even shaving soap, it accompanied the regiment all through its time in Palestine,

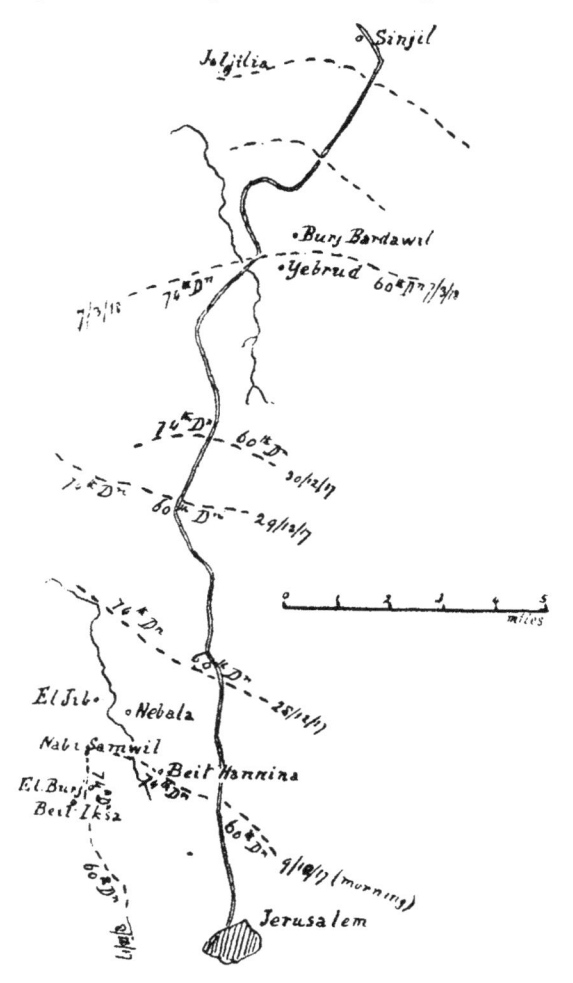

ADVANCE OF 74TH DIVISION NORTH OF JERUSALEM

and afterwards in France. In France it was presented with a collar of bells by a Frenchman, and was given a saddlecloth of the regimental colours with a badge on it. Abdul survived all this campaigning, and was taken safely to England by Major M. E. Barclay when the cadre of the regiment returned to Norwich.

On the evening of November 30th the battalion was up in second line about eight or nine miles west of Jerusalem facing north-east. Here it remained road-making till December 6th.

The attack which was to end in the capture of Jerusalem was fixed for December 8th. The 74th division was to advance eastwards towards the Jerusalem-Nablus road. In the front line of the 230th brigade the 12th Norfolk battalion was to lead on the left, with the 10th Buffs on the right, and the 15th Suffolk in reserve.

The advance began up a stony slope, on which little opposition was encountered, the Turks retreating from the 1st objective, a line of trenches which was occupied by 5 a.m. Just over the crest of the hill the enemy were found lined up behind rocks and walls on the reverse slope. The whole country was very rough and rocky, and it took the battalion one and a quarter miles of fighting inch by inch to reach the gardens and village of Beit Iksa, from which it was intended to assault the second objective, Khirbet El Burj. The whole advance had been under heavy artillery and machine-gun fire in front, supported by enfilade fire from Nebi Samwil on the left, which was supposed to be in British hands. This, and the fact that the 60th division was held up on the right, caused considerable delay, so that it was afternoon when Beit Iksa was reached. There the machine-gun and artillery fire was still severe, and there was enfilade fire from both flanks. Moreover, it was found that there was still another deep gully to be passed between Beit Iksa and El Burj. Under the circumstances it was decided to hold on to the gains so far made for the night, and to attack El Burj next morning. The exact position, at 3 p.m. on the 8th, was 10th Buffs on the ridge above and west of Beit Iksa and in the gardens immediately to the north. 12th Norfolk on the left of the Buffs, in gardens to the north, with one company of the 15th Suffolk supporting on their left. The night passed quietly, and in the morning the Turks had evacuated El Burj. The 1st Sussex then passed through and advanced on Beit Hanina, whilst the 12th Norfolk followed as far as El Burj, which they held for the rest of the 9th. The 229th brigade was astride of the Jerusalem-Nablus road about

Tel el Ful, the 230th on its left, and the 231st on Nebi Samwil ridge, still farther to the left. It was only on the following night, when the 12th Norfolk moved to Nebi Samwil, that the men's overcoats, which had been left behind for the advance of the 8th, were brought up. In the fighting at this time Captain Fenwick Owen and Lieutenant Cobon were severely wounded, the latter dying soon after as a result of his wounds.

From the 11th to the 16th the battalion occupied the outpost line facing north, sending out nightly patrols towards El Jib and Bir Nebala, and furnishing salvage and burial parties.

It was relieved on the 17th, and on the 18th and 19th was again at Beit Iksa, whence it returned on the 20th to its old quarters of the 5th and 6th.

On the 22nd it again moved up to the outpost line at Beit Izza, in relief of the Somerset Yeomanry, where it found the conditions very trying, owing to heavy rain. Here it remained till the 26th.

On the 27th the 60th division, on the right of the 74th, repulsed repeated heavy attacks made along the Nablus road towards Jerusalem, and at the same time the 229th and 231st brigades, on the left of the 230th, advanced, the former capturing the Zeitun ridge. During the night of the 27th-28th the rest of the 230th brigade closed up to the 12th Norfolk, the 15th Suffolk going through it, and being attached to the 231st brigade in support.

On the 28th the 230th brigade was ordered forward to fill the gap between the 60th division on its right and the 231st brigade on its left. In consequence, the Norfolk outpost line was extended and the 10th Buffs, 16th Sussex, and 15th Suffolk went through to attack at dawn on the 29th. During that day the 12th Norfolk only followed the attacking battalions, which had taken Rahm Allah by 9 a.m. unopposed. After halting at Beitunia for four hours, the battalion moved, at 4 p.m., to south of Rahm Allah.

That night the 230th brigade held a line from the left of the 60th division just north of Rahm Allah to the right of the 229th brigade. During the night the 60th division moved forward from Bireh, where they had been held up during the day, towards, Beitin, the 230th brigade conforming to its movement.

Near Rahm Allah, and in rear of it, the 12th Norfolk remained till the end of the year making up the roads in rear.

1918

NORTH OF JERUSALEM—FRANCE—NIEPPE FOREST—VIEUX BERQUIN—THE LAST ADVANCE

Road-making and training went on during the whole of January and February, though often interfered with by heavy rain.

There was to be a fresh attack by the 74th division extending over March 9th–12th, the ultimate objective being Abu-el-Auf and the high ground beyond it. For this attack, along and just east of the Nablus road, the 231st brigade was to be on the right of the 230th, which was astride of the road.

The attacking battalions on the 9th were the 15th Suffolk and 16th Sussex, with the 12th Norfolk and 10th Buffs behind. At Yebrud, just east of the road, the attacking battalions were held up and the 12th Norfolk moved up with the idea of a flank attack to assist them. But, as the resistance died out, the battalion moved by Raspberry Hill and Yebrud to Burj Bardawille. Their arrival and concentration at the latter place was delayed by shrapnel fire encountered at Yebrud.

At 2 p.m. the battalion, being ordered to attack, advanced downhill in artillery formation with " A " and " B " companies leading and taking direction by the 16th Sussex on the right; 15th Suffolk in support, 10th Buffs in reserve. As they reached the top of Burj Bardawille, they were greeted with very heavy long range machine-gun fire from front and right flank. They deployed into line, but were still held up by this fire and lost touch on their left. At dusk they were withdrawn to reorganize, and at 6.15 p.m. started again down a very rough hill, being compelled to move in single file in the darkness. Touch with the 16th Sussex was regained in Wadi-el-Tib.

At 2.30 a.m. on the 10th the advance was continued up a steep hill, the 16th Sussex being on the right of the 12th Norfolk, the latter directing.

There was heavy machine-gun fire from the left, but it was found possible to avoid it to a great extent by a judicious use of the terraces of the hillside. These were very difficult of ascent; in places men had to assist one another in getting up. At 3 a.m., believing it was close on the enemy, the 12th Norfolk charged with a cheer, only to find there were yet more terraces to be negotiated. In this stage Captain J. Harbord, well ahead of his men, met a party of seven Turks. He shot four and captured the other three, of whom one was an officer. For this feat Captain Harbord received the M.C.

At last the top of the hill was reached. Bursts of Lewis-gun fire kept the enemy's heads down, and the battalion charged. Unfortunately the men were so out of breath with the climb that most of the Turks got away.

"C" and "D" companies were now sent against an unnamed hill, with "A" in support. As the 231st brigade had not yet completed the capture of the high ground on the right, the right flank of this advance was threatened, and "C" had to face half right to meet any attack from this direction. It was now nearly dawn. "D" had advanced to the foot of the last ascent to the objective hill, but was held up there by machine guns in front and on both flanks. At this point Captain Fenwick Owen, commanding the battalion,[1] was wounded and his place was taken by Captain J. Harbord. Captain M. C. Bonsor was killed whilst rejoining the battalion from leave. The hostile machine guns and snipers were very active, but were presently compelled to move off by the excellent shooting of the British. After that the advance to the top of the hill was made with little opposition. The position was consolidated, with a company in reserve. During the night Lieutenant-Colonel J. F. Barclay took over command of the battalion. Water and supplies were brought up with much difficulty over this broken country.

---

[1] Captain G. Fenwick Owen commanded in this action as he was acting second in command during Major M. E. Barclay's absence on leave, and it was the turn of the commanding officer to be left out of this action. It was at times the practice in Palestine to order commanding officers to stay behind with reinforcements and to give over command in an action to the second in command.

On the 11th the advance was continued at noon by the 10th Buffs and 12th Norfolk, followed by the 15th Suffolk in support, and 16th Sussex in reserve. The brigade was under severe shelling as it moved over the high ground near Khirbet Sahlat, but casualties were few, and by 5.30 p.m. the 10th Buffs on the right and 12th Norfolk on the left had occupied the ridge overlooking Sinjil, just west of the Nablus road. Owing to the winding of this road through the hills, the Norfolk battalion had been during these days sometimes on one side of it and sometimes on the other. The 229th brigade was now astride the Nablus road, the 230th on its left, and the 231st in reserve.

The next three days were mostly employed in road-making. On the 20th medals and decorations were distributed by H.R.H. the Duke of Connaught.

At 7.30 p.m. on the 22nd an extensive raid was planned, under command of Lieutenant-Colonel J. F. Barclay, against the Turkish trenches. A picked squad of rifle bombers was detailed for it. At 9 p.m. " A " company and the rifle bombers advanced in artillery formation under Captain J. Harbord. " B " company provided one platoon, with an additional Lewis-gun section, as right flank guard, and another platoon as left flank guard. The remaining two platoons followed in rear. There was considerable hostile rifle and machine-gun fire, but it was very wild and caused no casualties. The companies deployed into line 200 yards short of the objective and opened fire with rifle grenades. This gave the enemy the impression that the British were close up, and they replied with hand grenades, which, of course, fell far short. The British artillery co-operated during this movement. At 9.30 the Turkish works were rushed without a check and two platoons took position beyond to repel counter-attacks. In the captured trenches eight Turks were bayoneted, one taken prisoner, and the dug-outs were bombed. Then the retirement was ordered, under protection of the two advanced platoons as rear-guard. The rest of March was occupied by road-making.

The great German offensive on the Western front had now necessitated calls for reinforcements from other points. Early in April the 12th Norfolk battalion marched for Ludd, where they arrived on the

11th. On the 14th and 15th they entrained for El Kantara on the Suez Canal, and remained in that neighbourhood till the 29th, when they entrained for Alexandria, embarked, with a strength of thirty-five officers and 835 other ranks, on the SS. " Caledonia," and sailed, with the rest of the 74th division, on May 1st for France.

On May 7th the " Caledonia " reached Marseilles without mishap, on the 9th the battalion entrained for the north, and detrained on the 12th at Noyelles-sur-Mer, whence it marched to camp at Bouvines, where it remained till the 20th. Colonel Morse had resumed command of the battalion on May 9th.

On the 22nd the battalion moved to the neighbourhood of Neuville-au-Cornet, on the 25th to Izel-les-Hameaux, where they continued training, varied by sports, etc., till June 20th, when the battalion was transferred to the 31st division, as the brigades of the 74th had to be reduced from four to three battalions. On leaving the 74th division the following letter was received by Colonel Morse :

" Dear Morse,
"As you will understand, I cannot issue a special order of the day on your departure. At the same time I feel I cannot let you and your splendid men go without writing to tell you how sorry I am to lose you and them. The whole Yeomanry Division, and particularly myself, suffer an irreparable loss by the transfer of your gallant battalion to another division. No man has ever been better served than I have by the Norfolk Yeomanry, or could wish to have under his command a finer battalion. Every objective that has been given them, and all I have ever asked them to do, they have done with never-failing success and undaunted gallantry. This is a record which few battalions can equal and none can surpass. We shall watch your deeds and follow your fortunes, wherever you may be, with intense interest, and the feeling that, although you are not with us, you are still of us, knowing the while that whatever you are given to do will be carried through with that gallant yeoman spirit which knows not defeat, and that devotion to duty which you have invariably displayed. On my own behalf, and that of the

whole Yeomanry Division, I wish you and your battalion God speed and good fortune.

"Yours sincerely,
"(Signed) E. S. GIRDWOOD, Major-General
"21.6.18.   Comg. 74th (Yeomanry) Division."

On the 21st the battalion entrained for Tinques and went into billets at Blaringham, where it was met by Brigadier-General A. Symons, C.M.G., commanding the 94th brigade, of which it was now to form part, along with the 12th Royal Scots Fusiliers from the 229th and the 24th Royal Welsh Fusiliers from the 231st brigade. The brigade thus remained one of yeomanry. Its head-quarters were at Pont Asquin.

On the night of the 25th the battalion had its first turn in front line trenches on the Nieppe Forest front. On the 27th it was relieved and temporarily attached to the 93rd brigade. There was an attack on the 28th by the 31st division, with the object of getting the Becque stream as an obstacle to the enemy close to the British front, and also securing more elbow-room east of the Nieppe Forest. In this attack the 12th Norfolk was not engaged. Next day it was returned to the 94th brigade, which took over the front line on the 30th. The Norfolk battalion was in reserve to the 12th Royal Scots Fusiliers on the right, and 24th Royal Welsh Fusiliers on the left. The casualties during June had been one officer wounded. This was Major M. E. Barclay, who was wounded during a relief. One other ranks was killed and five were wounded. The effective strength on the 30th was thirty-six officers and 780 other ranks.

On July 5th Colonel Morse was wounded and was unable to rejoin the battalion during its war service. Captain J. Harbord died of wounds received at the same time as Colonel Morse's.

Nothing else notable occurred till the night of July 8th, when one platoon each of "A" and "D" companies went out to try and blow up two bridges over the Becque. 2nd Lieutenant Wagner, with the platoon of "D," succeeded in blowing up his bridge. 2nd Lieutenant Knox, with the "A" platoon, finding himself up against superior forces of the enemy in a post and a farm, was unable to get near his bridge, and had to return without accomplishing his object.

On the 9th he again went out at night, intending to occupy the farm and blow up the bridge. Against the farm he was successful, establishing in it a post of one N.C.O. and six men. He then personally reconnoitred the bridge which he found to be swept by machine guns in front and on

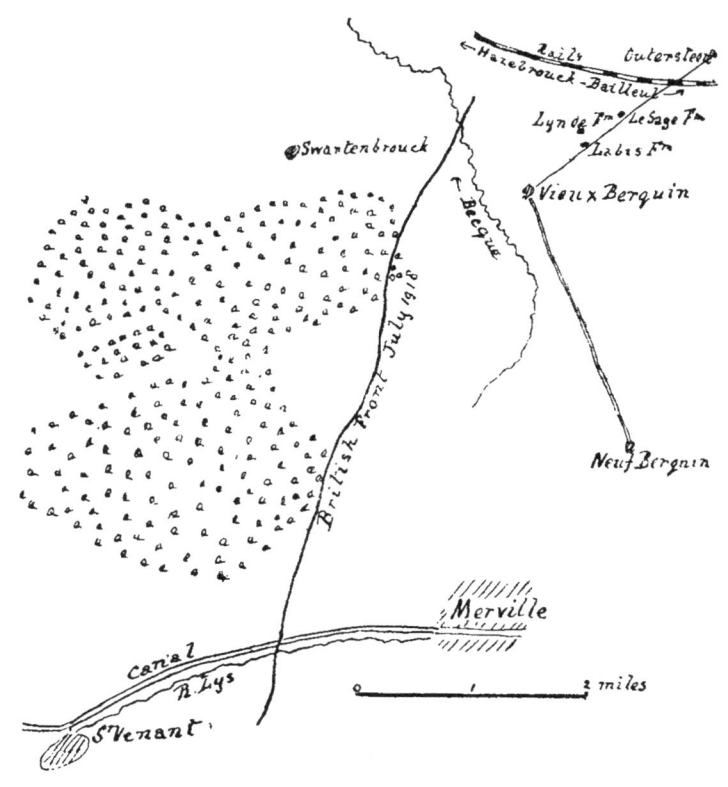

NIEPPE FOREST AND VIEUX BERQUIN

both flanks. He decided that any attempt to blow it up could not hope to succeed without artillery support, for which no arrangement had been made.

On the night of the 10th–11th the 94th brigade was relieved by the 93rd and went for six days into divisional reserve. On the 14th the battalion was inspected by the corps commander, Sir B. de Lisle, who expressed his satisfaction with the turn-out of men.

The 16th saw it again in front line, working hard at improving the defences.

In the night of the 26th–27th Major Birkbeck commanded a raid on the enemy posts East of the Becque. His force consisted of two platoons of " A " company, covered by our artillery barrage. The two platoons were commanded by 2nd Lieutenant Knox. Advancing at 11.30 p.m. behind the barrage, he found the first line of shell holes almost unoccupied. A few bombs were thrown at the raiders, and then the enemy ran back through the barrage towards Vieux Berquin. The casualties in this raid were five men wounded and two missing. A search party sent to look for the latter failed to find them, but brought back three German rifles. The strength of the battalion at the end of the month was forty officers and 956 other ranks.

On August 11th the battalion, which had gone back to rest, moved up into support, and on the 15th into the line. About this time a patrol under 2nd Lieutenant W. Stone was very successful in getting right behind the German front line, which, like the British, consisted of a series of small posts. 2nd Lieutenant Stone was unfortunately killed next day.

At 2.30 p.m. on the 15th 2nd Lieutenant E. P. Smith went out with a platoon of " D " company to raid some enemy strong points. Half an hour later, finding himself under machine-gun fire, he asked for artillery support, and a barrage was put down on the German supports behind the strong points. Nothing being seen of the raiders for some time, the British machine guns continued firing. Meanwhile, the left section of the raiding platoon, under Sergeant Walker, after advancing 150 or 200 yards, came upon three strong points, each garrisoned by ten or twelve men. The whole of the left section only numbered fourteen, and after a few minutes was forced to retire, owing to the enemy working round its right flank between it and the right section. There were two clumps of trees in the enemy's lines, and the strong points encountered by the left section were from thirty to fifty yards in front of the northern clump. Between them and the trees wire was being set up.

The left section now withdrew twenty yards down a small ditch and opened fire. Seeing that 2nd Lieutenant Smith (who was killed in the action) was not aware of the intrusion of the enemy between the two sections, Sergeant Walker sent Corporal Gent and another man across to warn him. They were too late, as the enemy had already begun bombing the right section before they could arrive.

As the right section began to retire, the left section opened fire to cover their retreat, and again did so after themselves retiring another fifty yards. Having given the right section time to retire, the left also fell back to its starting point.

We must now follow the earlier operations of the right section. They found a trench in front of the southern clump of trees held by from forty to sixty of the enemy. 2nd Lieutenant Smith at once ordered his section to charge. They lost heavily from bombs as they approached the trench. Only Smith himself with Corporal Neve and one other man, succeeded in getting into a section of the trench. Then, seeing that further progress was impossible, 2nd Lieutenant Smith gave the order to retire.

2nd Lieutenant Heading, in command of a supporting platoon, seeing the right section in difficulties, advanced to cover its retirement. Taking up a position, he opened fire, whilst the right section retired in good order through his platoon. Then he also withdrew his men. An enemy machine gun had worked round the right of the right section, and was engaged by a Norfolk Lewis gun. The British gunner was killed, and his gun, which was already damaged, was unfortunately lost.

The Lewis-gun section of the left section had crawled up to an enemy listening post in a ditch. The Germans at once ran away down the ditch. When these raiders advanced, they saw eight of the enemy running away and twelve pushing forward. This Lewis-gun section claimed to have caused twelve casualties by their fire. Sergeant Tannard claimed to have shot two out of eleven Germans whom he saw stand up to throw bombs. This account, taken from the battalion diary, had (owing to 2nd Lieutenant Smith's death, apparently in the retreat), to be made up from accounts given by N.C.O.'s and men. Of the officer and thirty men constituting this raiding party, the officer was killed and eleven other ranks were wounded.

On August 18th the battalion stood to, ready to attack again, but, owing to the battalions on its left not succeeding completely, was not taken into action.

Next day (19th) came the sequel of the partially successful attack of the previous day. The objective for that day had been to seize part of the road running south-west from Outtersteen to Vieux Berquin, including the two farms on it—Lesage on the left and Labis south-west of it. The first point to be taken was Lynde Farm, north of Labis and west of Lesage Farm. On the 18th the 12th Norfolk battalion was under orders to advance only when Lynde Farm was taken. The troops on their left having failed to take Lynde Farm, the occasion for their advance did not arise. Major J. F. Barclay having gone on leave, Major M. E. Barclay was now in command.

For the 19th zero hour was fixed at 5 p.m., the Norfolk battalion advancing on the right of the 87th brigade, which was to take Lynde Farm. The assembly was effected unobserved by the enemy.

At 5.10 a strong point on the line of advance of the 12th Norfolk was taken by the battalion, and by 5.30 Lynde Farm also had been captured by the 87th brigade. A heavy fire was met as the battalion advanced on the strong point behind the barrage, which caused heavy losses, especially of officers and N.C.O's. The strong points being just on the British side of where the barrage started, were untouched by it. Both flanks were checked by this fire. The two left platoons of "A" company bore too much to the left, thus leaving nothing in front of part of the strong point. The officer commanding "D," seeing this, pushed forward his right platoon to engage the enemy. Then, bringing up the rest of "D," he formed line with the right half of "A" and carried this and other strong points. The delay in mopping up these posts prevented the battalion from following as close to the barrage as was to be desired. The enemy fell back fighting.

The first check occurred a little farther on at a line of shell holes. Here a small party of "B" company pushed on close up to the final objective, Labis Farm, in the face of considerable opposition. This party, finding its flanks held up, sent back for reinforcements. When these arrived, the enemy was forced back, and the flanks were able to get forward, despite the opposition of bombers lying in the standing corn.

"B" company was commanded on this day by Lieutenant Richards, who for his distinguished services received the M.C.

The whole line was now in touch for the advance against the final objective. Lesage Farm on the left had been taken by 6 p.m., and twenty minutes later the enemy were seen to be leaving Labis Farm under stress of artillery fire.

The Norfolk battalion, having now overcome the resistance at the shell holes, was able to report the occupation of Labis Farm at 7.23 p.m. It had inflicted heavy casualties on the retreating enemy.

At 7.44 it took a point farther on, where a listening post was established whilst the line was being consolidated. A carrying party of "D" company did particularly good work in bringing up tools as the objectives were secured during the action. The battalion on this day had to fight for every inch of the ground they conquered. They did it splendidly, taking a good number of prisoners and killing a large number of the enemy.

The Germans now put down a heavy barrage in front of the new British line, of the exact position of which they seemed very uncertain.

The battalion on this day took sixty prisoners and twelve machine-guns, but its losses during the last few days were the heaviest it had yet suffered. The killed were eight officers [1] and thirty-eight other ranks; wounded one officer and a hundred other ranks. The officer losses in killed are very remarkable. The losses were particularly grievous to the battalion as they included several old yeoman who had been serving with their comrades left behind for many years, in smooth as well as rough times.

Of the enemy a hundred dead were counted.

On August 20th the battalion consolidated its newly won position, and next day went back to the support line. On the 28th it was in line in front of Bailleul, when, during the ensuing night, one of its night

---

[1] The names are not recorded in the battalion diary. They appear to have been : 2nd Lieutenant G. R. L. Jode, Lieutenant B. W. Ramsbottom, Lieutenant Knox, 2nd Lieutenant A. H. S. Joyce, M.M., 2nd Lieutenant H. Glanville-West; 2nd Lieutenant E. P. Smith ; 2nd Lieutenant W. Stone, M.M., and 2nd Lieutenant Place.

patrols came into collision with one of the enemy. In the fight which ensued one officer was wounded and missing, one other ranks killed, and two missing. The officer (2nd Lieutenant F. R. Watts) was never heard of again and was officially recorded as killed.

On the 30th, when it appeared that the enemy had evacuated Bailleul, patrols were pushed into the place and found the enemy were in position on a ridge 800 to 1,000 yards farther on.

The brigades to the right and left of the 94th now pushed forward, converging so as to necessitate the withdrawal of the 94th to divisional reserve.

On the 31st the following letter was received from head-quarters of the division :

"Please express to all ranks the divisional commander's appreciation of the most excellent work done by the officers, N.C.O's., and men during the minor operations yesterday. Success was largely due to the skilful planning of the operation, and the excellent co-operation between artillery and infantry. Plans, however good, do not succeed unless the men display the fine fighting spirit which enabled the 12th (Yeomanry) Battalion Norfolk Regiment to overcome strong opposition."

This letter, which referred to the operations of the 19th, followed on congratulations by the corps and army commanders.

On August 31st the effective strength of the battalion was twenty-nine officers and 786 other ranks.

On September 4th the 94th brigade moved forward to Bailleul to relieve the 86th and 88th brigades. On the 14th it was relieved in line by the 93rd, and again went into front line in the night of September 18th–19th. "A" company was attached to the Royal Scots Fusiliers on the right and "B" to the Royal Welsh Fusiliers on the left ; "C" and "D" in support.

On the 23rd command of the battalion was temporarily taken over by Lieutenant-Colonel J. Sherwood Kelly, V.C., from Major M. E. Barclay.

On the 24th the battalion moved back by rail to Hazebrouck, returning on the 28th to Bailleul and on to Neuve Eglise (Battery Post).

During an attack by the 93rd brigade on September 28th, the 94th followed it, but was not engaged. At 12.55 a.m. on the 29th orders were received by the division from the corps commander that the 93rd brigade was to be directed so that its left moved on Warneton. The reason of this was that the 30th division had crossed the Messines ridge and was advancing on the Comines-Warneton railway. It was too late to stop the advance of the 93rd brigade, which had already reached a point north of Warneton. In order to get into the position required by corps orders, or as near it as possible, the 93rd brigade now wheeled to its right and worked due south. Meanwhile, the 94th brigade had moved up to fill the gap between the 92nd and 93rd. It had been decided to advance the 12th Norfolk to the line of the Ploegsteert-Warneton road in conjunction with the 92nd brigade working south to the line of the Warnave Becque. " B " company, followed at a distance of 200 yards by " D," worked along the right of the road ; " A," followed in like manner by " C," along the left. By dawn the battalion had reached all its objectives, and was established along the road. Captain Bonsor, our Medical Officer, was killed in this advance. In this advance there was no attack, for the Germans were found to have evacuated their trenches. Such casualties as may have occurred were due to shells or stray bullets.

At 9.50 a.m. the battalion was preparing to advance its right, pivoting on the left, when orders were received that the advance was to be continued by the 92nd and 93rd brigades, the 94th being withdrawn.

On October 6th the 12th Norfolk was in the Ploegsteert sector, where t was engaged patrolling on the Lys till the 11th, when two feint attacks were made with the object of inducing the enemy to believe a general attack was coming. In these the 12th Norfolk only participated to the extent of sending out " A " company in the early morning to attempt a crossing of the Lys by a bridge. As heavy machine-gun fire was met, this attack was not pressed home.

On this day Colonel Sherwood Kelly went to command the brigade, and his place was taken by Major Birkbeck.

On the 12th the battalion went back to Bailleul to refit; on the 16th it moved up again into support, and next day to Ploegsteert. On the 18th it crossed the Lys at Warneton and went on to Quesnoy. Colonel Sherwood Kelly returned to the battalion command on the 19th. From the 20th to the 25th there was training at Lannoy, followed by a forward move, on the 26th and 27th, to Mouscron and Staceghem, and into line on October 29th.

On the 31st the 31st division attacked, with the 35th on its right, and 34th on the left. The attack was on the north of the Scheldt towards Audenarde. The 94th was the attacking brigade of the 31st division, the 12th Norfolk was in support of the Royal Welsh Fusiliers and Royal Scots Fusiliers and had no fighting. Though the resistance to the attacking battalions was strong at first, it weakened later, and support action was not required.

The casualties of the battalion in October were one officer (Captain H. E. Dodd) wounded, and of other ranks four killed, eight wounded, and four missing.

At the end of October the effectives were forty-two officers and 800 other ranks.

The following extract from a captured German regimental order was published on October 21st in army, corps, division, and brigade orders:

"The prisoners belong to a big patrol ordered to make good the occupation of a farm (apparently Hof Osternelle near Ploegsteert) to put out of action the machine guns conjectured to be there. The twenty-one prisoners, among whom were four N.C.O.'s, had all taken off their badges and could not, or would not, give a satisfactory reason for having done so. The great majority of the prisoners belong to the workman class. They make a good military impression, but in their statements are so extraordinarily reticent that one must assume that their superior officers have instructed them clearly, and warned them how to behave when taken prisoners."

This patrol was one of "C" company whilst the battalion was at Ploegsteert. The G.O.C. 31st division congratulated the C.O. and all ranks of the 12th Norfolk battalion on the fine spirit shown by the N.C.O.'s and men.

After the end of October the battalion had no more fighting. On November 3rd it was moved back to Courtrai, on the 4th to billets at Lauwe, whence it relieved the Royal Inniskilling Fusiliers on the banks of the Scheldt, on the 7th, returning next day to Lauwe.

On the 10th it moved to Avelghem on the Scheldt, where it was on the 11th when the Armistice was announced. Hence it crossed the Scheldt on the 11th and marched to Renaix.

Between the 16th and 22nd it was in billets successively at Renaix, Avelghem, Courtrai, and Lauwe, at which latter place there was a parade, on the 22nd, for distribution of medal ribbons gained since joining the 31st division as follows :

D.C.M.—Sergeant Lawn ; Corporals Lloyd, Benning, Gladwin ; Privates Watts and Blake.

The rest of the month was passed at Menin, Vlammertinghe, St. Eloi, Eeelingham, and St. Martin-au-Laert.

In December the following letter was received by the C.O. from Colonel Morse :

"I shall be very grateful if you will convey to all ranks of the battalion, at any rate those with whom I served, how sorry I was to leave them in July and to have to say good-bye now. Also how much I appreciate their good work all through the war, and their invariable loyalty and good-fellowship.

"I look upon them all as personal friends ; no man ever had better ; and I shall always be delighted to hear from any and to see any of them who come back to Norwich or anywhere near to have a chat about old times."

On December 24th, at the brigade competition, the battalion transport gained the following prizes :

Best battalion transport.
Best riding and pack animals.
Best pair of draught horses.

On the 29th the battalion was sent to Calais on strike duty, but returned on the 31st to the divisional area at St. Omer.

1st GARRISON BATTALION

Regarding this battalion very little information is forthcoming. It landed in India on December 23, 1915, under the command of Lieutenant-Colonel R. H. Martin, C.B. It was apparently doing garrison duty in Indian stations till the beginning of 1920, when it seems to have returned to England and to have been finally disbanded, in September, 1920.

Lieutenant-Colonel Martin was in command till he was succeeded on August 28, 1918, by Lieutenant-Colonel Norrie of the 4th Lincolnshire Regiment, who continued till the disbandment. During the latter part of Colonel Martin's command he was commanding the troops at Lucknow, and Lieutenant-Colonel Black acted for him. The stations of the battalion in India are not given in the Indian Army List.

APPENDICES

APPENDIX I

THE SUCCESSION OF COLONELS AND LIEUTENANT-COLONELS

1ST BATTALION.

Colonels.		*Lieutenant-Colonels.*	
June 12, 1685.	Henry Cornwall.	1685.	Sir John Morgan, Bart.
Nov. 20, 1688.	Oliver Nicholas.	1687.	James Purcell.
Dec. 31, 1688.	John Cunningham.	1689.	Thomas Hussey.
May 1, 1689.	William Steuart.	1705.	William Steuart (jun.)
July 17, 1715.	James Campbell.	1716.	Verney Lloyd.
Feb. 15, 1717.	Charles Lord Cathcart.	1720.	John Campbell.
Jan. 7, 1718.	James Otway.	1725.	Richard O'Farrell.
Dec. 25, 1725.	Richard Kane.	1741.	Michael Doyne.
Jan. 27, 1737.	William Hargrave.	1745.	Rowley Godfrey.
Aug. 28, 1739.	George Reade.	1749.	John Catillion.
Nov. 1, 1749.	Sir Charles Armand Powlett, K.B.	1751.	Peter Dumas.
		1754.	Richard Worge.
Jan. 26, 1751.	Hon. John Waldegrave.	1760.	Rowland Phillips.
Mar. 18, 1755.	Hon. Sir Joseph Yorke.	1763.	William Tayler.
Oct. 23, 1758.	William Whitmore.	1776.	John Hill.
Aug. 8, 1771.	Edward Earl Ligonier, K.B.	1784.	John Campbell.
		1795.	Gerrit Fisher.
June 19, 1782.	Thomas Lord Saye and Sele.	1799.	Gideon Shairpe.
		1800(?)	Henry de Bernière.

1ST BATTALION—*cont.*

Colonels.		Lieutenant-Colonels.	
July 4, 1788.	Hon. Alexander Leslie.	1807.	John Stuart.
Dec. 31, 1794.	Albemarle, Bertie.	1808.	John Cameron.
June 15, 1804.	Peter Hunter.	1822.	Nathaniel Blackwell.
Oct. 3, 1805.	Sir Robert Brownrigg, Bart., G.C.B.	1826.	David Campbell.
		1828.	Jeremiah Taylor.
May 31, 1833.	Sir John Cameron, Bart., K.C.B.	1832.	Holman Custance.
		1838.	Sir John McCaskill, K.C.B., K.H.
Dec. 7, 1844.	Sir Thomas Arbuthnot, K.B.C.	1846.	George Lenox Davies, C.B.
Feb. 18, 1848.	Sir James Archibald Hope, K.C.B.	1852.	Brownlow Villiers Layard.
Dec. 31, 1871.	Sir Henry Bates, K.C.B.	1853.	Arthur Borton, C.B.
Oct. 17, 1889.	Sir A. Borton, G.C.B., G.C.M.G.	1859.	Duncan Munro Bethune.
Sept. 8, 1893.	C. Elmhirst, C.B.	1861.	William Inglis.
Dec. 15, 1893.	T. E. Knox, C.B.	1864.	Henry Disney Ellis.
May 28, 1898.	H. J. Buchanan, C.B.	1873.	George H. Hawes.
Oct. 8, 1903.	H. R. Browne, C.B.	1878.	Francis G. C. Probart.
Dec. 24, 1917.	Sir E. P. Strickland, K.C.B., C.M.G. D.S.O.	1883.	Henry C. Vibart.
		1885.	William James Massy.
		1888.	Charles More Stockley.

From February 1, 1907, till his death H.M. King Edward VII was Colonel in Chief of the Norfolk Regiment, an honour which was continued by King George V. from December 2, 1910.

1891.	Archibald Graham Wavell.
1892.	H. Gunter.
1894.	Divie Knighton Robertson.
1897.	William Gibbs Straghan.
1898.	James Lorne Govan.
1901.	Andrew Cracroft Becher.

1ST BATTALION—*cont.*

Lieutenant-Colonels.

1904. William George Hamilton.
1905. Godfrey Massy.
1909. John Marriott, M.V.O., D.S.O.
1913. Colin Robert Ballard, C.B.
1916. John William Vincent Carroll, C.M.G., D.S.O.
1917. Francis Cecil Lodge, C.M.G., D.S.O.

2ND BATTALION.

1st Raising, 1799–1802.

Colonel Commandants.

1799. Robert Manners.
1800. Hon. John Knox.
1801. J. W. T. Watson.

2nd Raising.

Lieutenant-Colonels.

1804. Henry Craufurd.
1807. Sir John Cameron.
1809. George Molle.
1814. W. G. McGregor.

3rd Raising.

1857. Charles Elmhirst, C.B.
1865. Thomas E. Knox, C.B.
1873. Henry James Buchanan, C.B.
1879. William Daunt, C.B.
1883. Charles J. Cramer-Roberts.
1888. Charles Smith Perry.
1889. Gerard Septimus Burton.
1893. C. H. Shepherd.
1898. Lewis Horace Phillips.

2ND BATTALION—*cont.*

3rd Raising.

1901.	Charles Edward Borton, C.B.	1913.	Evelyn C. Peebles, D.S.O.
1905.	Fitzgerald Wintour.	1918.	William Fanshawe L. Gordon, C.M.G., D.S.O.
1909.	Arthur John Luard, D.S.O.		

3RD BATTALION.

1799–1802.
Colonel Commandant.
Gerrit Fisher.[1]

WEST NORFOLK MILITIA.

Colonels (as far as traceable).

1778. Horace Earl of Orford.
1882–1892. Sir Hambleton Francis Custance, K.C.B.

3RD BATTALION NORFOLK REGIMENT.

1896–1905. General Sir E. A. Bulwer, G.C.B.
1906–1908. Colonel Frederic Hambleton Custance, C.B.

---

[1] The above lists are based on those supplied by the Depôt. The writer feels some doubt about them in the period 1799–1805. The Army Lists of those years give the names of all officers of each rank in the regiment, but do not show which battalion each belongs to. Henry de Bernière was certainly lieutenant-colonel of the 1st Battalion in 1805, when he was taken prisoner on the Ariadne. The Depôt list shows him as commanding the 2nd Battalion, in which he never served. He has been omitted accordingly, in the above list, and Major Craufurd, who raised the battalion on the second occasion has been inserted.

Also Lieutenant-Colonel (later Sir John) Cameron, who was in command of the 2nd Battalion from October 1, 1807, till transferred to command of the 1st after Stewart's death at Roliça.

The name of C. Elmhirst, C.B., has been added in the list of colonels. He succeeded Sir A. Borton, but died a few weeks after appointment.

3RD BATTALION (SPECIAL RESERVE).

1908. Colonel Frederic Hambleton Custance, C.B.

Lieutenant-Colonels Commandant.

1778. John Barker (month of appointment not shown).
(No Militia Lists between these dates.)

1778–1792. Knipe Cobbett (no trace of appointment in Gazettes). Died March 20, 1792.

Mar. 20, 1792. Richard Lloyd. Resigned July 18, 1793.

July 18, 1793. William Earl of Albemarle. Resigned September 20, 1798.

Sept. 20, 1798. Theophilus Gurdon. Resigned April 3, 1799.

Apr. 3, 1798. George Nelthorpe. Died May 16, 1854.

May 16, 1854. Sir Hambleton Francis Custance, K.C.B. Resigned October 5, 1881.

Oct. 5, 1881. Randall Robert Burroughes. Resigned March 17, 1888.

Mar. 17, 1888. Frederick Willock Garnett. Resigned April 4, 1896.

Apr. 4, 1896. Frederic Hambleton Custance, C.B. Resigned September 17, 1904.

Oct. 15, 1904. Sir Kenneth Hagar Kemp, Bart. Resigned August 27, 1910.

Aug. 27, 1910. William Corrie Tonge, D.S.O. Resigned August 28, 1917.

Major Retired Pay Reserve of Officers.

Aug. 28, 1917. Evelyn William Margesson, C.M.G. Resigned June 30, 1923.

Lieutenant-Colonel Retired Pay.

Charles Maurice Jickling, O.B.E. (temporary Lieutenant-Colonel in command), August 28, 1917 to June 27, 1919.

EAST NORFOLK MILITIA.

Colonels (as far as traceable).

1759.	Sir Armine Wodehouse, Bart.	1821.	Hon. J. Wodehouse, M.P.
1779.	Sir John Wodehouse, Bart.	1843.	Hon. Berkeley Wodehouse.
1798.	John Lord Wodehouse.	1878.	Sir E. E. K. Lacon, Bart. (Honorary Colonel).
1799.	Hon. John Wodehouse.		

4TH BATTALION NORFOLK REGIMENT.

Colonel.

1889. The Earl Albemarle, K.C.V.O., C.B., V.D., A.D.C. (Honorary Colonel).

Lieutenant-Colonels Commandant.

1759.	Henry William Wilson.	1809.	William Durrant.
1779.	Jacob Preston.	1825.	William Mason.
1780.	Hon. H. Walpole.	1860.	Sir E. H. K. Lacon, Bart.
1793.	Richard Ward.	1882.	Henry C. Mathew.
1804.	Charles Lucas.	1891.	Thomas William Haines.
1805.	Sir George Berney Brograve, Bart.	1896.	Sir Charles Harvey, Bart.
		1900.	E. R. A. Kerrison, C.M.G.
1807.	John Patteson	1904.	W. E. Danby.

VOLUNTEERS.

NORFOLK VOLUNTEER INFANTRY BRIGADE.

Commanders.

1894. Colonel W. E. G. L. Bulwer, C.B., V.D.
1901. Colonel The Earl of Albemarle, K.C.V.O., C.B., V.D., A.D.C.
1906. Colonel C. E. Borton, C.B.

1ST VOLUNTEER BATTALION.

Colonels.

1884-1901. Colonel G. W. Boileau, V.D.
1907. Colonel the Earl of Leicester, G.C.V.O., C.M.G., A.D.C.

Lieutenant-Colonels.

1860-1864.	T. D. Brett.	1893-1895.	A. C. Dawson.
1865-1868.	G. Black.	1896-1906.	S. G. Hill, V.D.
1869-1883.	G. W. Boileau, V.D.	1907-1908.	J. R. Harvey, D.S.O.

2ND VOLUNTEER BATTALION.

Colonel.

1897-1905. H. E. Buxton.
1905-1908. The Earl of Albemarle, G.C.V.O., C.B., V.D., A.D.C.

Lieutenant-Colonels.

1876.	Major J. H. Orde.	1899-1902.	Colonel Walter Diver, V.D.
1876-1887.	Colonel Henry E. Buxton, V.D.	1903-1904.	Colonel C. J. Wiltshire, V.D.
1887-1896.	Colonel E. H. H. Combe, V.D.	1905-1908.	Colonel E. Harrison.
1896-1899.	Colonel H. J. Hartcup, V.D.	1904-1905.	Colonel R. W. Edis.

3RD VOLUNTEER BATTALION NORFOLK REGIMENT.

Colonel.

1878. Lord Suffield.

3RD VOLUNTEER BATTALION—*cont.*

Lieutenant-Colonels.

To 1886.	Lord Suffield.	1894–1903.	H. E. Hyde, V.D.
1866–1878.	J. Duff.	1903.	B. B. Sapwell, V.D.
1878–1894.	W. G. G. L. Bulwer, V.D.	1903–1908.	G. F. A. Cresswell, V.D.
	1913.	B. J. Petre.	

4TH VOLUNTEER BATTALION NORFOLK REGIMENT.

Colonels.

1888–1902.   R. T. Gurdon, V.D.
1904–1908.   H. T. S. Patteson, V.D.

Lieutenant-Colonels.

1862–1872.	Sir T. W. B. P. Beauchamp, Bart.	1888–1895.	C. W. J. Unthank.
1873–1887.	R. T. Gurdon, V.D.	1896–1901.	H. T. S. Patteson, V.D.
	1902–1908.	H. G. Barclay, V.D.	

BIOGRAPHICAL NOTES ON COLONELS AND FAMOUS SOLDIERS CONNECTED WITH THE REGIMENT

Henry Cornwall. First Colonel. Came from Royal Horse Guards. Resigned on landing of Prince of Orange.

Oliver Nicholas. Only held command for a month, when he was dismissed, as he refused to take the oath of allegiance to the Prince of Orange. Came to the regiment from Prince George of Denmark's Regiment (Marines).

John Cunningham. A supporter of the Revolution. Was appointed by William III, under whom he had served in the war against France in Charles II's reign. Came from Werden's Horse which was disbanded in 1690. Was dismissed by William III in May, 1689, for his recent conduct at Londonderry, which led to his arrest on suspicion of treason.

William Steuart. Being appointed to succeed Cunningham, he was colonel of the regiment till the accession of George I in 1715. He is said to have been connected with the family of the Earls of Galloway and Caithness, but nothing definite can be said on this subject. It seems that his family was settled in the north of Ireland, where some of his officers of the same name had estates. When appointed to the 9th he was lieutenant-colonel of the 16th. At Londonderry, and for some time afterwards, he personally commanded the regiment in the field, and when he became a brigadier-general it was still under his eye in his own brigade at the Boyne, at the first siege of Limerick, and at Athlone. He was wounded at the first siege of Limerick and at Athlone. He became major-general in 1693 and was employed in Flanders under William III. He was in command of the forces, including his own regiment, sent to Spain in 1794. Made a lieutenant-general in 1703, he was in Marlborough's campaigns, but not with his own regiment. It is clear, however, from Marlborough's despatches that he continued to take a lively interest in it, and it certainly contained a large number of officers of his name, presumably relatives. He was still in Flanders when the regiment went to Portugal for the War of the Spanish Succession there and in Spain. At the battle of Almanza the lieutenant-colonel of the 9th was William Steuart, nephew of the colonel. The two William Steuarts seem to have fallen out, as the elder cut the younger off with a shilling in his will on account of his "ingratitude," though what it consisted in is not known.

The colonel appears to have been born in 1652, and was evidently highly appreciated as a soldier by William III and Marlborough. He became general in 1711, and later was appointed commander-in-chief and privy-councillor in Ireland. The cause of his retirement, or sale of his commission in 1715, is obscure. We are reluctant to think that there is any truth in the story that he was suspected of disaffection to the new King. After that he appears to have lived in ease in London.

His first wife (Catherine Viscountess Grandison) had been insane for some years, when she died in January, 1726. A fortnight later the old general married again. On February 15th he had a stroke of apoplexy and died on June 4th. He is buried in the Duke of Buckingham's vault in King Henry VII's Chapel, Westminister Abbey. The inscription on his coffin-plate was as follows: "The Rt. Honourable William Steuart, Esq., General of the Foot and Commander-in-Chief of all Her late Majesty's forces in Ireland, colonel of a regiment of foot, and one of Her said Majesty's Privy Council in the aforesaid Kingdom. Died June 4th, 1726, aged 74." He was well off, as shown by his bequest of £5,000 Irish money for a school for boys in the parish of St. George's, Hanover Square, London. He was one of the few colonels of the regiment who personally commanded it in the field.

James Campbell. Succeeded Steuart. He was a distinguished officer of the Scots Greys, from the lieutenant-colonelcy of which he was promoted to the colonelcy of the 9th, and to which he returned two years after as colonel. His career is not closely indentified with the Norfolk Regiment.

Honourable Charles Cathcart, like Campbell, came from the Scots Greys and left the 9th in less than a year.

James Otway. Another cavalry officer who got the colonelcy as a reward for services in Spain and at Preston Pans. He is not particularly indentified with the 9th. It is understood that his family was recently represented in the regiment in the person of Major Otway Mayne.

Richard Kane. In his earlier career distinguished himself with the 18th Royal Irish under Marlborough. When Minorca was ceded to Great Britain he was appointed lieutenant-governor and commander-in-chief. There he showed himself to be an excellent administrator and did much for the improvement of the island, especially by constructing a road across it. When Colonel Otway died in 1725 the 9th was in Minorca and Kane was given the colonelcy. It was with him there still when he died in 1737, so that he was one of the few colonels who were in the same station with it during his colonelcy. He wrote a brief history of the campaigns of William III and Marlborough, and some essays on infantry formations and training.

William Hargrave. Apparently an average soldier of no particular note who was colonel successively of the 31st, 9th, and 7th.

George Reade. Equally calls for no special remark.

Sir Charles Armand Powlett, K.B. Yet another cavalry officer who only commanded the regiment for two years as a stepping-stone to the colonelcy of the 13th Dragoons.

Honourable John Waldegrave. Also only held the command for four years, when he went to that of the 8th Dragoons. Though he did well in the Seven Years' War, it is not necessary to go into details, as his career neither previously to being colonel of the 9th nor subsequently was specially famous.

Honourable Sir Joseph Yorke. Formerly of the Guards and A.D.C. to the Duke of Cumberland and George II, he held the colonelcy of the 9th for a little over three years before being promoted to a similar position in the 8th Dragoons.

William Whitmore. Held the colonelcy of the 9th for thirteen years. He was not an officer of any great distinction, and if it be true that it was owing to his parsimony that the badge of Britannia was discontinued on the colours of the regiment, his name will hardly be held in high honour in it. The dropping of the badge at this period would be particularly unfortunate, as it no doubt was the cause of the omission of mention of it in the printed description of recognized badges attached to the dress regulations of 1768.

Edward Earl Ligonier. His claim to the gratitude of the regiment is enhanced if it be correct that it was he who revived the use of the Britannia badge. He was appointed to the colonelcy in August, 1771, very shortly before the "Saratoga" colours were presented. Those it will be seen have not got the Britannia on them, but possibly they had already been made, if not taken into use, when he succeeded, or at any rate before he could be approached on the subject. The regiment was then in Ireland.

Thomas Lord Saye and Sele. Calls for no remark. Like several other colonels of line regiments, he was originally a Guardsman.

Honourable Alexander Leslie. Another Guardsman who had gained some distinction in the American War before being rewarded with the colonelcy of the 63rd in 1782, and that of the 9th in 1788. During the whole of his command the regiment was in the West Indies, whilst he was at home as second in command in Scotland.

Albemarle, Bertie. Again an officer who had served thirty years in the Guards. Appointed to the 9th as colonel in 1794, he left it in 1804. Unlike many of his predecessors, he actually commanded the 1st Battalion during the period of three battalions from 1799 to 1802. During the same period colonels commandant were appointed for the other two battalions: for the 2nd battalion Major-general Manners of the 3rd Guards, for the 3rd Colonel Gerrit Fisher of the 1st battalion of the 9th. This appointment was not revived when the 2nd Battalion was reconstituted in 1804.

Peter Hunter. Held the colonelcy for only sixteen months, and was in Canada as lieutenant-governor of Upper and commander-in-chief in both Canadas. He had previously served in three line regiments,— the 1st Royal Scots, the 92nd, and the 60th.

Sir Robert Brownrigg, Bart., G.C.B. Held the colonelcy of the 9th for the long period of twenty-eight years. Before his appointment his service had been varied, in the 14th (which at one time served on board ship as marines), the 100th, 35th, 52nd, 60th, 88th, and on the staff. When he was appointed colonel of the 9th he was quartermaster-general, an office in which he gained the approval of the Duke of Wellington. He was in that capacity in the Walcheren expedition, in which the 1st Battalion of his own regiment was engaged. He was afterwards, whilst still colonel of the 9th, employed as governor and commander-in-chief in Ceylon, where he distinguished himself and annexed the Kingdom of Kandy. He was made a G.C.B. and a baronet for these services. On the whole, he seems to have been the most distinguished of the colonels of the 9th since William Steuart.

Sir John Cameron, K.C.B. Of all the colonels of the 9th Sir John Cameron is the one most distinguished, not only by his achievements as a regimental officer, but by his long and intimate connexion with the regiment in its service in the field. Sir A. Borton alone rivals him as an officer who served throughout his active service with the regiment, but perhaps cannot claim to have led it in quite such notable campaigns as those of the Peninsula.

John Cameron of Calchenna, a collateral descendant of Lochiel, was born in 1773, and at the age of fourteen received his first commission in the 43rd, with which he was engaged, as was the 9th, at Martinique, St. Lucia, and Guadeloupe, and distinguished himself specially at the storming of Fort Fleur d'Epée in the last-named island.

At the age of twenty-one, owing to the ravages of disease amongst senior officers, he found himself in command of the remains of the 43rd as part of the garrison of Berville camp in Guadeloupe. When the camp was carried by assault by Victor Hugues' men Cameron was wounded and taken prisoner. Exchanged from France in 1797, he returned to his regiment in the West Indies, and brought it home as Major in 1800, when he was still only twenty-seven.

In 1807 he became lieutenant-colonel in the 7th West India Regiment, but almost immediately exchanged into the 9th and sailed in command of the 2nd Battalion for Portugal in July, 1808. At Roliça Colonel Stewart of the 1st Battalion was killed, and Cameron was promoted from the 2nd Battalion to command the 1st, after he had served with the 2nd at Vimeiro. His services in the Peninsula from 1808 to 1814 have been recounted in the body of this history and do not need to be repeated here.

From the date of his joining the regiment in 1807 till his death in 1844 Cameron's career was bound up with that of the 9th, of which he became colonel in 1833.

When with the 43rd in Guernsey in 1803, he married Miss Brock, a niece of Lord de Saumarez. Their son, Sir Duncan Cameron, G.C.B., commanded the Black Watch in the Crimea, and was later commandant of the R.M.C.

After the Peninsula, Colonel Cameron went with the 1st Battalion to Canada till 1815, when, on return to France, he was given command of a brigade of the army of occupation. For ten years (1823—33) he commanded as major-general (which rank he attained in 1821) the Western District, where, it will be remembered, his old regiment was under him in 1827 at Plymouth. He was promoted Lieutenant-general in 1837, and died at the age of seventy-one in 1844 in Guernsey.

Though a strict disciplinarian, he was beloved by officers and men.

In the 5th division he was known to the men as "The Devil," a soubriquet of which Colin Campbell afterwards remarked, "That, sir, was a compliment of which any man might be proud, and which I should prefer to the most elaborate epitaph on my tomb."[1] That refers to Cameron's intrepidity and determination. Another story, also told by the biographer of Clyde, illustrates his enforcement of discipline. Colin Campbell, as he then was, after being badly wounded at the first assault on St. Sebastian, was not yet cured of his wounds at the time of the passage of the Bidassoa. Nevertheless he was determined to be there in command of his light company. Without a proper discharge, he got out of hospital and was again badly wounded leading the company. Cameron, who had himself led the regiment, had him up and severely reprimanded him and a companion who had followed his example. He was given to understand that he only got off so lightly in consideration of his gallantry. The reprimand shows what high value Cameron placed on discipline, though it must have been a great regret to him to have to censure an action the temptation to which he would perhaps himself have been unable to resist under similar circumstances.

Cameron was not always quite fairly treated. His share in the taking of the convent at San Sebastian was not brought out in Sir Thomas Graham's report. Though Colin Campbell was mentioned, Cameron was not. When the latter, years afterwards, learnt of the omission, he wrote to his old subordinate Colin Campbell, who replied in the most generous terms. "It is twenty years," he said, "since I first saw this report. You were therein represented only as being in support, whereas not only did you lead the left attack all the while, but made it with your own regiment, unassisted by other troops. I can therefore enter into your feelings on perusing this despatch."[2] At Busaco Sir James Leith, commanding the 5th division, actually put himself at the head of the 9th in their great charge. With a man like Cameron commanding the 9th, it seems rather an unnecessary action for a general of division to lead a battalion. But probably no slur on the Colonel was intended.

Sir Thomas Arbuthnot, K.C.B. Was originally in the 29th Foot,

[1] Shadwell, "Life of Lord Clyde." [2] *ibid.*

a regiment which has always been intimately associated with the 9th since the two regiments fought together at Roliça.[1] He was on Sir John Moore's staff in the Corunna campaign, and when appointed colonel of the 9th in 1844, in succession to Sir John Cameron, was commanding the Midland and Northern Districts. He was transferred to the colonelcy of the 71st H.L.I. in 1848.

Sir James Archibald Hope, G.C.B. Joined the 26th Cameronians in 1800. Was at Lugo and Corunna and in the Walcheren expedition. Later he was at Cuidad Rodrigo and Badajoz, and was present as assistant adjutant-general at Salamanca, Burgos, Vittoria, San Sebastian, the Bidassoa, Nivelle, and Nive. In 1814 he was transferred from the Cameronians to the 3rd Foot Guards. He was employed, after retiring on half pay in 1839, as major-general on the staff in Lower Canada.

Sir Arthur Borton. Served in the Norfolk Regiment from ensign to colonel. He was born in 1814, the youngest son of the Reverend John Drew Borton, Rector of Blofield, Norfolk. Leaving Eton, he joined the regiment as ensign in July, 1832, in Ireland. He was with it in Mauritius and India, where he left it in 1838 for a year's study in the senior department of the Royal Military College. Returning to India in 1839, he went with it to Afghanistan in 1842. Of his services in that campaign, in the first Sikh war and the Crimea, the history has been written in the body of this work, in which we have so frequently quoted from his papers. It is unnecessary to repeat this here. After the Crimea he went to Canada with the regiment and returned with it.

In 1865 he was given command of the troops at Colchester, in 1866 of the Infantry Brigade at the Curragh, and in 1868 became major-general. In 1870—75 he commanded the Mysore Division of the Madras Army, and in 1877 his C.B. gained in the Crimea, became a K.C.B. In 1878 he was given the post of governor and commander-in-chief of Malta and created a G.C.M.G. On vacating this appointment he was raised to the G.C.B. He died in London in September, 1893, having held the colonelcy of the Norfolk Regiment from 1889. He was buried at Hunton near Maidstone, near the residence of his elder son, Colonel A. C. Borton of the Somersetshire Light Infantry. His younger son,

[1] See Appendix.

Lieutenant-Colonel C. E. Borton, C.B., followed in his father's footsteps in the Norfolk Regiment, which he joined in 1878, and after seeing much service commanded the 2nd Battalion as lieutenant-colonel from 1901 to 1905. Sir Arthur Borton was even more closely connected with the Norfolk Regiment than Sir John Cameron, for he was a Norfolk man by birth, and save for being colonel of the 1st Battalion West India Regiment from 1876 to 1889, was never connected with any other regiment. The whole of his active military service was in the Norfolk Regiment, of which he was a whole-hearted admirer and supporter.

His papers, letters, and sketches, placed at the writer's disposal by his elder son, Colonel A. Borton, have been of the greatest assistance.

General C. Elmhirst. Only held the colonelcy for three months. His service throughout had been with the 9th in the Afghan War and the Crimea, where he was Borton's second in command. His services with the regiment are recorded in the body of this history.

General T. E. Knox. Was with the 67th in China, and was lieutenant-colonel of the 2/9th from 1864 to 1872.

General H. J. Buchanan. Was mostly in the 47th Foot till 1873, when he became lieutenant-colonel commanding the 2nd Battalion Norfolk Regiment till 1879.

General H. R. Browne. Began his military career as ensign in the 9th Foot in 1846. After 1849 he was with several other regiments, and commanded in the West Indies.

Sir E. P. Strickland. Present Colonel. Has been an officer of the Norfolk Regiment since he joined the Army in 1888. Services, as stated in " Who's Who." Upper Burma, 1887—89 (Medal and clasp); Egyptian Army; Dongola Expedition, 1896 (despatches, medal, two clasps); Sudan 1897 (despatches, clasp); Khartoum campaign, 1898 (despatches, brevet majority, English medal, clasp to Khedive's medal); operations against Ahmed Fedil, 1889 (despatches, Distinguished Service Order, 3rd class Medjidie); operations Northern Nigeria 1906 (medal and clasp); temporary lieutenant-colonel 1906; temporary colonel Northern Nigeria Regiment, 1909; European War, 1914—18 (despatches, brevet colonel, promoted major-general, K.C B.), promoted lieutenant-colonel to Manchester Regiment, 1914, at beginning of the war, brigadier-general,

1915, temporary major-general, 1916, commanded Jullunder Brigade Indian Expeditionary Force, January to November, 1915; 98th infantry brigade in France, November, 1915 to June 1916; 1st division in France, June, 1916, to March, 1919; Western division Army of the Rhine, March to September, 1919; 8th division Irish Command, November, 1919, to May, 1922.

There remain two men who, though neither of them was ever colonel of the regiment or even rose to high rank in it, both began their military career in it, saw much active service with it, and must both be looked upon by it in the same way as an eminent man is regarded by the school at which he was educated and by the employers to whom his earlier services were rendered. Each of these men, Field-Marshal Sir William Gomm, and Colin Campbell Lord Clyde, rose to great military eminence, and the Norfolk Regiment must look with pride on their achievements as the outcome of their early military training in it.

Field-Marshal Sir William Maynard Gomm, G.C.B., was, as has already been related, the son of Lieutenant-Colonel W. Gomm who was killed at Pointe-a-Pitre in Guadeloupe. His early history as an officer of the 9th and on the staff in the Peninsula has appeared sufficiently in the body of this history.

In 1814 he was made a K.C.B. for his services in the Peninsula, and transferred to the Coldstream Guards. He was again on the staff at Quatre Bras and Waterloo. From 1817 to 1839 he was on Home service, and during that period he married twice, but had no issue of either marriage. In 1829 he became a full colonel, and in 1837 a major-general. In 1839 he was appointed to the command-in-chief of the troops in Jamaica till 1842, when he returned to England to command the Northern District, only to be appointed a few months later to the Governorship of Mauritius, which he held for seven years. In 1846 he had become a lieutenant-general.

In 1849 he had a disappointment. He had been appointed commander-in-chief in India, and proceeded direct from Mauritius to Calcutta. There he found that, owing to panic in England over the second Sikh war and other causes, his appointment had been cancelled and Sir Charles Napier having been appointed had actually arrived in Calcutta and gone on to the Punjab. Full explanations from the Duke of Wellington and Lord Fitzroy Somerset enabled him to bear the disappointment with dignity. He returned to England, and in August, 1850, had accepted the chief command in Bombay, when, just as he was starting, Sir Charles Napier resigned, and Gomm after all became commander-in-chief in India, till 1855. He was promoted full general in 1854. In 1868 he was made a field-marshal, and in 1872, on the death of Sir George Pollock, was appointed Constable of the Tower, an appointment which he held till his death at the age of ninety.

Colin Campbell Lord Clyde was born Colin Macliver in 1792. His mother was a Campbell and her brother, Colonel John Campbell, obtained for him a commission in the 9th Foot. When he was introduced to the Duke of York the latter, supposing him to be " another of the clan " Campbell, entered his name as Colin Campbell, a name which he adhered to for the rest of his life.

His commission as ensign was dated May 9, 1808, when he was still some months short of sixteen, and his lieutenancy was of June 29th of the same year. On July 20th he sailed with the 2nd Battalion, under the command of Cameron, for Portugal. His first action was Vimeiro, where he acknowledged his debt of gratitude to his captain, who led him out from the rear company and walked him up and down in front of the regiment under the enemy's artillery fire.

Cameron now succeeded to the command of the 1st Battalion in consequence of the death of Lieutenant-Colonel Stewart at Roliça, and Colin Campbell also was transferred from the 2nd to the 1st Battalion, with which he went through the Corunna campaign and the Walcheren expedition. After this he was re-transferred to the 2nd Battalion, then at Gibraltar, and was with the two flank companies of the 9th which formed part of Browne's battalion at Barrosa, where, owing to all the other officers being wounded, he found himself in command of the remains of the two companies. Here, he himself says, " the present Lord Lynedoch (then Sir Thomas Graham) was pleased to take favourable notice of my conduct." He went with Colonel Skerrett's expedition to Tarragona in June, 1811, and later in the year was attached to the Spanish armies in the South.

In January, 1813, he was once more returned to the 1st Battalion and to the command of his old Colonel Cameron in Portugal. The rest of his services with that battalion have already been sufficiently stated. The crossing of the Bidassoa was his last service with the 9th, for in November, 1813, he was given a company, without purchase, in the 60th. In 1818 he was transferred to the 21st, and was on the staff in British Guiana. It was not till 1835 that he was appointed lieutenant-colonel in the 9th, but only on condition of his at once exchanging to the 98th, which he commanded for some years, going to China with it, and, after commanding a brigade in Chusan, going with it to India in 1846. His excellent service in the second Sikh war earned him a K.C.B. In 1850 he was employed in clearing the Kohat Pass on the North-West Frontier, and later in other frontier affairs. In 1853 he was in England on half-pay. Then he was through the Crimean War as commander of the Highland Brigade at the Alma, commandant of Balaclava, and commander of the 1st division. He had a home command in 1856. His great opportunity came with the Indian Mutiny, when he was made commander-in-chief in India on the death of General Anson. To him belongs the honour of the capture of Lucknow and the final suppression of the Mutiny. Of all his doings between 1813 and his death in 1863 it is impossible here to give an account. They are to be found in full in General Shadwell's life of him. He was buried in Westminster Abbey.

His honours were many. He was made a C.B. for China in 1842, a K.C.B. for the Sikh war, G.C.B. for the Crimea, besides receiving several decorations from the allies. For his supreme services in the Indian Mutiny he received the newly created K.C.S.I., was promoted general, and raised to the peerage as Lord Clyde of Clydesdale. The East India Company voted him a pension of £2,000 a year. He was colonel of the 93rd Highlanders in 1858, and of the Coldstream Guards from 1860.

APPENDIX II

ESTABLISHMENT OF THE REGIMENT AT VARIOUS DATES

The following table shows the sanctioned establishment of the regiment at every date when it was materially changed from 1685 to the middle of the nineteenth century.

The colonel, lieutenant-colonel, major, adjutant, and other staff officers were generally the same, and it seems unnecessary to burden the body of the statement with an interminable repetition of the same figures year after year. Therefore it has been confined to the company organization. Changes in the above officers, and the gradual addition of sergeant-majors, drum-majors, colour-sergeants, staff-sergeants, etc., are noted in the column of notes against the years in which they were made.

Date	Number of Companies.	Captains.	Lieutenants.	Ensigns or 2nd Lieutenants.	Sergeants of Companies.	Drummers and Fifers.	Corporals.	Privates.	Notes.
1685 (June)	11	8	11	11	33	22	33	1100	1685 to 1803. The colonel, lieutenant-colonel, and major were also captains, and there was a captain-lieutenant instead of a lieutenant for the colonel's company. He is included among the lieutenants during that period.
1685 (July)	10	7	10	10	20	10	30	500	
1687 (May)	11	8	12	10	22	11	33	550	1687. The grenadier company now permanently added to the battalion had two lieutenants instead of one lieutenant and one ensign.
1687 (Sept.)	13	10	14	12	39	26	39	780	

352

Date	Number of Companies	Captains	Lieutenants	Ensigns or 2nd Lieutenants	Sergeants of Companies	Drummers and Fifers	Corporals	Privates	Notes
1694 (April)	13	10	14	12	51	38	39	910	1694 (April). Augmentation of twelve sergeants, twelve drummers, and 130 men.
1699 (March)	11	8	12	10	22	11	22	396	
1700	10	7	11	9	20	10	30	360	
1701 (June)	12	9	13	11	24	24	36	708	
1703 (Dec.)	13	10	14	12	39	26	39	790	1703. The establishment was generally fixed for a year from each December 24th. Unless a month is given, it should be understood the establishment was for this year. Where there was a revision during the year the month is stated. In this year battalion companies had sixty privates; grenadier company seventy.
1704	13	10	14	12	39	26	39	728	
1707	13	10	14	12	39	26	39	790	1707. Battalion and grenadier companies as in 1703 above.
1709 (April)	12	9	13	11	24	24	36	600	
1713 (June)	10	7	11	9	20	10	20	380	
1717	12	9	13	11	24	24	24	452	1717 and July, 1718. Battalion companies thirty-seven privates; grenadier company forty-five.
1718 (June)	10	7	11	9	20	10	20	380	
1718 (July)	12	9	13	11	24	24	24	452	
1729	10	7	11	9	30	20	30	500	1729. Number of privates fifty in all companies, grenadiers included.
1739 (June)	10	7	11	9	30	20	30	600	
1739 (Aug.)	10	7	11	9	30	20	30	700	
1750	10	7	11	9	20	10	20	290	1750. Irish establishment.
1754	10	7	11	9	30	20	30	700	

Date	Number of Companies	Captains	Lieutenants	Ensigns or 2nd Lieutenants	Sergeants of Companies	Drummers and Fifers	Corporals	Privates	Notes
1755	12	9	13	11	38	14	38	900	1755. The two additional companies added in October, 1755, each had four sergeants and four corporals, also two drummers and 100 privates. They appear to have been again reduced in January, 1756, when they had been only partly raised.
1757 (April)	10	7	11	9	30	20	30	700	
1759 (Feb.)	10	7	11	9	30	20	30	700	
1759 (June)	9	6	19	8	36	20	36	900	1759 (June). Two lieutenants and one ensign in each company, except grenadier, which had three lieutenants and no ensign. Two fifers for grenadier company. They appear in some years, but not in all, down to 1776, when they became permanent.
1760	9	6	10	8	30	20	30	700	
1761	9	6	19	8	36	20	36	900	1761. As above after reduction of 1760.
1763 (March)	9	6	10	8	18	9	18	423	
1769	9	6	10	8	27	18	27	378	1769 and 1770. Irish establishment.
1770 (Jan.)	9	6	10	8	27	20	27	378	
1771	10	7	12	8	20	12	30	380	1771. Light company introduced. British and Irish establishment equalized. 1772. From this year the captain-lieutenant ranked as captain, but only got lieutenant's pay, and is included among lieutenants in establishment lists. Light company established with two lieutenants and no ensign.
1776	12	9	14	10	36	26	36	672	1776. Grenadiers henceforward have two fifers.
1780 (Feb.)	12	9	14	10	36	26	36	672	
1781 (Jan.)	12	9	14	10	36	26	36	360	
1783 (June)	8	5	10	6	16	18	24	384	1783. Officers for a 9th and a 10th company to remain " en second."
1785 (May)	8	5	10	6	16	10	24	384	

Date	Number of Companies	Captains	Lieutenants	Ensigns or 2nd Lieutenants	Sergeants of Companies	Drummers and Fifers	Corporals	Privates	Notes
1787 (June)	10	7	12	8	20	12	30	370	1787. "Two sergeants exclusive of those here specified for whom an extra allowance of 6d. a day is to be provided on that establishment." So says the establishment warrant. Apparently these were the first staff-sergeants. They are shown in the body of the statement for 1791.
1791	10	7	12	8	22	12	30	300	
1792	10	7	12	8	22	12	30	400	
1798	10	7	20	8	50	22	50	550	1798. There was a surgeon and assistant surgeon, sergeant-major (a new appointment), and the two extra sergeants are called respectively quartermaster-sergeant and paymaster-sergeant. In addition there were the following officers "en second"—two captains, one captain-lieutenant, two lieutenants and two ensigns. There were two majors henceforward. Battalion companies had two lieutenants and one ensign. Flank companies three lieutenants only.
1799	11	8	24	9	44	24	44	836	
1800	10	7	22	8	40	22	40	760	1800. "En second" one captain, one captain-lieutenant, two lieutenants, one ensign.
1803	11	11	23	9	50	22	50	950	1803. In this year the captain-lieutenant disappears and the colonel, lieutenant-colonel, and major cease to be captains also, so that henceforward a captain is shown for each company. There was an eleventh recruiting company with the usual establishment in 1803, which was reduced at end of 1804.
1804	10	10	12	8	20	20	20	380	
1805	10	10	22	8	53	22	50	950	1805. Three staff-sergeants shown under sergeants, viz. quartermaster, paymaster, and armourer. No recruiting company.
1806	10	10	12	8	43	22	40	760	
1808	10	10	22	8	63	22	60	1140	1808. On transfer from Irish to British establishment.
1809	10	10	22	8	63	22	60	1140	1089. There was an eleventh recruiting company consisting of one captain, two lieutenants, one ensign, eight sergeants, eight corporals, four drummers, 1810. In this year the drum-major first appears on the official establishments of marching regiments, though he is said to have existed unofficially in marching regiments at an earlier date.

Date	Number of Companies	Captains	Lieutenants	Ensigns or 2nd Lieutenants	Sergeants of Companies	Drummers and Fifers	Corporals	Privates	Notes
1811	10	10	22	8	60	21	60	1140	1811. Recruiting company as above not shown in body of statement. Only nineteen drummers and two fifers.
1812	11	11	24	9	68	25	68	1140	1812. Body of statement includes recruiting company.
1813	11	11	24	9	58	25	58	950	1813. Recruiting company included. There were two assistant surgeons.
1814	10	10	22	8	40	21	50	950	1814. No recruiting company.
1815	11	11	24	8	48	21	58	950	1815. Includes recruiting company. Ten colour-sergeants appear for the first time, also a schoolmaster-sergeant.
1816	10	10	12	8	30	21	40	760	1816. No recruiting company.
1818	10	10	12	8	20	21	30	620	1818. Reduced establishment from June. 1817. Only one assistant surgeon.
1822	8	8	10	6	16	11	24	552	
1825 (June)	10	10	12	8	26	13	36	627	1825. Hospital sergeant added.
1826	10	10	12	8	42	14	36	704	
1836	10	10	12	8	26	13	36	703	
1838	9	9	20	7	36	17	45	926	1838. This is for the nine companies in India only. They had two lieutenant-colonels, two Majors, and two assistant surgeons.
1842	10	10	22	8	41	19	50	950	1842. Includes a recruiting company left at home when the rest (9) went to India.
1854 (May)	12	12	14	10	48	24	60	1140	1854. Augmentation for Crimean War.
1855 (Jan.)	16	8 (service	16	8 companies)	42	20	50	950	1855. The battalion had sixteen companies, of which eight were service (it was the Crimean War) and eight depot. There were three majors, of whom one was with the depot companies, together with eight captains, eight lieutenants, eight ensigns, one paymaster-sergeant, one schoolmaster-sergeant, and one orderly-room clerk. Attached to the service companies were the colonel, lieutenant-colonel, two majors, eight captains, sixteen lieutenants, eight ensigns; one each paymaster, adjutant, quartermaster, surgeon;
		8 (depot	8	companies	42	50	50	950	
1856 (Nov.)	12	12	14	10	48	24	48	952	
1857 (June)	12	12	14	10	48	24	36	804	

Date	Number of Companies	Captains	Lieutenants	Ensigns or 2nd Lieutenants	Sergeants of Companies	Drummers and Fifers	Corporals	Privates	Notes
									three assistant surgeons; one sergeant-major; one each quartermaster-sergeant, paymaster-sergeant, armourer-sergeant, hospital sergeant, orderly-room clerk. The depot companies had none of those mentioned after ensigns except one each paymaster-sergeant, schoolmaster-sergeant, and orderly-room clerk. They had no drum-major. The service companies had no schoolmaster-sergeant. The total establishment all ranks was 2,218.
									1877. The battalion was reduced to eight companies on formation of depots.

2ND BATTALION.

1st Establishment, (1799 to 1802).

Date	Number of Companies	Captains	Lieutenants	Ensigns or 2nd Lieutenants	Sergeants of Companies	Drummers and Fifers	Corporals	Privates	Notes
1799 (Aug.)	11	11	24	9	44	24	44	836	The colonel counted with the 1st Battalion; but the 2nd had a colonel commandant, lieutenant-colonel, two majors, and other establishment the same as the 1st.
1800 (Dec.)	10	7	23	8	40	22	40	760	The establishment remained unchanged till disbandment in December, 1802.

2nd Establishment.

Date	Number of Companies	Captains	Lieutenants	Ensigns or 2nd Lieutenants	Sergeants of Companies	Drummers and Fifers	Corporals	Privates	Notes
1804 (Oct.)	10	10	12	8	40	22	40	760	Colonel counted with 1st Battalion. The colonel commandant was not revived in 1804.
1805	10	10	12	8	20	22	20	380	
1808	10	10	22	8	50	22	50	950	
1809	10	10	12	8	40	22	40	760	1809 to 1811. In addition there was in these years a recruiting company of the usual strength.
1810	10	10	12	8	30	22	30	570	
1812	10	10	12	8	40	21	40	760	

Date	Number of Companies	Captains	Lieutenants	Ensigns or 2nd Lieutenants	Sergeants of Companies	Drummers and Fifers	Corporals	Privates	Notes
1814	10	10	12	8	10	21	20	570	1814. Reductions after Napoleon's first abdication. The battalion was disbanded on December 24, 1815.
1815	10	10	12	8	20	21	20	380	

3RD ESTABLISHMENT.

| 1857 | 8 | 8 | 10 | 6 | 24 | 16 | 32 | 608 | |

3RD BATTALION.

1799 to 1802.

During this period the establishment of the 3rd Battalion was the same as that of the 2nd. After its disbandment in October, 1804, it was never revived in the same form. The 3rd (Militia) Battalion and later the 3rd (special reserve) Battalion were in no sense descendants of this old 3rd Battalion.

APPENDIX III

UNIFORM, ARMS, AND BADGES

A regimental history is not the place for a general history and detailed descriptions of the uniform of the British infantry. No such history has yet been published, and it rests with some of the few who have made a special study of the subject to write one of uniforms in all branches of the service.[1]

We propose in this note merely to give some general idea of the changes which have taken place in the uniform of the Infantry of the Line during the two hundred and thirty-three years of the Norfolk Regiment's existence from 1685 to 1918. In this will be noted, as far as we have been able to ascertain them, all changes specially affecting the regiment, as distinguished from others.

The infantry soldier of 1685 was, as regards his clothing, a very different looking individual from him who fought in 1914–1918. A corporal of Colonel Henry Cornwall's regiment in 1686 has been depicted in an unpublished series of illustrations intended for the late Colonel Clifford Walton's History of the British Standing Army in its early days. The picture is imaginary, but authorities are quoted for colours, etc. The corporal's dress is a red coat with orange lining, orange cuffs edged with white lace or braid, and with three flat white buttons near the upper edge. There is also a line of white along the seam of the sleeve, round its junction with the body, and down the side seams of the coat. The buttons of the coat and lace, or braid, down the opening are white, as

[1] To one of these, Major Parkyn, Librarian, R.U.S.I., the author must render his special thanks for much assistance and advice received.

is the cravat, which has short hanging ends. There is no facing to the collar, which is soft. The breeches are plain grey. Stockings white with orange garters. Shoes black with orange bows. Shoulder belt brown or orange, with cases for cartridges hanging from it by two strings each. The waist belt is of the same colour, with a frog holding a long, straight, rapier-like sword with yellow metal hilt. The black felt hat is turned up on one side only, after the fashion of the modern Colonial soldier's hat.

The orange colour of the facings and the other colours are authorized, by advertisements in the "London Gazette," for deserters from the regiment, dated July 22 to 26, 1686, and June 2 to 6, 1687, describing the uniform as "red coat, lined with orange colour, grey breeches, and white stockings." Another similar advertisement (April 22 to 26, 1688) gives the undress as "grey coat lined with black." The corporal has a long, bright barrelled musket.[1] The grenadier of this period had a tall, mitre-shaped cap of cloth, turned up and richly embroidered in front. Of the officer's uniform nothing is known. Presumably it was a glorified edition of the soldier's. In 1695 companies of a strength of sixty men had fourteen pikemen. The pike, as a soldier's weapon, disappeared in 1701. There had been, in 1685, thirty pikemen to sixty musketeers. At this time captains carried pikes, lieutenants "partizans," ensigns half pikes, and sergeants halberds.

Somewhere between 1686 and 1733 the facings were changed from orange to bright green; for in the latter year[2] there is an order authorising Colonel Richard Kane, then commanding the regiment, to change its facings from bright green to bright orange, out of respect and regard

---

[1] Browned barrels were not introduced till 1816.

[2] We are indebted to Major Parkyn for this reference, which is to "C.-in-C.s' Letter Book, No. III," p. 270. That book is not traceable at the War Office or the Public Records Office. Major Parkyn does not remember where he got it, but its precision gives it the stamp of truth, and it is probable either that the old letter-book was destroyed, or that it has got inextricably mixed up in the rearrangement of documents at the Public Records Office. Captain Trimen's "The Regiments of the British Army" gives the facings as "blue 1685–1751." This is clearly wrong. The mistake was probably due to one in the "1742 Book," which will be dealt with presently.

for the House of Orange. When the change from orange to bright green had taken place is not traceable. The following suggestion is advanced by us as a possible answer to the question. Colonel Steuart, who commanded the regiment from 1689 to 1715, came from Ulster, where several of his family, officers in the regiment, owned property. It is possible green may have been adopted as an Irish colour in the early days of his command, and perhaps in memory of the green sprigs worn by William III's troops at the Boyne and elsewhere. In those days colonels of regiments had the provision of clothing for their men in their own hands (often making an iniquitous profit from it), and, provided they did not make very important changes in the general style, they could probably use a wide discretion as to facings, lace, etc.

In 1742 there appeared a book of coloured illustrations, published by authority, showing a private (battalion company) of each of the various regiments, with a list of the colonels on the opposite page. A man in blue facings appears opposite a list of colonels corresponding to those of the 9th Foot, whilst the list of colonels corresponding to the 8th Foot is faced by a man in orange facings.[1] It is quite clear that the two pictures in the original have got transposed in binding, and that orange was still, as we should expect, the facing colour of the 9th. The hat was black, cocked three cornered, and edged with white. Waistcoat and breeches red. Regimental lace on lappels, cuffs, and waistcoat. White gaiters (an article not hitherto mentioned) extending above the knee, with a black garter below it, and a white strap below the arch of the foot as in a modern "spat." A musket, sword, and bayonet were carried.

There had been a dress regulation, the first general one on record, in 1729, but it dealt with the kind and number of articles to be supplied to the men, rather than with the pattern or colour. The first real attempt

---

[1] In the modern reproduction of the plates only of the figures in this book these are printed, under the man with blue facings, words showing him as belonging to the 9th Foot, and the man with orange facings as belonging to the 8th; but there are no such words in the originals at the War Office and the British Museum. There are pencil notes in the War Office copy indicating that the figures have been transposed.

to introduce uniformity, and to control the idiosyncrasies of colonels, was in 1743. It does not go so fully as might have been expected into details of infantry uniform, and probably the "1742 book" was its basis and supplement. It did lay down:

(1) That drummers of marching regiments (other than "Royal" regiments) were to be clothed with the colours of the facings of their regiment (still orange for the 9th), faced and lappelled with red, and laced in such manner as the colonel should think fit for distinction's sake. The lace was to be of the colour of that on the soldiers' coats. That colour is shown for the 9th in the 1742 book as white, with a red "worm," or zigzag line, and a yellow straight line below it.

(2) The front of the grenadiers' caps was to be of the same colour as the facings of the regiment, with the King's cypher embroidered, and the crown over it. The "little flap," at the bottom of the front, was to be red, with the White Horse (of Hanover) and the motto of the regiment[1] over it. The back part was to be red, with a turn up of the colour of the front (orange for the 9th). The number of the regiment *might* be in figures in the middle part of the back. Regiments were still, in 1743, known officially by their colonel's name and not by numbers.

Another regulation, of 1747, may be passed by, and that of 1751 has already been given in abstract. It changed the facings of the 9th from orange to yellow, and yellow they remained till 1881. A note, furnished by Major Parkyn, shows the lace of the 9th in 1752 as white ground, red line down centre, with a blue one on each side, between it and the margin.

In January, 1753, it was laid down that grenadiers' coats were to have "the usual little ornaments" on the point of the shoulder, and drummers were to have short hanging sleeves like the Foot Guards. Sergeants' coats to be lappelled on the breast with yellow (for the 9th) with white metal buttons. An inspection report of October 10, 1755

---

[1] What appears really to have been meant was the motto "nec aspera terrent," which was not the motto of the 9th, but apparently one belonging to all grenadiers only. It will be remembered that in those days battalions of grenadiers were formed for an army by abstracting the grenadier companies of all its component infantry regiments.

shows the uniform of the 9th as red, faced and lappelled with yellow, bound and looped with a mixed braiding of purple and yellow.

In 1761 the colour of stockings was ordered to be white.

In 1768 appeared the most complete regulation so far issued, dealing in detail with the uniform of all ranks. At the same time there was prepared an illustrated book like that of 1742. Of this there is only one copy extant, in the Prince Consort's Library at Aldershot. It gives a picture of a grenadier private of each regiment. The principal changes and descriptions in this regulation are as follows :

Private (battalion company).—His coat was looped with worsted lace with a white ground and two black stripes on it towards the margins. The exact width of lace, lappels, etc., is prescribed. The lining was white, so as to make turn-backs of that colour at the bottom of the front of the skirt. His pewter buttons bore the number " 9 ."

His waistcoat and breeches were white; gaiters black canvas, with small stiff tops reaching above the knee, and black garters with buckles. The belts were white, and the arms carried were a musket and bayonet, but no sword.[1]

The *grenadier private* differed in having a black bearskin cap tapering into the old mitre shape ; he had a match case (a survival of the days of grenades) on his cross belt. He had " wings " with three loops each on his shoulder points, and he carried a sword, in addition to his musket and bayonet.

The *Drummer's* cap resembled the grenadier's, but had on the front trophies of drums and colours, and the number of the regiment on the back. His coat was yellow, as before, faced with red, and laced at the colonel's discretion, subject to the condition that the ground of the lace corresponded with that on the men's coats. This left the colonel a wide discretion in introducing lines and other ornaments. The yellow wooden drum had painted in front the King's cypher and crown, with the number " IX " under it. Waistcoat, breeches, gaiters the same as the men's, and a short sword with scimitar blade completed his get up.

Sergeants had their coats lappelled to the waist, instead of only on the breast, as with privates and corporals. All sergeants wore, round

[1] Musketeers had ceased to carry swords about 1745.

the waist, a crimson worsted sash with a yellow stripe and an epaulette. The latter was also worn by corporals. In battalion companies they carried halberds and swords, whilst sergeants of grenadiers had, instead of halberds, fuzils and pouches.

Officers' uniforms are described fully, as they had never been before. Their red coats might be plain, without embroidery or lace, but the colonel might, if he chose, require them to be embroidered or laced round the buttonholes. In the 9th the exercise of this discretion is shown in two inspection reports. That of June 1, 1771, at Charles Fort, Kinsale, shows the officers' uniform as having laced silver loops, whilst, on May 26, 1774, it is noted, at Waterford, that it had " silver embroidered holes." There had been a change of colonels in the interval which, no doubt, accounts for the change from lace to embroidery. Battalion company officers carried sword and " esponton,"[1] so did not require the cross belts or pouches of the grenadier officer, who was armed with sword and fuzil.

The sash, of crimson silk, was worn round the waist. The gorget was still worn, being a silver plate, the last relic of armour, with the King's arms and regimental number engraved on it.

The sword knot was crimson and gold, and swords in a regiment were to be uniform pattern, which seems to imply that no general pattern for the whole infantry was required. In a sort of summary for each regiment, at the end of the regulation, it is specially stated that the colour of lace is " white with two black stripes " for the 9th. Officers of battalion companies wore one epaulette, of silver embroidery with silver fringe, on the right shoulder. Grenadier officers had it on both shoulders.

In 1771 the left flank company of all infantry regiments became the light infantry company and introduced new variations in the uniform.

The light infantry wore, instead of a hat, a black leather skull cap, with a black leather upright front.

With the subsequent changes of uniform and arms we need only deal briefly, except where the Norfolk Regiment differed from the general rule for line regiments.

[1] This weapon resembled a light halberd and replaced the half pike.

The chief changes were as follows:

1769. The match cases and swords of grenadier privates were abolished.
1784. The sash to be worn over the right shoulder instead of round the waist.
1786. The "esponton" no longer to be carried by officers, and a new pattern of sword prescribed.
1790. Men supplied with tufts or feathers for hats—red and white for battalion companies, white for grenadiers, green for light infantry.
1791. Field officers to wear two epaulettes; officers of flank companies to have embroidered-on epaulettes, a grenade for grenadiers, or a bugle for light infantry.
1792. Sergeants (battalion companies) to have pikes instead of halberds. Officers of flank companies not to carry fuzils. Sergeants of grenadier companies to carry pikes; those of light companies to retain their fuzils.
1795. Hair powder abolished for non-commissioned officers and men. Non-commissioned officers, drummers, and privates no longer to wear lappels; lace to be put on their coats, as heretofore it had been on their lappels.
1799. Officers and men to wear hair in queues ten inches long.
1800. Cocked hats abolished for battalion companies, except for officers, who continued to wear them. Other ranks were given a black, lacquered, cylindrical hat with leather peak in front. This was also worn by the light company, and by the grenadiers when not wearing their bearskins, a matter left to the colonel's discretion. On the front of the hat was the regimental badge, in the centre of the garter on a brass plate, and the regimental number on each side of the lion. Also in the front there was a black cockade with a regimental button in its centre, or a grenade for grenadiers. Out of this rose a red and white plume for battalion companies, which was changed to white for grenadiers, and green for the light company.
1801. Greatcoats supplied to the men.

1802. Epaulettes abolished for non-commissioned officers.

1804. Queues shortened to eight inches.

1806. Hats not to be lacquered; otherwise not changed. The plate was thin and weak, easily damaged.

1808. Grey trousers replaced breeches and gaiters on active service, and queues, as well as hair powder, finally disappeared.

1809. Distinguishing badges of rank, for the first time introduced for field officers only. The colonel to wear, on the strap of his epaulettes, a crown and star; lieutenant-colonel a crown only; major a star only. The adjutant to have the usual epaulette on the right shoulder, on the left a laced strap only.

1811. The officers' dress on active service was assimilated to that of the men, to prevent their being easily picked off by riflemen. The coat at this time was cut short in front, with tails, something like a modern dress coat, but buttoned up and with shorter tails. It would have been more comfortable than the old coat on service, but for the fact that it had an upright stiff collar and stock, which was anything but an improvement on the soft turned down collar.

In this year a new form of hat was introduced for officers as well as men, and continued till after Waterloo. It was of hard felt with a sort of rounded front to the cylindrical back. In front was a plate, similar to but stronger than that superseded. Across the front were festooned cap lines or cords. Those for officers were gold and red cord; for other ranks white worsted. These terminated in two tassels on the right side of the hat. On the left side a red and white plume (white for grenadiers, green for light infantry) fitted into a socket, outside of which was a black cockade with a button in the centre.

1814. Abolition of brass cap plate for light companies, and substitution of a bugle with the regimental number.

1816. In this year the hat of 1811 was replaced by the heavy bell-topped hat copied from the Prussian army. In front a plume twelve inches high, of the usual colours, fitted into a socket covered, as before, by a cockade. Below the cockade was a brass plate with the regimental number surmounted by a crown, except in the light company which wore a bugle horn. All other devices were prohibited. Instead of the plate, officers wore a circular disc with the number, surmounted by a scaled loop passing up to the cockade, on which were inscribed the battle honours of the regiment. They had a brass scaled chin strap. Round the top of the hat was a two inch border of gold lace, and another, three-quarters of an inch in breadth, at the bottom. Grenadiers had bearskins with a brass chin strap, changed to leather in 1822. Cocked hats were finally abolished for officers.

1820. Short-tailed coats abolished in favour of coatee.

From 1822 the dress regulations were always printed.

1823. In place of breeches, gaiters, and shoes there were adopted for officers blue grey cloth trousers and half boots. The officer wore a coatee and a black beaver cap. Battalion officers wore one epaulette, field-officers two, officers of flank companies wore "wings." The officers' cap feather was upright of red and white, white in grenadier, and green in light company. Except for full dress, when breeches were worn, the officer wore white kerseymere pantaloons, a crimson sash, with bullion fringe ends, round the waist. In undress he had grey trousers.

1828. The officer was given a black beaver hat instead of felt. It was six inches deep, diameter of top, as before, eleven inches, peak of black patent leather, ornamented in front by a gilt star plate surmounted by a crown. The height of the feather was reduced to eight inches. Cap lines as before.

1830. Light companies had a green ball instead of a plume. In this year the lace of the 9th was changed from silver to gold.

1839. A universal brass plate was introduced for other ranks and continued till 1855.

1842. The depth of the officers' black beaver was increased to $6\frac{3}{4}$ inches, top as before, but communicating by black patent leather side straps, $3\frac{1}{2}$ inches apart at the top, with a band of the same round the bottom. There was a black patent leather peak, and the star plate was surmounted by the crown with a lion's head on each side, with a gilt device. In place of the plume was a ball of the usual colours.

This was almost at once replaced by the "Albert" hat, of which the body was beaver for officers, felt for others. It was bound, top and bottom, with black patent leather, and had a peak behind as well as in front. The chin strap was brass for officers, leather for other ranks.

1846. Officers of regiments with badges to wear them on forage caps, instead of the regimental number.

1855. A tunic was substituted for the coatee, and epaulettes were abolished. Rank distinctions were introduced for captains, lieutenants, and ensigns, who wore respectively the same badges as colonels, lieutenant-colonels, and majors, but carried them at each end of the collar instead of on the epaulette.

The shako was now adopted from the French in the Crimea. It was of black felt with patent leather binding and peaks before and behind. Its height was $5\frac{1}{4}$ inches in front, $7\frac{1}{2}$ behind. On the front was a gilt star plate $3\frac{3}{8}$ inches in diameter, and above a red and white ball.

The sash was now worn across the left shoulder.

1860. Shako made of blue stiffened cloth.

1864. Badge to be worn on cap plate, waist belt, and forage cap above the number.

1871. A new shako introduced. It was lighter, only four inches high in front and $6\frac{1}{4}$ behind. Most regiments only had the number in front, without the garter.

1874. The badge to be worn in silver on the shako plate, in addition to the number. Also on waist plate and forage cap.

1881. In this year came a great change in the facings which were to be, for all English and Welsh regiments, white. The Norfolk Regiment had worn yellow facings since 1751. To have lost their yellow facings, after wearing them for 116 years (and having worn orange, which is only a variety of deep yellow, for at least eighteen years before) must necessarily have been a blow to the regiment. Happily, by an order of April 5, 1905, the yellow facings were restored. Eight regiments (Norfolk, Somerset Light Infantry, East Yorkshire, Leicestershire, East Surrey, Loyal North Lancashire, York and Lancaster, and Connaught Rangers) were authorized to wear two black lines on the margins of the officers' gold lace. The origin of these two black lines is not mentioned in the dress regulations of 1884[1] or later. The Leicestershire Regiment claim theirs as being a sign of mourning for Wolfe. In the case of the Norfolk Regiment these two lines date back to the regulation of 1768. The drummers of the Norfolk Regiment had, at any rate, from 1859 to 1871, worn also a central black line in their lace which, it is claimed, was in memory of the presence of part of the regiment at the funeral of Sir John Moore in 1809. The sealed patterns of drummers' lace at the R.U.S.I. show this central black line, as well as those on the margins. These drummers' laces were done away with in 1871, but the following letter sanctions the black line for officers' gold lace :

"HORSE GUARDS.
"*8th July*, 1881.
"Her Majesty has been graciously pleased to approve of the officers of the Norfolk Regiment wearing a black line in their lace, in consideration of the part taken by the late 9th Foot at the burial of Sir John Moore."

Applications to have the black line restored to the drummers' lace have been refused, but the claim to the origin of that in the officers' lace is clearly recognized by the above letter. It might have been thought that the Norfolk Regiment would have worn the two black stripes sanctioned for them, with the seven other regiments, and also a third black stripe, probably in the centre, in consequence of the sanction above quoted. This would have made the lines the same as those on

---

[1] The dress regulations of 1884 were the first issued after the changes of 1881.

the drummers' lace of 1859—1871. This, however, is not so. The officers' lace, like that of the Leicestershire Regiment, who claim that their black stripes are a token of mourning for General Wolfe's death at Quebec, has only the two marginal black stripes. As the letter of 1881 speaks of a " black line," it is not very clear which of the two actually (and properly) worn is the commemorative one.

It seems unnecessary to go further into changes of uniform and arms after 1881, as they do not affect the Norfolk Regiment specially.

The Badge of Britannia.

The following letter speaks for itself:—

" Horse Guards.
" 30th July, 1799.

" Sir,

I have received His Royal Highness the Commander in Chief's directions to signify to you that His Majesty has been pleased to confirm to the Ninth Regiment of Foot the distinction and privilege of bearing the figure " Britannia " as the badge of the regiment.

" I have &c.,

(Signed) H. CALVERT.

" Adjutant General."

The letter was addressed to Lieutenant-General Bertie, the colonel of the Ninth. The word " confirm " should be noted as admitting a previous claim, and probably user.

Cannon rightly says that no mention of the badge appears in the regulation of 1751; he might have added the previous one of 1743.

Apparently he did not look up the original of the 1768 regulation, which he says also contained no mention of it.

We have turned it up in the Public Record Office. It is a lengthy printed document with supplements, one of which gives a list of recognized regimental badges. In print the badge of the 18th Royal Irish immediately follows that of the 8th Foot. But between the two are inserted in writing in ink, the following words: " 9th or East Norfolk Regiment—

HISTORY OF THE NORFOLK REGIMENT

the figure of Britannia as a badge—*vide* Letter book No. 10, page 236." Unfortunately, it is impossible to trace any letter-book of this number, either in the Public Record Office or the War Office. Officials at the former thought the writing was probably of the eighteenth century, but it is quite clear from the words " East Norfolk Regiment " that it could not have been made before 1782, when that title was first given to the 9th. On the whole, the probability seems to be that it was made in 1799, on the decision of July 30, 1799. Anyhow, it seems to show that the War Office recognized the title as extending back at least to 1768.

The regiment claim that it was granted by Queen Anne after the campaign of 1707 in Spain, when the regiment was practically annihilated at Almanza. Unfortunately, we have to confess defeat in our search for written evidence of this grant, just as Cannon had to. However, it is quite clear that the tradition was in full force long before 1799, when the badge was " confirmed," and all doubt as to the regiment's title to it ended.

It seems probable that the question was threshed out in consequence of the following report by Lieutenant-General Garth of his inspection of the 9th at Yarmouth in 1798. " The breast plates have a device-Britannia—upon them ; the drums are of brass,[1] and have the same device painted upon them ; the colours nothing but rags, so that nothing could be seen upon them."

The receipt of this report no doubt made the War Office start an investigation.

On October 31, 1890, the officer commanding the 1st Battalion received, from the Rev. J. Studholme Brownrigg, a copy of the letter of 1799 from the Horse Guards, and of the following one, both of which he found among the papers of his father, General Brownrigg, to whom they probably came from his great uncle, Sir R. Brownrigg, who was colonel of the 9th from 1805 to 1833 :—

" NORWICH, *9th March*, 1797.
" I had a long letter from Major Baillie, late of the 9th Regiment, about the badge of the 9th Regiment, of which he

---
[1] Brass drums replaced wooden ones in 1789.

gives the following account from Major Bolton and other officers who were in the Regiment long before him. 'That it was gained at the siege or battle of Saragossa in Spain, and also liberty to beat drums thro' the city of London, as well as the Buffs on the same occasion. This last was done by Captain Dobbyn with a company of the 9th, so late as the year 1781. The badge lay dormant for several years because General Whitmore (Colonel of 9th) *would not pay £5 5s. od for embroidering Britannia on the Colours.* That in 1776 the Regiment applied to Lord Ligonier to have it revived, which he immediately consented to, as far as I recollect with the King's approbation, and the officers in Canada in consequence wore Silver Britannias on their caps (the whole army there wearing Caps and Jackets) and Lord Saye and Sele had the Badge also put on the Colours, Drums, etc., when he got the regiment.' Since which time we have continued to wear it and *I hope with honour—who dare say to the contrary?*

"(Signed) ALEX LORAINE.

Captain, 9th Foot.

"Colonel Fisher,
"9th Regiment."

This carries back the tradition a long way, as Major Bolton joined the regiment in January 7, 1750, and "other officers who were in the regiment long before him" are referred to. The story about the "siege or battle of Saragossa" is doubtful, as the regiment was in Ireland at the time of Stanhope's battle of 1710, and does not appear to have played any part in the siege of 1707. We prefer Almanza. The part about the right to beat their drums through London is also interesting, but the claim would perhaps now be difficult to enforce, after being in abeyance since 1781.[1] If the story of General Whitmore's parsimony is true it will hardly raise his reputation in the regiment. According to Colonel Shepherd's history of the 2nd Battalion, there was an entry

[1] On this subject see an article in the Journal of the R.U.S.I. for May, 1923. No mention is made of the Norfolk Regiment or any claim by them.

HISTORY OF THE NORFOLK REGIMENT

in an old record book of the orderly-room that the badge " was granted by H.M. King George III to Colonel Hill, to be worn as an insignia of the corps for its bravery under the command of that officer during the contest between Great Britain and her colonies in North America." We have found no evidence of this version, which is hardly probable, and certainly not likely to be acceptable to the regiment as against the Almanza story.

The Britannia appears in several different forms:

(1) On a fragment of the colours presented in December, 1798, now at Sandhurst, with a mural crown instead of a helmet. She has a spear in her left hand and a laurel (? olive) branch in her right. She faces to her right. The shield in all cases bears the " Union."

(2) In a tailor's pattern book—with a helmet; facing to her left, with shield on right, and a lion lying on her left. Spear in right, olive branch in left hand.

Another drawing in the same book reverses this as regards aspect, shield, lion, spear, and branch.

(3) On a shako plate (1830—1844), in the same book. Britannia in silver, with trident in left and branch in right hand. Lion on her right, shield on left. The figure IX below in gold. Her badge is surrounded by scrolls with the then sanctioned battle honours, viz. Roliça, Vimiera, Busaco, Vittoria, Nive, Peninsula, San Sebastian.

(4) On a silver stamped shako plate of about 1809—1815, in the collection of Major Parkyn, with a wreath on her head, olive branch in right, spear in left hand, shield on left, facing to her right. Underneath " IX.R. E. G."

(5) On a shoulder belt plate of 1830; facing to her right, with branch in right, trident in left hand, lion on right, and shield on left. Nothing on her head.

(6) On a cap badge of 1860. Facing to her right and similar to above, except that she wears a helmet.

(7) In accordance with the dress regulations of 1884 she appears, on the waist plate only, with the castle of Norwich below. The castle is not prescribed for the badge on buttons, collar, helmet plate, or forage cap. The same order reappears in 1894, but not later. The

castle was the old badge of the Norfolk Militia, and was introduced on the waistbelt after 1881, when the Militia battalions were amalgamated with the regulars.

(8) In 1900 the Britannia on the field forage cap has below a tablet inscribed " The Norfolk Regiment."

(9) The dress regulations of 1911 describe the figure as " holding an olive branch in the right hand; the trident rests against the left shoulder."[1]

Militia Uniforms.

With regard to Militia uniforms, they appear to have been generally similar to those of regular regiments, but the Norfolk militia battalion wore gold lace, instead of silver, down to 1857, when silver was ordered.

In 1880, and onwards to 1830, both East and West Norfolk Militia had black facings.

In 1814 officers wore, on a red coat, black cuffs and collars, white breeches, gold lace and loops with square ends. The men's lace had, in the West Norfolk Militia, a red and a black worm. The East Norfolk had only a black one.

---

[1] The following notes on the figure of Britannia have been kindly furnished by the Keeper of Coins at the British Museum :—

" The modern type of Britannia, a free imitation of the old Roman type, first appeared in 1665 on the design for the farthing by Jan Roettiers. Frances Stuart, afterwards Duchess of Richmond, sat for Britannia (see " Pepys' Diary," February, 1666–7).

" She holds a spear in her left and an olive branch in her right hand. Under Anne the features of Britannia seem to resemble those of the Queen. The type continues substantially the same till 1797, when Küchler produced Britannia holding an olive branch in her right and a *trident* in her left hand. I do not know of a Britannia with a trident before this date.

" The figure faces to the left throughout until the reign of George IV, when she was turned round and provided with a helmet.

" You may, I think, assume that specimens of the badge with the spear are older than 1797. But there is nothing in the pose or other details which definitely fix the badge to Queen Anne."

The above was written with reference to the present regimental badge.

In 1859 the drummers' lace was thus:

1st or West Norfolk Militia.—White ground—two red lines and blue labels between.

2nd or East Norfolk.—White ground, one red and one black line. Labels red.

The badge of the regiment was the arms of the City of Norwich, representing the castle built originally by Offa first King of the East Angles. Below the castle was the lion of England from the arms of Henry IV, who had conferred considerable privileges on the city.

In 1881, when the militia battalions became the 3rd and 4th of the Norfolk Regiment, the castle was worn on the waistbelt of the amalgamated regiment. The lion also appears to have been there, but disappeared almost at once.

The castle is last mentioned in the dress regulations of 1894. The next regulation did not appear till 1902 when the waist plate disappeared on the officers' sash being worn round the waist, instead of over the left shoulder.

Motto.

In October, 1887, Colonel Massy wrote to Sir Arthur Borton: " I am now trying to get back our old motto " Firm," remembering the tradition when I joined the Regiment under you long ago. General Brownrigg told me the other day he recollected it."

Regarding this motto the only evidence we have come across is a marginal note, " Motto," to some notes on the Regiment prepared by Colonel Massy as follows :

" An old tradition asserts that, after the battle of Almanza, the motto ' Firm,' in addition to the badge Britannia, was conferred on the regiment for the determined valour evinced by officers and men alike on that trying occasion. In Ree's Encyclopædia (1820), under Heraldry, there is an engraving of a Ninth colour displaying the word ' Firm ' under the badge."

Colonel Massy does not appear to have been successful in his attempt to get back the motto.

APPENDIX IV

COLOURS AND BATTLE HONOURS

When Colonel Cornwall's regiment was raised in 1685 there were no such things as King's colours and Regimental colours. In each regiment of infantry the colonel, lieutenant-colonel, major, and the captains of companies had each his own flag. The colonel's was generally a plain colour throughout. Colonel Cornwall's was orange, the same as the facings of his regiment, and that was the ground colour of all the flags. The lieutenant-colonel's differed from the colonel's in having at the centre a small white square bearing the red cross of St. George. The major's was the same as the lieutenant-colonel's, with the distinction of a white " flame " in the top corner nearest to the staff or pike, extending diagonally down towards the centre. The first captain's flag had the white square with St. George's cross, as with the lieutenant-colonel's. It had not the major's flame, but over the white square there was a silver roundle. Some regiments had, instead of the roundle, a numeral, according to the seniority of the captain's company. Mr. Milne suggests that, as no numeral was used in Cornwall's regiment, the second captain may have had two roundles and so on. However, with a twelve or thirteen company regiment, the number of roundles would have run up to nine or ten (omitting the companies commanded by the three field officers) and there would hardly have been room for so many on the flag, if they were of the relative size shown on page 48 of Mr. Milne's book. He could find no definite information as to captains' flags of Cornwall's regiment other than that of the first.

Under William III the flags were reduced to three,—the colonel's, lieut-colonel's, and major's. It is not known what, if any, device was on them.

With the Union with Scotland, in 1707, came a change. If you place the red cross of St. George with its white edging on the top of the white cross of St. Andrew, the whole on a blue ground, you get as the result the old Union flag. Of this a small edition now appeared in the colonel's flag, in the top corner nearest the staff. The rest of the flag appears to have been decorated according to the Colonel's fancy, with his crest, or arms, or other devices.

The lieutenant-colonel's flag was probably the plain Union, but this is not quite certain. It is said the Union was first carried by the regiment at Almanza in 1707. Seeing that the Act of Union only received the Royal assent on the 6th March, and the battle was fought on April 25th the story seems improbable.

The first real regulation of the colours occurred in the clothing warrant of 1743, which commences with a prohibition, addressed to all colonels, against putting their own arms, crests, devices, or livery on any part of their regiment's clothing or equipment. This prohibition was repeated in subsequent regulations up to 1768. Previously to this colonels had exercised their own discretion in putting their crests, arms, or other devices in the centre of the colours. The first colour of every marching regiment was to be the great union, the second colour to be the colour of the facings of the regiment, with the Union in the upper canton, except regiments with white or red facings. The 9th, with their orange facings, were not covered by the exception.

In the centre is to be painted, in gold Roman figures, the number of the rank of the regiment within a wreath of roses and thistles on one stalk, except those regiments which were allowed to wear royal devices or ancient badges. In those cases the number was to be towards the upper corner. The length of the pike and size of the colours to be the same as those of the Foot Guards. Cords and tassels of all colours to be crimson and gold. The regulation then says " All the Royal Regiments the Fusilier and Marine Regiments, the old Buffs, the 5th and 6th Regiments, the 8th or King's Regiment, and the 27th or Inniskilling Regiment are distinguished by particular devices, and therefore not subject to the preceding articles for colours." There is no mention of Britannia for the 9th.

The regulation of 1751 is practically the same as this regarding colours, except that the first stand of colours is described as the "King's" and the second as the "Regimental." The ground of the regimental colour was orange in 1743, yellow in 1751, in accordance with the facings of the time. The regimental number "IX" appeared in the centre of the cross of St. George in the King's colour, and the centre of the regimental colours, with a wreath round it.[1]

We propose to deal with the history of the colours of the battalions successively. There is no record traceable of any colours of the (old) 3rd Battalion in its short period of existence from 1799 to 1802. As the 2nd Battalion did not apparently have any till 1806, two years after their second raising, it appears probable that the 3rd also had none during the period in question.

1st Battalion.

The oldest infantry colours of the British Army known to be still in existence appear to be those which Colonel Hill rescued in his baggage at the capitulation of Saratoga in 1777, which has been already alluded to in the account of that campaign. These colours are now in the Chapel at the R.M.C. Sandhurst. They appear to have been given back to Colonel Hill when he presented them to the King on his return from captivity. They eventually came into the possession of a descendant of Colonel Hill, the Rev. E. J. Rogers, who was chaplain at Sandhurst. He, with his son, Colonel Rogers of the Royal Irish Regiment, presented them for deposit in the R.M.C. Chapel.

---

[1] We have said elsewhere that regiments were only known by their colonel's name down to 1751, but this is not quite accurate. They were generally known by the colonel's name, but the "number of its rank" had been assigned to each regiment then in being so far back as 1694, and Mr. Milne quotes the "Gentleman's Magazine" of 1736 as speaking of the 1st, 2nd, etc., Regiments. Still, it is true that the colonel's name was generally used, even in official correspondence, up to 1751 and often later.

The following, with reference to them, is extracted from the regimental record of services :

"1887. May 7th. An escort consisting of Captain J. L. Govan, Lieutenants E. C. Peebles, H. G. Levinge, and A. J. Bateman-Champain ; Sergeant-Major Connors, six sergeants and fifty rank and file proceeded to the R.M.C. Sandhurst, to take part in the ceremony of trooping the old colours of the Regiment carried from about 1767 to 1777. These colours had passed into the possession of the Rev. E. J. Rogers, Chaplain to the Forces, a descendant of Colonel Hill, Colonel of the Regiment, and were by him presented to the R.M.C. The colours, having been trooped, were deposited by the above escort in the chapel of the College, and there placed beside the old Peninsular Colours of the Regiment which were deposited in the same place by General Sir Duncan Cameron, Governor of the College and son of Sir John Cameron who commanded the regiment during the Peninsular war, and who was subsequently appointed its full colonel."

Milne has shown clearly that the centre portion of the regimental colour was of much earlier manufacture than the rest, and that it was really cut out of an older colour and sewn on to a new piece of yellow silk. He remarks that the regimental colour " for various reasons, always wore better, and did not require replacing as soon as its companion." On a study of the style of this centre, he attributes its manufacture approximately to the year 1757. As we know, from an inspection report dated Dublin, May 9, 1768, that the regiment then had colours which had been presented in 1759, we may assume that this centre was finished in 1759 and that the "Saratoga" regimental colour, which was presented in 1772, thus represents, not only itself, but, to some extent, that of 1759. It does not bear the Britannia badge, but, as it was presented very early in the colonelcy of Lord Ligonier, it was in existence and commission before he had taken up the question of reviving the use of the badge, which had dropped out in General Whitmore's colonelcy.[1]

[1] *Cf. supra*, Lieutenant Loraine's letter of March 9, 1797.

In connexion with the "Saratoga" colours should be mentioned the colours of the New Hants (American) Regiment, which were captured by the 9th at Fort Anne. These appear to have been saved by Colonel Hill with those of his own regiment. They also were offered by Mr. Rogers to the R.M.C., but declined on the weak ground that to hang them in the chapel might offend American susceptibilities. They were afterwards lent for exhibition to the Royal United Service Museum, and eventually sold to the State of New Hampshire, U.S.A. There is a photograph of them in the "Holy Boy" of July, 1912.

The next colours after those of Saratoga were no doubt (though no record is traceable) presented when the Saratoga ones were returned to Colonel Hill, somewhere about 1782. This must have been the set which General Garth in 1798 described as "nothing but rags."[1]

The following from the "Norwich Mercury" of December 15, 1798, shows the fate of the "rags":

"On Wednesday the colours of the 9th Foot, worn by service literally to a rag, were burned, and the ashes buried with great ceremony, and new colours were received. Major Sandieman addressed the regiment in a very appropriate manner. The Yarmouth Volunteer cavalry, and both corps of Volunteer infantry, accompanied the regiment on the occasion."

Of the colours received at Yarmouth in December, 1798, after the burning of the old ones, there remains only a fragment of the centre of the regimental colour, which also is at Sandhurst. This bears the Britannia, on an oval shield of red cloth with a yellow scroll round it, the whole being surrounded by a wreath of roses and thistles only. As these colours were received more than a year before the Union with Ireland, the shamrock naturally does not appear in the wreath. Milne infers that the regiment probably received a new set, with the shamrock, soon after 1800. Britannia is seated facing to her right with the shield on her left. She wears a crown, not a helmet, and has no lion.

[1] Cf. *supra*, p. 371.

This brings us to a set of colours which require a somewhat lengthy discussion.

In the officers' mess of the 1st Battalion is a set of colours, framed. How they were acquired is shown by the following inscription on a brass plate: "These old colours of the 1/9th Foot were purchased in June, 1901, by Lieutenant-Colonel D. K. Robertson, late commanding 1st Battalion Norfolk Regiment, and presented to his old battalion—24th September, 1901."

The regimental colour is a faded yellow. In the top left hand corner is the Union. In the centre is a red heart-shaped shield on which are inscribed in gold letters the words "1st Battalion—IX Regiment." The shield is surrounded by a wreath of roses, thistles, and shamrock interwined. There is no badge of Britannia, and no battle honours.

The King's colour is the Union with wreath, etc., in the centre, the same as the regimental colour. As some doubts appear to have been expressed as to whether these colours are genuine, we shall endeavour to show that the suspicion is probably unfounded.[1]

Colonel Robertson purchased the colours in London, the vendor being a Mr. Crook. Other relics connected with the Duke of Wellington were sold by him at the same time. They were to have been auctioned, but Colonel Robertson, being anxious that this should not occur, made a private offer, of a not unreasonable amount, which was accepted. Before the sale Mr. Crook appears to have wanted to satisfy himself that the colours of the 9th were genuine, and received in reply to his inquiry a letter from his mother, dated March 7, 1901, in which she says: "Your flags are genuine. Have been in our families certainly thirty-five years at least; I do not know who gave them to Mrs. Baynton, but the Duke of Wellington was her great friend." Mrs. Crook evidently

---

[1] We are much indebted to Mrs. D. K. Robertson for allowing us access to her late husband's notes and correspondence on the subject, which are freely used in what follows. Another letter of July 7, 1903, from Colonel Robertson has since come to light. It differs from the others as to the name of the vendor, but Mrs. Baynton here also figures as having got the colours from the Duke of Wellington. She is stated to have married one Elsmlie, whose son by a former marriage is named as the vendor of 1901.

believed that the colours had been given to her relative, Mrs. Baynton, by the Duke.

To begin with practical considerations. Who would be in the least likely to fabricate a set of colours, and then pass them to a family who clearly did not buy them at a high price, and moreover had no apparent connexion with the regiment? Moreover, anybody attempting to raise money by a fraud would undoubtedly have put the badge of Britannia on the colours, as it was on the colours of 1798. Old colours in those days, when they were given to the colonel or Lieutenant-Colonel, would hardly fetch a high price, so their fabrication would not be a profitable business. These colours, if genuine, would certainly be of a date subsequent to 1800, as before that date colours would not have the shamrock in the wreath. It seems clear, therefore, that it is most unlikely that these colours were fabricated by anyone and foisted on to the Baynton-Crook family. The Mrs. Baynton referred to was perhaps the second wife of a Dr. Baynton, perhaps the Dr. Baynton mentioned in the "Dictionary of National Biography." At one time she lived in Paris, and it is possible she may have known the Duke of Wellington there.

Now we come to the question of what these colours could have been. It will be remembered that Milne surmises that the colours of 1798 were probably replaced soon after the Union, so as to get in the shamrock in the wreath. On the face of it, it does not seem likely that the colours of 1798 would be replaced so soon; but it must be remembered that they were carried in the very trying campaign in Holland in 1799, and may well have been considerably damaged in it. A note of Colonel Robertson's suggests that the colours he had bought could only have been carried in the period 1801 to 1809. In his letter of July, 1903, Colonel Robertson suggests 1809, on the ground that the colours replaced in 1827 would probably be about twenty years old when replaced.

What we would suggest is that the colours of 1798 were replaced in consequence of damage in the 1799 campaign, that they were replaced by Colonel Robertson's colours, and that these again were replaced, whilst the regiment was on service in the Peninsula under Wellington, after 1809. As they are in such condition as to indicate that they had not seen much service, it is possible they may have been replaced after Vimeiro, or on starting on that campaign. If they were replaced on service in the Peninsula (of which we can find no documentary evidence), it is quite comprehensible that they might have come into the possession of the Duke as commander-in-chief.

The great difficulty is the absence of the badge. It has been suggested that the badge may have been on them originally, but been taken off them and sewn on to the new colours, as was done with the centre of the colours of 1759. The badge was probably sewn on, not embroidered direct on the silk. The colours have been carefully examined by Lieutenant R. D. Ambrose and the master tailor of the 1st Battalion. Lieutenant Ambrose reports as follows : "*The Regimental Colour.*—This is composed of yellow silk. In the centre is a red (or crimson) piece of silk, heart-shaped. This has undoubtedly been sewn on, but whether to hide any stitches in the centre is hard to tell. The master tailor is of the opinion it is not an original centre piece. *The King's Colour.* This has a red background. The centre piece is also red ; shaped the same as the regimental colour centre piece. The master tailor is of the opinion that the centre piece is original, both background and centre piece being of the same colour, and where faded or torn, it is continuous. The centre piece is not a separate design, is part of the original." It was not safe to remove the colours from their frame.

This, though interesting, does not throw light on the suggestion that the Britannia was removed, and the idea remains hypothetical.

The next colours, after those of 1798, of which there is a record of the presentation are those presented by Lady Cameron, wife of Sir John, at Plymouth in 1827. It is hardly possible that the colours of 1798 should have lasted for twenty-eight years, all through the many trying campaigns in the interval, and that is another argument in favour of there having been an intermediate set between them and the colours which were replaced in 1827.

The colours purchased by Colonel Robertson may very well have been those hypothetical intermediate ones, and may have had their Britannia badge removed to be sewn on to those replaced by Lady Cameron's presentation. It must be admitted that this theory is not supported by any documentary or other positive evidence.

In the R.M.C. Chapel, Sandhurst, is a set of colours deposited there in 1875 by Sir Duncan Cameron, G.C.B., Governor of the College, and son of Sir John Cameron. Though Milne says it is doubtful if these colours belonged to the 1st or the 2nd Battalion, we must express a strong opinion in favour of their having been those of the 1st, which were replaced in 1827. Our reasons are as follows: Colonel Shepherd, in his history of the 2nd Battalion, states that it has been found impossible to trace the colours carried by that battalion at the time of its disbandment in 1815. Again, in 1815 Sir John Cameron was Lieutenant-colonel of the 1st Battalion. It is true he had commanded the 2nd from October, 1807, to May, 1809; but in 1815 the lieutenant-colonel of the 2nd Battalion was Lieutenant-Colonel W. Gordon McGregor. The probability is that the colours, on disbandment, would have gone either to Lieutenant-Colonel McGregor or to the Colonel of the regiment, Sir R. Brownrigg. We have referred to Sir Douglas Brownrigg the present baronet, but he is unable to find any trace of the colours having been presented to the first Sir Robert Brownrigg. For the present therefore Colonel Shepherd's conclusion must be accepted.

On the new colours of 1827 there are the following records. Major General Hawes, in a note of March 19, 1901, quoted by Colonel Robertson, says:

> "These colours, presented by Lady Cameron in 1827, were carried by me at the battles of Ferozeshah and Sobraon, 1845—46, the regimental at Ferozeshah, the King's at Sobraon.
>
> "The 1827 colours were mere shreds—the King's almost a bare pole, the regimental somewhat better, with figure of Britannia. One pole, part of top shot off, and one bent with a hole through it, where a colour-sergeant who carried it in the Khyber was shot in 1842."

Colonel Robertson had also heard from Colonel Hook, who was adjutant of the regiment in the Sutlej campaign, that he remembered the 1827 colours being sent to Sir Thomas Arbuthnot (then colonel of the regiment) in 1848. Sir Thomas, at that time, was commanding the troops at Manchester.

Colonel Hook also spoke of these colours being in shreds. The poles were continued in use with the new colours presented in 1848.

It appears that the whereabouts of the " shreds " of the 1827 colours have never been fully traced. Sir Thomas Arbuthnot's family were unable to throw any light on the subject. In a note to Colonel Robertson, Captain Inglis writes: " I fancy that the only portions of these colours now extant are the fragment in General Hawes' possession, and the Britannia given to the Depôt by Mrs. Gaynor. The shreds sent to Sir T. Arbuthnot, without the poles, are scarcely likely to have survived."

The Britannia presented by Mrs. Gaynor is at the Depôt at Norwich. It consists of the centre portion of the colour (Britannia looking to her left with a leaf of shamrock below) on a yellow silk background. The inscription, on a silver plate at the bottom of the carved oak frame, runs as follows :

"This relic of the Regimental Colour of the 9th Regiment carried through the 1st Afghan and Sutlej campaigns 1842—1845 was presented in 1889 to the Depôt Norfolk Regiment by Mrs. Gaynor, widow of Captain Charles Gaynor, late 9th Regiment. The frame is the gift of Colonel C. S. Perry, late commanding 2nd Battalion Norfolk Regiment, on relinquishing command of the 9th Regimental District 25th March, 1895."

The frame is surmounted by a figure of Britannia standing, with the figure IX below.

The 1827 colours were replaced in 1848 by those presented at Newry by Major-General Bainbrigge.[1] These were replaced, after being carried for nearly forty years, in 1887, and, as already narrated, were deposited in Sandringham Church.[2]

[1] Cf. *supra*, Vol. I, p. 326.   [2] Cf. *supra*, Vol. I, p. 384.

They had been repaired, about 1886, by Mrs. Robertson, Mrs. Terry, and Mrs. Sunderland, wives of officers in the regiment, and Miss Hawes, daughter of General Hawes. Some of the names of the older battles which had been lost were replaced at the same time, and the new honours " Kabul 1879 " and " Afghanistan 1879—80 " were added.

Captain Inglis writes regarding the date of repair, of which Colonel Robertson was not sure : " This must have been 1886, as at that time I handed over the old honour ' Sevastopol,' which had come off in my hands when carrying the regimental colour on the Queen's birthday parade in 1883, to be replaced. The present colours (new pattern) were taken out and used at Gibraltar from December, 1885, to July, 1886, prior to presentation, the old ones being sent to the Depôt at Yarmouth."

The 1887 colours were replaced, after twenty-one years' service, in 1909 and were also deposited in Sandringham Church.[1]

In concluding these notes on the 1st Battalion colours, we must refer to a private letter, written in 1901 by the late Mr. Milne to Captain Inglis, in explanation of the note at page 127 of his book, in which he says he saw parts of five stands of colours at Sandhurst. He writes: "There were therefore at Sandhurst (eliminating the two Saratoga colours) parts of three sets—

" (A.) part of the regimental colour of 1799.[2]

" (B.) Regimental Colour, in fair order, on its proper brass bound pole.

" (C.) the companion brass bound pole—that of the King's colour, but without any remains of the colour.

" (D.) centre of King's colour, of another stand altogether, with a scroll ' East Norfolk Regiment ' attached to it."

This is further explained by sketches with notes to them. In these sketches one pole is that of the regimental colour of the " Old Peninsula Colours " (those replaced as we hold, in 1827) with its proper regimental colour on it.

The other pole is that of the King's colour and companion to the

---

[1] Cf. *supra*, Vol. I, p. 390. [2] Should be December, 1798.

one above mentioned. It has no remains of the King's colour belonging to it; but there are attached to it as follows—

(1) To the upper part, the remains of the regimental colour of 1799 (really December, 1798);

(2) Below this is attached to the pole a small fragment, marked D on the sketch. Of this Mr. Milne notes, " D is a small fragment of a King's colour, it has a small scroll attached to it with ' East Norfolk.' A close observation led me to think that the scroll in question had originally been mounted on yellow silk; therefore that it must have appeared upon the regimental colour of which (*D*) is the King's."

To sum up, the colours of the regiment at Sandhurst appear really to be:

(1) King's and regimental colours of 1772 (saved at Saratoga), the centre of the regimental colour being a survival of the previous colours of 1759.

(2) Regimental colour carried in the Peninsula and replaced in 1827. This is on its own pole.

(3) The pole of the King's colour corresponding to (2) above.

(4) The regimental colour of 1799 (1798) attached to (3) above.

(5) Fragment of a King's colour, attached to pole (3) above, and attached to this a fragment of the scroll from the corresponding regimental colour.

The 2nd Battalion

After it was first constituted in 1798 the 2nd Battalion appears to have had no colours till a set was presented to them by Sir Robert Brownrigg, at Tamworth, on July 30, 1806.

As above mentioned, what became of these colours when the 2nd Battalion was disbanded for the second time in 1815 is unknown. After its third and last embodiment in 1857, the 2nd Battalion was first presented with colours, on March 3, 1859, at Corfu.

These colours were replaced in 1892 by the colours issued but never formally presented. The reasons for this have already been explained.[1]

On August 10, 1896 the old colours of 1859 were deposited in Norwich Cathedral, where they still are. There is little more than the pole of the King's colour, but of the regimental colour about half remains attached to the pole. The deposit was made with some ceremony by Lieutenant-Colonel Shepherd, D.S.O., and a party of officers and non-commissioned officers from Aldershot.

The colours of 1892 appear to have lasted till after the period with which this history deals, and to have been laid up on September 14, 1919. They were presented to H.M. King George V, after presentation of new colours, and deposited in Sandringham Church.

MILITIA COLOURS

Sir Charles Harvey, in his "History of the 4th Battalion Norfolk Regiment,"[2] quotes an order dated May 28, 1761, signed by Pitt, for the supply of new colours to both battalions of Norfolk Militia, whose old colours had been rendered unfit for service. There is nothing to show how or when the older colours were acquired.

Sir Charles makes no further mention of colours till April 8, 1854, when a full description of the presentation of new colours to the East Norfolk Militia Battalion is given. We cannot say whether the colours then replaced were those of 1761 There is no mention in the account of the presentation (by the Earl of Leicester, Lord Lieutenant of the county) of any old colours being on the field, and no reference is made to them in the account, or in the speeches. They probably disappeared during the long period after the Napoleonic wars when the militia was in abeyance.

The West Norfolk Militia received their colours, corresponding to the East Norfolk colours of 1854, on June 12 1855. The colours were presented with the usual ceremonial by the Countess of Albemarle,

---

[1] Cf. *supra*, Vol. I, p. 397.   [2] Page 42.

HISTORY OF THE NORFOLK REGIMENT

wife of the colonel of the regiment. The remarks above made, regarding older colours of the East Norfolk battalion, apply equally to the West Norfolk.

Sir Charles Harvey records that the colours of 1854 were still carried by the East Norfolk Battalion in 1898, and they and the 1855 colours of the West Norfolk Militia lasted till the disbandment of the Militia on the reorganization of the army in 1908.

Both sets are now in the Castle Museum, Norwich. They were presented to the Museum: (a) Colours of the 1st West Norfolk Militia (III Battalion Norfolk Regiment) in April, 1910, by Colonel Custance, C.B. and Colonel Sir Kenneth Kemp, Bt.; (b) colours of the East Norfolk Militia (IV Battalion Norfolk Regiment) deposited in May, 1908, through Colonel Danby.

A set of colours of the West Norfolk Battalion is stated to be at Wolferton, but the date of its presentation to the battalion is unknown.

The colours of the 4th and 5th Territorial Battalions were presented by H.M. King Edward VII on October 25, 1909, and are still in use.

COLOURS OF SERVICE BATTALIONS RAISED FOR THE WAR OF 1914—18

7th Battalion.—In January, 1919, H.R.H. the Prince of Wales presented to this battalion, then in France, its King's colour. On September 4, 1919, after a memorial service for all Norfolk men who had laid down their lives in the Great War, these colours were handed over to the care of the Dean and Chapter of Norwich Cathedral, where they now hang in the south nave.

8th Battalion.—Owing to its disbandment in February, 1918, this battalion appears never to have received any colours. Had it still been in existence at the Armistice, no doubt it would have received the same treatment as the 7th and 9th.

9th Battalion.—The King's colour was presented in Germany (Brühl) on February 1, 1919, by General Sir H. C. O. Plumer, G.C.B. The battalion ceased to exist on May 18th, and on September 4th the colour was deposited in Norwich Cathedral, at the same time and under the same circumstances as that of the 7th. It also hangs in the south nave.

The 12th Battalion (Yeomanry), being only temporarily part of the Norfolk Regiment, of course has its own Yeomanry colours.

Miscellaneous Flags, Etc.

With the 1st Battalion are :

(1) One of the banners presented in 1914 to the regiments of the first seven divisions. This is in the officers' mess.

(2) Each company has the " company flag " presented in France in 1915. In the centre is the Britannia, and round it the dates of the several actions in which the company was engaged. Above the badge is the name Mons.

(3) In the Orderly room is the flag taken with the headquarters in 1914 and carried till 1918.

Battle Honours.

The battle honours of the Norfolk Regiment, according to the Army List of 1922, are, so far, " Havannah," " Martinique, 1794," " Roliça," " Vimiera," " Corunna," " Busaco," " Salamanca," " Vittoria," " San Sebastian," " Nive," " Peninsula," " Cabool 1842," " Moodkee," " Ferozeshah," " Sobraon," " Sevastopol," " Kabul 1879," " Afghanistan 1879—80," " Paardeberg," " South Africa 1900—02."

The two 1st, " Havannah " and " Martinique 1794," were not authorized for any of the regiments which bear them till so late as November, 1909.[1] The dates of authorization of the others were as

---

[1] Colonel Marriott also applied at this time for the honours " Guadeloupe " and " St. Lucia," but these were refused. It will be remembered that at Guadeloupe only the flank companies of the 9th were employed. At the taking of St. Lucia only the flank companies were landed. Later the whole regiment was employed there, but only in suppressing insurrection.

follows : " Roliça," 1820 ; " Vimiera," 1820 [1]; " Corunna," 1835 ; " Busaco," 1819 ; " Salamanca," 1820 ; " Vittoria," 1820 ; " San Sebastian," 1820 ; " Nive," 1820 ; " Peninsula," 1815 ; " Cabool 1842," 1845 ; " Moodkee," 1847 ; " Ferozeshah," 1847 ; " Sobraon," 1847 ; " Sevastopol," 1857 ; " Kabul 1879—80," 1881 ; " Afghanistan 1879—80," 1881 ; " Paardeberg " and " South Africa 1900—02," 1904.

The narrative of the doings of the Norfolk Regiment during an existence of nearly 240 years has shown their title to all the honours so far awarded to them. There are others, previous to the great War, to which one would have thought them entitled. For Almanza, like other defeats, no battle honour was awarded. If it had been, the Norfolk Regiment should surely have had it. Belleisle also does not appear as a battle honour. Had it done so the Norfolk Regiment should have had it. There are three Peninsula honours for battles at which the Norfolk Regiment was present but received no honour. In the case of Badajoz they can hardly complain, for they took no active part in the assault ; at Fuentes de Oñoro likewise they were not seriously engaged, though the 5th division of which they were part, performed a very useful and important part in detaining a large French force in their front. With Barossa the case is different. The flank companies of the 2nd Battalion were in the very thick of the battle, as part of Browne's Battalion. The battalion lost very heavily for those days, but none of the regiments (9th, 47th, and 82nd) whose flank companies only were engaged bear the honour. The argument against them no doubt would be that the companies were only parts of a composite battalion, but it must be remembered that there are several instances where honours have been awarded notwithstanding the absence of head-quarters.[2]

---

[1] It is a curious fact that in 1819 the regiment had been authorized to bear the honour " Talavera." Neither battalion having been at that battle, this part of the order was cancelled in September, 1820, and " Rolica " and " Vimiera " substituted. The two authorizations are amongst the regimental records.

[2] For example, the 1st and 2nd Gurhka Regiments, each of which bears the honour " Bhurtpore," though each had only about 200 men at the siege. Other instances are given in Norman's " Battle Honours of the British Army," p. 435.

BATTLE HONOURS AWARDED TO THE NORFOLK REGIMENT 1914—1918

(Those printed in capitals are the ten to be borne on the **King's** colour.)

1. MONS
2. LE CATEAU
3. Retreat from Mons
4. MARNE 1914
5. Aisne 1914
6. La Bassée, 1914
7. YPRES 1914, 1915, 1917, 1918
8. Loos
9. SOMME 1916, 1918
10. Albert 1916, 1918
11. Delville Wood
12. Pozières
13. Flers-Courcelette
14. Morval
15. Thiepval
16. Le Transloy
17. Ancre Heights
18. Arras 1918
19. Scarpe 1917
20. Oppy
21. Pilckem
22. Langemarch 1917
23. Poelcappelle
24. Passchendaele
25. Cambrai 1917—18
26. St. Quentin
27. Bapaume 1918
28. Lys
29. Bailleul
30. Kemmel
31. HINDENBERG LINE
32. Epéhy
33. Canal du Nord
34. St. Quentin Canal
35. Selle
36. Sambre
37. France and Flanders 1914—18.
38. Italy 1917—18
39. Suvla
40. LANDING AT SUVLA
41. Gallipoli 1915
42. Egypt 1915—17
43. GAZA
44. Jerusalem
45. Tell 'Asur
46. Megiddo
47. Sharon
48. Palestine 1917—18
49. SHAIBA
50. KUT AL AMARA 1915—17
51. Ctesiphon
52. Defence of Kut al Amara
53. Mesopotamia 1914—18.

SCHEDULE OF COLOURS

1st BATTALION.

Description.	Presented.	Remarks.
1. Original Colours. James II.	1685	From a contemporary MS. in the Royal Library, Windsor Castle. By permission of His Majesty, The Colonel in Chief.
2. Saratoga. The oldest known Regimental Colours.	1772 The centre of this Regimental Colour probably taken from that of 1759	R.M.C. Chapel, Sandhurst.
3. Unknown	*Circa* 1782	Burnt on parade at Great Yarmouth, 1798, and solemnly buried. The exact place so far unknown.
4. Great Yarmouth	1798	R.M.C. Chapel.
5. Peninsular, Walcheren.	After 1800. A portion of the centre of the R. Colours, 1798, attached, and fragments of another King's and Regimental Colours (not identified).	R.M.C. Chapel. ,, ,,
6. Colours rescued from public auction by Col. D. K. Robertson. Peninsular.	*Circa* 1800	Presented to the 1st Battalion.
7. Kabul, 1842 Sutlej, 1845	Plymouth, 1827	A fragment at the Depot.
8. Crimea	Newry, 1848	Sandringham Church.
9. Presented by The Prince of Wales.	Aldershot, 1887	Sandringham Church.
10. Presented by H.M. King Edward VII, Colonel in Chief.	Buckingham Palace, 1909	In present use.

Note.—The 1st Battalion has a banner, given in 1914 in France. All Battalions in the first seven Divisions received the same. Company flags were given in 1915.

SCHEDULE OF COLOURS—*contd.*

2ND BATTALION.

Description.	Presented.	Remarks.
11. Jowaki, 1877–8 Kabul, 1879–80	Corfu, 1859	Norwich Cathedral, 1896.
12. Taken into use	1892	Sandringham Church.
13. Presented by H.M. King George V, Colonel in Chief.	Buckingham Palace, 1919	In present use.

MILITIA (3RD BATTALION).

Description.	Presented.	Remarks.
14. Post Union	*Circa* 1800	Wolterton Hall. See p. 136, Vol. I.
15. The Countess of Albemarle's.	1855	Norwich Castle, 1910.
16. Taken into use	*Circa* 1901	In present use.

MILITIA (4TH BATTALION).

Description.	Presented.	Remarks.
17. Colonel John Patteson's	Previous to 1800	Rainthorpe Hall.
18. Earl of Leicester's	1854	St. Nicholas Church, Great Yarmouth, 1904.
19. The Countess of Albemarle's.	1901	Norwich Castle, 1908.

SCHEDULE OF COLOURS—*contd.*

TERRITORIAL.

Description.	Presented.	Remarks.
20. 4th and 5th Battalions	By H.M. King Edward VII, Colonel in Chief, 1909.	In present use.

SERVICE BATTALIONS.

Description.	Presented.	Remarks.
21. 7th Battalion	Presented by H.R.H. The Prince of Wales. France, 1919.	Norwich Cathedral.
22. 9th Battalion	Presented by General Sir H. C. O. Plumer, G.C.B. Germany, 1919.	Norwich Cathedral.

APPENDIX V

REGIMENTAL BANDS AND MUSIC

At the time of its first raising in 1685 it appears that Colonel Cornwall's regiment had no military musical instrument beyond the drum. In 1717, even, no infantry regiment had got beyond this elementary stage, except some of the Guards. It was only in 1771 that two fifers were entered on the establishment lists for the grenadier company. In the inspection report by General Dilkes, dated Dublin, July 15, 1772, it is noted for the first time that the regiment has " a band of music," a statement which is repeated in the inspection report of May 18, 1773. No information is given as to its strength or what instruments it had.

After that the reports are silent on the subject of a band till we come to that of Lieutenant-General Garth, dated 1798, at Yarmouth, which says there were " two sergeants and nine privates clothed as musicians." Mr. Milne says this was a very strong band for the time.

As for the clothing of the band, that was a matter which had to be paid for by the colonel, and his taste in uniforms seems to have been little fettered by regulations. The general rule seems to have been that the bandsman's coat followed the colour of the facings, and no doubt it was faced like the drummer's with red.

We are indebted to Major S. D. Shortt for the following notes:

" The first Battalion band was at one period, I believe, about 1870 and onwards, one of the best bands in the service, and any reference to the band I hope will mention the bandmaster, Chevalier V. Bonicoli, who brought it to a very high state of efficiency. I remember years ago reading in a paper that in 1864 Mons. Bonicoli was known as one of the finest clarionet players in London. I also remember the story of how at Verdi's request he conducted an opera of Verdi's the first time it was produced in Milan before the King of Italy. At the conclusion, M. Bonicoli was summoned to the royal box and the king of Italy (*sic*) took a diamond ring off his finger and attempted to put it on the same finger on M. Bonicoli's hand, but found the ring too small, and, regretting the fact, was about to replace the ring on his own finger when M. Bonicoli said it would fit his little finger, and so it did, and M. Bonicoli always wore that ring. On guest nights M. Bonicoli always came in for a glass of wine and sat beside the president. Of late years— I am speaking of up to 1905—the band fell off and got to a very low ebb. They were very weak in numbers, and had very little support. Very different from the days when M. Bonicoli was bandmaster and Captain John Gillespie took the greatest interest in them.

"When M. Bonicoli was first made bandmaster he was not enlisted, but subsequently he was, and had, I believe, to be sent to Kneller Hall, and I believe he was at once offered the instructorship of the school, which he refused. He was very popular with officers and men.

"The drums have always been good. The 7th Fusiliers, who were friends of the regiment and who prided themselves on their drums, I believe taught our drummers 'the double tap,' I think that is the term."

During the European War of 1914—18 the following information has been gathered:

The 9th (Service) Battalion had a strong band of nearly thirty performers in Germany after the Armistice.

In July, 1917, when the 12th (Yeomanry) Battalion were in front of Gaza, the band instruments were brought up to the front and practised, and some new instruments bought. A band, under the rather depressing circumstances of that time, was no doubt a blessing.

The following note contributed by Colonel G. Massy gives an interesting account of the fortunes of a former musician in the Norfolk Regiment's band:

"When the 1st Battalion was at Bloemfontein (1905—06), the band, under Bandmaster Dean, was engaged to play for a fortnight at an exhibition at Capetown. During their stay there, they were accommodated in the A.S.C. barracks.

"They were visited there by Colonel the Chevalier O'Reilly, who formerly had commanded the local Volunteers and who had been Mayor of Cape town. Previous to this, the Chevalier O'Reilly had served in the 9th Regiment, and as a boy had been in the band. He left the regiment when it was at the Cape. He recognized several of the bandsmen and knew their names—owing to their likenesses to their fathers, who had served in the band in his time.

"He entertained the band at dinner in the Town Hall, and expressed a hope that when the 1st Battalion left South Africa for England they would be sent *via* Cape Town so that he might have the opportunity of giving the whole battalion a dinner in the Town Hall.

"When I heard of this I wrote and thanked the old chap for his hospitality to the band, and invited him to come and stay with me in Bloemfontein so that he could see his old regiment again, but he said he was too old for such a long journey, and again expressed a hope of being able to entertain the whole battalion at Cape Town.

"I had to go to Cape Town later on for a few days, and paid him a visit. He told me that during the South African War the Boers had a price (of I think £500) on his head.

"The band's engagement at Cape Town was extended for another fortnight, and at the end of this period the management presented a silver cup to the band and a baton to the bandmaster. They earned great credit there for their exemplary behaviour and general smartness, as well as for the excellence of their playing.

"The sergeant's mess have a photograph of O'Reilly which he presented to them."

For the 2nd Battalion there is a list of bandmasters in Colonel Shepherd's History.

APPENDIX VI

LIST OF OFFICERS OF THE NORFOLK REGIMENT WHO DIED IN THE WAR, 1914—18

The following list is taken from the official publication, the only change being the alphabetical rearrangement of order in the case of the territorial battalions.

In the last column we have endeavoured as far as possible to identify generally the locality in which each officer met his death.

The official publication explains that "it has not been possible to give the number of the battalion of officers in every case, as officers changed battalions so rapidly that the Army List was not always a guide, and in the notifications of casualties battalions were not always given."

We have succeeded in tracing, with the aid of battalion diaries, the locality of death in most cases. In a few a mark of interrogation indicates that correctness cannot positively be guaranteed. Cases of failure to trace are mainly due to the following causes:

1. Only the reserve battalion being given, without indication of the battalion abroad to which the officer was attached.
2. Officers losing their lives whilst attached to other units, such as the Royal Flying Corps, the Machine-Gun Corps, etc.
3. Omission in battalion diaries of the names of officer casualties.

On the other hand, several names are given in the diaries which do not appear in the official list for the Norfolk Regiment. These are probably mostly officers attached from other units, as was certainly the case in several instances. These names, which would appear in the official list under the unit to which the officers belonged, are given in a separate list. Though they were not perhaps, strictly speaking, officers of the Norfolk Regiment, they lost their lives whilst fighting on its strength. Whilst great care has been expended on these statements, we are unable to guarantee their absolute accuracy or completeness.

ABBREVIATIONS.

K. in A.	Killed in action.
D. of W.	Died of wounds.
Killed	Killed other than in action.
Died	From natural causes, etc.
Tp.	Temporary rank.

REGULAR AND NEW ARMY OFFICERS.

Batt.	Name and Casualty, etc.	Action or Locality of Death when Ascertainable.
	Abel, Frederick, 2nd Lieut. (Tp.), drowned 30/12/17	Not traced
8	Adams, Ernest Geoffrey, 2nd Lieut. (Tp.), D. of W. 26/6/18	Do.
	Adams, William John, 2nd Lieut., drowned 30/12/17	Do.
10	Alexander, J. W. E., 2nd Lieut., died 14/4/16	Do.
7	Allen, M. R. W., 2nd Lieut. (Tp.), K. in A. 2/8/17	Pick Avenue, near Arras
	Armstrong, G. H., Lieut., Died 28/10/18. (Attd. Nigeria Regt.)	Not traced
8	Attenborough, J. H., 2nd Lieut. (Tp.), K. in A. 1/7/16	Montauban
8	Ayre, B. P., Capt. (Tp.), K. in A. 1/7/16	Do.
	Backhouse, G. L., 2nd Lieut., Killed 2/8/16. (Attd. R.F.C.)	Not traced
1	Balders, A. W., Capt., K. in A. 27/11/15 (Attd. W.A.F.F. Nigeria Regt.)	Do.

Batt.	Name and Casualty, etc.	Action or Locality of Death when Ascertainable.
7	Barton, G. F., 2nd Lieut. (Tp.), K. in A. 10/4/17	Feuchy
9	Barton, H. F., 2nd Lieut. (Tp.), K. in A. 12/2/16	Trenches S. Jean, Ypres front
9	Bashforth, J. F. C., 2nd Lieut. (Tp.), K. in A. 15/9/16	Quadrilateral
1	Bates, A. W., 2nd Lieut., K. in A. 30/3/16	Trenches in front of Arras
2	Bell, F. de B., Major, D. of W. 24/4/15.	Shaiba. Died at Basra
8	Benn, B. W., 2nd Lieut. (Tp.), K. in A. 19/7/16	Delville Wood
7	Benn, W. H., 2nd Lieut. (Tp.), K. in A. 2/8/17	Pick Avenue, near Arras
1	Benton, S., 2nd Lieut. (Tp.), K. in A. 27/10/17	Stirling Castle
10	Bice, W. F., 2nd Lieut. (Tp.), K. in A. 4/9/16	Falfemont
	Bickmore, D. F., D.S.O., Lieut. (Act. Lieut.-Col.), K. in A. 19/7/18	Not traced
10	Bird, P. C. H., 2nd Lieut. (Tp.), K. in A. 5/4/16. (Attd. 6th L. N. Lanc. Regt.)	Do.
10	Blagden, R., 2nd Lieut. (Tp.), D. of W. 15/5/16. (Attd. 7th Battn.)	Trenches near Hohenzollern Redoubt (?)
3	Boast, T., 2nd Lieut., Killed 29/9/18. (Attd. 1st Battn.)	Banteux
10	Bolland, J. W. C., 2nd Lieut. (Tp.), K. in A. 9/4/17	Feuchy
7	Bonham, W. D., 2nd Lieut. (Tp.), K. in A. 14/10/17	Raid from Pick Cave
3	Boosey, F. C., Lieut., K. in A. 22/11/15. (Attd. 2nd Battn.)	Ctesiphon

Batt.	Name and Casualty, etc.	Action or Locality of Death when Ascertainable.
3	Bowlby, T. R., Capt., K. in A. 17/9/14. (Attd. 1st Battn.)	Missy-on-Aisne
1	Bradshaw, H. J., 2nd Lieut. (Tp.), D. of W. (Prisoner of War) 18/5/17. (Attd. 4th Battn.)	Palestine
9	Bray, R. B., 2nd Lieut. (Tp.), K. in A. 23/10/18	Final advance—Bois de l'Evêque
1	Briard, E. F. V., Capt., K. in A. 24/8/14	Mons
1	Brown, E. P. W., Lieut., K. in A. 4/9/16	Falfemont
1	Brown, T., 2nd Lieut., K. in A. 4/9/16	Do.
3	Brown, W. J. H. Capt., K. in A. 4/9/16 (Attd. 1st Battn.)	Do.
2	Brownrigg, J. H., Lieut., K. in A. 14/4/15	Shaiba
3	Brumbley, W. J., M.C., 2nd Lieut., K. in A. 27/3/18. (Attd. 7th Battn.)	German offensive near Albert
9	Brunger, R., D.S.O., Capt., K. in A. 8/10/18	Final advance near Brancourt
3	Buckell, C. J. A., 2nd Lieut., K. in A. 19/4/17. Attd. 4th Battn.)	Gaza
7	Buckland, T. A., Lieut. (Tp.), K. in A. 18/10/15	Loos
8	Bunting, W., M.C., Capt. (Tp.), K. in A. 11/8/17	Near Inverness Copse
1	Burlton, G. P., M.C., Lieut., K. in A. 5/6/16	Near Arras
	Butler, O. J., 2nd Lieut. (Tp.), K. in A. 16/10/18	Not traced
8	Byrne, H. V. E., M.C., Capt. (Tp.), K. in A. 15/4/18	Ypres front

Batt.	Name and Casualty, etc.	Action or Locality of Death when Ascertainable
9	Cadge, W. Capt. (Tp.), K. in A. 26/9/15	Hulluch Quarries
3	Cameron, H. S., Capt., K. in A. 4/9/16. (Attd. 1st Battn.)	Falfemont
7	Carley, H. V., 2nd Lieut. (Tp.), D. of W. 14/10/15	Loos
2	Carr, D. R., Lieut., K. in A. 23/2/17	Dahra Bend of Tigris
10	Carter, G. T., 2nd Lieut. (Tp.), K. in A. 10/3/16	Not traced
7	Case, F. M. B., 2nd Lieut. (Tp.), K. in A. 10/3/16	Not traced
7	Case, F. M. B., 2nd Lieut. (Tp.), K. in A. 10/8/16	Trenches near Pozières
8	Case, J. W., 2nd Lieut. (Tp.), K. in A. 21/10/16	Regina trench
7	Chaland, M. L., M.C., Lieut. (Tp.), D. of W. 1/12/17	2nd Battle of Cambrai
7	Charlton, A. N., M.C., Lieut. (Tp. Capt.), K. in A. 30/11/17	Do.
10	Chilvers, R. C., 2nd Lieut. (Tp.), K. in A. 19/4/17. (Attd. 4th Batt.)	Gaza
1	Clarke, F. A., 2nd Lieut. (T.P.) K. in A. 31/7/16	Near Longueval
3	Clarke, G. H., 2nd Lieut., K. in A. 22/4/18. (Attd. 1st Batt.)	Trenches, Nieppe Forest
3	Clements, L. W., Act./Capt., K. in A. 9/10/17	Polderhoek Château
10	Coath, L. C., 2nd Lieut., K. in A. 4/9/16. (Attd. 1st Batt.)	Falfemont
1	Cocksedge, R. J., 2nd Lieut., K. in A. 25/9/18	Near Ypres
3	Coleman, E., 2nd Lieut., K. in A. 31/7/17. (Attd. M.G.C.)	Not traced

Batt.	Name and Casualty, etc.	Action or Locality of Death when Ascertainable
3	Coleman, F. C., 2nd Lieut., K. in A. 23/4/17. (Attd. 1st Batt.)	La Coulotte, near Lens
7	Collins, W. G., Lieut., D. of W. 21/1/18. (Prisoner of War)	Not traced
	Cooke, S. P., 2nd Lieut., Died 4/11/18	Do.
1	Cresswell, F. J. Capt., K. in A. 24/8/14	Mons
7	Curwen, H. S., 2nd Lieut. (Tp.), K. in A. 13/10/15	Loos
8	Cutbill, B., Capt. (Tp.), Died 24/3/18. (Prisoner of War)	German offensive, Quéant-Pronville
3	Davis, H. G., Lieut., K. in A. 14/2/15. (Attd. 1st Batt.)	Trenches, Wulverghem. Buried Dranoutre
9	De Caux., W. T., Capt., K. in A. 15/9/16	Quadrilateral
1	Dickinson, L. A., 2nd Lieut. (Tp.), D. of W. 17/11/17	Wounded, Polderhoek
7	Digby, J. K., Lieut., K. in A. 4/8/15	Ploegsteert trenches
9	Dye, G. H. G., Lieut. (Tp.), D. of W.	Ribécourt
1	Edwards, L., 2nd Lieut., Died 8/6/16	Near Arras
	Entwistle, F., 2nd Lieut., K. in A. 9/10/17	Polderhoek Château
9	Everett, W. W., Capt. (Tp.), K. in A. 9/10/18	Final advance near Brancourt
9	Failes, G. W., D.S.O., M.C., Capt. (Tp.) K. in A. 15/4/18	Ypres front
2	Farebrother, H. S., Capt. (Tp.), D. of W. 24/7/16	Wounded Shaiba. Died in London
2	Farquharson, H. J., 2nd Lieut., (Tp.), Died 27/8/16	Mesopotamia
9	Faulke, W. J., Lieut. (Tp.), K. in A. 21/3/18	German offensive, Quéant Pronville
10	Flagg, A., Capt. (Tp.), K. in A. 27/9/15. (Attd. 1/58th Rifles)	Not traced

Batt.	Name and Casualty, etc.	Action or Locality of Death when Ascertainable.
1	Foley, T. A. F., Lieut., K. in A. 25/10/14	Near Violaines (Festubert)
1	Fox, H. N., 2nd Lieut. (Tp.), K. in A. 23/4/17	La Coulotte, near Lens
	Fox, J. J., 2nd Lieut. (Tp.), K. in A. 11/9/18. (Attd. 12th Batt.)	Near Bailleul (?)
9	Frederick, T., M.C., Capt. (Tp.), D. of W. 14/12/17	Wounded Ypres on 7/6/17; died 14/12/17
7	Gielgud, H. L. F. A., M.C., Major, Act. Lieut.-Col., K. in A. 30/11/17	2nd Battle of Cambrai
9	Glanfield, G., 2nd Lieut. (Tp.), K. in A. 12/11/15	Trenches near Ypres
	Glanville-West, H., 2nd Lieut. (Tp.), K. in A. 19/8/18. (Attd. 12th Batt.)	Final advance, Labis Farm
7	Goddard, A., 2nd Lieut., K. in A. 30/11/17	2nd Battle of Cambrai
9	Goddard, J. L., Lieut. (Tp.), K. in A. 15/9/16	Quadrilateral
9	Goodman, B. H., 2nd Lieut., K. in A. 25 or 27/9/15	Hulluch Quarries
7	Goosens, A. A., Lieut., D. of W. 17/8/16	Ration trench, near Pozières
7	Graham, D. C., Capt., K. in A. 28/4/17	Rifle trench, Monchy
7	Green, A. P., Lt. (Tp.), K. in A. 6/7/16	Ovillers
	Griffiths, L. H., 2nd Lieut. (Tp.), K. in A. 11/9/18. (Attd. 12th Batt.)	Final advance near Bailleul (?)
	Grissell, B. S., D.S.O., Major (Tp. Lieut.-Col.), K. in A. 19/4/17. (Attd. 1/5th Batt.)	Attack on Gaza
7	Haig-Smellie, H. H., 2nd Lieut. (Tp.), D. of W. 26/4/17	Trenches near Monchy Wood

Batt.	Name and Casualty, etc.	Action or Locality of Death when Ascertainable.
1	Hall, G. E., 2nd Lieut. (Tp.), K. in A. 25/4/17. (Attd. 9th Batt.)	Suburbs of Lens
2	Hall, H. E., Lieut. (Tp. Capt.), K. in A. 27/11/15	Ctesiphon
3	Hampton, W. O., 2nd Lieut., K. in A. 1/7/16. (Attd. 70 M.G.C.)	Not traced
9	Hancock, J. E., D.S.O., Capt. (Tp.), K. in A. 21/3/18	German offensive, Quéant-Pronville
	Hayter, A. C. T., Lieut., D. of W. 1/11/14	Trenches, Ploegsteert (?)
3	Hewitt, A. K., 2nd Lieut. (Tp.), K. in A. 20/9/17. (Attd. 1/8 King's Liverpool Regt.)	Not traced
7	Hewitt, T., 2nd Lieut., K. in A. 27/3/18	German offensive near Albert
9	Hill, J. E., Capt., (Tp.), D. of W. 24/3/18. (Prisoner of War)	Do. do.
1	Hoare, F. W., 2nd Lieut., K. in A. 23/4/17	La Coulotte near Lens
7	Hogben, F., 2nd Lieut. (Tp.), K. in A. 12/10/16. (Attd. 2nd Batt.)	Ctesiphon
	Hood, P. C., 2nd Lieut., D. of W. 20/9/18. (Attd. 1/5th Batt.)	Final battle near coast, Palestine
	Hullett, W. E., 2nd Lieut. (Tp.), D. of W. 7/12/17. (Attd. 7th Batt.)	Not traced
8	Inch, R. S. M., M.C., Lieut. (Tp.), K. in A. 22/10/17	Poelcappelle
7	Izard, G. H., 2nd Lieut. (Tp.), K. in A. 10/8/18. (Attd. 35th L.T.M.B.)	Not traced
10	Jephson, E. J., Capt. (Tp.), K. in A. 15/9/16. (Attd. 9th Batt.)	Quadrilateral
7	Johnson, G. B., Capt. (Tp.), K. in A. 23/11/15	Trenches near Béthune (?)

Batt.	Name and Casualty, etc.	Action or Locality of Death when Ascertainable.
9	Jones, C. G., Lieut. (Tp.), K. in A. 20/11/17	Ribécourt
7	Jones, W. J., Lieut. (Tp.), D. of W. 15/10/17	Raid from Pick Cave
1	Jones-Bateman, L. N., C.M.G., Lieut.-Col., Died 25/7/17	Simla, 2nd Batt.
	Joyce, A. H. S., M.M., 2nd Lieut. (Tp.) D. of W. 20/8/18. (Attd. 12th Batt.)	Final advance, Labis Farm (?)
9	Kendall, L. F. W. A., Lieut. (Tp.), D. of W. 22/11/17. (Attd. 11th M.G.Sqd)	Not traced
3	Kerkham, F. L., 2nd Lieut., K. in A. 14/10/17. (Attd. 7th Batt.)	Raid from Pick Cave
3	King, E. R., Capt., D. of W. 23/4/18	Not traced
7	Lancaster, R., 2nd Lieut. (Tp.), K. in A. 28/4/17	Rifle trench, Monchy
	Lane, S. F., Capt. (Tp.), K. in A. 18/9/18. (Attd. 9th Batt.)	Final advance, Holnon Wood
	Last, L. W., 2nd Lieut., K. in A. 22/8/18. (Attd. 1st Batt.)	Achiet le Petit
	Lawrence, J. G., 2nd Lieut., Died 15/2/18. (Attd. 2nd West India Regt.)	Not traced
9	Lewington, F. S., 2nd Lieut. (Tp.), K. in A. 21/3/18	German offensive, Quéant-Pronville
8	Lewton-Brain, J. A., 2nd Lieut. (Tp.), D. of W. 14/8/17	Gassed on Ypres front
9	Lightbody, W. P., Lieut. (Tp.), K. in A. 26/9/15	Hulluch Quarries
3	Ling, L. S., 2nd Lieut., K. in A. 23/4/17. (Attd. 1st Batt.)	La Coulotte, near Lens
3	Longfield, J. P., M.V.O., Capt., K. in A. 30/9/15. (Attd. 1st Batt.)	Trenches, Carnoy

Batt.	Name and Casualty, etc.	Action or Locality of Death when Ascertainable.
1	Lorimer, J. S., M.C., 2nd Lieut. (Tp. Capt.), K. in A. 5/11/17. (Attd. 95th T.M.B.)	Polderhoek Château
1	Luard, C. E., D.S.O., Major, K. in A. 15/9/14	Missy on Aisne
8	Macnicol, H. M., Lieut. (Tp.), K. in A. 19/7/16	Delville Wood
7	Maddison, G., 2nd Lieut. (Tp.), K. in A. 28/8/18	Final advance, Morlancourt
1	Magnay, J. C. F., Lieut., K. in A. 23/4/17	La Coulotte, near Ypres
	Maltby, C. T., 2nd Lieut. (Tp.), D. of W. 27/3/18. (Attd. 7th Batt. Suffolk Regt.)	Not traced
7	Manners, H. F., 2nd Lieut. (Tp.), K. in A. 28/4/17	Rifle trench, Monchy
8	Marsh, H. V., 2nd Lieut. (Tp.), D. of W. 22/10/16	Regina trench
1	Martin, E. W., 2nd Lieut. (Tp.), K. in A. 27/7/16	Longueval
1	Megaw, W. C. K., Capt., K. in A. 31/3/15	Farm near Hill 60. Buried, Ramparts, Ypres
9	Meire, W. H. G., 2nd Lieut. (Tp.), K. in A. 26/9/15	Hulluch Quarries
3	Miall-Smith, G. E., M.C., Lieut., K. in A. 25/3/17. (Attd. R.F.C., 11th Sqd)	Not traced
10	Mitchley, S. R., 2nd Lieut. (Tp.), K. in A. 12/10/16	Bayonet trench, near Montauban
1	Molley, J. G., M.C., 2nd Lieut. (Tp.), K. in A. 2/9/18	Final advance, near Beugny (?)

Batt.	Name and Casualty, etc.	Action or Locality of Death when Ascertainable.
8	Morgan, W. C., 2nd Lieut. (Tp.), K. in A. 19/7/16	Delville Wood
9	Nancarrow, W. T., 2nd Lieut. (Tp.), K. in A. 15/4/18	Ypres front
7	Nash, C. F. W., M.C., Capt., Killed 27/3/18	German offensive, near Albert
2	Northcote, G. B., Capt., D. of W. 4/12/15	Ctesiphon
1	Norton, R. L., 2nd Lieut., K. in A. 18/9/18. (Attd. 9th Batt.)	Final advance, Holnon Wood
1	O'Connor, A. C. Captain. (Tp), K. in A. 27/7/16	Longueval
1	Openshaw, H. M., Lieut., D. of W. 28/8/14	Retreat from Mons
1	Orr, J. B., D.S.O., Major, D. of W. 24/8/14	Mons
1	Otter, R. J. C., Capt., D. of W. 15/2/15	Trenches near Kemmel
9	Page, J. C., 2nd Lieut., K. in A. 18/10/16	Mild trench, near Gueudecourt
9	Page, T. S., 2nd Lieut. (Tp.), K. in A. 19/10/16. (Attd. 71st T.M.B.)	Do. do.
7	Parish, W. H., 2nd Lieut., (Tp.), K. in A. 30/11/17	2nd Battle of Cambrai
3	Peden, G. E., 2nd Lieut., K. in A. 25/3/17. (Attd. 133rd M.G. Co.)	Not traced
	Penn-Gaskell, L. Da Costa, Lieut. (Tp. Major), Died 4/2/16. (Attd. R.F.C.)	Not traced (accidentally killed)
7	Peyton, J. A. W., Lieut., K. in A. 22/8/18	Final advance, Morlancourt
9	Phelps, W. J., Lieut., K. in A. 15/9/16	Quadrilateral
7	Preston, P. C., Capt. (Tp.), K. in A. 13/10/15	Loos

Batt.	Name and Casualty, etc.	Action or Locality of Death when Ascertainable.
7	Proctor, C. E., Lieut. (Tp.), K. in A. 2/8/15	Final advance near Morlancourt
9	Randall, F. H., 2nd Lieut. (Tp.), K. in A. 18/7/17	Trenches near Lens
	Read, T. C., 2nd Lieut. (Tp.), D. of W. 22/4/17. (Attd. 1/5th Batt.)	Before Gaza
10	Riches, P. W., 2nd Lieut. (Tp.), Died 6/12/15	Not traced
3	Ritchie, R. A., Lieut., K. in A. 22/11/15 (Attd. 2nd Batt.)	Ctesiphon
9	Robinson, C. S., Capt. (Tp.), D. of W. 13/9/16	Trenches between Albert and Bray
10	Row, L. J., 2nd Lieut. (Tp.), K. in A. 4/6/16	Near Arras, 1st Batt.
	Rushbrook, S. H., 2nd Lieut., K. in A. 6/7/15. (Attd. Cycle Corps)	Near Ypres
3	Russel, A. R., Lieut., K. in A. 25/12/15 (Attd. 2nd Batt.)	Kut
10	Sarsby, R. A., 2nd Lieut. (Tp.), K. in A. 21/12/15	Not traced
9	Selfe, E. D., Capt. (Tp.), K. in A. 7/8/18	Trenches, Dickebusch Lake
3	Sharp, C. H., 2nd Lieut., Died 26/9/18 (Attd. R.A.F.)	Not traced
9	Shaw, A., 2nd Lieut. (Tp.), K. in A. 12/10/16	Bayonet trench, near Montauban
8	Shelton, C., Capt., K. in A. 21/10/16	Wounded and missing Regina trench
7	Shepherd, C., 2nd Lieut. (Tp.), K. in A. 12/10/16	Bayonet trench, near Montauban
7	Sizeland, C., 2nd Lieut. (Tp.), K. in A. 12/10/16	Do. do.

Batt.	Name and Casualty, etc.	Action or Locality of Death when Ascertainable.
3	Smith, B. A., 2nd Lieut., D. of W. 16/4/18. (Attd. 9th Batt.)	Near Kemmel
7	Smith, H., 2nd Lieut., K. in A. 12/10/16	Bayonet trench, near Montauban
1	Soddy, J., 2nd Lieut. (Tp.), K. in A. 23/4/17	La Coulotte, near Lens
8	Spencer, G. W. S., 2nd Lieut. (Tp.), D. of W. 24/2/16	Trenches near Albert(?)
9	Sprott, M. W. C., M.C., Capt. (Tp.), K. in A. 21/3/18	German offensive, Quéant Pronville
4	Steward, J. H., Major, Died 10/5/15	England (?)
	Stone, F. A., 2nd Lieut. (Tp.), K. in A. 20/9/17. (Attd. 1/8th K. Liverpool Regt.)	Not traced
8	Symonds, F. G., 2nd Lieut. (Tp.), K. in A. 22/10/17	Poelcappelle
1	Teeling, A. M. A. T. de L., Lieut., K. in A. 24/9/14	Chassemy-on-Aisne
7	Thorn, H., 2nd Lieut., D. of W. 13/10/16	Wounded, Bayonet trench, nr. Montauban
10	Thouless, A. C., 2nd Lieut. (Tp.), K. in A. 26/4/16. (Att. R.F.C.)	Not traced
7	Tilley, J., Capt. (Tp.), K. in A. 28/11/16	Inspecting wire near Hill 60 [Arras
3	Todd, A. F., Capt., D. of W. 21/4/15. (Attd. 1st Batt.)	
1	Trafford, E. T., Lieut. (Tp.), Died 10/5/16. (Garr. Batt.)	India (?)
10	Tucker, E. G., 2nd Lieut. (Tp.), K. in A. 13/10/15	Loos
	Tucker, S. W. J. B., 2nd Lieut. (Tp.) D. of W. 13/9/18. (Attd. 2/5th K.O.Y.L.I.)	Not traced

Batt.	Name and Casualty, etc.	Action or Locality of Death when Ascertainable
	Turton, Z. A., Lieut., K. in A. 23/4/15. (Attd. E. Yorks)	Not traced
1	Tyler, G. C., Tp. Lieut.(Act. Capt.), K. in A. 22/8/18	Final advance, near Achiet le Petit
1	Walsha, A. A., Lieut., K. in A. 18/9/18. (Attd. 9th Batt.)	Final advance, Holnon Wood
	Ward, A. E. M., Capt., K. in A. 12/8/15	Suvla Bay
9	Webber, F. H., M.C., 2nd Lieut., D. of W. 24/10/18	Final advance, Bois de l'Evêque (?)
9	Wellesley, E. E. C., Capt. (Tp.), K. in A. 30/4/16	Trenches, La Bassée Canal
1	West, E. L., Capt. (Tp.), K. in A. 31/7/16	Near Longueval
8	Wharton, S. A., 2nd Lieut. (Tp.), D. of W. 1/7/16. (Attd. T.M.B.)	With 8th Batt., Montauban
9	White, C. W. M., 2nd Lieut. (Tp.), K. in A. 26/9/15	Hulluch Quarries
3	Whitmore, H. C., 2nd Lieut., Killed 8/8/18. (Attd. 94th T.M.B.)	Not traced
8	Whitty, T., M.C., 2nd Lieut., K. in A. 5/10/16	Schwaben Redoubt
8	Williamson, W. R., M.C., Lieut. (Tp.), D. of W. 14/8/17	Gassed, Ypres front
3	Wilson, L. G., 2nd Lieut., D. of W. 12/8/15. (Attd. 1st Batt.)	Wounded, trenches, Ypres. Died in England
9	Wright, W. S., 2nd Lieut., K. in A. 21/3/18	German offensive, Quéant-Pronville
	Wroughton, H., 2nd Lieut. (Tp.), K. in A. 8/12/17	Not traced
2	Wynn, R. A., 2nd Lieut., K. in A. 14/4/15. (Attd. 2nd Batt.)	Shaiba

Missing and Believed Killed.

Batt.	Name and Casualty, etc.	Action or Locality of Death when Ascertainable.
1	Porter, A. J., 2nd Lieut., 19/4/17. (Attd. 4th Batt.)	Palestine
9	Setchell, A. K., 2nd Lieut., 21/3/18	German offensive, Quéant-Pronville

TERRITORIAL FORCE BATTALIONS

4th Battalion the Norfolk Regiment.

Name and Casualty, etc.	Action or Locality of Death when Ascertainable.
Badcock, H. J., 2nd Lieut., K. in A. 18/10/16. (Attd. 9th Batt.)	Mild trench
Barker, S. C., Lieut., K. in A. 21/3/18	Not traced
Beck, J. S., M.C., Capt., K. in A., 16/8/17	Trenches before Gaza
Beck, A., 2nd Lieut. (Act. Capt.), Died 21/3/18	Not traced
Blake, W. L., 2nd Lieut., D. of W. 27/3/18	Not traced
Coller, C. M., Capt., K. in A. 21/3/18. (Attd. 9th Batt.)	German offensive, Quéant-Pronville, 9th Batt.
Cole, F. J., Lieut., K. in A. 19/4/17	Gaza
Cockrill, A. C., 2nd Lieut., K. in A. 23/4/17	La Coulotte, near Lens, 1st Batt.
Collison, E. H., 2nd Lieut., Died 26/6/16	Not traced
Cozens-Hardy, R., 2nd Lieut., K. in A. 9/10/17 (Attd. 1st Batt.)	Polderhoek Château
Cubitt, T. A. K., M.C., K. in A. 22/8/18. (Attd. 1st Batt.)	Final advance, Achiet le Petit

Name and Casualty, etc.	Action or Locality of Death when Ascertainable.
Davey, S. G., Lieut. (Act. Major), Died 25/3/18 (Attd. M.G.C.)	Palestine
Fisher, G. K. T., Capt., K. in A. 3/9/17	Near El Arish
Gowing, W. L., 2nd Lieut., D. of W. 12/12/17	Stone Heap Hill
Hampton, G. K., Lieut., K. in A. 16/8/15	Gallipoli
Harvey, W. A., Lieut., Died 7/11/17. (Attd. R.F.C.)	Not traced
Hughes, B. M., Major, K. in A. 15/9/15	Gallipoli
Jennings, T. E., Act. Capt., K. in A. 11/12/17	Stone Heap Hill Palestine
Jewson, W. H., Tp. Major, K. in A. 19/4/17	Gaza
Kirby, K. C., Lieut., K. in A. 18/9/18. (Attd. 7th Batt.)	Final advance near Epéhy
Leamon, D. A., 2nd Lieut. (Tp. Lieut.), D. of W. 14/8/17. (Attd. 8th Batt.)	Gassed, Ypres front
Levy, J., 2nd Lieut., K. in A. 19/4/17	Gaza
Matthews, R. J., Lieut., Died 2/10/18	Not traced
Morgan, W. V., Capt., K. in A. 19/4/17	Gaza
Page, S. D., Capt., K. in A. 19/4/17	Gaza
Robarts, H. M., 2nd Lieut., D. of W. 26/9/17	Trenches, Palestine coast
Scolding, G. H., 2nd Lieut., K. in A. 26/3/18. (Attd. 7th Batt.)	German offensive, near Albert
Senior, R. M., 2nd Lieut., K. in A. 27/3/18	Not traced
Sharp, W. D. C., 2nd Lieut., K. in A. 9/10/17	Polderhoek, 1st Batt.
Steel, S. J., Capt., K. in A. 19/6/18	Kayak Tepe, Palestine
Thurgar, R. W., Capt., K. in A. 19/4/17	Gaza
White, S. J. M., Capt., K. in A. 15/1/17. (Attd. R.F.C.)	Not traced
Wylde, T. E., Lieut., D. of W., 27/6/17. (Attd. R.F.C.)	Do.
Wood, A. G., 2nd Lieut., K. in A. 11/12/17	Stone Heap Hill Palestine

5th Battalion the Norfolk Regiment.

Name and Casualty, etc.	Action or Locality of Death when Ascertainable.
Adams, R., 2nd Lieut., K. in A. 12/8/15	Suvla
Archdale, C. W., Capt., K. in A. 20/11/17. (Attd. 7th Batt.)	First Battle of Cambrai
Beck, A. E., M.C., Capt., K. in A. 19/4/17	Gaza
Beck, A. E. A., Lieut., K. in A. 12/8/15	Suvla
Beck, F. R., Capt., K. in A. 12/8/15	Suvla
Birkbeck, G. W., Capt., K. in A. 19/4/17	Gaza
Burroughes, R., 2nd Lieut., K. in A. 12/8/15	Suvla
Buxton, G. B., K. in A. 28/7/17	Trenches, Palestine coast (?)
Cubitt, E. R., Capt., K. in A. 12/8/15	Suvla
Cubitt, E. H., Capt., K. in A. 19/4/17	Gaza
Cubitt, V. M., Lieut. (Tp.), K. in A. 12/8/15	Suvla
Dodson, H. E., 2nd Lieut., K. in A. 28/4/17. (Attd. 9th Batt.)	Suburbs of Lens
Dover, W., Lieut., K. in A. 28/4/17	Rifle trench, Monchy
Gardiner, E. J., Lieut., K. in A. 19/4/17	Gaza
Gardiner, I. J., Lieut., Drowned, 27/5/18.	Not traced
Gay, E., 2nd Lieut. (Act. Capt.), K. in A. 12/8/15	Suvla
Hervey, D. F., Lieut., D. of W. 17/5/17	Wounded, trenches, Palestine coast (?)
Lambe, F. W., Lieut. (Tp.), D. of W. 10/11/16	Not traced
Markwick, W. P., Lieut., K. in A. 5/9/18. (With 7th Batt.)	Vaux Wood. Final advance
Norris, W. F., Lieut., K. in A. 25/8/15	Gallipoli trenches
Oliphant, M. F., 2nd Lieut., K. in A. 12/8/15	Suvla
Partridge, R. H., Capt., Killed 4/9/17	Trenches, Palestine coast (?)
Pattrick, A. D., Capt., K. in A., 12/8/15	Suvla

Name and Casualty, etc.	Action or Locality of Death when Ascertainable.
Parker, S., Lieut. and Qr.-Master, Died 1/11/15	Gallipoli (?)
Plaistowe, R. R., Lieut., K. in A. 19/4/17	Gaza
Proctor-Beauchamp, Sir Horace George, Bart., C.B., Lieut.-Col., K. in A. 12/8/15	Suvla
Proctor-Beauchamp, M. B. G., 2nd Lieut., K. in A. 12/8/15	Do.
Shaw, W. H., 2nd Lieut., K. in A. 2/11/17	Third Gaza battle
Smith, C. D., 2nd Lieut., K. in A. 23/10/18. (Attd. 9th Batt.)	Final advance, Bois de l'Evêque
Spencer, S., M.C., K. in A. 24/9/18. (Attd. 7th Batt.)	Final advance, Palestine coast (?
Tebbutt, A. B., Lieut., K. in A. 19/4/17. (Attd. M.G.C.)	Gaza (?)
Wenn, W., Capt., D. of W., 1/4/17	Gaza
Williams, C. A., 2nd Lieut., K. in A. 21/3/18. (Attd. 9th Batt.)	German offensive, Quéant-Pronville
Woodwark, E. R., Tp. Major, K. in A. 21/8/15	Suvla

6th Battalion the Norfolk Regiment (*Cyclists*).

NOTE.—As the 6th Battalion did not proceed overseas on active service the following casualties were incurred whilst the officers were attached to other Units. Except in two cases they have not been traced.

Name and Casualty, etc.	Action or Locality of Death when Ascertainable.
Brewster, B. S., Lieut., K. in A. 3/5/17	—
Callingham, S. B., Lieut., Died, 18/1/19	—
Coulton, A. E., Capt., K. in A. 20/7/16	—
Davies, F. L., Lieut., K. in A. 8/7/17	—
Fison, F. H., Lieut., K. in A. 19/7/16	—

Name and Casualty, etc.	Action or Locality of Death when Ascertainable.
Fowler, C. G., Capt., K. in A. 6/4/17	—
High, G. C., 2nd Lieut., K. in A., 14/3/17	—
Ireland, C. A., M.C., Lieut., K. in A. 14/10/17. (Attd. 7th Batt)	Raid from Pick Cave
Lee, F. G. D., Tp. Lieut., Died 1/3/16	—
Lee, R. H. D., Capt., Killed 23/6/17. (Attd. R.F.C.)	—
Lyon, R. A., Lieut., K. in A. 13/8/17	—
Miles, J. G., Capt., K. in A. 27/6/18. (Attd. 7th Batt.)	Near Senlis
Parkinson, G. H., Lieut., K. in A. 13/4/18	—
Watts, W. K., Capt., K. in A. 2/12/17	—
Wainwright, S. S., Lieut., K. in A. 11/3/17	—

Norfolk Yeomanry (later the 12th Battalion the Norfolk Regiment).

Name and Casualty, etc.	Action or Locality of Death when Ascertainable.
Birkbeck, G., Lieut., Died 19/2/15	England
Bonsor, M. C., Capt., K. in A. 10/3/18	North of Jerusalem
Buszard, S. G., Lieut., K. in A. 8/12/17	North of Jerusalem
Clapp, W. G. E., 2nd Lieut., D. of W. 29/4/17. (Attd. 7th Batt.)	Feuchy
Cobon, H. G., 2nd Lieut., D. of W. 24/1/18	North of Jerusalem
Ford, C. G., 2nd Lieut., Drowned, 10/10/18	Not traced
Gaskell, A. J., 2nd Lieut., K. in A. 2/11/18	Not traced
Goslett, J. S., 2nd Lieut., Died 11/11/15	Gallipoli trenches
Harbord, J., Capt., D. of W. 10/7/18	Nieppe Forest
Jode, G. R. L., 2nd Lieut., K. in A. 19/8/18	Labis Farm
Mason, A. H., Capt., K. in A. 21/8/15	Near Vieux Berquin

Name and Casualty, etc.	Action or Locality of Death when Ascertainable.
Notton, C. G., 2nd Lieut., K. in A. 3/12/17	Not traced
Plant, G. B. H., M.C., Lieut., K. in A. 18/9/18. (Attd. 7th Batt.)	Final advance, near Epéhy
Preston, T. F., Lieut., K. in A. 24/1/17. (Attd. R.F.C.	Not traced
Ramsbottom, B. W., Lieut., K. in A. 19/8/18	Labis Farm
Stone, W., M.M., 2nd Lieut., K. in A. 18/8/18	Day preceding Labis Farm
Tillard, T. A., Lieut., K. in A. 6/12/16. (Attd. R.F.C.)	Not traced
Watts, F. R., 2nd Lieut., K. in A. 29/8/18	Near Bailleul

OFFICERS WHOSE NAMES DO NOT APPEAR UNDER NORFOLK REGIMENT IN OFFICIAL LIST OF DEATHS. DERIVED FROM DIARIES, SUPPLEMENTARY LISTS, ETC.

Name and Casualty, etc.	Action or Locality of Death when Ascertainable.
Allen, G., 2nd Lieut., K. in A. 14/8/17	Gassed, Ypres front
Blackwell, Capt. S. F. B., K. in A. 20/11/17	Ribécourt
Briggs, Bt. Lieut.-Col. 8th Batt., Died 1916	
Burford, 2nd Lieut., K. in A. 9/10/18	Final advance near Brancourt
Clenshaw, J. S., Tp. 2nd Lieut. (Attd. 4th Batt.)	Accidental
Cockrill, A. C., 2nd Lieut., K. in A. 3/9/17. (Attd. from Royal Warwickshire Regt. to 4th Batt.)	Vimy Ridge
Collier, 2nd Lieut, K. in A. 2/11/17. (Attd. from Royal Warwickshire to 1/4th Batt.)	Gaza

Name and Casualty, etc.	Action or Locality of Death when Ascertainable.
Coxens, Lieut., K. in A. 9/10/17	Polderhoek Château
Davenport, B. T. W., 2nd Lieut., K. in A. 15/12/17. (Royal Warwickshire Regt, attd. to 4th Batt.)	Stone Heap Hill, Palestine
Dodd, H. E., Lieut., K. in A., Oct., 1918. (Attd. 12th Batt. from Essex Regt.)	Final advance, France
Dover, W., 2nd Lieut., 7th Batt., K. in A. 25/4/17	Rifle trench, Monchy
Fawkes, W. G. S., 2nd Lieut., K. in A. 12/8/15	Suvla
Giles, W. S., 2nd Lieut., K. in A. 3/9/17. (Attd. from Royal Warwickshire to 4th Battn.)	Near El Arish
Gleed, F. W. L., Lieut. and Quartermaster, Died 1917	Palestine
Hole, C. G., 2nd Lieut. (Royal Warwickshire attd. 4th Batt.)	Palestine
Holland, J. R., 2nd Lieut., K. in A., 19/3/18. (Attd. 7th Batt.)	Trench raid, Ypres front
Humphries, Lieut.-Col., D. of W., 22/8/18. (Attd. 1st Batt.)	Final advance near Achiet le Petit
Knowles, S. J. G., 2nd Lieut. (Royal Warwickshire, attd. 4th Batt.), K. in A. 15/12/17	Palestine
Knox, Lieut., K. in A., 19/8/18 (12th Batt.)	Vieux Berquin
Lecky, J. J., Capt., K. in A. 27/9/17. (Attd. 2nd Batt. from Royal Fusiliers)	Near Kut
McCurdy, Lieut., K. in A. 3/3/15. (Attd. 1st Batt.)	St. Eloi
Mason, A. H., Capt., K. in A. 12/8/15	Suvla
Myers, Capt. and Adjt., K. in A. 31/3/15. (1st Batt.)	St. Eloi
Paget, S. J., Capt. (8th Batt.), Killed 1918	
Payne, 2nd Lieut. K. in A. 30/11/17. (Attd. 7th Batt.)	Second Battle of Cambrai

Name and Casualty, etc.	Action or Locality of Death when Ascertainable.
Porter, A. J., Lieut., K. in A. 19/4/17 (1st Batt.)	Vimy Ridge
Rolfe, T., Capt., K. in A. 24/8/18. (Attd. 7th Batt. from A.S.C.)	Final advance, Morlancourt
Rumbold, Major (Royal Scots, attd. 2nd Batt.) K. in A. 22/11/15	Ctesiphon
Sharpe, 2nd Lieut., K. in A. 9/10/17 (1st Batt.)	Polderhoek
Shilcock, Lieut., D. of W. 24/11/15. (Attd. 2nd Batt.)	Ctesiphon
Simpson, 2nd Lieut., K. in A. July, 1918	Trenches, Ypres front
Smith, E. P., Lieut., K. in A. 19/8/18 (12th Batt.)	Vieux Berquin
Smith, N. M., D. of W. 12/8/15	Suvla
Spencer, Lieut., K. in A. 24/9/18. (Attd. 7th Batt.)	Final advance near Nurlu
Wallis, 2nd Lieut., K. in A. 27/3/18. (Attd. 7th Batt.)	German offensive near Aveluy
Walters, S. A., 2nd Lieut., K. in A. (5th Batt. attd. 4th)	Palestine
Wood, 2nd Lieut., D. of W. 20/9/18	Wadi Ikba, Palestine

APPENDIX VII

(A) EXTRACTS FROM MESS BOOK. (B) EXAMPLES OF SENTENCES OF COURTS MARTIAL IN THE EARLY PART OF THE 19th CENTURY IN THE EAST NORFOLK MILITIA.

(A)

Extracts from East Norfolk Mess, Bet, and Presentation Book

The following are to be considered as customary presentations to the mess by Officers on first joining the regiment. :—

    A Captain .. .. 1 Dozen of Claret.
    A Subaltern .. .. ½ dozen of Port.

On promotion in the regiment, the same quantity to each rank.

One bottle of wine to be given by each officer on

    First appearing at the Mess in Regimentals.
    First Commanding a Company.
    First Mounting Guard.
    First Sitting President of the Mess.
    First Sitting on a Regimental Court Martial.
    First Writing in the Mess Book.

The following are long-established fines at the Mess, and are to be strictly enforced :

    1. Having a Drawn Sword in Ye Mess Room.
    2. Speaking three words of Latin.

3. Throwing across the Table.
4. Taking the Newspaper or Books belonging to the Regiment out of the Mess Room.
5. Tearing or otherwise defacing the Mess Books or Newspapers.
6. Indecent conversation at Dinner during the time servants are in the Mess Room.

. . . .

Captain Orr in the most handsome manner *presents* the Mess with a bottle of wine to commemorate the anniversary of his birthday. 5th April, 1810.
Paid. Sheerness.

Captain Dawson *fined* one bottle of wine for not paying his Mess Bill. Mr. Tiffin the same.
Paid.

Capt. Lloyd, Mr. Mayes, and Capt. Orr, each fined a bottle of wine, for tearing the newspaper. 16th April, 1810.
Paid.

Mr. Beals *gives* the Mess a bottle of wine on Mr. Mayes performing a most extraordinary and wonderful feat, viz. drinking a bottle of wine out of a decanter at one draught. 16th April, 1810.
Paid.

Capt. Orr *fined* a bottle of wine for speaking three words of Latin: " Oh, Bolus, Bolus."
Paid.

Capt. Ruffel *bets* Mr. Hope one bottle of wine that Capt. Orr is dead before 9th December, 1811; to be paid when decided.
Lost by Capt. R. 9th December, 1810.

Capt. Orr *fined* a bottle of wine for buying a pennyworth of orange at the Mess Table.
Paid.

Mr. Mayes *fined* a bottle of wine for selling the above pennyworth to Capt. Orr.
Paid.

Mr. Beals politely *gives* the Mess " One penny."
Sheerness 6th March, 1811.   Paid.

Maj. Mason *fined* a bottle of wine for having a drawn sword in his hand in the Mess Room.
20th March, 1811.   Paid.

Mr. Ficklin *fined* a bottle of wine for an irregularity in filling the president's glass.
                                                          Paid.

Mr. Love *fined* one bottle of wine for dining in dirty boots.
                                                          Paid.

Capt. Falkner *fined* a bottle of wine for terrifying the vice president Mr. Boardman.
1st March, 1814.   Paid.

Mr. Hope *fined* one bottle of wine for making a bargain at the Mess table in selling three letters to Mr. Boulter for three farthings.
23rd April, 1814.   Paid.

Mr. Francis *fined* a bottle of wine for talking on his fingers at Mess.
Plymouth Citadel, 20th May, 1814.   Paid.

. . . .

Capt. Inglis, Norfolk Regt., *presents* the Mess with a goblet on his retiring from the Adjutancy.
Gt. Yarmouth, 1897.

EXAMPLES OF SENTENCES PASSED BY COURTS MARTIAL IN THE EAST NORFOLK MILITIA

1. Private John Wilson charged with stealing from a comrade a watch and half a guinea.
Verdict—Guilty.

Sentence—300 lashes, of which 200 administered and the rest remitted.

2. Private James Honeygold. Absent from 10 o'clock roll call on 11th April, 1808, and not returning to barracks till 11.30 p.m.

Verdict—Guilty.

Sentence—150 lashes, of which 50 inflicted. The rest remitted on ground of good character.

3. Private John Bird. 27th April, 1808. Charged with stealing 19s. 6d. from a comrade.

Verdict—Guilty.

Sentence—400 lashes, administered in full.

4. Private William Goward. 9th March, 1809. Having in his possession straw plait supposed to have been manufactured by prisoners of war.

Verdict—Guilty.

Sentence—200 lashes, of which 50 remitted by C.O.

5. Private John Smith. 12th April, 1809. Charge: Forging name of Sergeant on an order to obtain straw plait from prisoner of war.

Sentence—300 lashes, remitted on his volunteering into 40th Foot.

6. Private James Hardingham. Stealing regimental white trousers and selling to prisoner of war.

Sentence—400 lashes, of which 200 remitted by C.O.

7. Private James Ollett. 28th September, 1809. Desertion in August, 1808.

Sentence—400 lashes, of which 150 remitted.

8. Private John Cooper. 22nd October, 1810. Repeated irregular conduct. In particular making a disturbance in Blue Town, Sheerness, for which he was arrested by the watchman.

Sentence—300 lashes, of which 250 inflicted.

9. Sergeant William Woods. Drunk on parade and refusing to go to barrack room when ordered.

Sentence—Reduced to ranks and 200 lashes. Lashes remitted.

10. Private John Ames. 28th August, 1812. Obtaining forged certificate with name of C.O. permitting him to marry.

Sentence—Two months' solitary confinement.

11. Privates John Marshall and John Bailey. 11th May, 1811. Obstructing and ill-using Corporal Smith in execution of his duty.

Sentence—500 lashes each.

All these sentences of flogging were passed by Regimental Courts Martial and appear to have required no confirmation, except that of the commanding officer. The lashes were administered by the drummers of the regiment with a cat-o-nine tails on the bare back of the convict. When we consider the effect of a modern flogging (in the civil courts) of say fifteen or twenty lashes it is hardly possible to characterize these sentences as anything but savage.

The only thing to be said for them, in cases of theft, is that at that time the civil courts' sentence for a theft of five shillings was death. The soldier was too valuable to the state to be put out of the way by death, so he was flogged and generally kept for further use.

John Smith's case is curious in its remission of the flogging on condition of his enlisting in the regular army. That was compulsory service and no mistake.

APPENDIX VIII

THE WRECK OF THE "ARIADNE" IN 1805

Sir William Gomm's diary on this subject has already been referred to. Lieutenant Ambrose, D.C.M., has endeavoured, by reference to the French authorities, to clear up this matter. All that can be ascertained is the following. The transport "Ariadne," with the headquarters of the 9th Regiment, went ashore on the Sangatte near Calais early in November, 1805. All on board were saved. The ship broke up a day or so after. If any papers were saved from the wreck they would certainly have been destroyed at the close of the war, if not before. There was no record of any papers or cargo having been landed. The above is from a note of the D.A.Q.M.G. to the Quartermaster-General, dated 22nd May, 1880, giving the result of his inquiries at the Ministry of the Marine and Colonies in Paris.

Lieutenant Ambrose's inquiries from the municipal offices at Calais have elicited little beyond the fact that several English vessels were wrecked in this neighbourhood in November and December, 1805, besides the "Ariadne," and that there was some difficulty in lodging the numerous prisoners of war in the neighbourhood. There is an echo of the wreck in a letter of July 6, 1810, from the Adjutant-General to Lieutenant-Colonel Cameron, 9th Regiment, which advises the despatch to him of a sergeant and a private of his regiment who had been shipwrecked in the "Ariadne." They had escaped from France and turned up in the Peninsula. They were ordered to be clothed by the regiment and given two months' leave of absence to visit their families in England. It is to be regretted that there is no record of their adventures. The existing

Record of Service of the 1st Battalion, commenced in 1830, begins as follows:

"In recording the circumstances and events connected with the Regiment since its formation, we have to regret that the numerous achievements and important services rendered by the Corps for a period of 120 years and which are alike honourable and creditable to its character, cannot now receive the sanction of higher authority than Traditionary Reports, the whole of the Regimental Books and Records having been lost by the wreck of the 'Ariadne' Transport on the coast of France in the year 1805, with the exception of the following which are derived from an unquestionable source."

"In August, 1805, the 1st Battalion marched from Dublin and joined the army encamped on the Curragh of Kildare, and in the month of September it received orders to proceed to Clonmel. On 3rd October Major-General Brownrigg was appointed Colonel of the Regiment *vice* General Hunter deceased. On the 24th October the battalion marched from Clonmel and proceeded to the Cove of Cork, where it embarked on board the 'Ariadne,' 'Jane,' and 'Harriett' transports and sailed on the 10th November. Contrary winds compelled the two latter vessels to put back to the Downs, but the former, carrying the Head Quarters of the Regiment, was driven on the coast of France and wrecked near Calais, when all the Staff Officers and 262 men were made Prisoners of War, and the whole of the General Regimental Baggage Stores and Books, etc., were taken possession of by the enemy, thus causing the loss of all official documents and other data up to the period alluded to in the introductory page. Major Molle as senior officer took command of the remnant of the Battalion, and after its return from the expedition to the Weser it moved from Canterbury to Brawbourne Lees, to Shorncliffe, where in the spring of 1806 Lieutenant-Colonel John Stuart, appointed from the 52nd Regiment, joined and assumed command, and in December following, embarked with the Battalion at Dover and sailed for Ireland."

How the colours were saved has already been recorded in the body of this history on the authority of Sir W. Gomm.

APPENDIX IX

FRIENDLY RELATIONS BETWEEN THE NORFOLK REGIMENT AND THE WORCESTERSHIRE, ROYAL FUSILIERS, MIDDLESEX, AND DORSETSHIRE REGIMENTS

For many years there had existed the tradition that the Officers of the 1/9th and the 1/29th (WORCESTERSHIRE REGIMENT) were permanent honorary members of each other's mess. In the year 1889 correspondence passed between the two battalions of which the following is a summary:

Extract from the History of the 29th Foot by Major H. Everard.

"On the 9th of October (1835) in consequence of the removal of the 9th Foot to Bengal, the Headquarters of the 29th returned to Port Louis, and the strength of the various detachments was reduced."

"The close friendship," writes General Sir A. Borton, "which existed in 1833—34 between the 29th and my old Regiment, the 9th, when we were quartered together in the Mauritius, owed its origin to the traditions of Roliça, when, if I remember rightly, the gallant impetuosity of the 29th led them into trouble until timely supported by the 9th, when the two Regiments were enabled to hold their own against long odds until victory crowned the efforts of our Army, each Corps losing its Commanding Officer during the fight. In the days of which I speak, such events remained in the memory of Corps long after they ceased to retain in their ranks any of those who had taken part in them." Major Everard continues: "Having, some years ago, been told by an officer of the 29th, that in his time it was understood that the 9th and 29th were permanent honorary members of each other's mess, I took the liberty of writing to the P.M.C. of the 1/9th to inquire if there was any foundation for this report, and in answer received the following communications." Here follow about nine letters, of which the following is a précis:

Captain Shortt, P.M.C., 1/9th (dated May 17, 1889) states: "He can find no record of the two regiments being honorary members of each other's regiments."

Major Terry, late 9th Foot (dated June 11, 1889) states: "That he always knew that between both Regiments there was a very keen brotherly feeling, and that he had heard that they were permanent honorary members of each other's mess."

On inquiry of Major-General Hawes, Major Everard received the following letter: "I have a vague recollection that the 9th and 29th were permanent members of each other's mess, which either dated from the Sutlej Campaign or the Peninsula. The 29th relieved the 9th at Kussowlie. They joined the 9th the day after Moodkee by forced marches, and were almost destitute of baggage, etc. The 9th shared tents, etc., with them and made them permanent honorary members of the mess then or shortly before."

Captain Cook, Adjutant 9th Foot in 1845, corroborates the above statement, and states: "The 29th relieved the 9th at Kussowlie, just before the Sutlej War; on the arrival of the 29th at Kalka, at the foot of the hills, there was such scarcity of carriage that they could only send one Company up at a time, and the 9th sent one Company down with the return coolies, so it took some time before the relief was completed. During this time they were honorary members of each other's messes. The 9th kept up their mess at Kussowlie, and the 29th at Kalka, and both Regiments were very friendly. The 9th and the 29th got orders to advance on the Sutlej, the latter without tents. After the battle of Moodkee, the 29th caught the 9th up, who shared their tents with them. Finally, the very best feeling existed between the Regiments, and I have heard the old officers often talk of the good fellowship at the Mauritus and Roliça as a 'matter of History.' I am unable to say I recollect the 29th being made members of the mess, but I can fully believe they might have been."

No definite proof was to be obtained from the sources available, but apparently Lieutenant-Colonel Lascelles, who left the Norfolk Regiment to take over the command of the 1st Battalion Worcestershire Regiment, revived the old controversy, for the following welcome letter was received by the Mess President of the 1st Battalion The Norfolk Regiment:

" Parkhurst,
" Isle of Wight,
" *September 20th,* 1912.

" DEAR MESS PRESIDENT,

"At a Mess Meeting of the Officers of the 1st Battalion the Worcestershire Regiment, held at Parkhurst on July 15th, 1912, the following was unanimously passed :

" ' (7) It was definitely and unanimously decided to consider both Battalions of the Norfolk Regiment, late 9th Foot, permanent honorary members of this mess, in confirmation of substantial tradition to this effect.'

" Yours sincerely,
" (Signed,) M. K. PARDOE, Captain,
" P.M.C. 1st Battalion Worcestershire Regiment."

An extraordinary mess meeting was held at Aldershot on October 1, 1912 by order of Major A. L. Bellamy, in the absence of Lieutenant-Colonel Marriott, M.V.O., D.S.O., when the following minute was passed :

" (1) It is hoped that Lieutenant-Colonel A. E. Lascelles and the Officers the 1st Battalion the Worcestershire Regiment will also consider themselves permanent honorary members of their old comrades' mess."

A reply was also written in suitable terms and passed at the meeting. The wording of the letter was arranged by Lieutenant-Colonel Marriott, M.V.O., D.S.O., who was informed by letter of the case.

The following was received from the 1st Battalion Worcestershire Regiment :

" DEAR MESS PRESIDENT,

" The officers 1st Battalion Worcestershire Regiment have very much pleasure in receiving the kind invitation of the Officers of the 1st Battalion the Norfolk Regiment to consider themselves permanent honorary members of their mess, of which privilege they will gladly avail themselves.

" Yours sincerely,
" (Signed.) C. F. G. CRAWFORD, Lieutenant,
" P.M.C. 1st Battalion the Worcestershire Regiment."

Tradition has now become an established fact.

It may be recalled that previously to Roliça the two regiments had served together in the Saratoga campaign, when the flank companies of both were detached to serve together.

The regiments were also together in Grenada in 1796.

The 57th Regiment, commanded by Lieutenant-Colonel Tredennick, arrived at Limerick from Dublin in January, 1881. Although their head-quarters were in the castle, the officers combined their mess with that of the 1st Battalion of the 9th in the New Barracks, sharing everything alike in sport and social life. This happy arrangement continued till September, 1881, when the 9th left for Templemore. On Albuera night, May 16th, the mess was completely in possession of the " Die Hards," who celebrated their glorious anniversary alone. Later in the evening the officers of the 9th became their guests.

In memory of this pleasant comradeship, the 57th gave the 9th a shield, which was brought to Templemore for presentation by Lieutenant R. D. Longe. That officer, then Brigadier-General, died in 1918 and was buried at Sprixworth, the Norfolk seat of his family.

In 1876 the 1st Battalion of the 7th Royal Fusiliers at Dublin, and in 1914 the 1st Battalion of the Dorsetshire Regiment at Belfast, lived in the mess of the 1st Battalion Norfolk Regiment for some considerable time. The former presented a silver jug and the latter a cup to commemorate these occasions.

It will be remembered that, at one time, what is now the 1st Battalion Dorsetshire Regiment was known as the 54th or West Norfolk Regiment, when what is now the 1st Battalion Norfolk Regiment was the 9th or East Norfolk Regiment.

APPENDIX X

THE NICKNAME "HOLY BOYS"

There is more than one story as to the origin of this. One which ascribes it to the men having sold Bibles presented to them in order to purchase liquor seems improbable and may be disregarded. The same may be said of another which describes the origin as the theft by the men in Spain of a valuable Bible from a church. The most probable story, and the one generally accepted in the regiment, is that the figure of Britannia was mistaken by the Spaniards for one of the Virgin. The mistake is a very probable one. An ignorant Spaniard, seeing the Britannia on the colours, would be very likely to suppose it to be a figure of the Virgin on a banner, such as is carried in Roman Catholic countries in church processions. He would probably cross himself, or make an obeisance to it, and it is easy to suppose that the British soldiers of the regiment itself, or of other regiments, would jocularly ascribe the mark of respect as due to the regiment, rather than to the symbol they were supposed to be carrying.

APPENDIX XI

THE NORFOLK REGIMENT WAR MEMORIAL

At the end of the great War Major-General Sir E. P. Strickland, the present colonel of the regiment, raised the question of a memorial to those officers and men of the regiment, some 6,000 in all, who had laid down their lives in the defence of their country.

At the same time the County of Norfolk and City of Norwich had started two schemes as war memorials: one an agricultural college, and the other a chapel to be built on to the cathedral.

General Strickland's proposal was to build cottages for soldiers who had been disabled in the war, and the feeling of the regiment was strongly in favour of this proposal, especially as neither of the other schemes indentified itself with the regiment.

A committee was set up under the presidency of Colonel the Earl of Leicester. The prospect of raising money was not very bright, as a considerable sum had already been collected for or promised to the two other county schemes, and consequently very few subscriptions were forthcoming either from the County of Norfolk or the City of Norwich for the regimental memorial.

However, a total of over £18,000 was raised, inclusive of the Government subsidy of £2,600. The money was raised entirely by subscription and from various regimental funds. None of the usual money-raising devices, such as fêtes, concerts, dances, etc., were employed. Consequently the Cottages as they stand to-day are in truth a memorial worthy of the regiment, and raised solely by the personal efforts of the various battalions, past and present members of the regiment, and their friends.

The memorial consists of ten cottages erected on Mousehold at Norwich, and the grounds are tastefully laid out. The ten most deserving cases were selected from those men of the regiment who were totally disabled in the war.

On February 2, 1921, the King, Queen, and Princess Mary, during a visit to Norwich, inspected the cottages, which were then almost completed.

The Prince of Wales was to have formally opened the cottages early in April, 1921, but his visit was cancelled at the last moment.

The cottages were then occupied and the memorial was formally inaugurated on August 11, 1921, when the Earl of Leicester (Lord Lieutenant of the County), in the presence of the Lord Mayor of Norwich, the Mayor of Great Yarmouth, and the Mayor of King's Lynn, unveiled the memorial stone erected in front of the cottages. The inscription on the bronze panel is:—

IN MEMORY
OF THE 6,000
OFFICERS AND MEN
OF THE
NORFOLK REGIMENT
who fell in the
GREAT WAR
1914—1919
THESE COTTAGES
WERE ERECTED
FOR
DISABLED SOLDIERS
OF THE REGIMENT
1920.

The total cost of the Cottages and ground was about £15,000, so that over £3,000 were available as an endowment fund for their repair and upkeep.

When the present generation of disabled soldiers have passed away the cottages will be available for the most deserving cases of old soldiers of the regiment.

APPENDIX XII

NORFOLK REGIMENT PRISONERS OF WAR HELP ORGANIZATION

This organization was originally started in 1914 by Mrs. Bernard Grissell, and was taken over early in 1916 by a committee of which the Earl of Leicester was president, with Lieutenant-Colonel R. Lombe and later, Lieutenant-Colonel H. Y. Beale, D.S.O., as chairman, Miss F. W. Burton as Secretary (and later Miss M. I. Burton), and Colonel Kerrison, C.M.G., as Treasurer.

It undertook the care of prisoners of war of all battalions of the regiment.

The numbers of these reported were 694 in Germany and 376 in Turkey and thirty-six in Bulgaria. Of these thirty-three died in Germany and 237 in Turkey. The terrible mortality in Turkey should be noted in connexion with Captain Shakeshaft's account of the ill-treatment of prisoners by the Turks.

At first operations were confined to finding a patron for each prisoner reported, who would undertake to send a weekly parcel. As numbers increased, in March, 1915, Miss Burton started the sending of parcels by the organization and raising funds for the purpose. A packing room and office, lent by Mr. Hugh Davis, were opened in Prince of Wales Road, Norwich, and Miss Florence Burton superintended the packing by a large number of voluntary workers of food parcels and all clothing sent to the prisoners till the war ended; latterly the food parcels alone amounted to over 900 a week.

Much help was received from voluntary workers throughout, and subscriptions were most generous, including grants from the Norfolk County Council of £2,000, Lynn Borough Council £300, the Central Prisoners of War Committee £2,500, and Norwich Lord Mayor's Fund £1,500. The receipts amounted to over £32,000. Of this over £30,000 was expended, of which more than £22,000 represent provisions and bread, £850 tobacco and cigarettes, and remittances in cash to prisoners in Turkey and Bulgaria £3,340. The cost of boxes, packing materials, postage and carriage came to £2,330.

The balance of the Lord Mayor's fund, (£1,300) being handed over to them, the committee in May, 1920, allocated the sum of £1,500 to the " Norfolk Regiment War Memorial Cottages Fund " for the building of cottages for Norfolk Regiment Prisoners of war, and in 1922 the committee transferred £550 to the Norfolk Regimental Fund, the income to be used for relief primarily of former prisoners of war. The small remainder of the Fund was used by the committee for the immediate relief of prisoners in need.

APPENDIX XIII

NORFOLK NATIONAL RESERVE

Originating from the " Veteran Reserve " (A.O. 142 of June, 1910) and eventually becoming the Royal Defence Corps, this force took its title in September, 1911 (A.O. 240).

Membership required the qualification of at least three years' efficient service in any branch of the land or sea forces.

Colonel the Earl of Albemarle, K.C.V.O., C.B., V.D., A.D.C., was appointed commandant, with Major W. H. Besant as organizing staff officer, Major E. H. Evans Lombe as A.D.C., and later Lieutenant T. W. Spurling, secretary.

On August 4, 1914, there were 2,720 officers and other ranks enrolled, of whom some 500 were in Class I for service at home or abroad, 1,000 in Class II for garrison duties at home, and the remainder for general duties.

The whole of Class I were enlisted forthwith on the outbreak of war, and those of Class II were formed into supernumerary companies of the Norfolk Regiment and dispatched to various points for guards and other duties.

The earliest-formed companies were commanded by Major D. G. Astley, Lieutenant-Colonel S. G. Hill, Captain W. E. Hansell, Captain Worship, Lieutenant-Colonel P. E. Back, Lieutenant-Colonel J. A. Clarke, Captain Donovan, Lieutenant-Colonel Robin Gray, Captain Combe, and others.

Colonel A. C. Dawson, C.B.E., Lieutenant-Colonel S. G. Hill, V.D., and Major J. A. Berners took the places of the original staff, the members of which were detailed for other duties.

When Colonel Dawson was appointed section commandant, Colonel H. T. S. Patteson, V.D., became county commandant.

APPENDIX XIV

MISCELLANEA

(1) RECORD OF SERVICE OF JAMES WARD, A PENINSULA VETERAN—EXTRACT FROM THE "HOLY BOY."

This is interesting as showing the very early age at which boys were sometimes enlisted in the early 19th century. James Ward when he was discharged on account of "infirmities of advanced life" was only 35 years of age, of which he had served all but seven. He was in Walcheren at the age of ten.

NINTH REGIMENT OF INFANTRY

WHEREOF MAJOR-GENERAL SIR JOHN CAMERON, K.C.B. IS COLONEL.

No. 2 James Ward, Private, *Born in the parish of* Ipswich, *in or near the town of* Ipswich *in the county of* Suffolk, *by trade a* labourer.

ATTESTED for the Ninth *Regiment of Foot in the County of* on the 10–7–1800 *at the age of* 7 *years*.

FIRST SERVICE after the age of 18 years which he is entitled to reckon, up to 31st March, 1835 is 22 years and 237 days.

Regiment	Promotions Reductions	Rank	Period of Service From	Period of Service To	
9th Foot	—	Private	10th July, 1806	24th April, 1806	under age
	—	Drummer	25th April, 1806	24th Jan., 1810	
	—	Private	25th Jan., 1810	9th July, 1811	
	—	Private	10th July, 1811	12th May, 1814	
	Promoted	Corporal	13th May, 1814	24th April, 1815	
	Reduced	Private	25th April, 1815	29th April, 1832	
	Promoted	Corporal	1st March, 1832	27th December, 1832	
	Reduced	Private	28th Dec., 1832	31st March, 1835	

For Soldiers Enlisted Previous to March 15th, 1815.

		Years	Days
East Indies West Indies	3rd April, 1819—3rd February, 1827 (Half period)	3	336
Total of Foregoing statement		27	237
Further Service from 1st April, 1835, to 12th May, 1835, When finally discharged			42
Total Service allowed to reckon to the day of discharge		27	27

Served 3 months in Holland, 4 years 11 months in the Peninsula, 1 year in America, 3 years 2 months in France, 7 years and 10 months in the West Indies; was present at the following actions, viz. Roliça, Vimiera, Busaco, Salamanca, Vittoria, St. Sebastian, and Nive, in one of which he was severely wounded.

Disability or Cause of Discharge.—By authority of the General Commanding in Chief, as per letter dated Horse Guards, 21st March, 1835, and according to the Surgeon's report annexed, it appears that Private James Ward, 9th Regiment of Foot, is unfit for the service, from infirmities of advanced life, and worn out by repeated attacks of fever in the West Indies. The Board concur in the opinion with the Surgeon by the proceedings hereto attached.

Character.—The Regimental Board is of the opinion that his general character has been good.

Pay and Clothing.—He has received all just demands since his entry into the service up to 31st March, 1835.

I, James Ward, acknowledge to have been settled with my pay and clothing and allowances and all just demands whatever, to the above date.

(His)
James **X X** Ward.
(Mark)

(Certified) A. C. Chichester, Captain 9th Regiment.

(2) GERMAN PROPAGANDA. TRANSLATION OF A GERMAN LETTER THROWN INTO THE TRENCHES HELD BY THE 1ST BATTALION NORFOLK REGIMENT AT YPRES ON MAY 6, 1915.

" MY DEAR ENGLISHMEN,

" I will write you a few lines. We are quite well and are also not weary of the war or hungry as one falsely informs you. We have also soldiers enough. We are well, but wish to be allowed to rest. You are told that we kill prisoners and ill treat wounded. This is not the case. If you only knew how well your companions are with us, working here with us and doing it willingly, for we do not wage war against unarmed prisoners or wounded men. And then yourselves must see that you are being deceived, for according to your reports and to those of the French you should already long ago have been in Berlin, for they write nearly every day—we have gained so many kilometres. But I do not think that liar Kitchener reports that you have lost 64 guns at the last German attack at Langemarck; amongst these 9 were heavy ones.

" I will close with that—The Russians are already finished with, and then it will be Italy's turn.

" Were you ten times more powerful the Germans would stand fast.

" From

" Your neighbour,

" May 6th, 1915."

(3) Portrait of the Duke of Braganza.

Major-General Wintour, who was commanding the 2nd Battalion at Pietermaritzburg in August, 1907, writes that, when the Duke of Braganza was staying there on his way to the Portuguese South African colonies, he was invited to dine at the regimental mess, and was much pleased with his evening there. Next day he sent his photograph in memory of the occasion to Colonel Wintour, who handed it over to the mess. The memory is a sad one, as this unfortunate young man was murdered, with his father the King of Portugal, in Lisbon on February 1, 1908.

(4) Mess Table of the 2nd Battalion

The following information is from a letter written to the "Army and Navy Gazette" in 1895:

"An infantry regiment now quartered at Aldershot, with which I was dining a few nights ago, are the possessors of what is undoubtedly one of the handsomest dining tables in England. It is of abnormal width, of a deep rich mahogany colour, and cut, as the clearly and beautifully-marked grain shows, from timber of very large girth (Bombay black wood or American rose wood). There is enough of it, I was told, to seat 45 persons. This table is said to have a history connecting it with one of the most sanguinary battles ever fought in India. The story is that, on the evening of the battle of Chillianwallah, the bodies of 12 officers and the sergeant-major of Her Majesty's 24th Regiment, killed on that disastrous day, were laid out upon the leaves of this table. The table, however, was not the property of the 24th, but of another British regiment belonging to the force engaged. As the survivors of Chillianwallah are daily becoming fewer in number, and must ere long be as extinct as are now the survivors of Waterloo, I asked and readily obtained permission from the officers to invite, in the columns of the 'Army and Navy Gazette,' those who are in a position to do so, to throw any light they can upon the question of the identity of this table with the one on which there is direct testimony that the officers of the 24th were laid before burial; also to trace the history of the table from 1849 to 1874. The 2nd Battalion 9th Regiment, in whose possession it now is, bought the table from the 36th Regiment at Meean Meer in 1874. The 36th are said to have bought the table from the 42nd in 1868, and though nothing positive is known before that date, it is said to have been the property of the 61st. The 61st was one of the few British regiments engaged at Chillianwallah, and may therefore have been its possessors when it was requisitioned for so tragic a purpose."

104, Arundel Road,
Newtown,
13th October, 1924.

To J. C. Miles, Esq.,
The Denes,
Great Yarmouth.

Sir,

Having read the 1st Volume of the History of the Norfolk Regiment I am desirous to thank you most sincerely for the loan of the same and for your kindness in sending it to me and finding a messenger to carry it back to your house. I have read every page of the History with great pleasure, but some parts in particular, such as Cabul and Sutledge Campaigns, having known some of these and also the Crimea men. When I joined the Regiment at Sunderland, Colonel Borton was in command, and I knew Colonel Elmhirst; but what always gives me pleasure when I think of the past is that I saw and heard the voice of that famous old general, Sir Harry Smith, who inspected the Regiment at Sunderland on the 28th April, 1858 (Wednesday). At that date we had a few Cabul men and Sutledge and of course Crimean men. Standing in the ranks next to me was a man (we both belonged to the Grenadier Company), and being on the right of the line Sir Harry came to us first. As I stood next to John Potter I heard what Sir Harry had to say to Potter. He asked him what company he was in at Ferozeshah. "The light company, sir," said Potter. "My God," said Sir Harry, "I remember it well." I have a note from Major Colgan, 3rd Battn., dated 18th October, 1918, in which he states that he bought at Spinks & Son, Piccadilly, London, the six medals of No. 1520 John Potter, late 9th Foot. They are Kabul 1842, Sutledge with 2 clasps, Crimea with clasp, Sebastopol, Turkish Medal, Long Service and Good Conduct, and Medal granted for Distinguished Conduct on the Field. Sir Harry had something to say to all the old Indian soldiers, as he knew them by the medals they were wearing. Corporal Cook, whose name is mentioned in the History as having thrown a live shell clear and thus being the means of saving his own life and others, was, when I joined the Depot at Limerick on the 19th September, 1857, drilling a squad, and I was sent to him for instruction. Cook afterwards joined the Hd. Quarters of the Regiment and was promoted Sergeant, he wore the French Legion of Honour.

On page 347 of the History of the Regiment is the Farewell Address of the Municipal Council of Corfu. During my Service abroad with the 9th I wrote regular to my mother, and when she died some 34 years since all her letters and correspondence fell into my hands. In looking in the letters I found the Farewell Address. I brought it with me to Yarmouth, and after having it in my possession some years I thought I would try and get it photographed. The Address was in English and Greek. I ordered five copies; two I gave to old friends who had served in the Ionian Isles; one copy to the 1st/9th; and one copy to the 2nd/9th. One copy I sent to Colonel Bayley, East London, South Africa, who was several years Adjutant of the 1st Battn. It gave me great pleasure when Colonel Bayley wrote to me to say that he had received it and that he would have it framed and that it should be placed in the best part of his house. After Mr. Ayres had taken the photo he returned the address to me on a card from which he had taken the photo. I wrote to the Officer Commanding the Depot, Norwich, asking if he would like to have it for the Depot. I received a letter from Major Hadow stating that he would be pleased to have it and would find a suitable place for it in the Officers' Mess or elsewhere. I was forgetting to say that I kept one copy, which I got framed, and which I should be pleased to show you, sir, if I ever have the opportunity.

Once more I thank you for the History which I have spent some pleasant time in perusing its contents,

I am, Sir,
Yours faithfully,
(Signed) JOHN WALL,
Late Colour-Sergeant, 1st Battn. 9th Foot,
Norfolk Regiment.

INDEX

VOL. II

(This Index only contains such of the names shown in Appendix VI as are also mentioned elsewhere.)

Abbott, Lt., 243
Abbott, 2nd Lt. W., 103
" Abdul," 315
Achiet le Petit, 49
Adams, 2nd Lt. R., 122, 127
Adams, 2nd Lt. (7th Bn.), 192
Aisne, battle of the, 8
Allen, 2nd Lt. G., 243
Allen, 2nd Lt. M. R. W., 178, 191, 192
Allenby, General, 149, 154, 158, 309
Amara, 73–76
Ambrose, Lt., 34
Anable, 2nd Lt., 196
Anafarta, 123, 124
Ancre, R., 199, 201
Anthony, 2nd Lt., 256
Anzac, 136–138, 302–304
Archdale, Capt., 190–194
" Ariadne," wreck of, 427, 428
Arras, 20, 180, 183–190
Ash, Lt. B. N. (R.A.M.C.), 302
Ashdown, Capt. C. F., 212, 230, 243
Atkinson, Major J. C., 171, 173
Atrocities, 101
Attenborough, 2nd Lt., 218
Aylmer, Major-General, 99
Ayre, Lt. B. P., 212, 218
Azizieh, 78, 87, 108

Badcock, 2nd Lt., 261
Bakubah, 109
Ballard, Lt.-Col. C. S., 2, 4, 5
Balme, Capt., 135
Bampton, Lt. C. K., 121, 131
Bands, 396–399
Banks, 2nd Lt., 234, 235, 243
" Bantams," 104
Barclay, Major J. F., 301, 309, 311, 313, 320, 326
Barclay, Major M. E., 301, 309, 311, 313, 316, 322, 326
Barker, Lt., 287
Barrington, Lt., 228
Barter, 2nd Lt., 200

Bartley, 2nd Lt., 231, 243
Barton, Major, 121
Barton, Lt. H. F., 252
Barton, 2nd Lt. G. F., 187
Bashforth, Lt. J. F. C., 256
Basra, 64, 67
Bates, Lt. A. W., 20
Bates, Private, 156
Bayonet trench, 181, 182
Beale, Lt., 28
Beale, Sergeant, 156
Beck, Capt. F. R., 121, 126
Beck, Lt. E. A., 122, 126
Beck, 2nd Lt. A. E., 122, 147n
Beck, 2nd Lt. A., 122
Beckerson, Lt., 212
Beckwith, Brig.-General, 203
Beersheba, 309–312
Beesley, 2nd Lt., 261, 291
Beit Iksa, 316
Bell, Major F. de B., 61, 71
Bell, 2nd Lt. (7th Bn.), 201
Bell, 2nd Lt. F. St. J., 103
Benn, 2nd Lt., 191, 192, 220
Bennet, Capt., 180
Bennett, 2nd Lt. (9th Bn.), 266
Berners, Lt., 107
Berney, Lt.-Col. Sir T., 154
Berney-Ficklin, Major H. P., 208, 212, 218, 246
Berney-Ficklin, Lt. A. T., 212
Beugny, 48, 49, 50
Bice, 2nd Lt. W. F., 32
Bindley, Corporal, 155
Biographical Notes, 340–351
Bird, 2nd Lt., 296n
Birkbeck, Lt. G. W., 122, 137, 146, 147n, 324
Birkbeck, Capt. H. A., 301, 313, 314, 329
Birrell, 2nd Lt., 206
Blackborn, 2nd Lt., 218, 243
Blackwell, Capt. S. F. B., 261, 268, 275
Blake, Capt. J. R. W., 249
Blake, 2nd Lt., 200

Blakiston, Lt. L. W., 61, 73, 85, 107
Blyth, Capt., 159
Boast, 2nd Lt., 52
Bonain, actions near, 295–297, 299
Bois de l'Evêque, action, 297–298
Bolland, 2nd Lt. J. W. F., 187
Bonsor, 2nd Lt., M.C., 301
Boom Ravine, action, 229–231
Boosey, 2nd Lt. F. C., 2, 85
Borthwick, 2nd Lt. L. C., 171
Borton, Lt., 19
Boswell, Capt. B., 121
Bowlby, Capt. T. R., 2, 9
Bowstead, 2nd Lt., 47
Brackley, 2nd Lt., 197
Bradley, 2nd Lt., 203, 205
Bradshaw, 2nd Lt. H. J., 122
Brand, 2nd Lt., 294
Bray, 2nd Lt. R. B., 298
Briard, 2nd Lt. E. V. F., 2, 5
Briggs, Col. F. C., 212
Bright-Betton, 2nd Lt., 180
Britannia badge, 370–374
Broadwood, Lt. E. H. T. B., 2, 10
Brooks, Major W. T., 25
Brown, 2nd Lt. A. R., 196
Brown, Lt. E. P. W., 32
Brown, Lt. F., 108
Brown, 2nd Lt. G. P., 246
Brown, Lt. T., 31, 32
Brown, Capt. W. J. H., 32
Brownrigg, Lt. J. H., 61, 71
Brudenell Bruce, Capt. R. H., 2
Brumbley, Lt., 200
Brunger, Capt. R., 295
Bryans, Lt., 16
Buckland, Lt. T. A., 171, 174
Budgen, Lt., 10
Bullock, 2nd Lt. H. J., 61, 64, 66
Bullen, 2nd Lt., 271, 291
Bunting, Capt. W., 243
Bureid Ridge, 156
Burford, 2nd Lt., 295
Burlton, Lt., 18, 21, 22
Burnett, 71
Burrell, Capt. C. W. W., 121
Burrell, 2nd Lt. R. E., 122
Burroughs, 2nd Lt. R., 122, 126
Burry, Lt., 50
Burj Bardawille, 318–319
Burton, Corporal, 46
Burton, 2nd Lt., 287
Buxton, 2nd Lt. M. B., 122, 129, 138, 139, 141, 145,
Buxton, Capt. H. J., 250
Buxton, Major A. R., 301
Byrne, Capt. H. V. E., 291

Cadge, Capt. W., 250, 251
Cambrai: 1st battle, 194, 272–279; 2nd battle, 194–195, 279–280

Cameron, Lt. H. S., 20, 32
Camilleri, 2nd Lt., 157
Campbell, Lt. T., 74, 85, 95
Campbell, 2nd Lt. B., 265, 298
Cannan, 2nd Lt. A. C., 301
Carley, 2nd Lt. H. V., 171, 174
Carnoy, 215
Carr, Lt., 108, 146
Carroll, Lt.-Col. J. W. V., 37, 171, 173
Carroll, Major H. A., 99
Case, Major H. A., 99
Case, 2nd Lt. F. M. B., 39, 179
Case, 2nd Lt. J. W., 227
Catherell, Lt., 152
Caton, 2nd Lt. R. P., 122
Chaland, 2nd Lt., 196
Chapman, Lt., 39, 40
Chapman, 2nd Lt. B. E., 241, 243
Chappell, Lt. B. H., 85, 103, 108
Charlton, 2nd Lt. A. N., 171, 196
Christmas, 1914, fraternization, 13
Cistern Hill, 154
Clark, Capt. R. C., 2
Clark, 2nd Lt. S. W., 296
Clarke, Lt., 33
Clarke, 2nd Lt. J. W., 261
Clarke, 2nd Lt. J. H., 298
Clements, Capt. L. W., 42
Clode, Lt., 27, 28, 38
Coates, Lt. W. V., 249, 298
Coath, 2nd Lt., 32
Cobon, Lt. H. G., 314, 317
Cockrill, 2nd Lt. A. C., 38
Coe, R.S.M., 218
Coleman, 2nd Lt. F. C., 38
Coleman, 2nd Lt. (9th Bn.), 266
Coller, Capt. C. M., 287
Collier, 2nd Lt., 150, 151
Collins, Lt. W. G., 196
Collins, Lce.-Corporal, 23
Collins, Private, 47
Collison, 2nd Lt. F. H., 122
Colonels and Lt.-Colonels, succession of, 333–340
Colours and Battle Honours, 376–395
Connor, 2nd Lt., 294
Connors, 2nd Lt., 107
Cook, Corporal, 34
Cooke, Lt., 78, 84, 85, 102
Cooke, Major J. E., 249
Cooke, 2nd Lt. (M.I.), 266, 287
Cooper, Lt.-Col. F. S., 201
Corke, Lt. V. C. C., 121
Cosham, 2nd Lt., 49
Cour d'Avoué Farm, 35
Court Martial Sentences, 422–426
Covell, C.S.M., 157
Cowles, 2nd Lt., 261
Coxens, 2nd Lt., 42
Coxon, Capt. A. G., 121, 126, 127n

Cozens-Hardy, 2nd Lt. S. N., 213, 218, 221, 294
Cramer Roberts, Major W. E., 61, 69, 84, 91, 95
Cresswell, Capt. F. J., 2, 4
Cresswell, Col. G., 166
Crosbie, Sergt.-Major, 165
Crosby, Capt. P., 187
Crosse, 2nd Lt., 39
Crosse, 2nd Lt. J. E., 249, 251, 256, 265, 278
Crow, 2nd Lt., 292
Croxford, 2nd Lt., 291
Ctesiphon, battle of, 80–87
Cubitt, Lt. A. T. K., 47, 49, 258, 259–261, 275, 278
Cubitt, Capt. E. R., 121, 126
Cubitt, Lt. E. H., 122, 147n
Cubitt, Lt. V. M., 122, 126
Culley, 2nd Lt. G. H. C., 122
Cullington, 2nd Lt., 32
Culme-Seymour, Lt. A. G., 122
Cumberland, Lt., 152
Cumberland, 2nd Lt., 252, 256
Curwen, 2nd Lt. H. S., 171, 174
Cuthbert, Lt., 275, 278
Cuthbertson, 2nd Lt., 204, 205
Cutbill, Capt. B., 282, 287
Cuttrill, Lt., 243

Daniel, Lt. A. E. C., 103
Daunt, Capt. W. J. O'B., 61, 66
Davenport, 2nd Lt. B. T. W., 156
Davie, 2nd Lt., 206
Davies, Capt. R. G., 35, 38
Davies, Lt. L. F. St. J., 212, 221, 225
Dawkins, 2nd Lt., 192, 205
Day, Lt.-Col. F. R., 290, 292
Dean, 2nd Lt., 154
De Caux, Capt. W. T., 256
De Falbe, Lt.-Col., 140
De Grey, Major G., 49, 51, 61, 70n, 85, 103, 105, 108, 110
Delamain, General, 62, 80, 86, 89
Delville Wood, action, 24–28, 219–221
De Poix, 2nd Lt. R. B. C., 122
Dermott, C.S.M., 92
Diala River, 108, 109, 111
Dickebusch, 41
Dickinson, Capt., 42
Digby, 2nd Lt. J. K., 171, 173
Dillon, Lt., 206, 233, 234
Dilworth, 2nd Lt., 202, 205
Dodd, Major H. E., 313, 330
Dodson, 2nd Lt. H. E., 265
Done, Major H. R., 2, 18
Doughty, Private, 18
Dover, 2nd Lt., 190
Downs, Lt. R. A., 61, 64, 65
Drenon, 2nd Lt. L. C., 171
Dugdale, Revd. R. W., 52

Dunbabbin, Sergt., 18
Dye, Lt. G. H. G., 274, 275
Dye, 2nd Lt., 291
Dyer-Bennett, Lt.-Col. R. S., 261

Edwards, Lt. L., 21
Egerton, Lt.-General Sir R. G., 112
El Arish, 140
El Burj, 315, 316
El Kutunieh, action, 79, 80
Elliott, 2nd Lt. (9th Bn.), 291, 294
Elliott, 2nd Lt. C. H. B., 122
Emmerson, 2nd Lt., 296n
Elouges, action, 3–5
Entwistle, 2nd Lt., 42
Establishments, 352–358
Evans, 2nd Lt., 38
Evans, Lt. J. F., 212, 221
Everett, 2nd Lt. W. W., 250, 295
Everitt, Sergeant, 205
Ewin, Colour-Sergeant, 71

Failes, Lt., 253, 256, 276, 283, 287, 288, 289, 291
Failes, Lt. G., 291
Falfemont Farm, 29–32, 205
Farebrother, Lt. H. S., 61, 67, 69
Farmer, 2nd Lt., 107
Farquharson, Lt. M. J., 103, 104
Faulke, Lt. W. J., 287
Fawkes, 2nd Lt. W. G. S., 122, 127
Feetham, Brig.-General, 270, 271
Fellows, Capt. A. R., 171
Fenwick-Owen, Lt. G., 301, 314, 317, 319
Ferguson, Major-General Sir C., 2
Ferguson, Lt.-Col. H. G. de L., 212, 214, 225, 239, 241, 243
Ferguson, 2nd Lt., 191, 192
Ferrier, Capt., 206
Festubert, 10
Field, Lt. and Adjt., 50
Finch, Lt., 39
Finch, Lt. A., 250, 251
Finnigan, 2nd Lt., 291
Fisher, Capt. J. H. K., 121
Fisher, Sergt., 106
Flatt, Lt. T. W., 121, 154
Flers, 182
Fletcher, Major L., 212
Flower, Capt. N. A. C., 301
Floyd, Lt. A. B., 61
Foley, Lt. T. A. F., 2, 10
Forster, Lt., 206, 256
Fothergill, 2nd Lt., 291, 294
Fowell, 2nd Lt., 202, 204, 205
Fox, 2nd Lt. R. H. S., 212
Fox, 2nd Lt. J. F., 250, 251, 253
Francis, Capt., 26, 30, 32
Franklin, 2nd Lt. H. V., 171, 174, 176
Frederick, Lt. T., 250, 251, 253

French, F.-M. Sir J., 7
Frere, Lt. R. T., 61, 64, 71
Frere, Lt. J. G., 301
Fresnoy, 40
Fretwell, 2nd Lt., 50
Frost, Lt. and Q.M. F.W., 171
Fry, Major-General C. I., 62, 79
Funnell, 2nd Lt., 157

Garbutt, 2nd Lt., 291
Gardiner, Capt. W. C., 212
Gardiner, Lt. E. J., 147
Garnham, 2nd Lt., 253, 256
Gas, 16
Gay, Lt. E., 122
Gaza battles, 142, 144, 145, 149–152, 308, 314
Geldart, 2nd Lt., 151
Gethen, Capt. R., 174, 193, 201, 202
Gielgud, Lt. H. L. F. A., 171, 181, 190, 193, 196
Giles, 2nd Lt. W. S., 151
Gillett, Lt., 102
Gimson, 2nd Lt. A. T., 301
Girdwood, Major-General E. S., 308, 322
Givenchy, 10
Glanfield, 2nd Lt. G. E., 250
Glanville-West, 2nd Lt., 327n
Gleed, Lt. and Q.M. F. W. L., 213
Gleichen, Brig.-General Count, 1
Glencorse Wood, 236–238
Glover, 2nd Lt., 256
Goddard, 2nd Lt. J. L., 196, 256
Golder, R.S.M., 199
Goodman, 2nd Lt. V. H., 249–251
Goosens, Lt. A. A., 180
Gordon, 2nd Lt., 153
Gorringe, Brig.-General, 75
Goslett, 2nd Lt., 301
Gough, General Sir H., 176n
Gowing, 2nd Lt., 154
Graham, Capt. D. C., 190, 250, 251
Graham, Lt. (2nd Bn.), 108
Grand, 2nd Lt. R., 213
Gravestock, 2nd Lt., 261
Green, Lt. A. P., 171, 173, 174, 178
Greatorex, 2nd Lt., 287
Grissell, Lt.-Col., 140, 147n, 148
Grover, Capt., 32
Gundry-White, Lt., 220, 225
Gurmat Ali, 103

Haig-Smellie, 2nd Lt., 189
Hall, Capt. J. H., 212, 218
Hall, 2nd Lt. G. E., 264
Hall, Lt. H. E., 61, 87
Hall, Lt. (1st Bn.), 20, 23
Hall, Capt. T. B., 165
Hallam, 2nd Lt. S., 250
Hamilton, General Sir Ian, 124, 125

Hamilton, Brig.-General W. G., 79, 80, 83, 86, 89, 92, 94
Hammond, Capt. J., 171
Hammond, Lt., 49
Hampson, 2nd Lt., 218
Hancock, Lt. J. E., 277, 278, 284, 287, 289
Harbord, 2nd Lt. J., 301, 303, 319, 320, 322
Hare, Corporal, 262
Harrison, 2nd Lt. A. E., 238
Harrison, 2nd Lt. V. M., 233, 234
Harrison, 2nd Lt. C. F., 35, 38
Harrison, 2nd Lt. R. F., 296
Harvey, Lt.-Col. R. J., 121, 134
Havers, 2nd Lt., 200
Haward, Capt., 192, 196
Hawkesley, 2nd Lt., 296n
Hayes, 2nd Lt. H. F., 213
Haylock, 2nd Lt., 191, 200
Hedges, 2nd Lt. R. F., 194
Helsby, Lt. W. G. (R.A.M.C.), 250
Hendry, Capt. A. (R.A.M.C.), 61
Henshall, 2nd Lt., 261
Heselton, 2nd Lt., 200
Hewitt, 2nd Lt. T., 200
Hickie, Brig.-General, 213
High Wood, 23
Higson, Capt. F., 103, 110
Hill, 2nd Lt., 200
Hill, 2nd Lt. J. E., 249, 251, 287
Hill, Lt. L. S., 301
"Hill 60," action, 15
Hoare, Lt. F. W., 20, 21, 29, 38
Hodgson, Brig.-General H. W., 302, 305
Hogarth-Swann, Lt., 191, 194, 205
Hogben, Lt., 85
Hoghten, Brig.-General, 80, 89
Hohenzollern Redoubt, action, 175
Holland, Lt. J. R., 2, 9
Holnon Wood, action, 292–294
"Holy Boys," nickname, 433
Hook Trench, 191
Hopegood, 2nd Lt., 295
Hopton, 2nd Lt., 200
Horner, Capt. E. T., 103, 106, 108
Hosken, J. C. F. (R.A.M.C.), 122
Howe, 2nd Lt., 46
Howlett, Capt. J. M., 171, 174
Howlett, 2nd Lt., 26, 28
Hudson, Lt. F. W., 61, 85, 103
Hughes, Capt. B. M., 121
Hughes, Lt. H. V., 212
Hulluch Quarries, action, 250
Humphries, Lt.-Col., 49
Humphrey, Lt., 189
Hunn, Lt., 26, 28
Hurt, 2nd Lt., 200

Impson, Lt. H. J., 212
Inch, 2nd Lt., 225, 246

Ingle, 2nd Lt., 38
Ingram, 2nd Lt., 198, 200
In Seirat, 140, 143
Ireland, 2nd Lt., 193
Ironmonger, 2nd Lt., 218
Irles, action, 231-233
Italy, operations in, 43, 44
Izard, 2nd Lt., 198

Jackman, Lt., 28
Jackson, 2nd Lt., 180, 190
Jackson, Lt. F., 256, 291
Jackson, C.S.M., 204
James, 2nd Lt. W. C., 122, 159
Jarvis, 2nd Lt., 271
Jeary, 2nd Lt., 223
Jebel Hamrin, 109, 110
Jennings, Capt. T. E. A., 154
Jephson, Capt. E. J., 256
Jephson, Lt. M. D., 2, 5
Jephson's Post, 129
Jerusalem, capture of, 154, 316
Jewell, 2nd Lt., 151
Jewson, Capt. W. H., 121, 147n, 156
Jewson, 2nd Lt. J. H., 122
Jobson, Sergeant, 157
Jode, Lt. G. R. L., 327n
Johnson, Capt. G. B., 171
Johnson, Sergt. J. S., 191
Jolimetz, 53
Jones, 2nd Lt. A. J. N., 291
Jones, Lt. C. G., 278
Jones, Capt. R. A., 291
Jones, 2nd Lt. W. J., 182, 193
Jones-Bateman, Major L. N., 104, 110
Jordan, 2nd Lt., 50
Joyce, 2nd Lt. A. H. S., 327n

Kayak Tepe (Palestine), action, 157
Keighley, Lt. G. C., 103
Kelly, Capt., 36, 39
Kemp, 2nd Lt., 196
Kendall, Lt. F. W. A., 250
Kenny, 2nd Lt. H. T., 103
Keppel, Lt. F. G., 171
Kerkham, 2nd Lt., 193
Ketteringham, 2nd Lt., 181, 192
Khanikin, 110
King, H.M. George V, 18, 48, 203, 221
King, Capt. (1/4th Bn.), 156
King, 2nd Lt. (7th Bn.), 204, 205
King, Lt., 102
King, Private, 156
Kinsman, Lt.-Col. H. J., 134
Kirby, Lt. K. C., 206
Kirby, 2nd Lt., 38
Kizil Robat, 109, 110
Klein, Lt., 18
Knights, 2nd Lt. A. E., 197
Knox, 2nd Lt., 320, 321, 324, 327n
Kontill, 2nd Lt., 196

Kurna, 64-67
Kut el Amara, 78; siege of, 89-94

La Boiselle, action, 177
La Coulotte, action, 37
Lajj, 81, 82, 83, 87
Laden, Capt. R. G. (R.A.M.C.), 122
Laker, 2nd Lt., 221
Lambton, Major, 41
Lampard, Lt., 243
Lancaster, 2nd Lt. R., 190
Lane, 2nd Lt. J. R. C., 287
Lane, Capt. S. F., 293
Lanyon, Capt. C. V., 61, 64, 65, 71, 99
Lark, Private, 34
Lark, 2nd Lt., 200
Larkman, 2nd Lt., 296n
Lawrence, 2nd Lt., 206
Leamon, Lt. D. A., 243
Le Cateau, battle, 5, 6
Lecky, Capt., 77, 78
Lee, Capt. F. W., 294
Lee, 2nd Lt., 206
Leggatt, Private, 34
Lens, battle, 268
Lewell, 2nd Lt., 152
Levy, 2nd Lt. J., 147n
Lewington, Lt. F. S., 287
Lewton-Brain, Lt. J. A., 243
Lightbody, Lt. W. P., 250, 251
Lightfoot, Lt. M. F. R., 2
Lightfoot, Capt. (8th Bn.), 243
Lindsay, Capt., 102
Ling, Lt. L. S., 38
Little, Lt. (Norsets), 102
Livingston, 2nd Lt., 42
Llewellyn, 2nd Lt., 221
Lloyd, 2nd Lt. R. S., 103, 105, 107, 108
Lloyd, Lt. (7th Bn.), 206
Lodge, Major F. C., 76, 84, 85, 95
Longfield, Capt. J. P., 18
Longueval, 24-28
Lovell, 2nd Lt., 159
Luard, Capt. C. E., 2, 9
Lucas, Capt. (R.A.M.C.), 177
Lucas, 2nd Lt., 151
Lyle, Lt. G. C., 2
Lyus, 2nd Lt. A. O., 103, 107

McCurdy, Lt., 14
MacLean, 2nd Lt., 218
McMurrough Kavanagh, Capt. J. T., 302
MacNicol, 2nd Lt. H. M., 213, 221
McNeill, Brig.-General, 308
Maddison, 2nd Lt., 195, 205
Magnay, Capt. J. C. F., 38
Major, 2nd Lt., 296n
Mallett, Corporal, 47
Mann, Capt., 47
Manners, 2nd Lt., 179, 190
Mansura Ridge, 142

Marden, Major-General, 254, 271, 283
Markwick, Lt., 206
Marsh, 2nd Lt. H. V., 227
Marshall, Capt. R. D., 61, 71
Martin, Lt. E. W., 19, 27, 28
Mason, Capt. A. H., 121, 126
Maxse, Major-General, 213, 218, 228
Mazera action, 64-66
Megaw, Capt. W. C. K., 2, 15
Meire, 2nd Lt. W. H. G., 250, 251
Melliss, Brig.-General Sir C., 72, 90, 96, 98
Mena Camp, 138
Merville, 45
Merryweather, Private, 155
Mess Books, extracts, 422-424
Miall-Smith, 2nd Lt. G. E., 213, 217, 221
Michell, 2nd Lt. J. H., 301
Middleton, 2nd Lt., 291-295
Mild Trench, action, 257
Miles, Capt. J. G., 202
Miller, 2nd Lt. A., 291, 298
Miscellanea, 439
Mitchley, 2nd Lt., 182
Monaghan, Lt. and Q.M., 103
Monchy-le-Preux, action, 189
Mons, battle, 3; retreat from 5-7
Montauban, action, 216-218
Montgomerie, Lt.-Col. E. W., 46, 121, 127-134, 136, 137
Montgomery, Lt. H. R. G., 171, 182
Montreuil aux Lions, action near, 8
Moore, Q.M. R. W., 122
Morgan, Lt. W. V., 121, 147*n*
Morgan, Lt.F. J., 212, 227, 233, 234, 239, 243
Morgan, 2nd Lt. W. C., 212, 221, 256
Morland, Major-General, 34
Mormal Forest, 53
Mornement, Col., 160
Morse, Lt.-Col. A. F., 301, 306, 309, 321, 322, 331
Morval, capture of, 32
Munro, Lt.-General Sir C., 213
Murphy, 2nd Lt. J. L., 291
Musters, Capt., 47
Mutimer, 2nd Lt., 262, 295
Myson, 2nd Lt., 296

Nalin (Palestine), 153
Nancarrow, 2nd Lt. W. T., 291
Nasariyeh, 75
Nash, Capt., 197, 200
Natusch, 2nd Lt., 203
Neale, Sergt.-Major, 267-277
Needham, Lt., 39
Neilson, 2nd Lt. E. E. M., 213
Neuve Chapelle, action, 11
Nevill, Capt. R. H. R., 212
Nieppe Forest, 45, 323
Nixon, General Sir J., 67, 80
Nixon, Lt. R. C., 206
Norfolk, National Reserve, 438

"Norsets" (composite Battalion of Norfolk and Dorset Regts.), 99
North, Capt. Hon. W. F., 212
Northcote, Capt. G. B., 61, 85
Norton, 2nd Lt. R. L., 293
Norwack, 2nd Lt., 192
Nurlu, 206

Oakes, 2nd Lt. J. B., 2, 5
O'Connor, 2nd Lt. A. C., 7*n*, 9, 19, 21, 27, 28
O'Donnell, 2nd Lt., 178
Officers killed, etc. (1914-1918), 400-421
Ogilby, Capt., 178
Oldman, Brig.-General, 46
Oliphant, Lt. T., 122, 126
Openshaw, Lt. H. M., 2, 5
Oppy Wood, 39
Orams, Major, 248, 249
Orchard, 2nd Lt., 291
O'Reilly, Capt., 256
Orr, Major J. B., 2, 4
Orton, Lt. J. O. C., 61, 71
Otter, Capt. R., 171, 174
Owen Lewis, 2nd Lt. F. A. H., 212

Padfield, 2nd Lt., 218
Page, Capt. S. D., 121, 147*n*
Page, 2nd Lt. E. C., 196
Page, 2nd Lt. T. S., 261
Page, 2nd Lt. J. C., 261
Paget, Capt. S. J., 212
Paget, 2nd Lt. G. N., 2, 5
Painter, Lce.-Corporal, 155
Pallett, Lt., 152
Palmer, 2nd Lt. H. G., 204, 205, 298
Parish, 2nd Lt., 196
Parker, Lt. and Q.M., 122
Patten, 2nd Lt. A. J. H., 212, 237
Patteson, Lt. R. W., 2, 36
Pattrick, Capt. A. D., 121, 126
Paul, Capt. J. D., 301, 307
Payne, 2nd Lt., 196
Peacock, Lt. H. L., 61, 95
Peake, Lt. (Norsets), 102
Peddie, 2nd Lt., 271
Peden, 2nd Lt. G. E., 103
Peebles, Lt.-Col., 61, 70, 71*n*, 74, 75
Pelly, 2nd Lt. A. R., 122, 127
Percival, 283, 287
Petrie, 2nd Lt., 238
Peyton, 2nd Lt. J. A. W., 204, 205, 231
Phelps, 2nd Lt., 200, 256
Phipps, 2nd Lt., 200
Pick Cave, 192, 193
Pike, 2nd Lt., 296*n*
Piper, 2nd Lt., 218, 234
Place, 2nd Lt., 327*n*
Plaistowe, 2nd Lt. R. R., 147*n*
Plant, Lt. G. B. H., 206
Platten, 2nd Lt., 246

Playford, Sergeant, 278
Poelcappelly, 243–246
Polderhoek Château, action, 41
Pollington, Sergeant, 198
Popham, 2nd Lt., 187
Portsmouth, Lt. F. V., 95
Potter, 2nd Lt., 180, 190, 196
Pratley, 2nd Lt., 196, 204, 205
Preston, Capt. P. C., 171, 174
Preston, Capt. T. F., 301
Price, 2nd Lt. C. T., 103
Prior, Lt.-Col. B. H. L., 167, 179, 181, 256–258, 259, 261, 262, 264–278, 280–282, 291
Prisoners of War, help for, 436, 437
Proctor, Lt. G. E., 126, 171, 173
Proctor-Beauchamp, Col. Sir H. G., 121, 125, 126
Proctor-Beauchamp, 2nd Lt. M. B. G., 122, 127
Pryer, C.S.M., 34
Pryor, 2nd Lt. E. J., 213
Purdy, Major T. W., 121, 127

Quadrilateral, 255–257
Queant-Pronville, battle, 280–289

Ramsbottom, Lt. B. W., 327n
Ramsden, Capt. Sir J. F., 301
Randall, 2nd Lt. F. H., 270
Ration Trench, action, 179
Raven, C.S.M., 217
Read, Lt., 33
Read, Lt. J. F. W., 95
Read, 2nd Lt., 295
Rees, Lt.-Col. E. T., 196, 199, 200
Reeve, 2nd Lt. A. E., 2, 5
Regiments, relations with other, 429–432
Regina Trench, 226
Reynolds, Capt. R. T. H., 171, 176
Rhine, march to, 299
Richards, Lt., 327
Richardson, 2nd Lt. H., 71, 85, 103
Richardson, Lt. and Q.M. J. T., 61, 95
Riches, Private, 35
Rickwood, Lt., 51
Ridge Trench, action, 179
Rifle Trench, action, 189, 190
Ritchie, Lt., 85
Rivett, 2nd Lt., 49
Robartes, 2nd Lt., 193
Robertson, Lt. N., 250
Robinson, Capt. C. S., 250, 253
Rolfe, Capt. T., 204, 205
Room Trench, action, 206
Rose, Lt., 33
Row, Lt. L. J., 21, 22
Rowell, Lt.-Col. H. E., 166n
Rowell, Capt., 261
Ruggles-Brice, Capt. E. C., 301
Rumbold, Major, 74, 85
Russians, 109

Sahil action, 62, 63
St. Elie, 173
St. Eloi, 14
St. Venant, 45
Sannaiyat, 76, 99
Sayer, Q.M. J. A., 301
Scarlett, Lt.-Col. Ashley, 202
Schulter, German Lt., 183
Scobell, Major S. J. P., 172
Scolding, 2nd Lt., 200
Scott, Major-General A. B., 173, 175
Scott, Capt. (R.A.M.C.), 28
Scott, 2nd Lt. R. P., 39, 40, 42
Scott, 2nd Lt. (8th Bn.), 235
Scott-Murray, Capt. A., 172
Selfe, Capt. E. D., 291
Semmence, Sergt.-Major, 71
Senior, 2nd Lt., 200
Setchell, Lt., 287
Shaiba, battle, 68–72
Shakeshaft, Lt. A. J., 89–98
Shand, Capt. N. P., 103, 107
Sharp, 2nd Lt., 42
Shaul, 2nd Lt., 48, 49
Shaw, 2nd Lt. A., 182
Shawe, Colour-Sergeant, 47
Sheikh Abbas, 142, 144
Sheikh Hassan, 152
Sheldrake, Private (diary), 54–58
Shelton, Lt. C., 212, 228
Shepherd, 2nd Lt. C., 182
Sheria, action, 313–314
Sherlock, 2nd Lt., 231, 234, 235, 243
Sherwood-Kelly, Lt.-Col. J., 328–330
Shilcock, Lt., 85
Shilta (Palestine), 153
Shutes, Capt., 206
Shumran Bend, passage of Tigris 105–107
Sibree, Capt., 32
Sidi Bishr Camp, 138, 305, 306, 308
Simpson, 2nd Lt., 291
Sizeland, 2nd Lt., 182
Smith, 2nd Lt. B. A., 290
Smith, 2nd Lt. C. B., 42
Smith, 2nd Lt. C. D., 268, 298
Smith, 2nd Lt. E. P., 324, 325, 327n
Smith, Lt. and Q.M. E., 2, 54, 250
Smith, Lt. H., 182
Smith, Capt. N. M., 154
Smith-Dorrien, Lt.-General Sir H., 2
Snepp, Capt. E. N., 10, 243
Soames, Capt. (R.A.M.C.), 200
Soddy, Lt. J., 33, 38
Sollum, 306, 307
Solly Flood, Brig.-General, 175
Somme, battle, 23
Spackman, 2nd Lt. C. B. S., 122
Spencer, Lt., 33
Spencer, 2nd Lt. G. W. S., 213
Sprott, 2nd Lt. M. W. C., 253, 256, 287

Spurrell, Lt. W. J., 250, 256, 291
Steel, 2nd Lt. S. G., 122, 157
Steer, 2nd Lt., 27, 28
Stephens, Major-General, 22
Stocker, Lt. (Norsets), 102
Stone, Lt.-Col. P. V. P., 16, 19, 20, 25, 26, 32, 33, 36
Stone, 2nd Lt. W., 324, 327n
Stone Heap Hill, action, 155, 156
Stracey, Lt.-Col. E., 249, 262
Stracey, Capt. A. H., 249, 251
Stuart, 2nd Lt., 38
Stubbs, 2nd Lt., 196
Suez Canal, 138, 139, 305
Summers, 2nd Lt., 196
Summerskill, 2nd Lt., 179
Suvla, 122–138
Swift, 2nd Lt. T. R., 301
Swift, Lt., 32
Symons, Brig.-General, 322
Symonds, 2nd Lt. F. F. G., 246

Tapply, Capt., 200
Tarrant, 2nd Lt., 192
Tayler, Capt. and Adjt., 193
Taylor, Capt., 46, 49
Teal, 2nd Lt., 298
Teeling, 2nd Lt. A., 10
Thiépval, 222
Thompson, 2nd Lt., 278
Thorn, 2nd Lt., 182
Thornley, 2nd Lt., 246, 287
Thurgar, 2nd Lt. R. W., 122, 147
Tidd, Sergeant, 23
Tigris River, passage of, 105–107
Tilley, Capt. J., 171, 177, 178, 183
Todd, Capt. W. A. (R.A.M.C.), 213, 246
Tonge, Lt.-Col. W. Corrie, 114–119
Tool Trench, 191
Torkington, Lt.-Col., 148
Tower, 2nd Lt., 38
Townshend, Major-Gen. Sir C., 72, 73, 76
Trench warfare, 12, 262, 263
Trimble, Lt.-Col., 262
Tuck, Capt. M. J., 39
Tuck, Capt. M. J., 171, 174
Tucker, Capt., 174
Turner, Capt. H. E. M., 249, 253
Tyce, Lt., 283
Tyler, Capt. G. C., 49

Umm-el-Hannah, 99
Umm-al-Tabul, 88
Uniform, 359–375
Upcher, 2nd Lt. C., 250–251

Van Straubenzee, Brig.-General C. H. C., 171, 175
Vieux Berquin, action, 323–327
Vimy Ridge, action, 36
Vos, 2nd Lt., 218

Wadley, 2nd Lt., 221
Wagner, Lt., 322
Walker, Major H. S., 50
Walker, Capt., 159
Walker, 2nd Lt. E. B., 250, 251
Walker, Sergeant, 324, 325
Waller, Corporal, 69n
Wallis, 2nd Lt., 200
Walsha, 2nd Lt. A. A., 271, 293
Walter, Lt.-Col. F. E., 171, 173, 176, **178**, 181, 184, 193
Ward, Capt. A. E., 121, 126
Wardropper, Sergeant, 156
War Memorial, Norfolk Regiment, 434–435
Watson, 2nd Lt., 32
Watts, 2nd Lt. F. R., 328
Weaver, Capt., 199, 200
Webber, 2nd Lt., 291, 296n
Wellesley, Capt. E. E. C., 252
Wenn, Capt., 143
West, 2nd Lt., 29, 46
Wharton, 2nd Lt. J. A. G., **174**
Wharton, 2nd Lt. S. A., 218
White, 2nd Lt. C. W. M., 250, 251
White, 2nd Lt. D. G., 194
White, 2nd Lt. S. J. M., 122
White, 2nd Lt. J. W. L., 187
Whitty, 2nd Lt., 225
Willett, Capt. H. L., 61
Williams, Lt. C. A., 283, 287
Williams, Sergeant, 106
Williamson, Lt. W. R., 243
Willoughby, 2nd Lt., 268
Wills, 2nd Lt. O. S. D., 2
Wilson, Lt. L. C., 16
Windham, 2nd Lt., 27
Wing, Major-General, 172, 173
Wittington, Lt., 16
Wood, Capt. (1st Bn.), 48, 49
Wood, 2nd Lt. A. G., 152, 154
Wood, 2nd Lt., 122, 159
Woodger, 2nd Lt. J. H., 103
Woodham, 2nd Lt., 180
Woodthorpe, Lt., 33
Woodwark, Lt.-Col. G., 162, **164**
Woodwark, Capt. E. R., 121, 126
Woolsey, 2nd Lt., 192
Worn, 2nd Lt., 278
Worster, 2nd Lt. F. G. L., 301
Wright, Capt. A., 121
Wright, 2nd Lt. F., 213, 223
Wright, Lt. W. S., 287
Wyatt, 2nd Lt. C. P., 301
Wynn, 2nd Lt., 71

Youell, Capt., 32
Younden, Lt.-Col. W. A., 138, **148**
Ypres: 1st battle, 11; 2nd battle, 14; 3rd battle, 40

Lightning Source UK Ltd.
Milton Keynes UK
UKHW050839270219
338106UK00003B/25/P